Praise for the authors of *Flash 8: Projects for Learning Animation and Interactivity*

"Rich Shupe can be admired for his encyclopedic knowledge of all things Flash, but it is the combination of creative ingenuity and teacher's intuition that make him a writer of rarefied skill. When Rich talks about Flash he manages to strip the mystery out and replace it with imagination. He is, at once, artisan and guru."

—*Lori Piquet, Editor-in-Chief,* DevX

"Hoekman's approach is clear and unpretentious—attributes not always associated with software how-to books. He leaves the reader who actually ventures into the lessons with the feeling of 'Hey! I can do this!' It's a nice bonus that he doesn't show off his prowess in the jargon department."

—*Michael W. Dominowski,* Staten Island Sunday Advance

Flash 8

Projects for Learning Animation and Interactivity

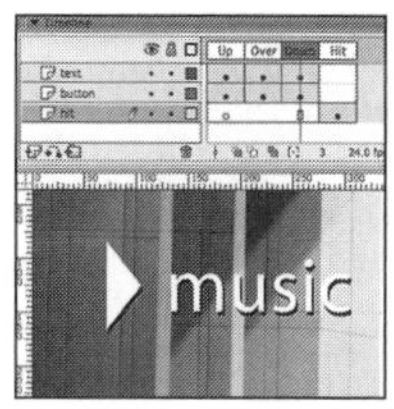

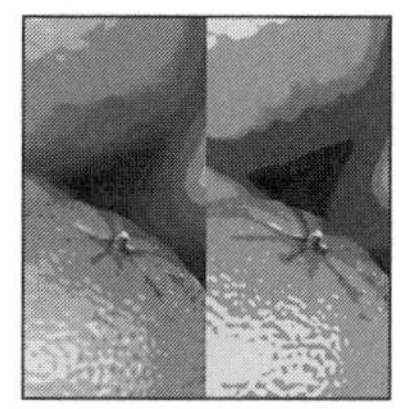

Rich Shupe and Robert Hoekman, Jr.

O'REILLY®

BEIJING • CAMBRIDGE • FARNHAM • KÖLN • PARIS • SEBASTOPOL • TAIPEI • TOKYO

Flash 8: Projects for Learning Animation and Interactivity

by Rich Shupe and Robert Hoekman, Jr.

Printed in the United States of America.

Published by O'Reilly Media, Inc., 1005 Gravenstein Highway North, Sebastopol, CA 95472.

O'Reilly books may be purchased for educational, business, or sales promotional use. Online editions are also available for most titles (*safari.oreilly.com*). For more information, contact our corporate/institutional sales department: 800-998-9938 or *corporate@oreilly.com*.

Print History:

March 2006: First Edition.

Editor: John Neidhart

Production Editor: Genevieve d'Entremont

Copyeditor: Rachel Wheeler

Proofreader: Sada Preisch

Indexer: Johnna VanHoose Dinse

Cover Designer: Linda Palo

Interior Designer: David Futato

Illustrators: Robert Romano, Jessamyn Read, and Lesley Borash

This book uses RepKover™, a durable and flexible lay-flat binding.

0-596-10223-2
[C]

Contents

Preface

Welcome to *Flash 8: Projects for Learning Animation and Interactivity*, a project-based introduction to the newest version of Flash. This book includes everything you need to get started in Flash—a robust animation and interactive development tool—right out of the box, including a CD-ROM with trial versions of the software and all of the example files from the exercises herein.

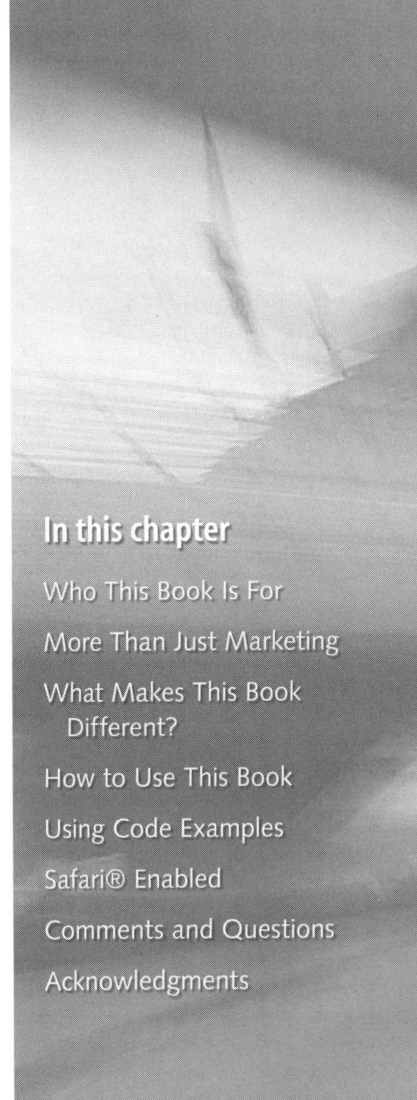

In this chapter

Who This Book Is For

This book is primarily geared toward beginning Flash users who want to bring their project ideas to life. This is not an exhaustive look at every feature available in Flash, nor is it an ActionScript dictionary. This book offers a different perspective.

Flash 8: Projects for Learning Animation and Interactivity has been designed as a project-based introduction to the Flash world. Easy-to-follow exercises, content-rich sidebars, and plenty of illustrations work together to guide you through the application's major features. You will never find yourself overwhelmed by unnecessarily complex exercises or dry, labored discussions. At the same time, however, you will be inspired to create in new and different ways.

This book was written with a few simple assumptions in mind: that even if you're a beginner, you are relatively intelligent and motivated, you have a general familiarity with typical graphics programs and web browsers, and you have some basic HTML experience. However, you do not need to be well versed in ActionScript to enjoy this book. In fact, quite the contrary is true.

No programming experience is required. ActionScript fundamentals are slowly introduced throughout the book to help guide you through each new topic. You can take advantage of the sample files supplied on the enclosed CD-ROM and learn to program at your own pace. You needn't fully understand all the code examples right away, but when you feel comfortable, the

ActionScript foundation presented in this book should prepare even the greenest of beginners to take your Flash skills to the next level.

Not Exactly a Beginner?

While essentially an entry-level work, this book is not just useful for the uninitiated. It is also an excellent choice for readers who have a superficial familiarity with Flash and want to learn more about the new features introduced with Version 8.

This book should also be effective for programmers with no prior Flash experience who need to learn the Flash development environment. If, however, you want a more in-depth look at ActionScript, take a moment now to refer to the resource listing in Chapter 15. You may find a pointer to a book better suited to your needs.

If you're looking for a broader focus, and you want to get up to speed in Flash with minimal effort, this book is for you. It follows the success of tutorial instruction, providing information on a need-to-know basis, without muddying the waters unnecessarily.

More Than Just Marketing

The subtitle of this book is more than just a catch phrase, it emphasizes two important themes that run throughout. First, this book will show you how to use Flash right out of the box. You'll dive right in and learn how to animate, play audio and video, program basic interactivity, and more. Second (and just as important), as you make your way through these pages, you'll learn how to think outside the box. The last two chapters, in particular, show you a few examples of how to create with Flash in nontraditional ways.

In this book, a box will serve as a unifying element. It will be the basis for graphic layouts, buttons, animations—even a cartoon character. It will be there to remind you of what is possible without additional resources, as well as what is possible when you think without boundaries.

Boxes are allegorical of many aspects of design and development. A box can suggest form and structure, but it can also represent an empty container that you can fill with ideas. This book will help you develop some of the skills you need to fill that box.

What Makes This Book Different?

Most entry-level books are structured with a rigid, linear sequence of chapters planned with the hope that one topic will logically lead to the next. Sometimes, however, this approach may not cover a subject when you really need it or, perhaps worse, may thoroughly cover a topic in which you have no interest. By contrast, this book tries to pair topics with goals, making learning the material a more organic process. Much like peeling an onion, this book will expose new concepts layer by layer, sometimes revisiting a point more than once to make it easier to grasp.

Several techniques are used in this book to help you better understand and retain the information you are given. This approach is what makes this book a more effective learning tool than other books on the shelf. Here's a breakdown of the approach:

Learning by doing
: People learn by repetition, so you should perform all the exercises contained in this book. Techniques presented in one chapter are often used again in later chapters, offering practice while you learn new concepts. Subsequent uses will require less description and tutorial focus, until eventually accomplishing basic tasks becomes second nature. You aren't expected to master skills at the first use, and this approach means that you won't have to absorb too much information at once.

Shortcuts
: Shortcuts and alternative techniques are introduced after you have performed an operation at least once. Becoming more familiar with each operation from multiple perspectives reinforces the material, helping you to transfer your newly acquired knowledge from short-term to long-term memory.

Chunking
: Information in this book is grouped together in small digestible parts. This process is known as *chunking*. To see how this works, try to remember the following nine-letter sequence: *pnggifjpg*. Not too easy. Now try to remember the chunks PNG, GIF, and JPG. Simple, eh? The difference is in the presentation. Chunking makes it easier for you to understand broader ideas, instead of just repeating things by rote.

Need-to-know basis
: As previously mentioned, this book doesn't try to teach you everything about a given topic before you're ready. Instead, it features "progressive disclosure," in which a topic is revisited in more depth as your knowledge and needs grow. For example, don't be concerned if a specific chapter doesn't describe all of the settings in a particular dialog. You may learn about portions of the dialog in one discussion and revisit the options in the remainder of that dialog later. This reduces the chance that you'll feel overwhelmed.

Sidebars
: In addition to presenting new information, sidebars are also used to expand upon topics introduced in the main text. Subjects are usually explained in the text just enough to convey the main ideas, or for you to perform an exercise. If warranted, additional detail may appear in a

sidebar. This allows more experienced readers to move on without interruption, while beginners can learn in stages (but see "A Few Important Words About Sidebars," later in this Preface, for a caution).

Suggesting the next step
: Each chapter ends with a section called "What's Next?" This conclusion not only prepares you for the upcoming chapter, but also offers simple suggestions for you to expand on what you've learned. These unguided goals push you to develop related skills by accomplishing tasks *without* numbered steps or sample files. They are designed to motivate you into taking your skills to the next level and to start you down the road of self-teaching.

How to Use This Book

If you read this book from cover to cover, you'll find many tidbits in unlikely places that you'd miss if you skipped around. You're strongly encouraged to perform all the exercises, even if they don't appear to relate to tasks that you specifically want to accomplish, in order to gain familiarity with Flash. Most of the exercises build on concepts and operations learned earlier, so unless you're already familiar with Flash, you should start at the beginning. The exercises are refreshingly brief, so give them a shot and pick up the finer points hidden along the way.

Getting Started

Nothing is more frustrating than a tutorial book in which you can't get the examples to work. If you run into trouble, bear the following in mind.

Flash 8 is sold in two versions: Basic and Professional. Think of the Professional version as a full product and the Basic version as an entry-level, or functionally limited, product. (See *http://www.macromedia.com/software/flash/basic/* for a comparison of the two versions.) Many of the basic features are common to both versions, but the two start to diverge when it comes to more in-depth capabilities. To cover the most ground, this book and some of its sample files assume you are using the Professional version, but you can still get a lot from these pages if you're using Flash 8 Basic. Installers for both versions are included on the enclosed CD-ROM. If you don't already have Flash 8 installed, it's a good idea to evaluate the Professional version.

NOTE

If you have lost the CD-ROM and have a high-speed connection, you can download the trial software from Macromedia's web site (http://www.macromedia.com). You can also download the sample files, as well as any updates or corrections, from the book's support web site at http://www.flash8projects.com.

A Few Important Words About Sidebars

The use of sidebars in this book differs from their use in many other books, in that they do not merely contain supplemental material that tangentially relates to the topic at hand. Instead, sidebars are used to pull important or lengthy topics out of the body text, where they might otherwise be too weighty or significantly interrupt the flow of the chapter. This is especially true in the step-by-step projects.

Therefore, it is highly recommended that you read every sidebar. ActionScript topics, in particular, are introduced or expanded upon throughout the book in sidebars. This book has been designed to allow you to work through the projects quickly and to learn by doing. Rather than dedicating a full chapter or more to ActionScript theory, we introduce these topics as you go, in smaller pieces that are easier to digest and are presented just when you need them most.

Again, you are highly encouraged to embrace sidebars as content that is as valuable as the main body of the text. Skipping sidebars because you assume they are of lesser importance will almost certainly reduce the effectiveness of this book.

Conventions Used Herein

The following typographical conventions are used in this book:

Keyboard shortcuts
: Windows and Mac OS keyboard shortcuts are often listed for commands, especially the first few times they are mentioned. If only one shortcut is specified, it is the same on both platforms. Typically, the shortcuts only differ because they begin with the Control key on the Windows platform and the Command key on the Macintosh platform. These modifier keys are usually cited as "Ctrl-G (Win) or Cmd-G (Mac)." For brevity, they may be listed as "Ctrl/Cmd-G."

Menu commands
: Menu commands are indicated using the arrow symbol (→). For example, Edit→Copy indicates that you should select the Copy command from the Edit menu. The same convention is used to indicate that you should choose a tab or suboption in a dialog box, such as File→Publish Settings→Flash→ActionScript Version.

Italic
: Indicates new terms, ActionScript references (names of functions, methods, parameters, properties, etc.), symbol names, symbol linkage identifiers, frame labels, and URLs, as well as the names of layers, files, directories, and similar items requiring emphasis.

`Constant width`
: Indicates code samples, named instances of movie clips, XML tags, HTML tags, the contents of files, or the output from commands.

`Constant width bold`
: Shows commands or other text that should be entered literally by the reader. This font is also sometimes used within code examples for emphasis, such as to highlight an important line of code in a larger example.

NOTE

This icon signifies a tip, suggestion, or general note. Many tips are integrated throughout the text, but notes set aside in this manner may be particularly important.

WARNING

This icon indicates a warning or caution. Ignore it at your own peril.

Using Code Examples

This book is here to help you get your job done. In general, you may use the code in this book in your programs and documentation. You do not need to contact us for permission unless you're reproducing a significant portion of the code. For example, writing a program that uses several chunks of code from this book does not require permission. Selling or distributing a CD-ROM of examples from O'Reilly books does require permission. Answering a question by citing this book and quoting example code does not require permission. Incorporating a significant amount of example code from this book into your product's documentation does require permission.

We appreciate, but do not require, attribution. An attribution usually includes the title, author, publisher, and ISBN. For example: "*Flash 8: Projects for Learning Animation and Interactivity*, by Rich Shupe and Robert Hoekman, Jr. Copyright 2006 O'Reilly Media, Inc., 0-596-10223-2."

If you feel your use of code examples falls outside fair use or the permission given above, feel free to contact us at *permissions@oreilly.com*.

Safari® Enabled

When you see a Safari® Enabled icon on the cover of your favorite technology book, that means it's available online through the O'Reilly Network Safari Bookshelf.

Safari offers a solution that's better than e-books: it's a virtual library that lets you easily search thousands of top tech books, cut and paste code samples, download chapters, and find quick answers when you need the most accurate, current information. Try it for free at *http://safari.oreilly.com*.

Comments and Questions

Please address comments and questions concerning this book to the publisher:

O'Reilly Media, Inc.
1005 Gravenstein Highway North
Sebastopol, CA 95472
(800) 998-9938 (in the United States or Canada)
(707) 829-0515 (international or local)
(707) 829-0104 (fax)

We have a web page for this book, where we list errata, examples, and any additional information. You can access this page at:

http://www.oreilly.com/catalog/flashprojects

To comment or ask technical questions about this book, send email to:

bookquestions@oreilly.com

For more information about our books, conferences, Resource Centers, and the O'Reilly Network, see our web site at:

http://www.oreilly.com

Acknowledgments

Rich Shupe would like to thank the following people for their help, support, and distractions during his work on this book:

- John Neidhart, Steve Weiss, and everyone at O'Reilly Media, as well as Robert Hoekman, Jr., and Bruce Epstein
- Jodi Rotondo, Thomas Yeh, Kawai Sin, Joseph Shoemaker II, and everyone at FMA, including my students
- Bruce Wands, Joe Dellinger, Russet Lederman, Mike Barrons, Jaryd Lowder, Diane Field, and everyone at the School of Visual Arts, including my students
- Lori Piquet and everyone at DevX
- Stewart McBride, Lynda Weinman, Kevin Skogland, Christoph Wiese, Gaylynn Firth, Kim Vandyk, and everyone at FlashForward

- Paul Kent, Rachael Jones, Kate Greene, Heather Meninno, and everyone at Macworld, IDG, and Mactivity
- Steve, Cindy, and Brian Shupe; Abigail Jannsens; Dennis, Elaine, Denise, and Doug Rotondo; and Cheri Strand
- The Jungle (especially Penn Jillette and Teller), The Residents, Tony Fitzpatrick, Tim Jenison, Emily Z. Jillette, Paul Provenza, and all aristocrats everywhere
- Extra special thanks to Jodi, Thomas, Brian, and Jesse Freeman; and welcome Kaito, Enzo, Moxie, and...?

Robert Hoekman, Jr., would like to offer his sincerest gratitude to the following people:

- Bruce Epstein
- O'Reilly Media, Inc. (especially Tim O'Reilly, Rob Romano, Claire Cloutier, Glenn Bisignani, and Norma Emory)
- Robert Eckstein (and Scrappy)
- Liatt Bailey
- Beta readers Sham Bhangal, Paul Catanese, Lisa Coen, Marc Garrett, Mark Jonkman, Andy Rayne, Darron Schall, Drew Schiffman, Dana Stokes, Karen Vagts, and Edoardo Zubler
- Macromedia (in particular Mike Downey, Mike Chambers, Ed Sullivan, and Amy Brooks)
- FMUG.az (Flash and Multimedia Users Group of Arizona): John C. Bland II, Shane Anderson, Bob Wohl, Ron Haberle, Muharem Lubovac, Shaun Jacob, Jeff Garza, and everyone else in the group
- Above all else, my wife, Christine Rose Pearson

Getting Started, Right Out of the Box

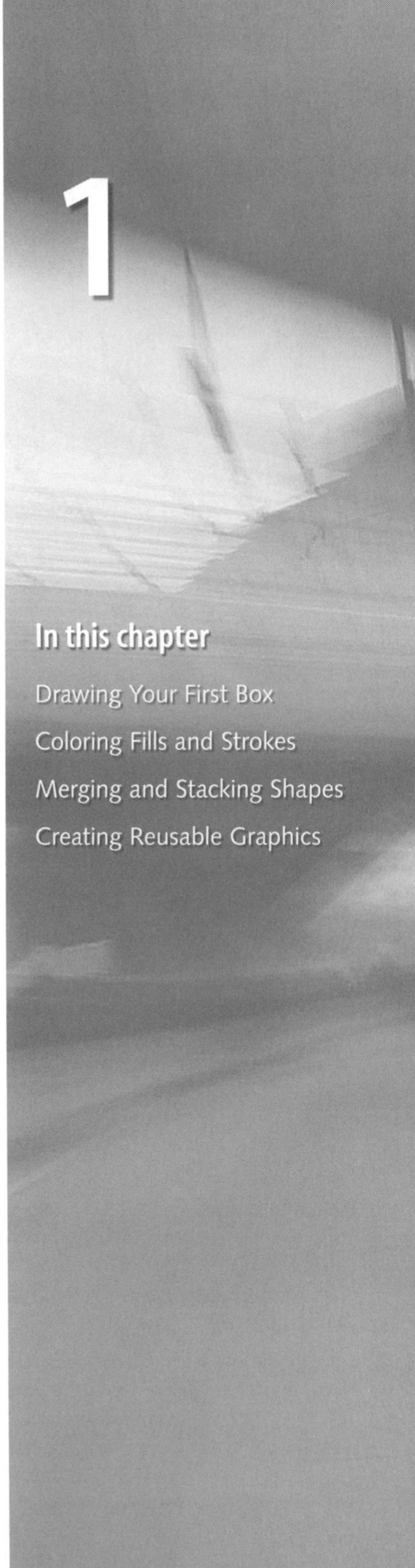

In this chapter, you'll gain your first experience with Flash's vector drawing tools. Many of Flash's tools are similar to those available in other applications, so you may be able to apply some of what you already know to Flash. However, some of Flash's tools behave in unique ways. For example, Flash builds everything you draw using vectors. So, although using Flash's Brush tool will feel similar to using a brush tool in a bitmap editing application such as Photoshop, what you draw will actually be a vector shape.

Flash's selection tools also behave a bit differently than those in a typical drawing application. You can select a shape's fill or stroke independently, and even separate the two. Also, using the Lasso tool, you can freely draw a selection path across any shapes and work only with the selected portion of those shapes. This combination of pixel- and vector-based drawing approaches makes creating Flash assets a natural and immediate experience.

If you are comfortable with traditional vector drawing applications, don't worry; you will also find a Pen tool for creating Bezier curves complete with vertices and control points in Flash. However, even if you are unfamiliar with these terms, you'll still be able to jump right in and start creating.

Your first project is to create a graphic you might use in a psychedelic poster illustration of guitar legend Jimi Hendrix. You'll begin by drawing a *box*, which is one of the most commonly used shapes in design and a frequently used metaphor in this book. Next, you'll customize your lines and fills, add a vibrant array of colors, and draw Jimi's silhouette. The techniques used in this chapter are the first steps in learning to create assets within Flash, and they are commonly used for animation, illustration, game development, application design, and virtually anything else you'll do in Flash.

Drawing Your First Box

Drawing a box is easy, so in this project you'll also look at a few ways to enhance your drawing with color and stroke properties. If you're new to Flash, fear not—you'll feel comfortable in no time.

When you launch Flash for the first time, the Start screen appears, as shown in Figure 1-1. This is merely a handy launch utility, and if you find it intrusive, you can disable it in the lower-left corner of the panel. One of the reasons you may want to use the panel is that it keeps track of the last 10 documents you opened (although you can also access this list via the File→ Open Recent menu command).

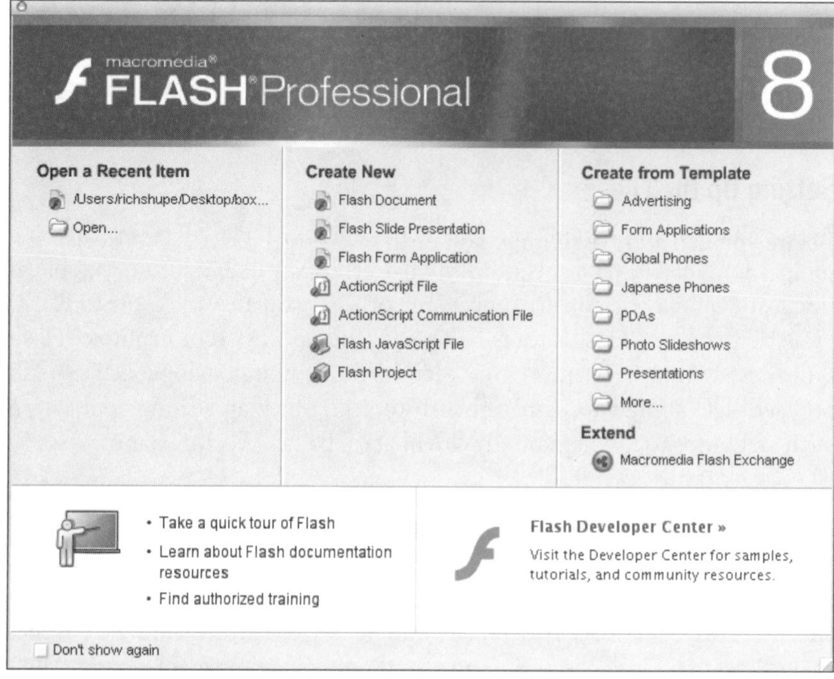

Figure 1-1. The Start screen knows what you've been doing

Exercise Files and Trial Software

All of the exercise files in this book are available on the accompanying CD-ROM and from *http://www.flash8projects.com*. Copy or download the examples, and put them somewhere on your hard drive where you can find them easily. Hereafter, this will be called your "working directory."

The assets you need for each exercise (images, sound files, and so on) have been grouped into numbered folders for your convenience. For example, any assets required for Chapter 1 can be found in the *01* folder. It's a good idea to preserve this directory structure to make it easier to find any referenced files.

In many cases, completed exercise files have also been included. Occasionally, you may want to start with a specific instruction and continue from there. However, you'll benefit most by going through the exercises step by step.

If you haven't already installed Flash 8, a 30-day trial version is also included on the accompanying CD-ROM. Installing the Professional version of Flash 8 will allow you to get the most out of the exercises in this book.

The second column of the Start screen allows you to create a new Flash document. Figure 1-1 shows the Start screen from Flash 8 Professional, which includes additional file types. You'll learn a little more about some of these files later in this book. In Chapter 13, you'll also learn how to use templates. For now, though, you'll focus on your first steps.

NOTE

The bottom portion the Start screen provides quick links to Internet resources to help you learn Flash. This area may reflect automatic online updates provided by Macromedia, so your screen may vary slightly.

Setting Up the File

Before you can start designing, you need to create a new Flash file:

1. If you haven't already, copy the CD-ROM source files and folders to your hard drive. Hereafter, the location where you store these files will be called your "working directory." Also, be sure you're running Flash 8. (Some features of this book require the Professional version. See "Getting Started" in the Preface for more information.)
2. Under the Create New heading of the Start screen, or by using the File→New→Flash Document menu command, create a new Flash document. You will save this file using the *.fla* extension (sometimes pronounced "flah"). This file type is the basis for virtually every Flash project.
3. Save your new document as *box.fla* in your working directory, using the File→Save menu option. Alternatively, you can press Ctrl-S (Win) or Cmd-S (Mac) to save the file.

NOTE

Flash documents are often called FLA files. This is the convention used in this book, although some developers reserve this term for the final compressed file format used to distribute Flash files. Files in this format use the .swf (pronounced "swiff") extension. SWF files are compiled when you test or publish your FLA files.

NOTE

Throughout this book, exercises will frequently build upon previous exercises. Usually, you'll be told when you no longer need a file, or when to start another file for a new topic or for experimentation. So, as a new series of steps begins, assume you're continuing your work, unless otherwise stated. You will also occasionally be prompted to compare your work to the sample files at major milestones. Feel free also to check your progress against interim steps at any time.

Now, take a moment to look around the world of Flash. Notice the Tools panel, shown in Figure 1-2. (If your Tools panel isn't visible, open it using the Window→Tools menu command.) Many tools will look familiar if you've worked with other graphics programs. As you roll your cursor over each tool in the panel, a tool tip indicates its name and shows its keyboard shortcut in parentheses. For example, you can select the Rectangle tool by pressing R. The Options portion at the bottom of the Tools panel reflects options for the currently selected tool. This context-sensitive area changes depending on which tool is active.

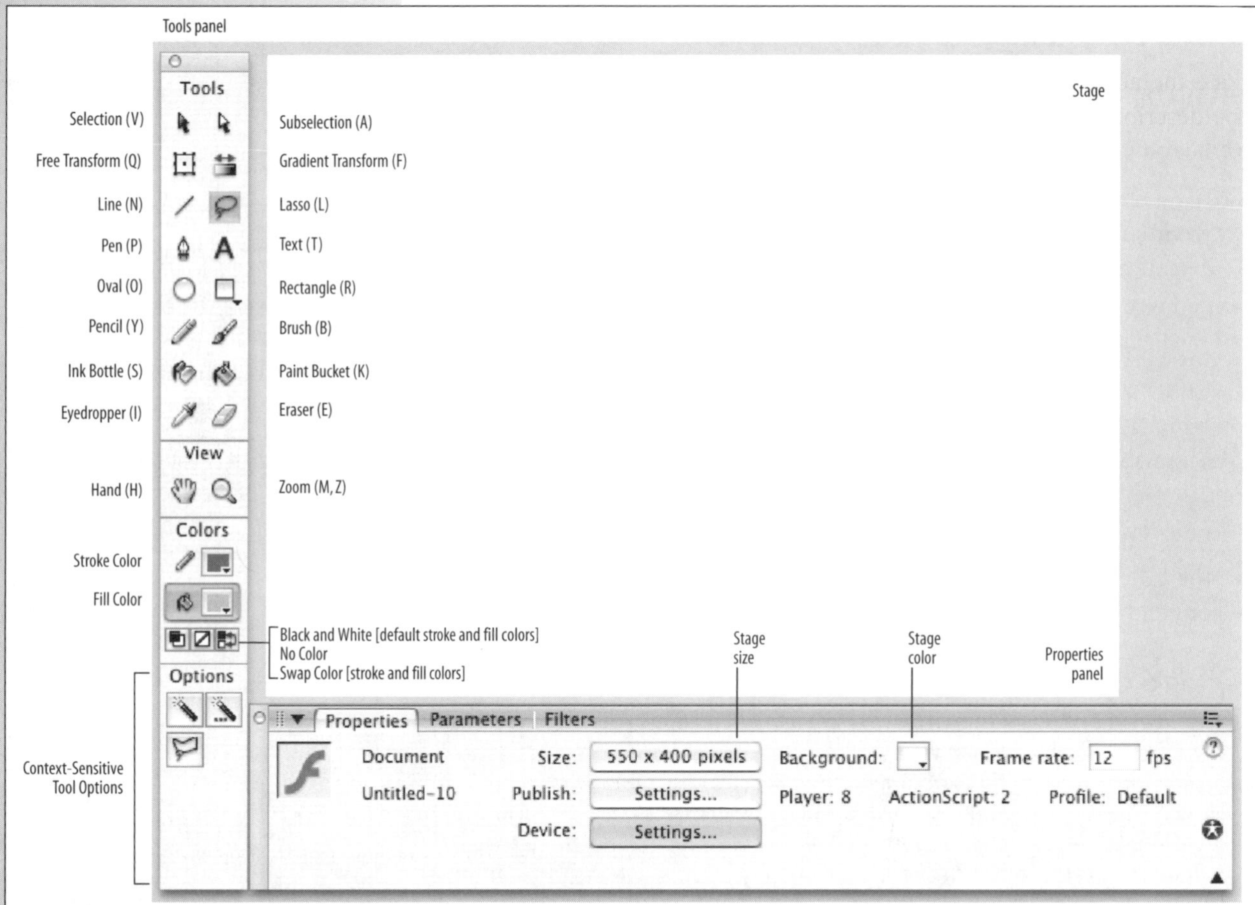

Figure 1-2. The Flash interface, showing the Tools panel, Stage, and Properties panel

Drawing a Rectangle

Begin by drawing a rectangle as a starting point for a new design:

1. In the Tools panel, select the Rectangle tool, indicated in Figure 1-2.
2. Roll your cursor over the Stage (the large white area in the document window, also seen in Figure 1-2). Your cursor should look like a crosshair.

3. Click and drag somewhere on the Stage to create a rectangle. As you can see, using the Rectangle tool in Flash is similar to using the same tool in other programs.

Using Undo and the History Panel

You are probably familiar with the Undo command from your experience with other programs. When you use the Edit→Undo menu command, or press Ctrl-Z (Win) or Cmd-Z (Mac), Flash will attempt to undo your last action. (Some things can't be undone; in this case, Flash will try to warn you before proceeding.)

Take a moment now to undo your rectangle creation. If you followed the steps described previously, you should now have an empty Stage. If not, continue to use the Undo command until your Stage is empty.

By default, Flash will store the 100 most recent undoable changes you have made to your open documents. Several hundred levels of undo can be stored, but they require memory. With each additional step you store, more system memory is consumed. Refer to Appendix A for information on how to change this setting.

You can see the undo list in action by opening the History panel, shown in Figure 1-3, using the Window→Other Panels→History menu command. Once you have opened this panel, draw a few boxes on the Stage again, and watch the history list grow. After adding a few items, use the draggable arrow on the left side of the panel to slide up the list. As you move further back in history, you will see your boxes disappear as your actions are undone. Great, huh? It gets better. In Chapter 2, you'll learn how to use the History panel to help automate tasks.

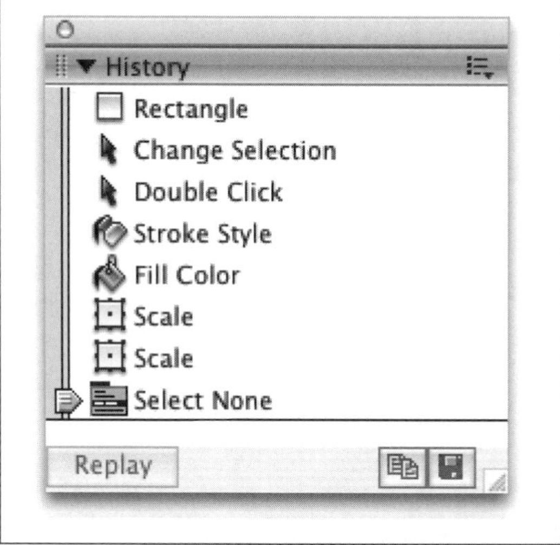

Figure 1-3. The History panel

Flash 8 now offers both *Document Undo* and *Object Undo* modes. Document-level undo maintains a single list of all undoable actions for the entire Flash document. Object-level undo maintains separate lists of your actions for each major object (such as buttons and similar items) in your document. Object-level undo is more flexible, because you can undo an action in one object without having to also undo more recent actions in other objects.

However, it can sometimes be advantageous to use document-level undo, and you should bear in mind that switching between the two modes will clear your current history. (Your document will not be affected, but your history list will be emptied.) So, experiment to see which you prefer, and be cautious when switching undo modes.

Drawing a Perfect Square

Drawing a perfect square is simpler than it sounds. All you need to do is hold down the Shift key while drawing the square. This technique, common to many graphics applications, is called "constraining." This is because the Shift key constrains the shape into a square while it's being drawn, even if you accidentally describe a rectangle with your mouse movement. This is a great way to ensure that your squares are actually square. The same rule applies to the Oval tool for drawing perfect circles and the Line tool for drawing straight lines.

What if you want to create a box that is exactly 300 × 300 pixels? In this case, you can use numeric input to get the exact shape you want. Here's how:

1. If you haven't already done so, delete everything on the Stage.
2. Select the Rectangle tool, and click and drag on the Stage to draw a rectangle.
3. When you're done, choose the Selection tool (shown in Figure 1-2) from the Tools panel.
4. Double-click inside the box you just drew to select both the box and its border.

NOTE

Flash allows you to select individual fills and strokes separately, so be sure you select both when desired. See the "Fills and Strokes" sidebar for more information.

5. With the box selected, locate the Properties panel, shown in Figure 1-4. (If necessary, open it with the menu command Window→Properties.) The Properties panel looks different in this figure than it did in Figure 1-2 because its contents change depending on what is selected. At the bottom of Figure 1-2, the Properties panel displays the Stage's properties. In Figure 1-4, it displays properties for the selected rectangle.
6. The *W* and *H* fields in the Properties panel represent the rectangle's width and height. The relative proportions of width and height can be constrained by clicking on the lock icon to the left of these fields. In this case, this is fine, as you are drawing a square. However, if you want freedom to enter any width or height, you'll need to click on the icon to unlock it, as pictured in Figure 1-4. Enter 300 for the width and 300 for the height. You now have a precisely sized rectangle—a perfect square.
7. Save your work.

NOTE

Don't worry if you can't get an exact number when entering property values. Flash does its best to give you the value you request, but it isn't always easy to achieve exact sizing or positioning at the sub-pixel level. If you get values like 299.9 or 300.1, the difference will usually be unnoticeable.

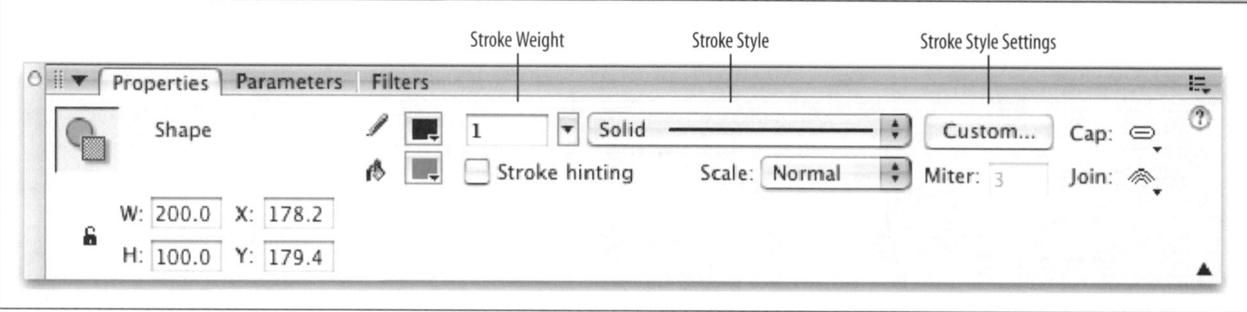

Figure 1-4. The Properties panel, as it appears when a shape is selected

Adjusting Caps and Joins

You may have noticed, during your experimenting, that you haven't been getting nice sharp corners. Flash's default behavior uses rounded stroke corners and end caps, but Flash 8 finally introduced the ability to customize the cap and join settings of your strokes. The *Cap* setting dictates the appearance of the ends of the lines, while the *Join* setting defines the appearance of corners. As you can see in Figure 1-4, both settings can be found in the far right of the Properties panel when a shape with strokes is the active selection.

Caps can be set to *None* (the line ends precisely at the end point), *Round* (a round cap is placed on each end of the line), or *Square* (a square cap is placed on each end of the line). Joins can be set to *Miter* (sharp corner), *Round*, (rounded corner), or *Bevel* (two-point corner).

Figure 1-5 shows the results of each setting. All the line widths are the same, and all shape end points terminate at the dotted lines. From top to bottom, the features used are: 1) Cap: *None*, Join: *Miter*; 2) Cap: *Round*, Join: *Round*; and 3) Cap: *Square*, Join: *Bevel*.

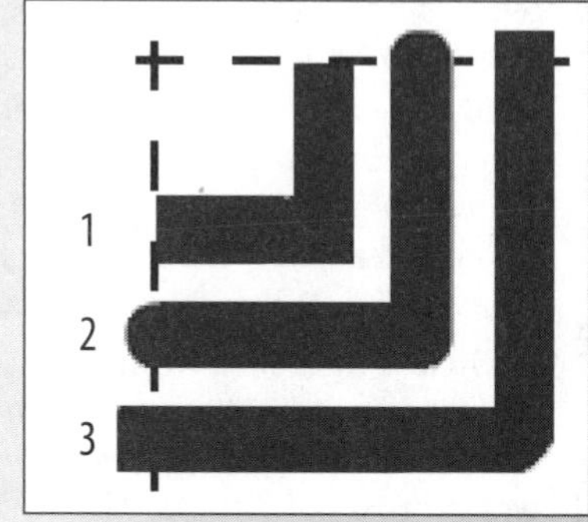

Figure 1-5. Cap and join differences

NOTE

Cap settings add to the apparent length of a line. Notice in Figure 1-5 that although all the lines end at the same horizontal or vertical positions, those with caps appear longer.

Coloring Fills and Strokes

When you're drawing or editing a shape, Flash independently colors fills and strokes. You can change the colors via the Tools panel or the Properties panel when a shape or shape tool is active. In both locations, a small pencil icon indicates the stroke color, and a small paint bucket icon indicates the fill color.

There are two simple ways to change a shape's fill or stroke color. First, you can change the fill color of a selected shape using the pop-up color swatch utility:

1. Choose the Selection tool from the Tools panel, and click once inside the box on the Stage. The fill area will appear as if seen through a screen, indicating that it is selected.
2. In the Properties or Tools panel, click on the Fill Color swatch. A palette of colors will pop up, and you'll be allowed to select from the default web-safe swatches. A white box with a red line through it at the top of the pop-up indicates that no fill will be used, allowing underlying assets to be visible within the borders of the shape.
3. Deselect the box to view the results. You can deselect by using Edit→ Deselect All, or by clicking in any unoccupied area of the Stage or Work Area (the area surrounding the Stage). Deselecting is often required to avoid editing an active element, and it will soon become second nature.

Fills and Strokes

Unlike in many other drawing programs, Flash elements are drawn using separate *fills* and *strokes*. Although this can take some getting used to, it can also be very helpful. The best way to understand how fills and strokes work is to do a little experimenting. You may want to open a new document so that you can tinker while reading without affecting your ongoing exercises.

A *fill* is the area of color that fills the inside of a stroked shape or constitutes the body of a borderless shape. For example, if you draw a free-form blob on the Stage, the colored area inside its border is its fill. The colored area is called a fill even if no border surrounds it.

A *stroke* is the border or line surrounding a shape. Strokes can have six styles, the most common of which are solid, dotted, and dashed. Each stroke type can be customized with a variety of settings, all of which can be found within the Properties panel when a line or line-making tool is active.

Flash allows you to select individual fills and strokes separately, if you desire. You can select only a fill, or even only one side of a multi-sided stroke. Selecting a contiguous fill, or a single part of a multi-part stroke, requires one click. To select an entire contiguous stroke, double-click on the stroke only. To select both a fill and its stroke, double-click on the fill. See Figure 1-6 for a comparison of single-clicking and double-clicking a multi-part stroke.

Figure 1-6. Stroke selection by single-click (left) and double-click (right)

If you want to work with an entire shape (fill and stroke) but accidentally only select one, the remainder of the shape will not be edited. This can happen when dragging—for example, you may drag a fill and leave the stroke behind.

If this happens, undo your change and double-click, or press the Shift key while selecting multiple objects, to include all the desired elements in your efforts.

You selected just the fill to practice, and to show that the colors of selected shapes can be changed directly with the color swatches. Next, you'll use the Ink Bottle tool to exclusively change the color of a stroke, regardless of whether or not it has been selected. The Ink Bottle tool is adjacent to the Paint Bucket tool in the Tools palette.

You may be familiar with the Paint Bucket from experience with other graphics tools. You can use it to change a fill color by single-clicking within the fill area. Think of the Ink Bottle tool as a Paint Bucket for lines. It will apply your preferred stroke attributes to any shape stroke you click on:

1. Choose the Ink Bottle tool, click on the Stroke Color chip (indicated by the pencil icon), and pick a color for your stroke.
2. If you wish, experiment with some of the other stroke attributes in the Properties panel, such as thickness, cap, and join settings. Editing strokes will be discussed further in a few minutes.
3. To view the results, with the Ink Bottle tool active, click on a shape stroke. The stroke should change to reflect your chosen attributes while the fill remains unaffected.

Solid Fills and Gradients

Now that you know how to add colors to shapes, you're probably asking yourself, "What if I don't want to use one of the default colors available in these tool swatches?" No problem. There are a few ways to create your own custom colors.

If you just need a quick color, which you may not use often, you can create a color on the fly, you can take advantage of two options in the color swatches pop-up palette that appears when you select a stroke or fill color. The first option is to use the hexadecimal entry field in the top left of the swatches pop-up. This field allows you to enter hex color values to specify any color numerically. If you are familiar with HTML, you will likely be comfortable with this method.

The second option is to use the color picker icon in the upper right of the swatches pop-up. This will bring up your operating system's color picker, which will allow you to select colors using a variety of methods used by your system. If you work with color in other applications, you may be familiar with this utility already.

Another handy feature in Flash 8's swatches pop-up (Figure 1-7) is the ability to control your color's opacity via the Alpha setting. Colors with an alpha value of less than 100% have some transparency, allowing your colors to mix on the Stage.

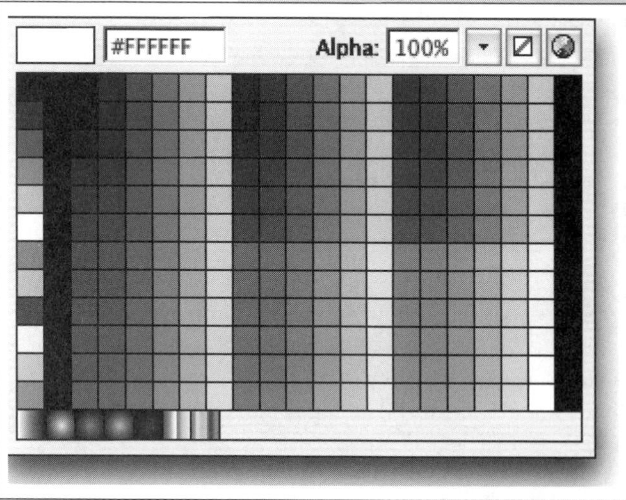

Figure 1-7. The color swatches pop-up, accessible via the Tools and Properties panels

The swatch pop-up utility is great for quick access, but what if you need more control? Enter the Color Mixer.

The Color Mixer

The Color Mixer panel, shown in Figure 1-8, gives you some great options for changing strokes and fills, and even enables you to change the fill completely by converting it to a gradient.

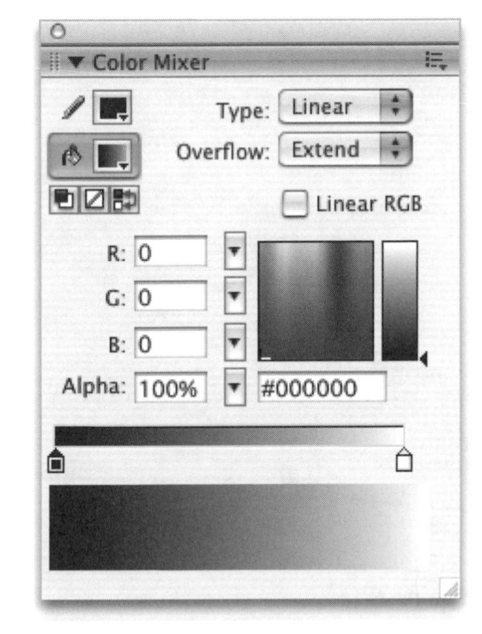

Figure 1-8. The Color Mixer panel

Here is a breakdown of the options for the Color Mixer:

Stroke color
: Changes the color of the stroke. You can access your operating system's native color picker using the icon in the upper right of the pop-up palette. This allows you to specify colors from spaces other than RGB, such as hue, saturation, and brightness (HSB).

Fill color
: Changes the color of the fill. See Stroke Color for additional information.

Swatch utilities
: Sets the stroke and fill colors to black and white, respectively; removes the selected stroke or fill; switches the stroke and fill colors.

Fill Type (menu)
: Changes the fill style. Options include None (which deletes the fill), Solid (for a solid, one-color fill), Linear (for a gradient that blends on a linear path), Radial (for a gradient that blends outward, in a circular path, from a focal point), and Bitmap (for a fill made of tiled bitmap images). Additional gradient options are discussed in the main text.

Gradient Overflow (menu)
: Visible only when a gradient fill type is selected; determines how the gradient is mapped when exceeding the range of the Gradient Transform tool. Options include Extend, Reflect, and Repeat.

RGB input (three separate entry fields, pop-up sliders)
: Changes the density of the red, green, and blue (RGB) colors in a fill.

Alpha
: Sets the percentage of opacity for a solid fill (or the currently selected Color Proxy slider for a gradient fill). Zero percent alpha makes it invisible, while 100% alpha makes it opaque.

Color chooser
: Provides a quick, visual way to choose any color. Simply click on the color chooser and drag the cursor around to locate the color you want.

Brightness slider
: Changes the brightness of the current color.

Hexadecimal input
: Changes the color by accepting hexadecimal values. Commonly used in HTML, hex values are six-digit number and/or letter (A–F) combinations that represent colors, such as #000000, which represents black, or #FFFFFF, which represents white.

Gradient color swatches
: Changes the colors used in gradients. Between 2 and 15 colors can be used for each gradient.

Current color
: Displays the currently selected color.

When creating *solid* colors, like the colors you've been using so far, in some ways the Color Mixer is not unlike the color swatches pop-up. However, instead of limiting custom color creation to hexadecimal value entry and the system color picker, it has its own color chooser. A small box presents a graduated tone of hues from left to right, and decreasing brightness from top to bottom. You can pick a color value with your mouse and then use the vertical slider to increase or decrease brightness. As you'll see in a moment, you can also save your color choice for later reuse. See the sidebar "The Color Mixer" for a look at its interface and a little more detail on its functionality.

Gradient Psychedelia

When creating *gradients*, the Color Mixer is required. Next, you'll use it to create a gradient that will be the basis for a psychedelic look in a 1960s-style Jimi Hendrix poster illustration:

1. If you've been experimenting, undo your changes or use the File→Revert menu option. As long as you haven't saved since last instructed to do so, this will revert your file back to where you left off—a 300 × 300 pixel square with fill and stroke.
2. Select the fill and choose Window→Color Mixer to open the panel shown in Figure 1-8, in the sidebar "The Color Mixer."
3. In the Color Mixer panel, select Linear from the Type drop-down menu. The solid color automatically changes to a linear gradient. A thin bar, showing the gradient in progress, allows you to edit the gradient via the mini-swatches below it. (A new menu, called *Overflow*, also appears; you'll learn about that later.)

The small color chips beneath the gradient color bar have arrows pointing to the focus point of each color. These swatches define the colors used in the gradient and slide left and right to define the position of each color.

To change the gradient, change the color of these swatches in one of two ways. Double-clicking a chip enables you to choose a color from the familiar swatch pop-up utility. For more flexibility, you can select a chip with a single click and enter RGB or hexadecimal values in the input fields, or use your mouse with the color picker and brightness slider. Both techniques allow you to add an alpha value to a color to achieve transparencies of 0 to 100%.

You can use from 2 to 15 swatches, and you can remove swatches by dragging them down and away from the gradient preview bar. Change the gradient hues now, and add two more for big splashes of color:

1. Double-click on the leftmost gradient color swatch, and pick a bright yellow color from the color palette. If you want to try to match the sample files (although there's no reason you must), the yellow is HEX #FFFF00, or RGB 255, 255, 0.

NOTE

Be sure to hit Enter/Return to update the color each time you put in a value.

2. Next, double-click on the rightmost gradient color swatch to change the end color for the gradient. Choose a vibrant purple. The sample file uses HEX #660099, or RGB 102, 0, 153.

3. Now add a new chip by clicking directly beneath the gradient color bar, approximately one third of the way along the span of the gradient, from the left. It will assume the color immediately above it. Change its color to HEX #FF0000, or RGB 255, 0, 0, for bright red.

4. Add another color halfway between chips two and four, or approximately one third of the way along the span of the gradient, from the right. This time enter a HEX value of #3399FF. You now have a colorful linear gradient.

5. Experiment by dragging the chips left and right to give each color more or less prominence. When you're done, place the first chip at the far left, chips two and three at one-third and two-thirds from the left, and the last chip slightly short of far right. This will give purple a bit more weight and will help demonstrate another feature in a minute or so.

6. To create a background more like the psychedelic posters from the 1960s, change the Type drop-down menu choice to Radial. This changes the gradient so it blends outward from a central point instead of along a linear path.

7. If you're satisfied with your gradient, save it for later use. If it's not already visible, choose Window→Color Swatches to view the Color Swatches panel. When you move your mouse over the empty white area, the pointer will change into a paint bucket. Click the mouse and, since the currently active new color is a gradient, the gradient will appear in the bottommost row of swatches. Now you can use the gradient anytime later in this file, even if you create a new gradient in the meantime.

8. Save your work and leave this file open.

Custom Stroke Styles

The stroke for this image could be improved to better fit with the illustration style, so change it from a solid line to something funkier:

1. Deselect the fill of the box, and double-click the stroke to select the entire stroke.

2. In the Properties panel, give the stroke a dark maroon color.

3. Click on the Stroke Style drop-down list, shown in Figure 1-4, and choose the next-to-last style. (The styles aren't named in the menu, but it looks a bit like splattered paint.)

4. Using the Stroke Height text field or slider in the Properties panel, set the stroke weight to 10.

NOTE

Flash 8 now supports gradients as stroke colors. If you want your image to be really colorful, you can try to make a new gradient for the border. Don't worry too much if your file differs from the sample. Think outside the box!

5. Deselect the stroke to see what it looks like. Your stroke should be 10 pixels wide and appear as an array of spots that resemble paint splatters. Things are looking good now, but the stroke doesn't seal off the border as well as it could, so modify it to fix the problem.
6. Select the entire stroke again. In the Properties panel, click the Custom button to open the Stroke Style dialog box. The Type drop-down should already be set to Stipple (unless you chose a different type of stroke earlier).
7. Set Dot Size to Medium, Dot Variation to Varied Sizes, and Density to Very Dense. This tightens up the stroke to seal up the edges of the fill it surrounds. Click OK and deselect the stroke to see your work by clicking somewhere outside of the box. Nice, huh?
8. Save the file, but leave it open.

Scaling Shapes

Often, you can't tell when starting a drawing how big or small it needs to be, and sometimes creative tangents bring about change. Here, you need to make your illustration more impressive by filling up the Stage.

Quick, inexact scaling is very simple in Flash. All you need to do is activate the Free Transform tool (Q) and use your mouse to drag one or more of the active drag locations. You can resize by dragging any of the handles; the cursor will temporarily change to a double-headed arrow to indicate that scaling is possible. (You can also skew by dragging the sides, or rotate by dragging *outside* one of the corner handles. Temporary cursor changes will also indicate that these features are possible.)

Here, however, you need exact resizing and positioning capabilities, so you'll use the Properties panel. The Stage is rectangular, but the image is square, so you have to make one change first. If you resize the background box as is, changing its shape from a square to a rectangle, the radial gradient fill will distort. You'll learn later how to position and scale gradients directly, but in this exercise you'll delete the fill and replace it after resizing the box. Here's how:

1. First, make sure your background gradient has been saved in the Color Swatches panel, as described earlier. If not, use the Eyedropper tool to pick up the gradient from the background and then click anywhere in the empty white area of the Color Swatches panel.
2. Now you can safely select the gradient fill and delete it using the Backspace or Delete key on your keyboard.
3. Select the box's stroke and, using the Properties panel, set the width (W) to 550 and the height (H) to 400. Remember, you may need to unlock the padlock icon to change the box's width and height independently. The stroke now matches the dimensions of the Stage.

4. Also in the Properties panel, change the box's X (horizontal) and Y (vertical) coordinates to 0. After pressing Tab or Return to register the values, this aligns the stroke to the upper-left corner of the Stage.
5. Activate the Paint Bucket tool and switch the fill color using the pop-up swatches. You should now see your gradient in the bottom row with the default gradients. Select it.
6. Look in the Paint Bucket tool's Options area, located in the lower portion of the Tools panel, and make sure the Lock Fill option is disabled. Use the Paint Bucket tool to apply the gradient to the background box. Notice that the radial gradient's center point is determined by the position of your click. Click several times inside the box to change the center point for the gradient until you are happy with the look.
7. Next, activate the Lock Fill option and try to apply the fill again. The Lock Fill option prevents the fill from being changed. Now that you've seen the effect of this option in both states, disable it once again, so you can edit the fill later. If the scale or position of the gradient isn't exactly the way you want it, don't worry. You'll soon learn how to change that.
8. Save your work. If you want to compare your work with the sample files, your file should look like *box_03.fla* in the *01* folder in your working directory.

Drawing Strokes Freehand

Adding a silhouette of Jimi Hendrix in the foreground of this gradient will finish off the design nicely. If your drawing skills aren't great, don't sweat it. The silhouette of Jimi, just like the rest of this image, can be as psychedelic as you want. The objective is to see how the Pencil tool can be used to draw shapes freehand:

1. Choose the Pencil tool from the Tools panel. In the lower portion of the panel, the context-sensitive Options area includes two options. You'll use the Object Drawing option in a moment. For now, this should be disabled. The Pencil Mode option offers you a choice of Straighten, Smooth, and Ink. These options will help you draw straighter lines, create smoother curves, or work freehand, respectively. Set the option to Smooth. In the Properties panel, set the stroke weight to 5, set the stroke color to black, and change the stroke style back to a solid line.
2. Click and drag inside the box to draw a silhouette of Jimi, like the one in Figure 1-9. Don't let the ends of the stroke touch the border of the box. (You'll learn why in a moment.)

Figure 1-9. A silhouette of Jimi Hendrix drawn with the Pencil tool

NOTE

If you prefer not to draw the silhouette yourself, open hendrix_silhouette.fla, located in the 01 folder in your working directory. Double-click to select the entire stroke, choose Edit→Copy to copy it to your clipboard, and then return to box.fla and choose Edit→Paste in Center to paste it into box.fla. Close hendrix_silhouette.fla by choosing File→Close when you're done.

You can stop and start as much as you want using the Pencil tool, so feel free to use as many lines or curves as you need. If you make a mistake, either undo it or just go with it. In creative situations like these, mistakes can sometimes be as inspirational as the lines you draw intentionally.

If you're not satisfied with your drawing, try smoothing the stroke with the Selection tool's Smooth option in the Options section of the Tools panel. This is similar to the Pencil tool's Smooth option, but it allows you to smooth strokes after they've been created. Try this:

1. Select the stroke you wish to smooth. If the lines are all connected, double-clicking will select them all. If not, press Shift and select each line individually until you have selected all of them.
2. Click once on the Smooth option at the bottom of the Tools panel. This makes the stroke smoother. If you're happy with the new look, leave it alone. If not, click Smooth one or two more times until you're satisfied. The trick is knowing when to stop smoothing it. Making it too smooth

will diminish the hand-drawn quality. Deselect the stroke when you're done.

3. Choose the Paint Bucket tool, and change the fill color to black using the Properties panel. With the Paint Bucket tool active, click once inside the outline to fill in the silhouette of Jimi.

Did the entire image turn black? If it didn't, that's fine. In fact, this is the desired result, as it shows that when you drew your line you fully enclosed the area within it (either by connecting the stroke's end point with its starting point, or by connecting both ends of your stroke with the border of the box).

If the entire image did turn black, don't worry. What this means is that when you drew the silhouette, you didn't fully complete the Hendrix outline—a gap remained that allowed the fill color to "spill out" and fill any connected area with the black color. You can fix this by closing the stroke and sealing off the fill area:

1. Undo the last step to remove the black fill from the image.
2. Using the Pencil tool, make sure the entire outline is complete, including a line across the bottom of the silhouette.
3. Activate the Paint Bucket tool again, and display the Gap Size menu from the Options section of the Tools panel. The Gap Size option dictates how large a gap Flash will bridge for you when applying a fill with the Paint Bucket tool. Choose Close Small Gaps from the menu and click inside the shape to see if the fill is applied properly. If not, choose Close Medium Gaps and try again. If that doesn't work, choose Close Large Gaps, and the fill should be applied.
4. Save your work.

If you connected your silhouette border to the box stroke, your results may differ slightly from the descriptions in some upcoming exercises. Feel free to continue with that in mind, or open *box_05.fla* to continue.

Merging and Stacking Shapes

So far, you've been using Flash's default *Merge Drawing mode*. In this mode shapes can interact with one another, merging together when they overlap. For example, if the corners of two squares overlap, the frontmost shape will "knock out" the underlying shape, effectively deleting it, as seen in the top of Figure 1-10. This behavior contrasts with that of the newly introduced Object Drawing mode, which will be discussed shortly.

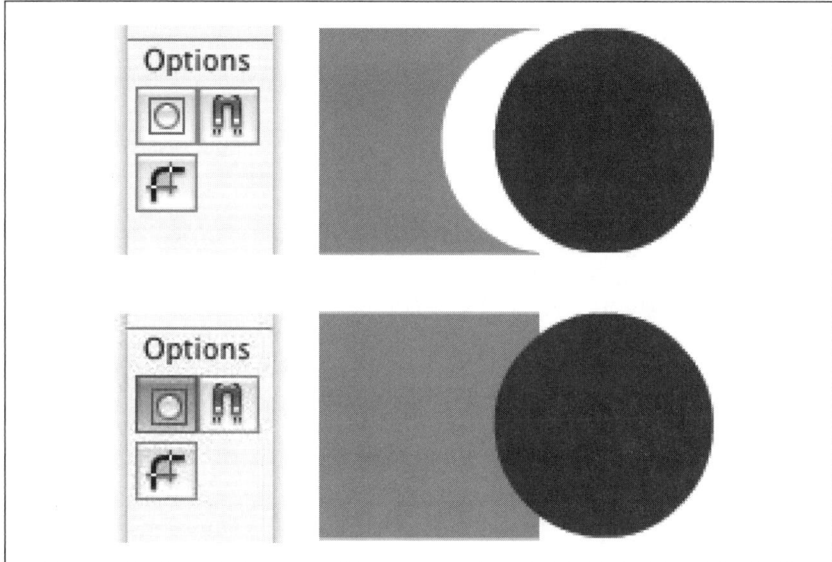

Figure 1-10. Merge Drawing mode (top) and Object Drawing mode (bottom) compared

What are the implications of shapes merging? If you didn't save your work at the end of the last sequence, do so now, and then try this with your current file:

1. Activate the Selection tool, select the black fill you just applied to the silhouette, and then delete it. Everything inside the fill area is removed, including the gradient previously behind the silhouette's fill!
2. Undo the last step. You'll need the silhouette fill for something else in a minute.

At first you may think this is a problem, but it can be very useful, *and* you can prevent it from happening, if you wish. First, however, look at a few simple examples of how Merge Drawing mode can be advantageous. If you recently saved your work, feel free to experiment.

Select the Line tool and draw a line all the way through your artwork, from outside left to outside right. (This is arbitrary, but ensures that the line goes completely through the box and protrudes on either side.) Now choose the Selection tool and click once in various regions of your art. You'll see that the line has effectively segmented your art, allowing easy selection of smaller pieces.

Next, select the Brush tool. This will show you a good example of how unprotected shapes can be altered in creative ways. In the tool's Options area, experiment with the different Paint modes. Paint Normal will behave the way you likely expect. Paint Fills, however, will paint only fills, leaving strokes unaffected. Try Paint Behind and Paint Inside to see how they work, too.

Finally, try one last thing. Select the Lasso tool, and freely select any combination of fill and stroke. With a selection active, you can move it, or delete it, as before. The Merge Drawing mode and the Lasso tool make selecting partial fills and strokes very easy and natural.

Groups

When you don't want shapes to merge together, there are a few ways to prevent this from happening. In just a few minutes, you'll learn how to convert shapes into another type of Flash asset. Also, in Chapter 3 you'll learn how to add new layers to prevent shapes from ever touching each other. However, you still need to know how to protect existing shapes in the same layer. The first approach you'll practice is making a *group* from a shape:

1. Select the fill and outline (stroke) of the Hendrix silhouette. Press Ctrl-G (Win) or Cmd-G (Mac). This creates a group of the fill and stroke so they can easily be moved together (i.e., they cannot be edited separately). A light blue bounding rectangle appears around the silhouette when it's selected, indicating that this is no longer a shape. In this case, it is now a group.
2. Drag the group to the right. You'll see that the area under the silhouette is still empty, but if you deselect the silhouette and then move it again, you will find that this time the move does not affect the gradient beneath it.
3. Save your work. If you wish, compare your file to *box_06.fla*.

Traditionally, you probably think of a group as two or more items treated as a single entity, and the same is certainly true in Flash. However, as you've just seen, a group in Flash has another important purpose. By grouping the parts of a shape, you ensure that the shape can no longer be altered by another shape. Thus, grouping single items is an attractive solution to unwanted shape merging.

Editing groups

What if you want to edit a shape that has been grouped? Although the shapes no longer seem editable, there are two ways to satisfy this need.

First, if you double-click a group, the surrounding assets will appear to dim, and the group will become editable. This is because you are effectively "inside" the group and can edit it as if it were a shape. When you are finished editing, you can double-click elsewhere on the Stage to go back "outside" the group. This is useful when you want the shape to continue to be protected from interaction with other shapes.

NOTE

When inside a group, if you look at the very top of the main document window (to the right of the word "Timeline"), you will see a series of icons from left to right that represent a nested hierarchy of objects that you are editing. The last one will likely say "Group," indicating where you are. You will read about this in greater detail later in this book, but for now bear in mind that if you ever get stuck and don't know what you're editing, you can look to this area and click icons to the left until you've walked your way back to where you want to be.

Second, if you *break apart* a group, it will return to behaving like a shape. To do this, first select the group and then access the Modify→Break Apart menu command (Ctrl/Cmd-B). Be sure you want to do this, though, because it means that other overlapping shapes will again affect the shape.

Both of these techniques are very useful and can be applied to many different types of Flash assets. You'll see them again when you look at other types of native Flash assets, such as buttons, but they apply to other editable items as well. For example, if you break apart a block of text, the selection will turn into a group of individual letters. If you again use the Break Apart command, those letters will turn into shapes—they will not be editable as text, but can be fully manipulated as shapes.

Think of breaking apart assets as "going down to the next smallest editable item." This will become clearer with more practice.

Gradients Transformed

Now that you know about groups, you can prevent existing shapes from being deformed by other shapes. But you still have a big hole in your gradient background that needs repair. Here's how to fix it:

1. In the Color Mixer panel, change the Fill Type from Solid to Radial. Your previous gradient should appear again. If not, use the eyedropper to pick it up from your saved color swatch or the remaining background.
2. Next, use the Selection tool to select the remaining gradient and delete it.
3. Switch to the Paint Bucket tool so you can fill the border with an intact gradient, but first check again to make sure the Paint Bucket tool's Lock Fill option is still disabled. This time, click in the upper-left corner of the background box to apply the gradient. The effect you're looking for is a bright, vibrant sun radiating rays of color. Deselect the gradient to see how it looks.
4. With the gradient deselected, activate the Gradient Transform tool (F). Click the gradient fill to position and scale the gradient the way you want it. The Gradient Transform tool will display a circle with five control points on it, as seen in Figure 1-11.

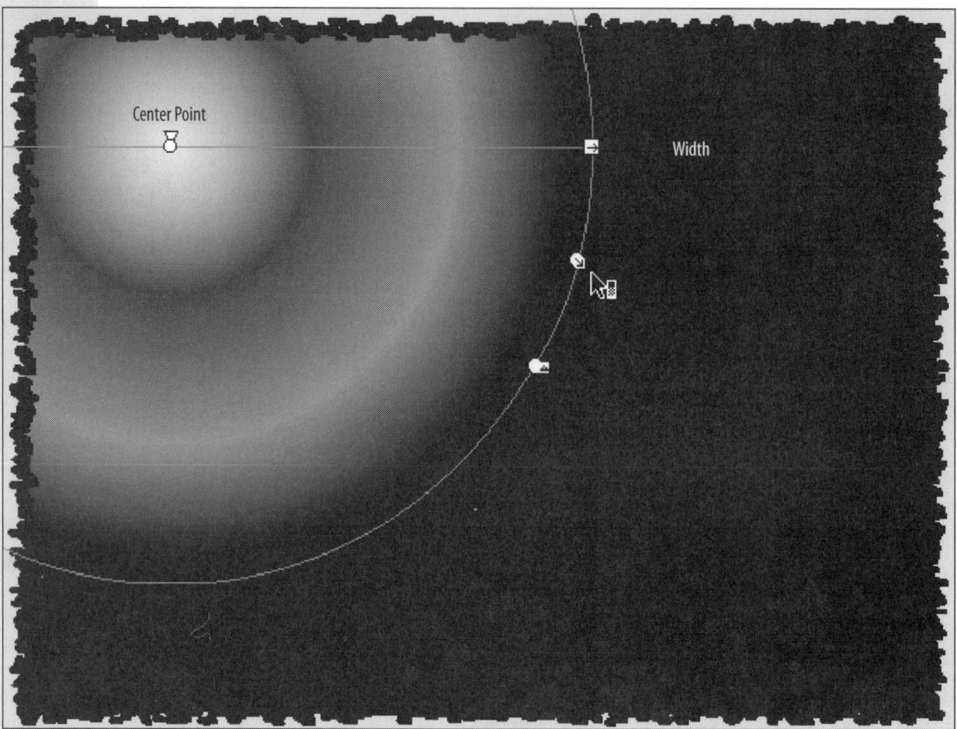

Figure 1-11. The Gradient Transform tool in action

5. Use the Center Point control point (the circle in the upper-left corner of Figure 1-11) to position the sun where it appears in the figure. (The triangle is the Focal Point control, which is not used in this exercise.)

6. Use the Scale control point (the second icon down on the right side of the circle) to scale your gradient until it resembles the gradient in Figure 1-11. As you can see, the last color in the gradient (purple) extends to fill the rest of the box. This is more like a traditional sun. Save your work so you can revert to this design if you prefer it.

7. See if you can make your sun a bit more psychedelic. Switch to the Selection tool and select the gradient. In the Color Mixer, change the Gradient Overflow setting to Reflect. Your file should now look like Figure 1-12.

Figure 1-12. Your poster with the gradient applied

8. The Gradient Overflow option dictates what the gradient will do when it extends beyond the size you set with the Gradient Transform tool. You've seen two of the overflow options in action: Extend continues the last color, and Reflect reflects the gradient, reversing the order of its colors until the area is filled. A third option is Repeat, which starts over at the first color in each cycle until the area is filled. Pick the look you prefer and save your work.

Object Drawing Mode

You've already learned how to protect a shape from merging with other shapes by grouping it, but there's a faster way to achieve this result as you are drawing. The *Object Drawing mode*, introduced in Flash 8, essentially draws shapes that are "pre-grouped." (The results are actually called *drawing objects*, but the effect is the same.)

Add a couple of stars to your illustration to practice:

1. Click and hold the Rectangle tool, and select PolyStar Tool from the pop-up menu. You can use this tool to create polygons or stars with your preferred number of sides or points, respectively.
2. In the Properties panel, choose no stroke color and a white fill color. Then look in the context-sensitive Options section of the Tools panel, and enable Object Drawing mode.
3. Back in the Properties panel, select the Options button in the lower-right corner. Change to the Star style and click OK.
4. Draw stars of different sizes in the lower-left and upper-right corners. Feel free to move them around—your background gradient will be unaffected, just like when you moved your grouped shapes around.
5. Save your work. If desired, compare your file to *box_07.fla*.

Stacking Graphics

The image's composition is good, but not great. The silhouette looks a bit odd on top of the stroke for the box. If you fix that, the stroke will appear as a frame for the entire image:

1. Double-click, or Shift-select, the entire border. Press Ctrl/Cmd-G to create a group from the stroke.
2. If the gradient border doesn't also now appear in front of the silhouette, choose the Modify→Arrange→Bring to Front menu option while the border is still selected.
3. Save your work.

The stroke now appears in front of the silhouette, so it looks like a frame for the image. This occurs because Flash creates a visual *stacking order* for assets that exist in a single layer (layers are discussed in Chapter 3). If you draw a shape, and then draw a second shape, the second shape will appear in front of the first. Additionally, grouped shapes and drawing objects will appear on top of shapes in their own stacking order. You will quickly get the hang of the stacking order after a short time working with shapes, drawing objects, and groups.

WARNING

It is possible to draw a shape only to watch it disappear behind a grouped item or drawing object. If this happens, or if you are having trouble achieving the desired results with the Modify→Arrange menu options, remember that drawing objects are always drawn on top of shapes, and groups are always stacked on top of both shapes and drawing objects.

Finished! You're all done with your first project. It's hard to believe this image started as a simple box, but it did. Making use of a few drawing tools, some fill and stroke options, and a bit of ingenuity turned this simple shape into a background for a 1960s rock concert poster. Great work!

Before you move on, though, you need to discover how to make your graphics reusable and your files more efficient.

Creating Reusable Graphics

You may find that you need to use a graphic several times in one movie, whether it's a box, a logo, or a character. To avoid adding substantially to the file size of the finished project as a result, use symbols.

A *symbol* is a reusable asset that resides in a Library in every Flash document (see the sidebar "The Library"). When a symbol is dragged from the Library to the Stage, the on-Stage element is called an *instance* of that symbol. This is because the element is not removed from the Library. Instead, the instance references, or points to, the Library symbol. Multiple instances can be spawned from a single symbol, without significantly increasing file size. On-Stage changes (such as adjustments to width, height, rotation, opacity, etc.) can be made to individual instances of a symbol, and the original symbol will remain intact. However, if persistent changes are made to the symbol in the Library, all instances derived from that symbol will be affected.

Think of symbols this way: a symbol is analogous to an actor in a movie. Each instance of that symbol is analogous to a character played by the actor. The actor can play multiple characters in the movie, simply by changing costume or make-up. However, if the actor is replaced with another actor, all of the characters will also be changed.

This discussion is focused on reusability and file optimization, but in nearly every remaining chapter of this book, you will see that symbols are central to Flash development. Most notably, they are the building blocks within every Flash file that can be controlled by ActionScript. You'll learn more about that throughout this book. For now, take a look at how to create and use symbols.

Creating Symbols

It's time to create a reusable box symbol that you can use in your designs:

1. Create a new, blank document using File→New.
2. Select the Rectangle tool, and in the Properties panel set the stroke weight to 1, the stroke color to dark gray, and the fill color to light gray.
3. Draw a square box and then select both the fill and stroke for the box by double-clicking the fill with the Selection tool.
4. Choose Modify→Convert to Symbol (F8). This opens the Convert to Symbol dialog box, shown in Figure 1-13. In the Name field, type the word **box**.
5. For the Behavior type, choose Graphic. A graphic symbol is typically thought of as a type of animation that can be played in three ways without requiring any ActionScript: using the Properties panel, you can set a graphic symbol to loop, play once, or display a specific frame. Because they require no ActionScript, using graphics is a convenient way to start learning about symbols.
6. Click OK to close the dialog box. You should see a blue line around the box you just drew. This indicates that the art is no longer a shape. In this case, it is now a symbol.

NOTE 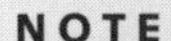

If you create a graphic symbol with an animation inside it, the symbol must span the same number of frames in the main timeline that the graphic itself contains. For example, if a graphic symbol contains a 10-frame animation, the graphic must span 10 frames in the main timeline. If the symbol spans only five frames in the main timeline, the animation inside the graphic will only play to its midpoint.

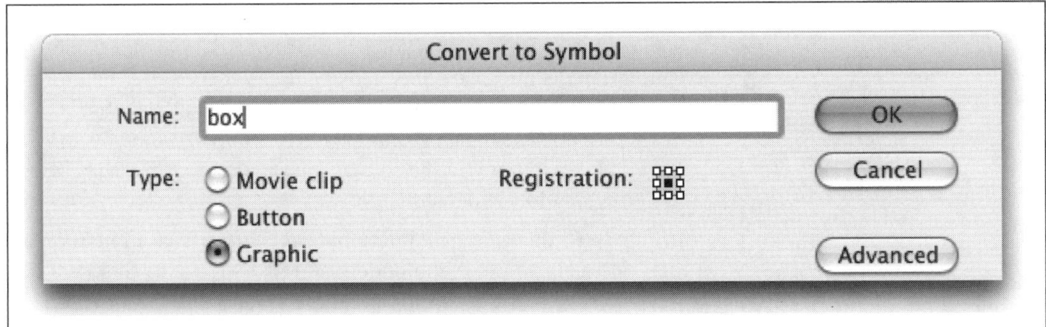

Figure 1-13. The Convert to Symbol dialog box

It's important to understand that a grouped image is not the same as a symbol. A grouped image is raw graphic data on the Stage, whereas a symbol is the defined blueprint for one or more instances of the same asset. If you made a copy of a group, you would literally be copying the vector data required to draw that group and, therefore, measurably increasing the file size. If you made a copy of a symbol instance, on the other hand, you would essentially be creating another reference to the single symbol residing in the Library. As you'll see next, the duplicated instance contributes negligibly to the size of your file.

Reusing Symbols

Now that you have a symbol, you can reuse it as many times as you want without re-creating the drawing or adding significantly to the file size of the project:

The Library

Figure 1-14. The Library

Every Flash file has its own Library, which serves as a repository for many of the file's assets. You can open the Library panel (shown in Figure 1-14) using Window→ Library, Ctrl-L (Win), or Cmd-L (Mac). When you import an asset, such as a JPG file, it is accessible from the Library. The same is true for sounds, video clips, and similar assets. The Library also holds all symbols, which you will continue to learn about in future chapters.

The Library can help you organize your internal assets by enabling you to collect them into folders; rename, edit, update, and delete them; view thumbnails; set symbol properties; and more. Libraries can be shared among multiple published SWFs, and you can easily copy a specific Library element from one Flash file to another.

In fact, Flash 8 now collects the Libraries of all open documents into one panel, making it easier than ever before to move between them. You can create multiple Library panels for simplified dragging and dropping, and you can pin a Library to a file so that focusing on that file will also switch to the pinned Library.

You'll be using the Library panel often, so take some time to get used to it and understand its features. In Chapter 5, you'll take a closer look at the Library and how to organize it effectively. Finally, be sure not to confuse an internal Flash Library with, say, a collection of ActionScript files, which may also be referred to colloquially as a library (as in "a library of scripts")!

1. Currently, you have a single instance of a graphic symbol on the Stage. To begin, test your movie using the Control→Test Movie menu option. This will publish your file to a SWF and open it in a Preview window so you can check your progress. Right now, you just have a box sitting there doing nothing.
2. With the Preview window open, choose View→Bandwidth Profiler. This utility, seen in Figure 1-15, shows you how much bandwidth your movie is using at any given time and can help you optimize your files. The third line down displays the file size of your movie. It should say something close to "0 KB (120 B)", but this may vary slightly. This means your movie is approximately 1/10th of 1 KB (kilobyte). That's very small, which is good because a smaller file size means that less time will be spent waiting for your file to download.
3. Close the Preview window. Now it's time to see how much the file size will be augmented by several additional instances of the symbol.
4. Drag the *box* symbol from the Library 10 more times. (It doesn't matter what your file looks like, as you are only testing file size in this exercise.)
5. Test the movie again (using Control→Test Movie). In the test case from which this exercise was derived, the movie size read "0 KB (190 B)," indicating that increasing the number of on-Stage symbol instances by 10 times added only 70 bytes to the file size. In fact, because of economies of scale you would need to add approximately 400 on-Stage instances of the symbol before the file grew larger than even 1 KB!
6. Close this file, but don't bother saving it. You won't need it again.

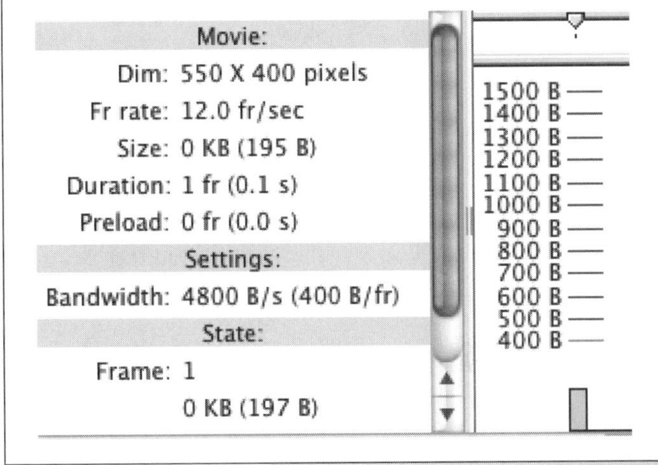

Figure 1-15. The Bandwidth Profiler

NOTE

You should try to memorize the shortcut key for Test Movie mode (Ctrl-Enter on Windows or Cmd-Return on Mac), as you'll use it frequently.

What's Next?

You may notice that many Flash terms and concepts, such as "the Stage" and "movie," were borrowed from the film industry. Using a filmmaking metaphor can help you grasp many Flash concepts. For example, much like in a film, anything that appears on the Stage appears in the finished movie. A graphic that resides off-Stage is not seen in the final movie unless it moves onto the Stage at some point. To help cement this analogy, think about what other aspects of Flash development might be similar to filmmaking. (Hint: Look back over the section on symbols and instances.)

If you want to experiment some more before moving on to the next chapter, try editing the two stars you created earlier. To edit drawing objects, use the same technique you used for editing groups. Double-click each star, and the rest of the Stage will dim, allowing you to focus on editing the drawing object in place. Experiment by selecting the star, clicking on the fill color swatch, and changing the white fill's Alpha value to 50% in the pop-up color palette.

Next, try cutting a star out of the background by breaking it apart, selecting it, and deleting it. (By breaking apart the drawing object, you're allowing it to merge with the underlying background shape.) Finally, try something totally new: finish off the Hendrix poster image by adding some text with the Text tool.

With your new knowledge of the basic drawing tools in Flash, you can start drawing everything from cartoon characters and backgrounds to logos and layouts—so get to it! This book is all about playing around, so have some fun.

In the next chapter, you'll learn how to make creating Flash magic quicker and easier by customizing your workspace. You'll focus on:

- How to create your own panel layout
- How to change document settings
- Several ways to align objects on the Stage
- How to automate simple production tasks

Creating Quickly: Customizing Your Workspace

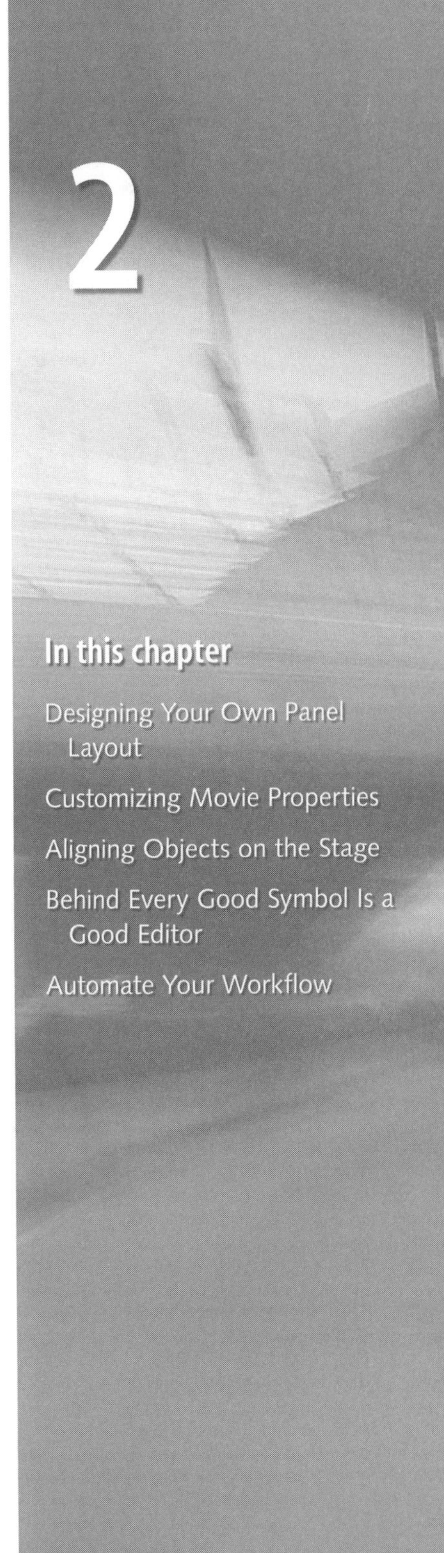

2
In this chapter
Designing Your Own Panel Layout
Customizing Movie Properties
Aligning Objects on the Stage
Behind Every Good Symbol Is a Good Editor
Automate Your Workflow

Think about it: you do your best work in Flash when you're creating, not when you're struggling with the interface. One of the downsides of working with a powerful program with a lot of depth is that the program... er... has a lot of depth. Wading through the interface can be a drag, so it's important to get working comfortably as quickly as possible, so you can concentrate on the good stuff.

The Flash design team has worked hard to organize Flash's many features in ways that are approachable and useful. However, you likely have your own preferred way of working that may not match the out-of-the-box Flash configuration. The good news is that the interface is *customizable*. This chapter's project is to set up your work environment the way you feel most comfortable.

Designing Your Own Panel Layout

One of the first things you'll notice when exploring the Flash interface is that a lot of features require a lot of interface elements to manipulate them. Flash has dozens of panels that provide access to design, scripting, and administration settings. Navigating all of these panels can be a challenge, particularly on laptops or smaller or low-resolution monitors. Creating your own panel layout can help un-clutter your screen, making it easier to focus.

Basic Interface Layout

The interface layout you are likely to use on a daily basis consists of the main document window, the Tools panel, and the Properties panel. As shown in Figure 2-1, the main document window typically anchors these elements, with the Tools panel on the left and the Properties panel below.

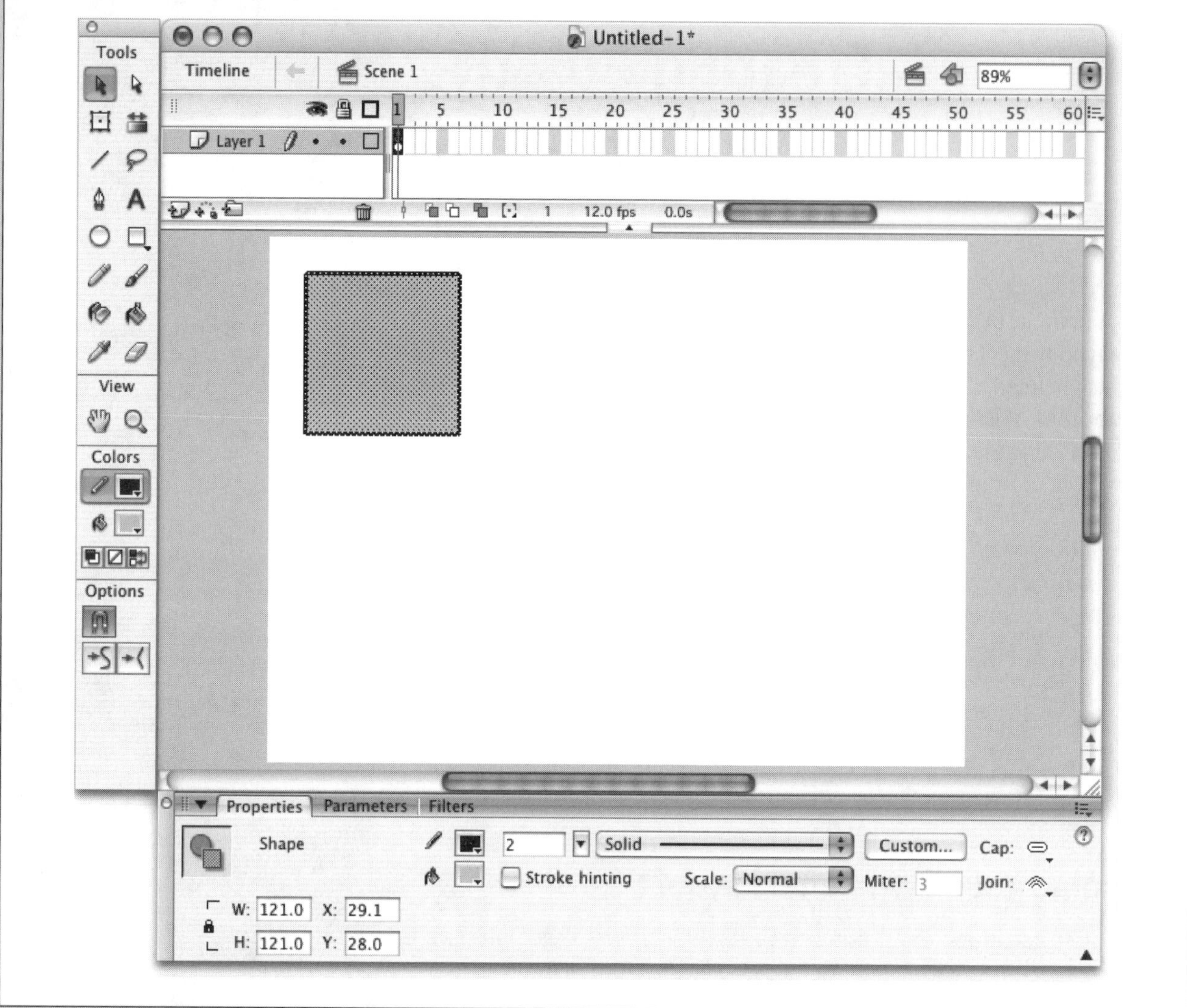

Figure 2-1. The basic Flash interface layout: Tools panel, document window, and Properties panel

This layout is entirely optional, however, so you can reorganize at will. For example, if you have a small monitor, you may wish to fill your screen with the main document window and open the Properties panel only when needed.

NOTE

Note that you can "undock" the timeline by dragging it away from the main window using the standard vertical "grab lines" (seen in every panel) in the upper-left corner. You can then "re-dock" the timeline where it was, to show fewer layers and lots of frames, or in a vertical position along the left side of the window, which is helpful when you have many layers and fewer frames. The timeline can also be hidden and restored using the "Timeline" button in the upper-left corner of the main document window.

A Plethora of Panels

You can add a variety of additional helper panels to this basic layout. You have experience with some of these panels from your work in Chapter 1, including the Color Mixer, Color Swatches, and Library panels. You'll work with more of them soon, including the Align panel in this chapter and a few ActionScript-related panels in future chapters. To see a list of available panels, browse the Window menu.

By default, each panel resides in its own palette. (*Palettes* are the mini-windows that float above the main document window at all times.) This can be a great benefit, because you don't have to juggle many windows to get to the panel you need. The trick is making effective use of these panels without being overwhelmed. This is especially important for users with laptops and small monitors. Fortunately, Flash provides a few ways of organizing the panel utilities you use the most.

First, each palette will conveniently snap to the nearest edge of another palette or to the edges of your screen. This makes it easy to arrange your panels into an ordered grid, to keep things tidy. Even if you're not the compulsive type, you may find yourself enjoying this nicety if you frequently use many panels.

Second, panels can be freely stacked within a single palette. When each individual panel is collapsed or expanded, using the familiar arrow in the panel's title bar, the palette adjusts its size. Combining panels is easy. In the far left of the panel's title bar is a pair of vertical dotted lines that mimic the appearance of a no-slip palette handle. You can use your mouse to drag the panel by this area and drop it into another panel to stack them. A dark horizontal bar will indicate whether you are dropping the new panel above or below the target. You can reorder the stacking of the panels the same way, by dragging a panel up or down in the palette.

Figure 2-2 shows the merging process. On the left, the Transform panel is being dragged to the bottom of the Info panel. On the right, the two panels appear together. The Transform panel has been collapsed using the arrow button in the panel title bar.

Finally, new to Flash 8 is the ability to combine panels into a tabbed set within a single palette window. This makes it even easier to find what

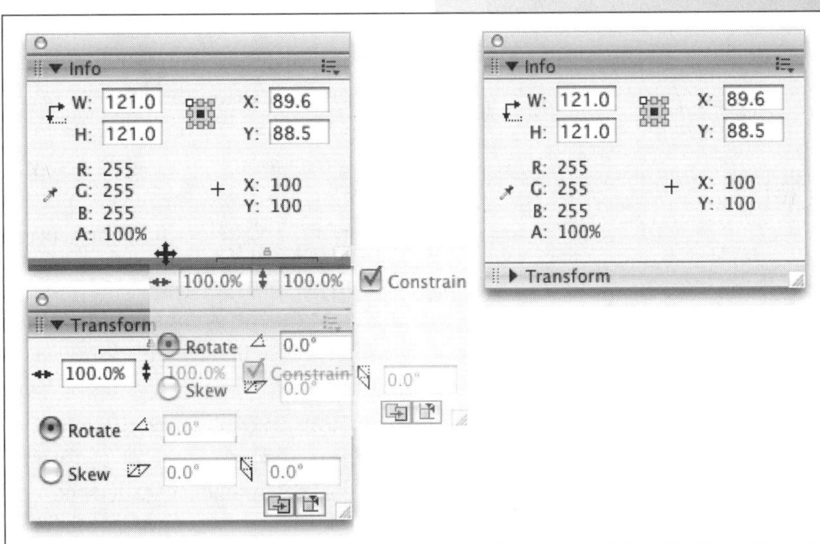

Figure 2-2. Merging panels into one palette window

you need, because you can group panels with related purposes, or the panels that you use most often. To group panels, you need to access a panel's menu using the icon in the far right of its title bar. You can group a panel with any other panel(s), and even rename the new panel set.

Figure 2-3 illustrates grouping panels. On top, using its panel menu, the Transform panel is being grouped with the Info panel. In the bottom of this figure, both panels appear as tabs in one palette window.

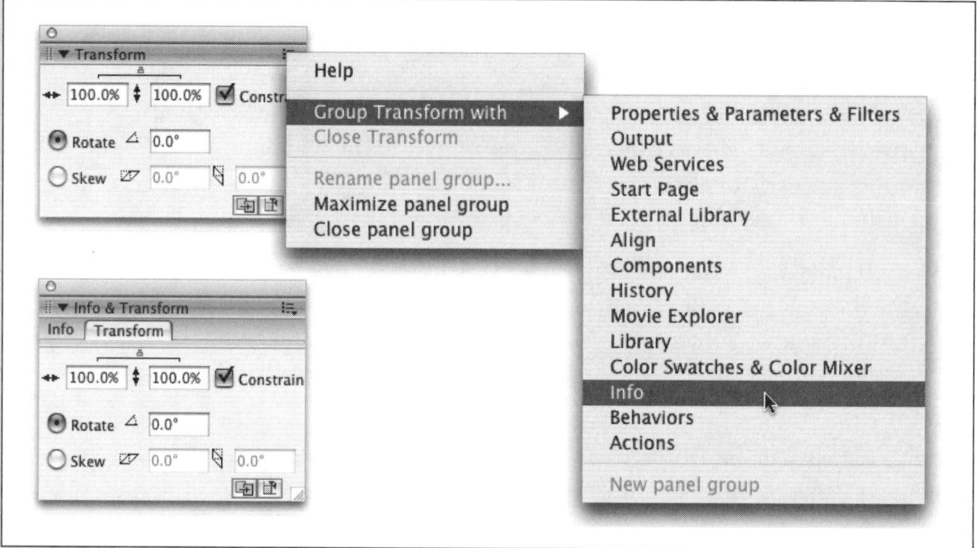

Figure 2-3. Grouping panels into one tab set

Saving Your Setup

Once you've configured your setup the way you like it, you won't have to do it again until you want to change it. When you're happy with the merging, grouping, positioning, and overall state of all your panels, save your layout using Window→Workspace Layout→Save Current. If you scatter your layout during a busy afternoon and yearn for a little order and method, simply restore your saved layout by using the Window→Workspace Layout menu command and selecting it by name.

A couple of sample layouts, such as the one seen in Figure 2-4, have been included on the accompanying CD-ROM in the *02* directory. The setup file has been conveniently packaged as a Macromedia Extension. With a simple double-click, the Macromedia Extension Manager—a simple but powerful utility that will install extensions for many Macromedia products for you—should take care of everything. If you do not have the Macromedia Extension Manager installed, you can download this free utility from *http://www.macromedia.com/exchange/em_download/*. You'll read more about Flash Extensions in Chapter 15.

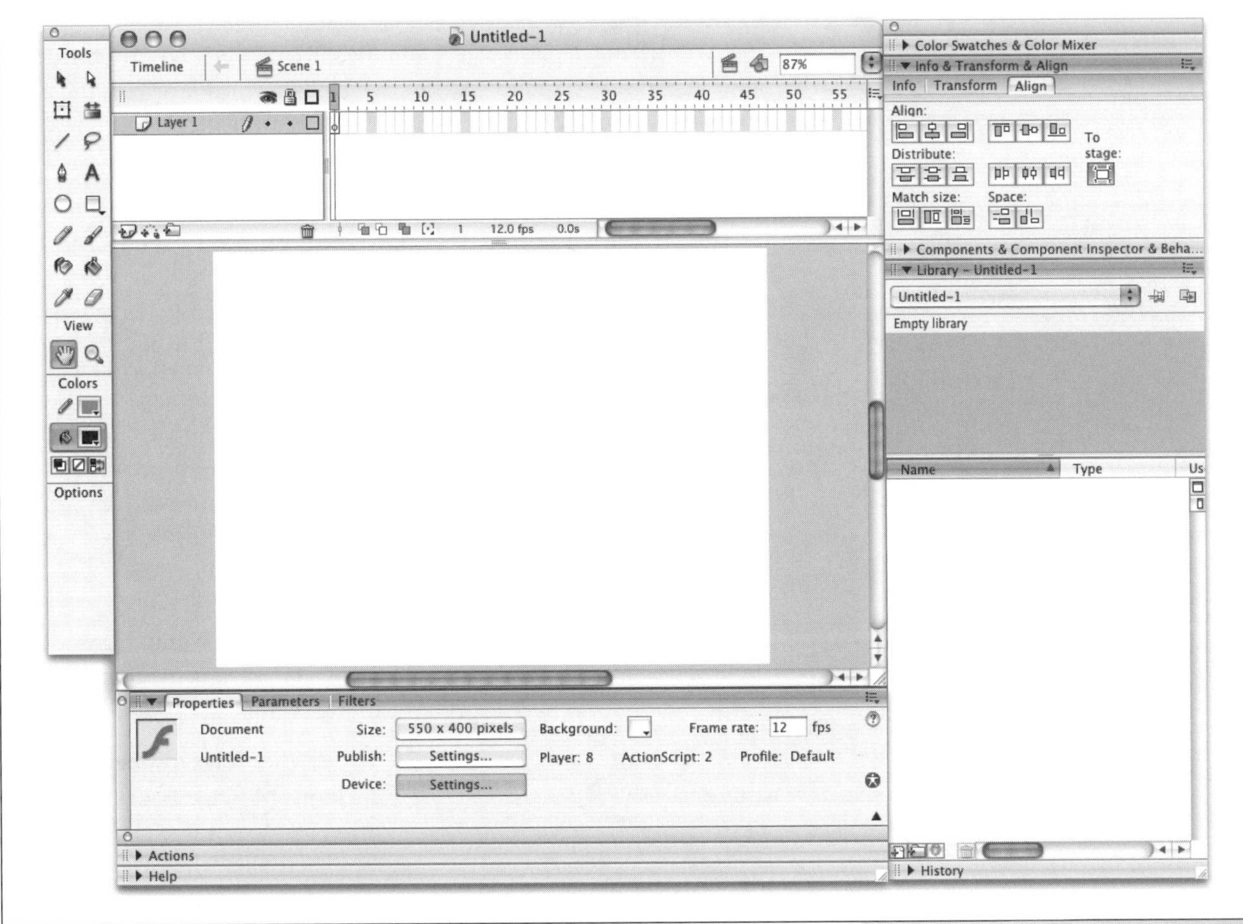

Figure 2-4. An economical, accessible sample workspace layout

Keyboard Shortcuts and Context-Sensitive Mouse Menus

You can really speed up production by learning Flash's keyboard and mouse shortcuts. Showing and hiding panels speedily is really important if you want to move around the Flash interface quickly—especially when screen real estate is limited. For example, showing and hiding the Info or Transform panels discussed earlier can quickly be accomplished by pressing Ctrl/Cmd-I or Ctrl/Cmd-T, respectively.

Learning to use the context-sensitive mouse menus also helps. A right-click (multi-button mouse) or Ctrl-click (single-button mouse) can reveal many normally scattered menu options, collected into one convenient mouse menu related to the object you've selected. For example, you can show or hide the document rulers discussed later in this chapter by right/Ctrl-clicking on the Stage. Similarly, by right/Ctrl-clicking on a symbol and accessing the Arrange option from the mouse menu, you can quickly change its stacking order.

See Appendix A for more workflow and workspace tips.

Customizing Movie Properties

Now that you have a version of the interface that suits your current needs (they may change over time, particularly when you start writing more ActionScript), it's time to talk about customizing your files.

The Stage's size determines the dimensions of your published Flash movie. The default Stage size is 550 × 400 pixels, but sometimes you'll want to work in other sizes. To learn how to change the dimensions, you'll set up a new file for the animation you'll create in the next chapter. It's usually a good idea to set the Stage properties before starting the animation, to avoid having to redo a lot of work later if you decide to change the document settings.

If you do need to change the Stage dimensions after you create a movie, keep in mind that the content doesn't scale or move during the process. Increasing the Stage's height adds pixels to the bottom edge of the Stage, and increasing its width adds pixels to the right edge. However, the content remains in its prior configuration, relative to the Stage's top-left corner.

Start by setting the Flash movie's properties:

1. Create a new, blank Flash document and save it as *animation.fla* in the *02* folder.
2. To set the Stage properties, first click on the Stage's background to make sure nothing else is selected. Then click the Size button in the Properties panel to open the Document Properties dialog box, shown in Figure 2-5.
3. Set the Stage dimensions in the dialog box by entering **500** for the Width and **100** for the Height.
4. Click on the Background Color swatch in the dialog box, and set the background color of the movie to black. If you'd like new Flash documents to always open with a black background, you can click the Make Default button in the dialog box to change the default color as well.

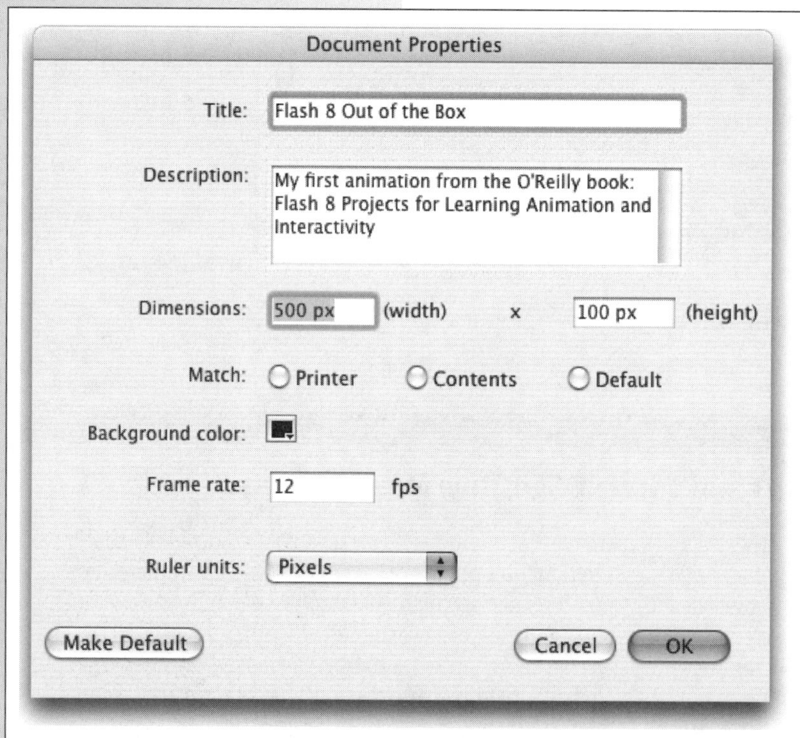

Figure 2-5. The Document Properties dialog box

5. New to Flash 8, you can optionally enter a title and description for your movie. This metadata feature will be searchable by popular web search engines, making it easier for your audience to find your Flash work.
6. Click OK to close the dialog box. This sets the Stage dimensions to 500 × 100 and the background color to black.
7. Save your work.

Aligning Objects on the Stage

Laying out your Stage elements well can improve the user experience of most projects and ensure that you're communicating effectively. However, planning and organizing a complex layout can quickly become cumbersome. Fortunately, the Flash designers planned for this possibility and built in several utilities to help you manage your designs.

Rulers and Guides

Create and position the first box in your layout using *rulers* and *guides*. In this exercise, you'll also practice some of the drawing principles you've already learned:

1. Select the Rectangle tool and enable Object Drawing mode. Shift-constrain your drawing, and draw a square on the Stage.
2. With the square still selected, use the Properties panel to enter a width of 90 and a height of 90.
3. Use Modify→Convert to Symbol (F8) and choose Movie Clip as the symbol type. Call the movie clip **box_mc**. You'll learn more about the "_mc" extension later.
4. Choose the View→Rulers menu option. Rulers appear, using pixels for measurement, along the top and left sides of the Stage, as shown in Figure 2-6. Notice that the upper-left corner of the Stage is aligned to (0, 0).
5. Zoom in pretty closely on the upper-left corner of your Stage. This can improve accuracy when working with small measurements.
6. Click on the horizontal ruler, which is parallel to the top edge of the Stage, and drag downward. This creates a *guide* (a green line). Drag the guide down past the top edge of the Stage, and watch the vertical ruler (which runs parallel to the left edge of the Stage) as you do it. Release the guide when it is aligned to 5 pixels below the top edge of the Stage (when the ruler measurement mark for 5 turns white).

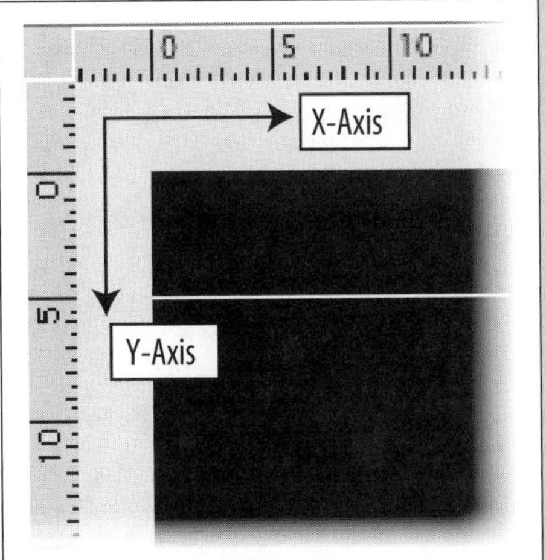

Figure 2-6. Rules and guides help you align objects

NOTE

If the green guide color is ever difficult to see because of a Stage color or background graphic, you can change the color used for guides with the View→Guides→Edit Guides menu command.

7. Click on the vertical ruler and drag a guide to the left edge of the Stage, or until it is aligned to the 0 mark on the top ruler. Note that this is not just for extra practice—guides are also helpful when you have a background image or other graphic covering up the edges of the Stage.
8. Drag the *box_mc* instance so that its upper-left corner is aligned with the intersection of the guides you just drew. When the bounding box for the *box_mc* instance is directly over a guide, the color of the bounding box line will change. If you have a hard time positioning it perfectly, use the arrow keys on your keyboard to nudge the object one pixel at a time.

You've just used guides to align the first box for your layout to the point (0, 5), or the x- and y-coordinates of 0 and 5, respectively.

Snap It in Place

You need to align several more boxes to create a complete layout. However, dragging guides onto the Stage is time-consuming and can clutter your view. Instead, get Flash to help you align graphic elements using one of its automatic alignment features to speed things up:

1. Alt-click (Win) or Option-click (Mac) on the *box_mc* instance and drag it down and to the right approximately 50 pixels to copy a second instance of the *box_mc* symbol. (The 50-pixel distance is arbitrary but will give you some room to work with in the following steps.)
2. Drag the new instance back up and to the left, aiming to align the top edges of both boxes, with approximately a 10-pixel horizontal gap between the two instances. As you drag, you will see vertical and horizontal dashed lines appear on the Stage. These are called *snap align guides*. You may see a few lines appear as you drag your box, which will be explained in just a second. When a horizontal dashed line appears across the top of both boxes and a vertical dashed line appears approximately 10 pixels or so to the right of the first box, release the mouse button to stop dragging. Figure 2-7 shows the snap align guides in action.

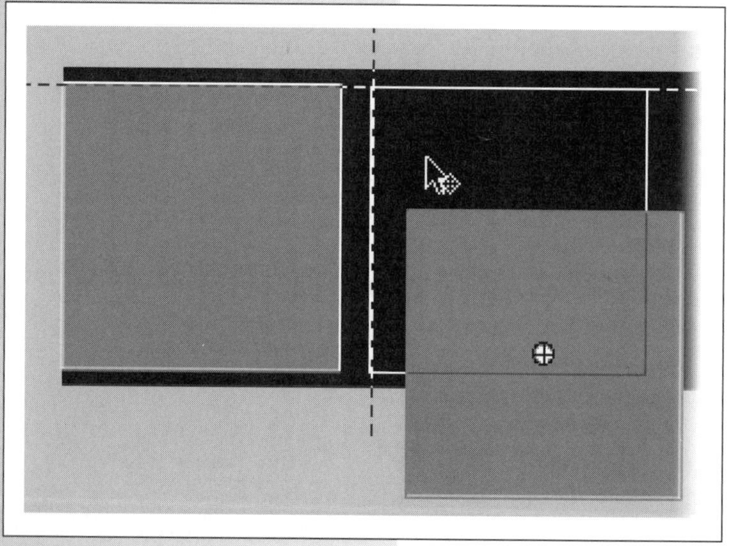

Figure 2-7. Snap align guides in action

The snap align guides tell Flash to "snap" objects along invisible, intersecting gridlines. Positioning an object creates a virtual grid based on that object's position and objects in close proximity, including the edges of the Stage. The Snap Align feature is enabled by default, but you can toggle it on and off by choosing View→Snapping→Snap Align.

You may have seen more than one snap align guide appear, because the default settings include options such as snapping 18 pixels from every Stage edge. You can edit these settings using the View→Snapping→Edit Snapping dialog. For example, you can opt to change the virtual grid from 10 × 10 to another measurement of your liking, or to enable snapping to object horizontal and vertical centers. See Appendix A for more tips on customizing your workspace.

Precision Alignment with the Properties Panel

Using guides isn't always an accurate method of aligning objects, but you've already seen that the Properties panel can position objects at precise x- and y-coordinates. Review this approach by adding another box:

1. Alt-drag (Win) or Option-drag (Mac) a new *box_mc* instance to the right of the previous instance.
2. With the new *box_mc* instance selected, use the Properties panel to set the X and Y values for the *box_mc* instance to **200** and **5**, respectively. This aligns the new instance perfectly to the same y-coordinate as the other boxes and positions it approximately 10 pixels to the right of the previous instance (depending on where you dropped box two when using the snap align guides).
3. Save your work.

As you can see, using the Properties panel to align objects eliminates the guesswork.

Auto Alignment with the Align Panel

You'll often need to align one object with another, and the Align panel can really make this painless. Create a fourth box and see how the Align panel works:

1. Alt-drag (Win) or Option-drag (Mac) another new *box_mc* instance, a bit down and to the right of the previous instance.
2. If it isn't already visible, choose Window→Align (or press Ctrl/Cmd-K) to open the Align panel, shown in Figure 2-8.
3. Using the Shift key, or dragging a mouse selection that surrounds all of the boxes, select all the instances currently on the Stage. Click the Align Top Edge button, which is located

Figure 2-8. The Align panel

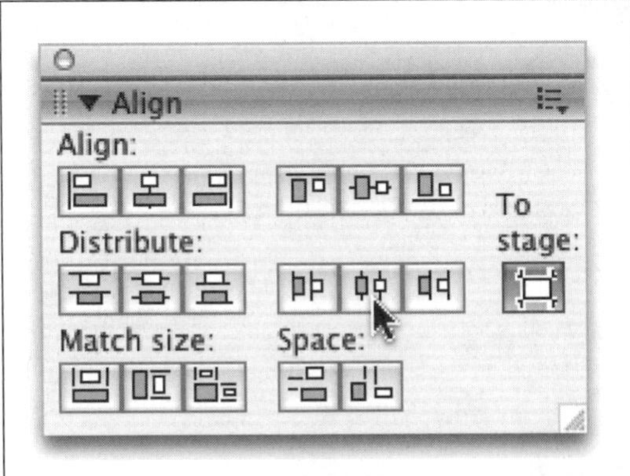

at the left of the second group of three buttons in the first line of the panel. This will vertically align all of the boxes along their top edges.

4. You'll align the boxes horizontally in the next step, so save your work and move on.

Distributing Objects

Often, a layout of repeating patterns is helpful for displaying a series of objects. You'll be building just such a pattern for your first animation in the next chapter. When using the Align panel, you are usually just aligning objects relative to each other. However, in some cases, it helps to add the Stage itself into the calculation. For example, it is possible to evenly distribute objects across the entire Stage in one step using the Align/Distribute to Stage feature:

1. Alt-drag (Win) or Option-drag (Mac) one final *box_mc* instance to the right of the previous instance.
2. Repeat steps 3 and 4 from the previous section to align the box vertically. All five boxes should now have a y-coordinate of 5. Feel free to adjust them, if necessary.
3. In the Align panel, enable the Align/Distribute to Stage option. Clicking the To Stage button in the right of the panel toggles this feature on and off.
4. Select all five boxes again and click the Distribute Horizontal Center button, found in the middle of the second group of three buttons in the second row of the Align panel.
5. Save your work and close your file.

With the Align/Distribute to Stage feature enabled, the first box is aligned to the left of the Stage, the last box is aligned to the right of the Stage, and the gaps are calculated based on these outer boundaries. If this feature were not active, the positions of the left- and rightmost boxes would have been used to calculate the gaps between all the boxes.

Timeline Effects: Assistants

Flash also contains two "assistant" utilities that can be used for alignment and distribution. The Timeline Effects, introduced in Flash MX 2004, provide a way of adding effects, transitions, and other features through guided wizards.

While the effects are less likely to be used in Flash 8 due to new runtime bitmap effects that you'll examine in Chapter 10, some users may still find some of the Timeline Effects helpful. The two assistants, for example, can be useful for repeated copy and transform, or "step and repeat," actions during authoring. The Copy to Grid assistant will create an evenly spaced grid of copies from a selected object. The more feature-rich Distributed Duplicate assistant can offset, scale, rotate, color, and fade a number of copies of a selected object, resulting in a single graphic symbol that can easily be reused.

Next, you'll look at how the Copy to Grid assistant can automatically accomplish what it took you several steps to do in the previous sections:

1. Create a new Flash document and use Modify→Document to configure its document properties like the *animation.fla* canvas you just created. Give it a width of 500, a height of 100, and a black background. This is just an experiment, so there's no need to save it.
2. Select the Rectangle tool, hold down the Shift key, and draw a square on the Stage. Timeline Effects can work with most any object, so it doesn't matter if you use Object Drawing mode or not.
3. Select the entire square, use the Properties panel to give it a width and height of 90, and position it at x- and y-coordinates (0, 5).
4. With the square still selected, use the Insert→Timeline Effects→Assistants→Copy to Grid menu command. Just like when creating a grid or table, enter 1 row and 5 columns. As in your earlier examples, use a row spacing of 0 pixels and a column spacing of 10 pixels.
5. Press Update Preview to check your values, and then hit OK if you're satisfied.

Look familiar? If you want an easily reusable single asset, you're done. To create a file similar to the prior examples, you need to break apart the new graphic symbol. The wizard will work whether you start with a shape, a group or drawing object, or a symbol, because it first creates a symbol to work with and then uses that symbol to create the final single asset. So, breaking apart the final asset will leave you with the five graphic symbols you need. If you plan to control your new boxes with ActionScript, you can convert them to movie clips as you did in Chapter 1.

Discard this file when you're through experimenting.

Behind Every Good Symbol Is a Good Editor

An important factor in feeling good about your design choices is knowing that you can experiment now and change them later. You've now created several symbols, in a variety of ways, but you may be wondering how to change an existing symbol. As an example, you'll get rid of the stroke in the *box_mc* symbol you created in your *animation.fla* file. This will refine the look of your layout and eliminate any possible distraction from distorting lines during your eventual animation.

Pick up where you left off, and edit the *box_mc* symbol:

1. Open the *animation.fla* file you recently finished. For quick access, it should be in the left column of your Start panel; if you have disabled this feature, use the File→Open Recent menu command to access the file.
2. Select any instance of the *box_mc* symbol on the Stage.
3. Choose Edit→Edit Selected.

Figure 2-9. The Edit bar, while in Symbol Editing mode for the box_mc symbol

You've just entered the fourth dimension, where there are no physical boundaries and space exists endlessly. Actually, you've entered *Symbol Editing mode*, but some strange things have happened nonetheless. For starters, the other content on the Stage has disappeared. Also, the Edit bar now says *Scene 1, box_mc*, as shown in Figure 2-9.

If you edit symbols in this way, they appear on their own canvas, without distraction from surrounding elements in your main movie. However, this is a double-edged sword, because your other movie elements are not visible for reference. In most cases, it is helpful to use a different menu command, Edit→Edit in Place. This will bring you to the same editing environment but will merely dim the surrounding elements without hiding them, allowing you to edit the symbol with some degree of visual context. For more information about editing symbols, see the "Symbol Editing Mode" sidebar.

Symbol Editing Mode

As discussed in Chapter 1, a symbol is a single *object*, from which all instances of that object are derived.

Although all instances of a symbol share a common instruction set, each instance can have its own characteristics, or *properties*. For example, instances of the *box_mc* symbol can have different colors, dimensions, and levels of opacity while still being derived from a single symbol. Altering the properties of a single instance will affect only that instance, which means that you can use the same symbol in many different ways.

However, if you edit a symbol—for example, removing a stroke from a shape therein—all instances created from that symbol will be changed. Symbol Editing mode is the editing environment that allows you to modify any symbol.

As you'll learn in Chapter 4, a button is a special type of symbol that has a predefined structure. However, editing graphic and movie clip symbols is very much like editing your main document. This is because graphics and movie clips are, in some ways, like Flash movies within a Flash movie. They share most of the same characteristics of your main movie, which can sometimes lead to confusion.

The Edit bar at the top of the main document window, shown in Figure 2-9, is the key to keeping track of where you are in the Flash environment. When in Symbol Editing mode (or simply "Edit mode"), the Edit bar tells you that, instead of editing Scene 1, you are now editing a symbol that is used in Scene 1.

This distinction is important to remember, because if you accidentally enter Edit mode by double-clicking a symbol (which has the same result as choosing Edit→Edit in Place), you'll have to undo any inadvertent changes made to the symbol and find your way back to your main document.

All that remains is to delete the stroke from the *box_mc* symbol:

1. Select the entire stroke of the shape and delete it. (If you used Object Drawing mode when creating the box, either double-click again to edit the object, or select it and break it apart. You will then be able to select and delete the stroke.)
2. Use the Edit bar to return to Scene 1 (by clicking on *Scene 1*).
3. Save your work and close your file.

You will see that every instance of the *box_mc* symbol has been updated to reflect the change. The layout on the Stage is unaffected, but those ugly strokes are gone for good.

Automate Your Workflow

Having to manually repeat common tasks, such as drawing a box, can slow you down. To speed up development, Flash can automate many of your efforts. One simple way for users of all skill levels to automate repetitive tasks is to save steps from the Undo History as Flash macros called *commands*. To start, you need to understand the History panel.

Making History

The History panel begins as a blank slate and tracks your actions while you are editing your movies. This allows you to undo and redo your actions, step by step. As you'll see, it also allows you to replay single actions and save sequences of actions for later use. To take advantage of these features, you need to make history:

1. Create a new, blank document with which to experiment. Name it *history.fla* and save it in your *02* directory.
2. Choose Window→Other Panels→History to open the History panel.
3. Activate the Rectangle tool (R), choose any fill and stroke colors you like in the Properties panel, and draw a square box (remember to hold down the Shift key to constrain the shape).
4. Use the Selection tool (V) to select the fill, and then change the fill color to light gray.
5. Select the stroke by double-clicking on any edge, and change the stroke color to dark gray. Then deselect the stroke.
6. Double-click in the fill area of the square to select both its fill and stroke. Then move it off-Stage.

Have you noticed the History panel filling up with information? It tracks each task you perform in order, resulting in something like the history list shown in Figure 2-10.

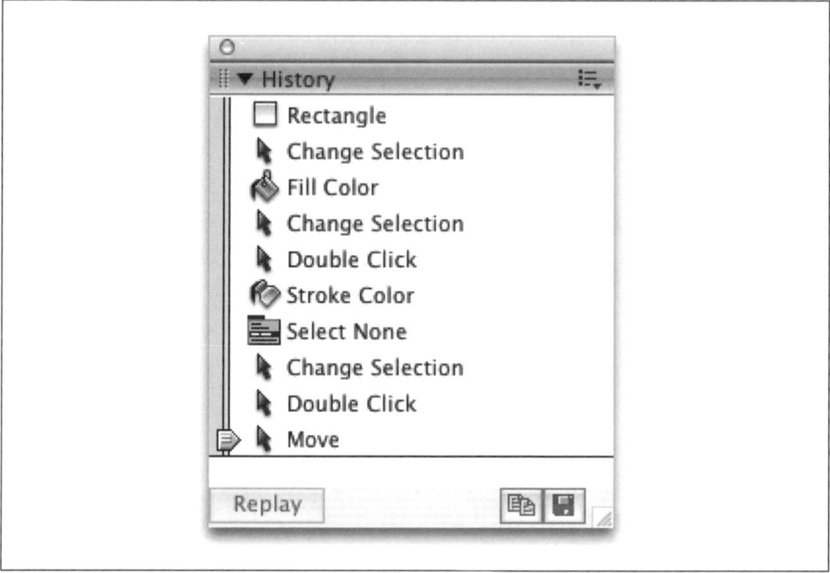

Figure 2-10. The History panel

You've already seen how the Undo command can help you travel back in time, but the History panel allows you to retrace as many steps as you please by stepping through a written list of the tasks you have performed. At any point, you can step backward in the History panel and start again from a previous step, or simply repeat a sequence by choosing the steps to replay. Take a look at how it works:

1. Drag the history slider, indicated in Figure 2-10, up two steps to the step marked Double Click. The box on the Stage becomes selected again and moves back to its original position. Essentially, you're going back in time.
2. Click once on the first step (Rectangle) in the history list, then hold down the Shift key and click on the last Move action that appears. (This is probably your last step, or possibly next to last if you deselected.) Shift-clicking highlights the entire sequence, selecting the steps in between.
3. Click on the Replay button at the bottom of the History panel, as indicated in Figure 2-10, to replay the sequence.
4. Save your work.

Instantly, the steps selected in the History panel are replayed, creating a box in the same position as the first one you drew.

You now know how to perform a sequence of steps and replay them, but the process of drawing the box needs to be simplified so Flash can replay the sequence faster. In this case, you drew a box and immediately changed its colors. It is easier for Flash to replay the sequence if you choose the colors you want *before* drawing the box, so it's time to simplify.

Economizing a Sequence

A long list of actions in the History panel, like the one you have now, can be difficult to read, and you need to be able to identify which steps to save as part of the sequence. So, the first step in simplifying the creation of your box is to clean up the History panel:

1. Delete the two boxes from the Stage.
2. Open the History panel's Options menu and choose Clear History, as shown in Figure 2-11. Flash warns you that the action cannot be undone. Click Yes to continue.
3. Save your work.

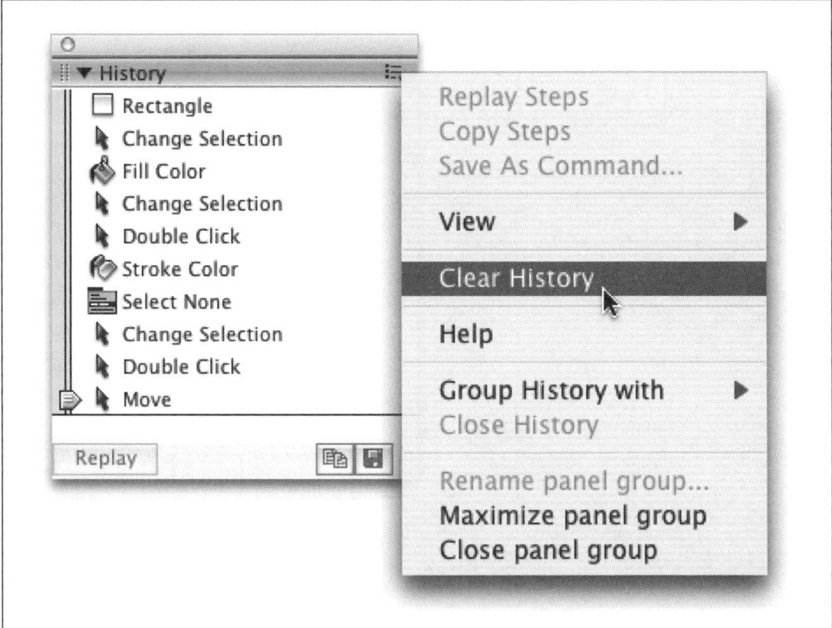

Figure 2-11. The History panel

Now you can cut the drawing process down to four steps, for an economical sequence that can be saved and quickly replayed by Flash. While you're at it, you can add a step that converts the graphic to a symbol, so Flash will also do that when you replay the sequence.

Perform the following steps exactly as they are listed, without any extra clicks or other actions:

1. Activate the Rectangle tool, disable Object Drawing mode if it is enabled, and choose light gray and dark gray for the fill and stroke colors, respectively.
2. Draw a square box on the Stage.

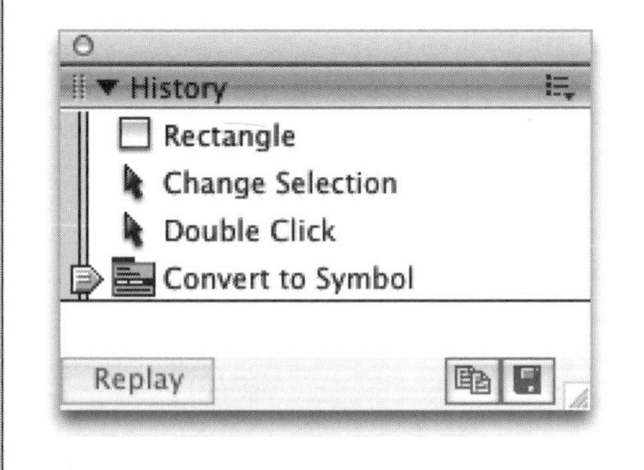

Figure 2-12. The history of a box

3. Using the Selection tool, double-click the box to select both its fill and stroke.
4. Convert the box to a movie clip symbol (using Modify→Convert to Symbol or F8) and name it **box_mc**, being sure to set the Behavior radio button to Movie Clip and the registration point to the center. The list in your History panel should match Figure 2-12, or be very similar. It doesn't have to be exact; the goal is just to avoid having many unneeded steps in your sequence.

Your new, more efficient sequence is easier to read and faster for Flash to execute. Next, you'll see how to save and reuse the sequence.

Commands: Next-Generation Macros

To make a sequence of steps reusable (like the macros common to many other applications), you need to save it as a command, as follows:

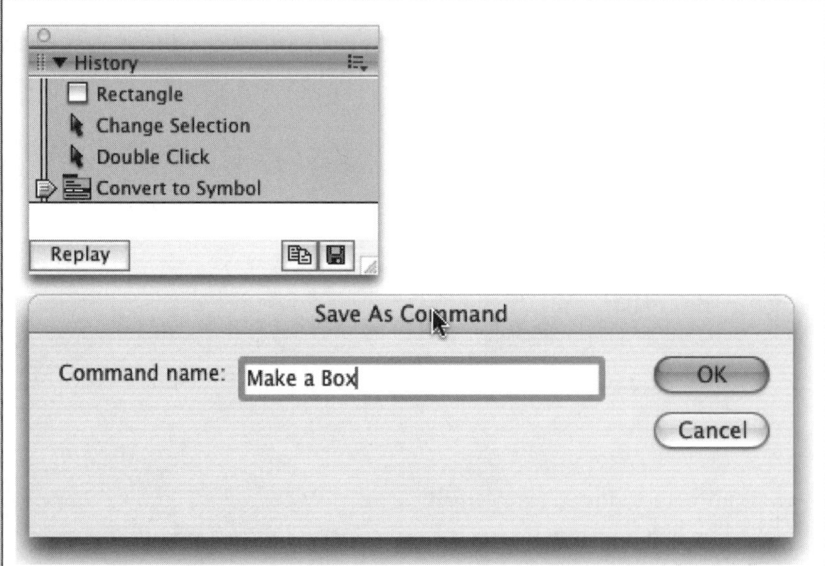

Figure 2-13. Saving selected steps as a command

1. Select the first step (Rectangle) in the History panel, and then press the Shift key and select the last step (Convert to Symbol) to highlight all four steps. (You can also click and drag from the top of the list to the bottom to select all the steps simultaneously.)
2. Click the Save Selected Steps as a Command button in the History panel, as indicated in Figure 2-13. This opens the Save as Command dialog box.
3. In the Command Name field, type **Make a Box**, and click OK to close the dialog box.

Now you have a command that creates a gray box any time you need it. Try starting over to see if it works:

1. Create a new Flash document. There's no need to name or save it, as you won't use it again.
2. Open the Commands menu at the top of the document window, as shown in Figure 2-14. The Commands menu shows your brand-new Make a Box command. Congratulations—you've permanently added a new command to the Flash interface (you can rename or delete it using Commands→Manage Saved Commands).
3. Choose the Make a Box command from the Commands menu.
4. Open the Library (Ctrl/Cmd-L). You should see a graphic named *Symbol 1*, which was created via the Make a Box command. Flash names new symbols using the default naming convention *Symbol 1*, *Symbol 2*, and so on, unless you enter custom names.

Figure 2-14. The Commands menu showing the custom Make a Box command

Each time you execute the command, Flash creates a brand-new box and places it in the same position as the box you drew originally. Why? Because the History panel, in addition to tracking steps, tracks the position of the box as you draw it. Also, each time you run the Make a Box command, Flash converts the box to a symbol for you, eliminating the need to repeat the process manually. This is a great time-saver.

So why doesn't Flash use the name *box_mc* every time you run the Make a Box command? If Flash named every new symbol *box_mc*, there would be no way to distinguish among them without renaming each symbol. The default naming convention used by Flash (*Symbol 1*, *Symbol 2*, etc.) keeps each symbol identifiable in the meantime.

Just as you saved your own command, you can download and install commands created by others. In Chapter 15, you'll learn more about customizing Flash this way. First, however, you'll concentrate on your first animation.

What's Next?

In this chapter, you learned how to customize your workspace to make your work easier and faster. You know how to use tools such as the Align panel, Timeline Effect assistants, and the History panel to make production more efficient. Now you can get through the sometimes tedious tasks that require a little extra precision, and get on with creating.

To expand on your work so far, replace each box instance in the file you built with custom content. Try text, a logo, or perhaps an animation piece to bring your file to life. If you don't yet feel sure enough to take on a project like this, keep reading—you'll soon feel your confidence grow.

If you're interested in extending Flash, Chapter 15 discuss this briefly. If you can't wait that long, visit the Macromedia Flash Exchange at *http://www.macromedia.com/exchange/flash/*. The Flash Exchange features many commands, as well as components (pre-made widgets, such as buttons, menus, and other user interface controls) and other extensions (tools, panels, and other utilities) that you'll learn more about later. These add-ons allow you to further customize your workspace, enabling you to do more than Flash can do out of the box and saving you lots of time and energy.

In the next chapter, you'll create your first animation. You will:

- Work with layers and the timeline
- Learn how to animate symbols using keyframes and tweening
- Animate a symbol along a specific path
- Add a touch of realism to your animations with custom easing
- Write your first ActionScript
- Publish your movie for playback in a web page

Your First Animation

3

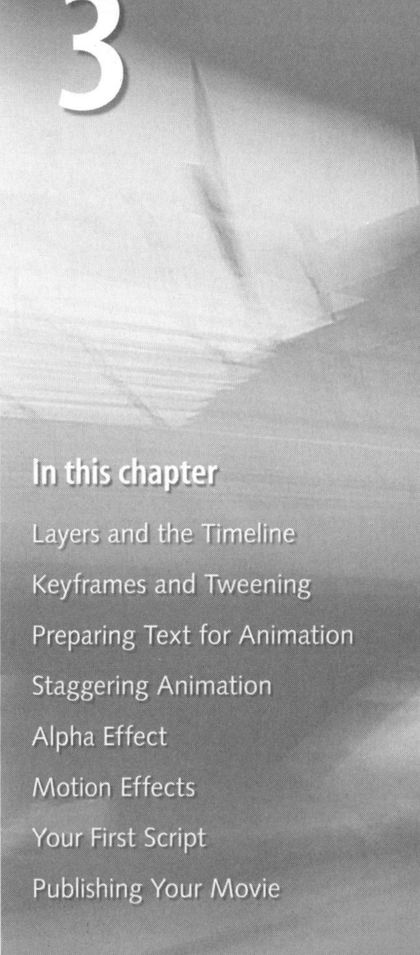

In this chapter

Flash started as a web animation tool and remains one of the most popular on the market. Now that you have some drawing and organization skills under your belt, you're ready to start making graphics move. The trick is knowing how to do so in ways that are both creative and aesthetically pleasing. Coupling inspiration and restraint can often lead to animation that makes a better first (and lasting) impression.

As your design experience and skills grow, you'll begin using Flash for more than just simple eye candy. Often, animation can be the key to more engaging presentations, effective charts and graphs, and more entertaining online advertisements. Flash animation has been used for everything from movie credits and DVD menus to billboards on the roofs of taxicabs.

In this chapter, your project will be to use a few essential techniques to create your first animated Flash movie. You won't need anything more than what comes with Flash, and this ease of use will be emphasized with a theme: "Flash 8 Out of the Box." When the project is complete, you'll publish a Flash *.swf* file for use on the Web.

The animation itself is straightforward. You'll first draw a series of colored boxes and then add text, as seen in Figure 3-1. Next, you'll jazz it up a little by making the boxes grow and the text slide into place—just enough to catch the reader's attention without being overbearing.

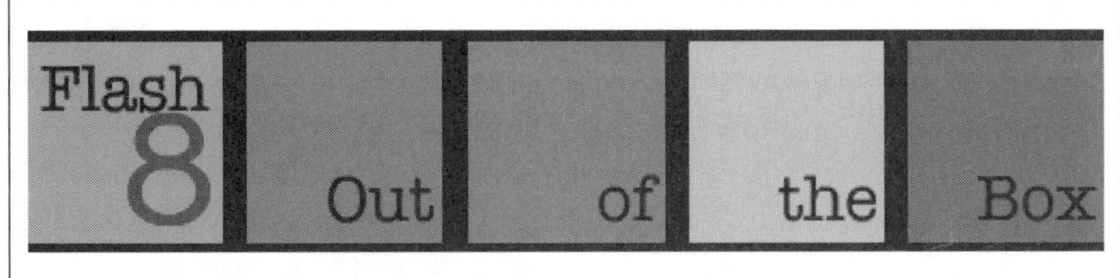

Figure 3-1. The Flash 8 Out of the Box animation

Layers and the Timeline

You may have noticed in the previous exercises that you placed everything on the Stage within a single *layer* of the timeline. Layers are used to determine which elements appear in the foreground and which appear in the background, creating a visual stacking order for objects on the Stage. This is in addition to the visual stacking order of graphics within each layer, discussed in Chapter 1.

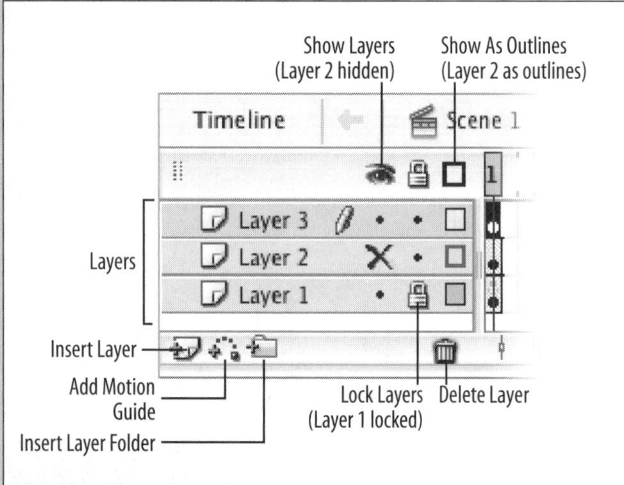

Figure 3-2. Layers in the timeline

While a single layer is sufficient for static graphics, computer-assisted animations require their own layers. To create multiple animations, you need multiple layers. Layers appear above the Stage in the main Flash document window, in a *timeline*. The timeline actually resides in its own panel (Figure 3-2), which is anchored at the top of the main document window by default.

If you don't like the default position of the Timeline panel, you can move it. To do so, grab and drag the panel using the small textured grab handle to the left of the expandable arrow in the panel's title bar. If you want to see more layers but minimize the number of panels you must juggle, you can anchor the Timeline panel to the left of the Stage by dragging it to the lower-left side of the window. This is especially handy when you have many layers that you would like to see all at once, without scrolling. If you need to switch back to seeing fewer layers so that you can see many frames at once, simply drag the timeline loose again, or re-anchor it to the top of the Stage window.

Establishing Layer Order

It's time to get started working with layers:

1. Pick up where you left off in the last chapter by opening the *animation.fla* file. If you didn't create this file, you can find it in the *02* folder in your working directory.

2. To get ready to animate the boxes, move each box to its own layer. Select all five boxes and choose Modify→Timeline→Distribute to Layers. This command automatically adds five layers to the timeline and places each box instance on its own layer. Each layer will be named with the name of the instance that appears on that layer, or the symbol name if the instances are unnamed. In this case, all five layers are named *box_mc*.

3. *Layer 1* is now empty, and you don't need it anymore. To get rid of it, select *Layer 1* by clicking on its name in the timeline, and click the Delete Layer button (the trash can icon indicated in Figure 3-2).
4. Select the bottom layer in the timeline. Doing so also selects the box instance on the Stage that resides on the bottom layer. Select the other layers, from bottom to top, to see which layer each instance is on.

Having five layers with the same name makes it difficult to identify which box is on which layer, so rename and rearrange the layers to correspond to the positions of the boxes:

1. Determine which layer contains the leftmost box instance, and double-click on the layer's name in the timeline. Change the layer name to **box 1**.
2. Rename the remaining layers **box 2**, **box 3**, **box 4**, and **box 5**, according to which box the layer contains, from left to right, respectively.
3. Click on the *box 1* layer name, drag it to the top of the layer stack, and drop it above the other layers, thereby moving it to the foreground.
4. Drag the *box 2* layer and position it below the *box 1* layer. Repeat for the remaining layers, in numerical order, so *box 5* is at the bottom.

NOTE

Content on the top layer is displayed in the foreground. Content on the bottom layer is displayed the background. You can drag and drop the layers to rearrange their stacking order.

The Timeline at a Glance

The Timeline panel contains information about your Flash file, as represented over time. If you think about a simple linear animation, the timeline is akin to a film in which each *frame* (i.e., column) represents a moment in time, just like a frame in a film. The *playhead* indicates the current frame, the content of which is rendered on the Stage, much like the light of a projector depicting a single frame on a screen.

Each *layer* (row) in the timeline represents a plane in which graphics are rendered. Imagine each character in the film residing in his or her own layer. Content in the bottommost layer is rendered in the background, like a set. Characters make up a scene in various layers in front of (or on top of) the background, allowing them to walk behind and in front of each other. Finally, foreground elements, such as opening titles and closing credits, are placed in the top layer.

Quick-access buttons throughout the timeline make it very easy to work with layers. Using the button bar below all the layers, you can delete or add new layers and create folders for additional organization. Once you've created a layer folder, you can drag and drop layers into that folder. You can also reorder layers by dragging and dropping.

To make it easy to identify its contents, you can name a layer (either upon creation, or later by double-clicking the layer name). You can also show or hide a layer by clicking in the column marked with an eye and lock or unlock a layer's edit capability by clicking in the column marked with a lock icon. The last in the column of quick buttons will convert anything in the clicked layer to outlines in the shown color. This can sometimes make it easier to see obscured layer contents.

You can also see all of these settings in one convenient place by double-clicking on a layer, which will display the Layer Properties dialog. This allows you to specify other types of layers, such as guide layers, which you'll discover later in this chapter, and masks, which you'll learn about in Chapter 7.

If you've followed the preceding steps, the layers in your timeline should match Figure 3-3.

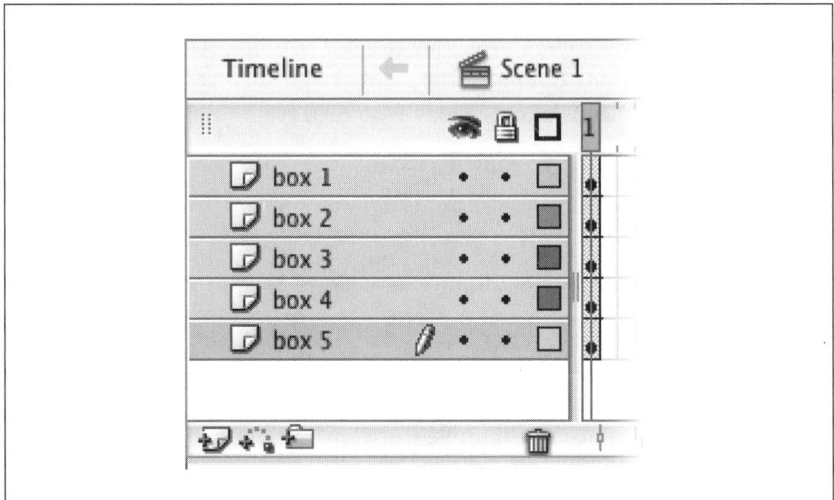

Figure 3-3. Each layer, from top to bottom, corresponds to a box on the Stage, from left to right

You've created a more intuitive way to view the assets by arranging the layers on which they reside. For convenience, "the *box_mc* movie clip symbol instance on layer *box 1*" will hereafter be called *box 1*, even though you haven't given it an instance name yet. This is just a shortcut, since you don't have to name each box individually yet; it will be true of the other boxes as well.

Organizing Layers into Groups

You'll be adding more layers later for the text in the animation, and the timeline will be full of layers, making it harder to locate the ones you want. To avoid potential confusion, you can organize the box layers into groups in the timeline:

1. Select the *box 1* layer and then click the Insert Layer Folder button, indicated in Figure 3-2. (In the contextual menu, this command is called Insert Folder to distinguish it from the Insert Layer command.) A layer folder named *Folder 1* appears above the *box 1* layer. Layer folders are used to organize layers into groups.
2. Shift-select the box layers, drag them onto *Folder 1*, and then release the mouse button. This moves the layers into the *Folder 1* layer folder and indents the layer names. Compare your layers to Figure 3-4.
3. Click the expand/collapse arrow next to *Folder 1* to collapse the layer folder. This hides the layers, giving you room to view new layers without resizing or zooming the Timeline panel.

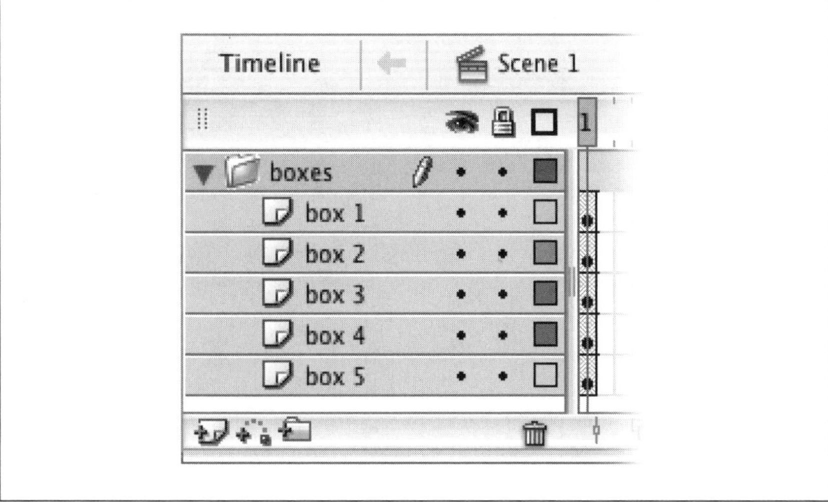

Figure 3-4. The boxes layer folder

4. Rename the *Folder 1* layer folder to **boxes**. Using a custom name makes the layer folder easier to identify.

Now that your boxes are on their own layers in the timeline and are stored neatly within a layer folder, you're almost ready to animate them—but first you'll jazz them up a bit.

Changing the color of the boxes

In this animation, you'll start each box very small and increase its size over time so it appears to be growing or coming toward the viewer. Instead of using five gray boxes, you'll make the animation more colorful by changing the color of each box instance. Later, you'll change the colors to create a color-fade effect over time:

1. Open the *boxes* layer folder to see the box layers.
2. Select the *box 1* instance and choose Tint from the Color drop-down list in the Properties panel, as shown in Figure 3-5. This changes the color of the movie clip instance on the Stage without affecting the original symbol in the Library. Editing the symbol directly changes every instance, but here you want each instance to be a different color. This symbol color effect lets you use boxes of different colors without adding to your file size. (If your Properties panel doesn't contain the Color drop-down list, click on the box symbol on the Stage to make sure you've selected the graphic instance and not just the layer containing it.)
3. Click on the Tint Color swatch and choose any color, or enter specific values for red, green, and blue. The instance's tint value changes to the new color. (Later, you'll be adding black type on top of these colored boxes, so light colors are preferable.)

NOTE

When manipulating an instance, be sure to click on the instance rather than the frame. Clicking on a frame in the timeline will select everything on that layer that is in that frame. This makes it hard to change properties for one instance.

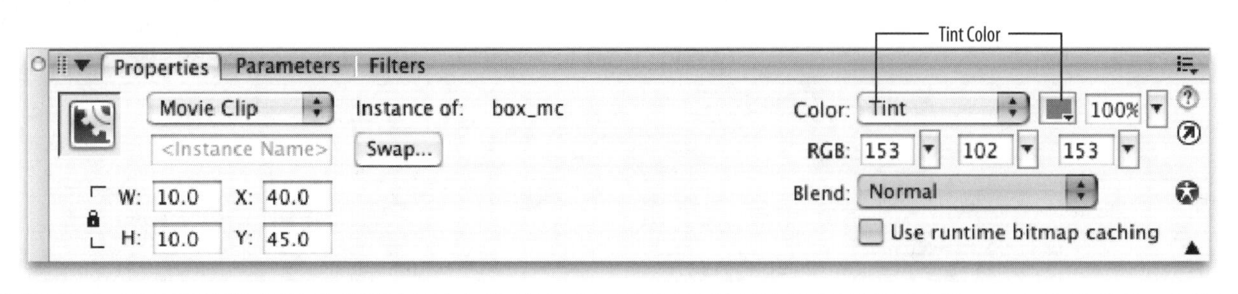

Figure 3-5. Setting the tint color in the Properties panel

4. Select each of the remaining box instances and give them new tint colors.

5. Save your work. If you want to check your progress, your file should now look like *animation_01.fla* in the *03* folder of your working directory.

Keyframes and Tweening

Now it's time to animate the boxes. The first step in doing so is to add a second *keyframe* in each layer. A keyframe is essential to all timeline-based animation techniques in Flash. While not a perfect analogy, perhaps the easiest way to understand keyframes is to think of each one as a place where *you* can define new information about the layer.

For example, every item placed on the Stage on a unique layer creates at least one keyframe. Why? You, the animator, have dictated at least one piece of new information—the position, or x- and y-coordinates, of the asset. If you want to move the asset across the Stage or, as in this case, increase its size, you'll need to define at least one new keyframe to add that new information.

Once you have at least two keyframes, you can create a *tween*. A tween is an instruction to the computer to fill in all the interim frames between (hence the name) the two keyframes you've defined. The computer will calculate the changes in each relevant characteristic and automatically adjust the animating elements in all the interpolated frames.

Creating and Moving Keyframes

The biggest benefit of computer-assisted animation is that it's a big timesaver. In this case, many steps can be applied to all five boxes at once. The first part of the animation will feature your boxes scaling and changing colors, so get started:

1. To make this animation last approximately one second on as many machines as possible, use Flash's default frame rate of 12 frames per second (fps), and add a keyframe for each layer at frame 12. Click in the top layer at frame 12 and drag down, selecting all five layers at once. Use the Insert→Timeline→Keyframe menu command to create a new keyframe in each selected layer. The content will be duplicated in the new keyframes so you can easily make changes.
2. Currently, your two keyframes contain the same information, so when you animate your file, no change will be visible. To scale the boxes and include a color fade, you must first change the starting keyframe. (Remember, keyframes are a chance for you, the animator, to dictate information the computer will use in the tweening process.) Click in frame 1 and select *box 1*.
3. Use the Info panel (Window→Info) to change the size of the box. In the center of the panel, you'll see a nine-point grid, allowing you to change the point around which the box is transformed. Click the center of this grid, placing the black box in the center to indicate your selection, so the transformation will be centered instead of relative to the registration point of the box. (Later, you'll learn how to use the Free Transform tool to set any point around which to transform the box, not just the center or upper-left.)
4. Enter 10 for the width and 10 for the height.
5. Use the Properties panel to change the color tint, as you did in the previous exercise. Choose any color that might look good fading to the color you started with, again trying to stay with lighter hues that might contrast well with black superimposed text.
6. Repeat steps 3 through 5 for the remaining four boxes.
7. Save your work.

Sometimes it's helpful to be able to move a keyframe to make an animation longer or shorter. Practice this by first single-clicking to select any keyframe in the timeline, and then reselecting it and dragging it to another frame. (If you immediately attempt to drag a frame, you will instead select the frames you drag your mouse over.) You want a one-second segment, so don't save your experiment. Undo your changes and move on to create your first tween.

Your First Motion Tween

Now that you've set up your first and last keyframes and varied the content to cause a change (in this case, in both scale and tint), you can add a tween and see the results. For the desired effect, you want to create a *motion tween*.

NOTE

You can also insert an empty keyframe by using Insert→Timeline→Blank Keyframe. However, when tweening, it usually helps to start with keyframes populated with content.

In simple terms, a motion tween is applied to symbol instances (such as the movie clips in your current example) or other non-shape assets, such as groups or text elements, and is used to vary properties of these assets over time:

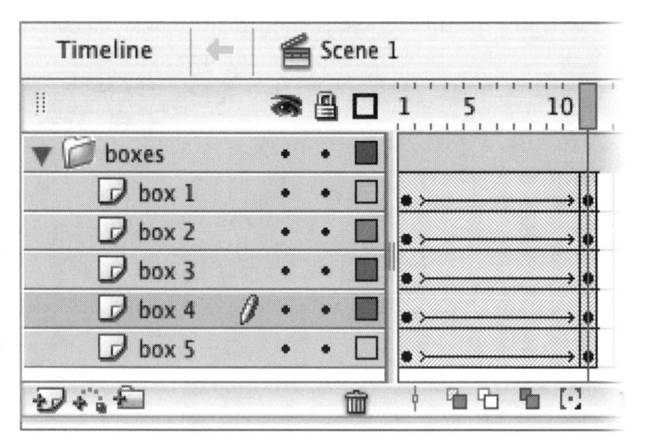

Figure 3-6. Motion tweens applied to each layer

1. Shift-select all the layers in the first frame.
2. Choose Motion from the Tween drop-down list in the Properties panel. An arrow appears on each layer in the timeline, starting at the first keyframe and ending at the second keyframe. The *frame span* (everything from one keyframe to the next) turns blue, indicating a motion tween has been applied, as shown in Figure 3-6. You may need to deselect the layers to see this color change in the timeline.
3. Play the animation by pressing Enter/Return. You should see the colors change gradually over the second or so the animation plays, and the boxes should grow larger until they reach their final size in frame 12.
4. Save your work and compare your file to *animation_03.fla*.

Preparing Text for Animation

Text is often an integral part of an animation, drawing the eye to key terms that need to stand out in the design. In the completed version of your animation, the text "Flash 8 Out of the Box" appears one section at a time, moving in from different directions. In this project, the boxes serve to initially attract the user's attention, and the animated text completes the effect. A short animation such as this one serves its purpose without being gratuitous.

When choosing a font, be sure to pick one that matches the needs of the piece. Be mindful of the fact that too many fonts can be distracting. Try to use as few fonts as are required to get the idea across—preferably no more than two or three. Make sure they are dissimilar enough that the user can appreciate the difference instead of merely viewing the choices as byproducts of inconsistent design.

Later, when you start using ActionScript to control text in text fields, you will learn that you must embed fonts in your file to make sure they display correctly on any machine. Reducing the number of fonts used will help to keep the *.swf* file size down.

Next, add the text to the movie:

1. Add a new layer folder to the timeline above the *boxes* layer folder. Remember, to create a layer folder, click the Insert Layer Folder button in the Timeline panel. Name the layer folder **`text`**. If the *boxes* folder is open or selected at the time, the new *text* layer folder may appear inside it. If this happens, practice rearranging the timeline by dragging the *text* folder outside the *boxes* folder.
2. Add a new layer and drag it into the *text* layer folder.
3. Activate the Text tool from the Tools panel, shown in Figure 3-7, and click once on the Stage to create a text field. Set the value in the Field Type drop-down list in the Properties panel to Static Text, pick an appropriate font, and set the size to 30, as shown in Figure 3-7. Return to the text field on the Stage and enter the word **`Flash`**.

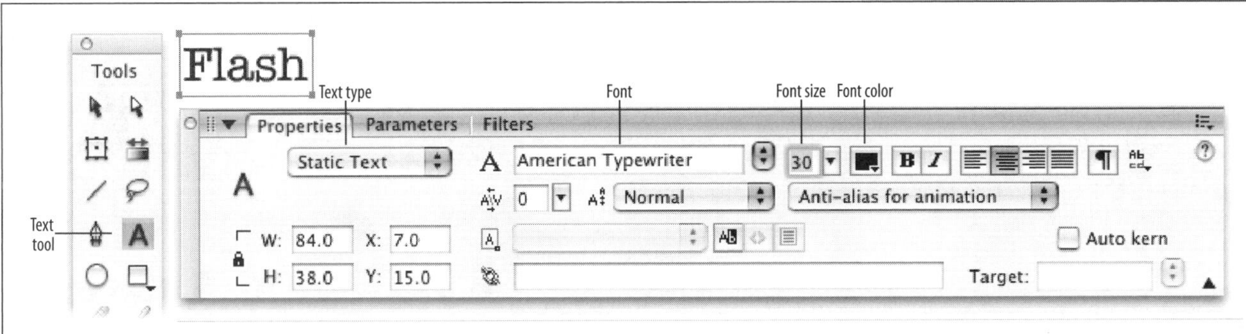

Figure 3-7. The Text tool, used to create a static text field for the word "Flash"

4. Switch to the Selection tool, and Alt/Option-drag the text element to create five additional copies of the text element.
5. Switch back to the Text tool and change the copies to say **`8`**, **`Out`**, **`of`**, **`the`**, and **`Box`**, respectively.
6. Shift-select the five text elements and change their color to black using the Text Color swatches pop-up in the Properties panel.
7. Select the text field containing the number 8 and increase its font size to 72. If you wish, give it a color that will contrast well with the other colors you've chosen for the underlying boxes.
8. Save your work.

You now have the text you need for your animation, but you can't animate these elements separately if they are all in one layer. To separate the text into five layers:

1. Convert each separate text element to a movie clip symbol, naming them appropriately.
2. Just as you did with the boxes earlier, use Modify→Timeline→Distribute to Layers to create a new layer for each symbol instance.

3. Delete the empty layer in the *text* layer folder (by selecting the layer and clicking the trash can icon).

4. Arrange the five word text layers so that *Flash* is on top and *Box* is on the bottom.

5. You'll do something special with the number 8 later in this chapter, so move that layer out of the *text* folder into a new folder of its own, called *eight*. When you're through, your file layer structure should match what you see in Figure 3-8 and in the *animation_04.fla* file.

NOTE

Text, unlike other elements in a Flash movie, does not need to be converted to a symbol before a motion tween is applied to it, because Flash treats it as a symbol automatically. However, it is a good practice to convert objects on the Stage to symbols before applying a motion tween. This makes it easier to make global changes when necessary.

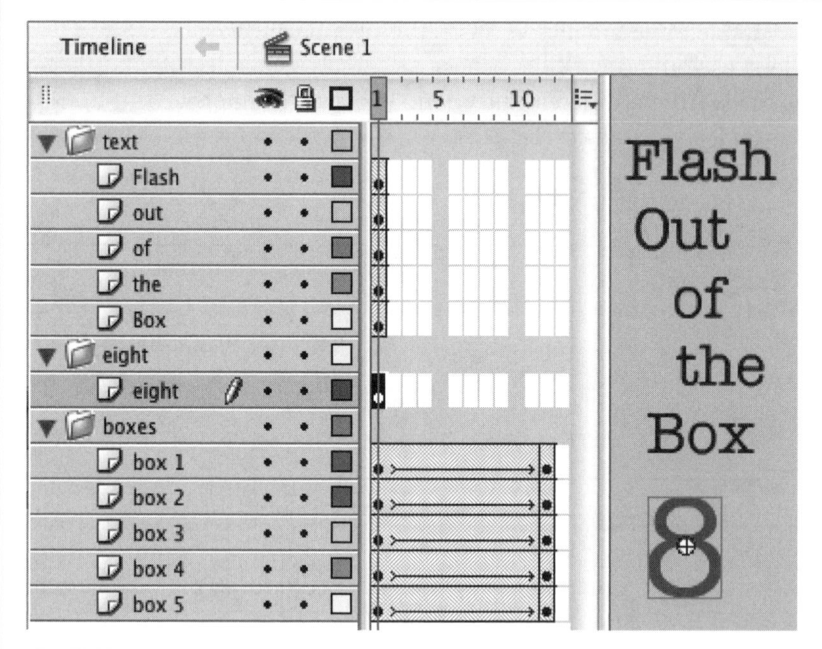

Figure 3-8. The new text layers, with each element converted into a symbol

Types of Text

The *static* text type is used when you don't need to change the content of the text with programming at runtime. Essentially, the type is treated like any other vector shape when compiled. This means that you can use a custom font without fear of it changing from machine to machine.

However, although the font will remain intact when compiled into a SWF by its creator, if the FLA is edited without the custom font installed, the SWF will not render as expected. Therefore, to ensure that the sample files you see on the CD-ROM match the screenshots in this book—even if you don't have the font used in these files—the text elements have been broken apart into vectors. They are no longer editable, but they will appear as intended.

When you're more experienced with Flash, you may want to use a custom font even when programming text content. In this case, you can opt for *dynamic* (programmable) or *input* (programmable and user-editable) text types, and embed a font in your file for use at runtime. This increases the file size but allows for more flexible and customized design possibilities.

Dynamic and input text types are assets that you can try working with later in the book, as your ActionScript skills grow.

Sliding Text

To complete the animation, instead of having the text resize and change colors, as you did with the boxes, you need to make each word slide onto the Stage from a different direction. To create a simple design from these elements, you can have the text on the ends slide in from the left and right edges, respectively, and you can have the text in the middle slide in from the top or bottom.

Soon, you'll tween the text animation as you did for the boxes. First, however, you need to make sure the text doesn't appear until after the box animation is finished.

To make sure the text doesn't appear until the boxes are in position:

1. Select the keyframes on frame 1 of all five layers in the *text* layer folder by clicking on the *Flash* layer's keyframe and dragging downward.
2. Click again and drag the keyframes to frame 14, and then release the mouse button.

Now, the text does not appear until the playhead reaches frame 14. The box animation completes in frame 12, and the text animation starts a few frames later for effect.

To animate the text:

1. At frame 48, select all layers and choose Insert→Timeline→Frame (F5) to add frames to every layer, allowing content to be visible until the end of the animation.
2. Still in frame 48, for each text layer in turn (including the *eight* layer), position the text symbol instances to match the positions indicated in Figure 3-1. These positions are where the instances land at the end of the animation, but it is easier to work backward in this case.
3. When you're finished, select frame 48 in all the text layers and choose Insert→Timeline→Keyframe (F6) to convert the frames to keyframes. Your box tweens should still end at frame 12.
4. Click on frame 14 in the timeline to move the playhead back to that frame. Move each text symbol instance to match the positions indicated

in Figure 3-9. This is where the instances appear at the beginning of the animation.

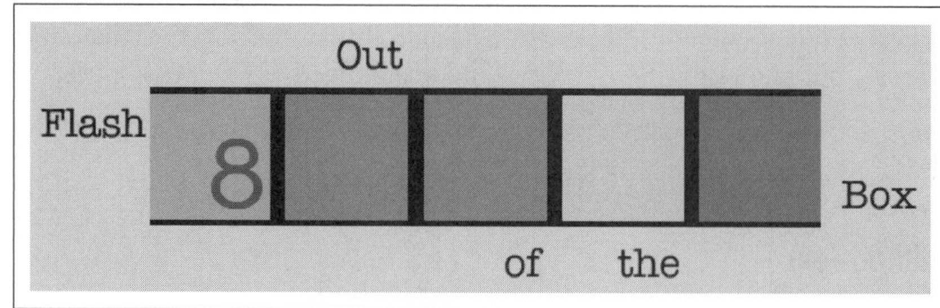

Figure 3-9. The position of each word at the beginning of the animation

5. Select frame 14 on all text layers and choose Motion from the Tween drop-down list in the Properties panel to apply a motion tween to each frame span.
6. Your timeline should now match Figure 3-10, or the *animation_06.fla* file.

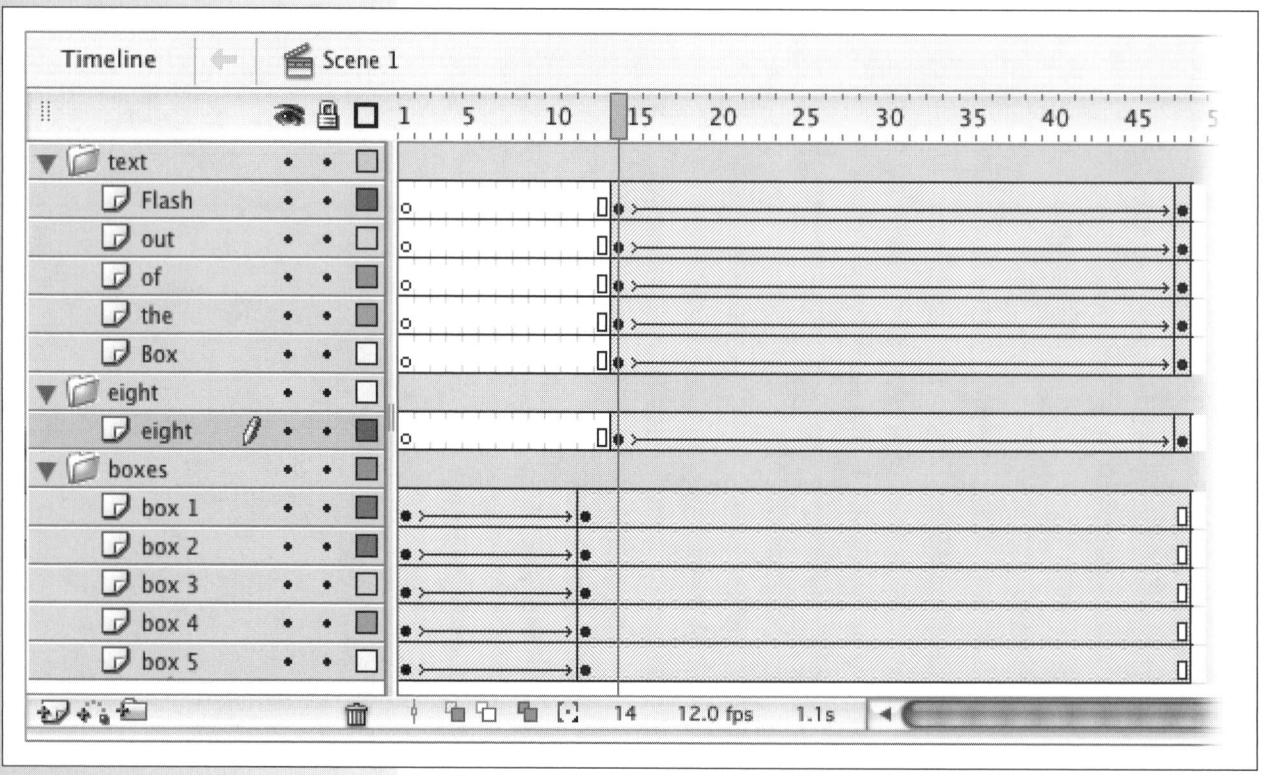

Figure 3-10. The text layers after applying the tweens

7. Press Enter/Return to play the animation in its entirety. The boxes grow and change colors, the words slide in from different directions, and the 8 appears in place.

Staggering Animation

The animation you have is getting there, but it's still slow and pretty boring. One way to spice it up easily, and simultaneously speed up the text tweens a bit, is to stagger the animation of the words. The word *Flash* should appear first, then *Out*, and so on. When you're done, you'll cap it off with a little flourish using the *8*. To stagger the words in time (i.e., start them in succession), you need to shorten the animation span for each text segment and adjust the positions of the keyframes:

1. Starting with the *Flash* layer, click once on the ending keyframe, and then click again and drag the selection to frame 26.
2. On the *Out* layer, select the first keyframe and drag it to frame 22. Select and drag the last keyframe to frame 33. You'll start this movement a frame or two later than the others to give the 8 a little extra time to show itself. You'll get to that in a second.
3. Select and drag the starting keyframes of the *of*, *the*, and *Box* layers to frames 28, 34, and 40, respectively.
4. Select and drag the ending keyframes of the same layers to frames 37, 43, and 48 (where it should already be), respectively.
5. Leave the starting keyframe for the *eight* layer where it is, but select and drag the ending keyframe to frame 32.
6. Play the animation (Enter/Return). In the revised animation, each word moves onto the Stage at a different time. The staggered animation guides the eye from the first word to the last.
7. Save your work. Your timeline should now look like Figure 3-11 and mirror the *animation_07.fla* file.

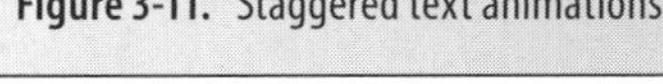

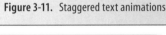

Figure 3-11. Staggered text animations

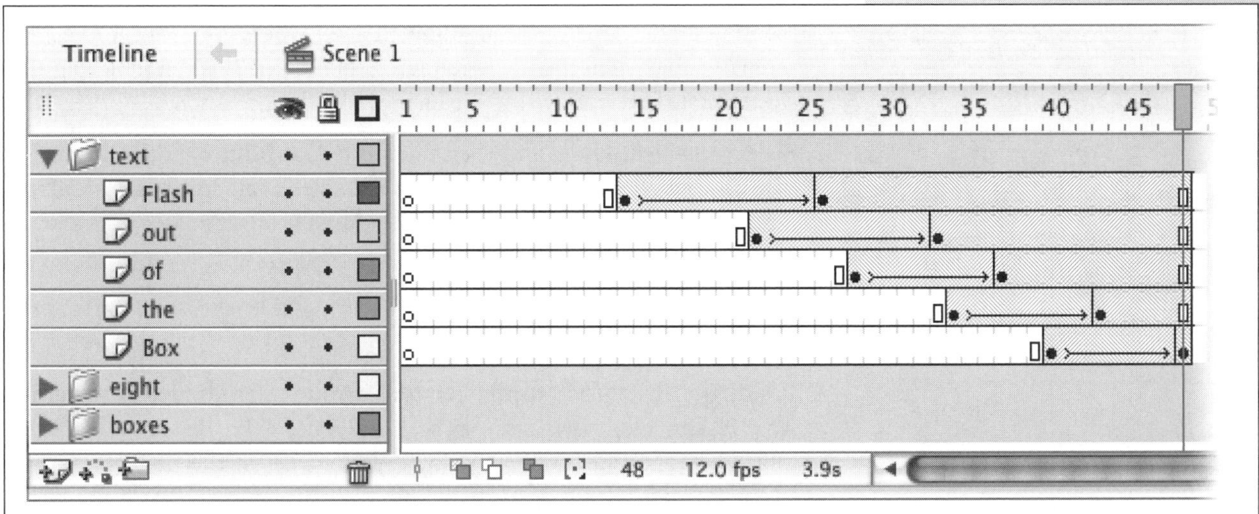

> **NOTE**
>
> *When you click on a timeline frame with content in it, all the Stage elements in that frame are selected. Sometimes that's handy, but it may be easier to select items on the Stage if you don't first click in the timeline frame. To move to a frame without selecting anything, click on the frame number in the top span of numbered notches (above all the layers, rather than in a specific layer).*

Alpha Effect

The final step to complete the first version of your animation is to add an alpha effect. Currently, the 8 just pops in immediately, and it's a little jarring. If you make one small adjustment, it will fade in nicely:

1. Move the playhead to frame 14, which is the frame that contains the first keyframe of the 8 animation.
2. On the Stage, click on the 8. In the Properties panel, choose Alpha in the Color effect menu, and enter a value of **0**.
3. Play your animation again. Now the number 8 fades in nicely.
4. Save your work.

Motion Effects

Successful designers communicate in myriad ways. Themes are communicated through type, blocking, pacing, color, and movement. Combining these elements can have a powerful effect. Convoluted intros on web sites are virtually extinct now (fortunately), but motion design is still alive and well, as it should be. How, then, can motion help bring your files to the next level?

Animating Along a Motion Guide

So far, your animated sequences have been linear and fairly conventional. True, you've added some color changes and an opacity fade, but mostly you've focused on scaling and sliding along straight lines. Now it's time to add a little spice by leading an asset along a stylized path:

1. Using a *motion guide*, it's possible to draw a path for an object to follow. Motion guides are lines that guide an asset where you want it to go but aren't visible when the file is rendered. Next, you'll add a motion guide to the *eight* layer, so that it waves in with a bit of punch.
2. Select the *eight* layer, and then click the Add Motion Guide button at the bottom of the timeline. Its icon resembles a red arc guiding a shape, and it sits between the Insert Layer and Insert Layer Folder buttons you used earlier.
3. Insert a keyframe in frame 14 of the motion guide layer so it starts at the same time as the *eight* layer.
4. Using the Pencil tool, or the Pen tool if you prefer, draw a flowing line that resembles a sideways S, as seen in Figure 3-12. Be sure it starts off Stage bottom and ends in the lower-left corner of the first box. If you want to start with a predrawn line, open *animation_09.fla* in the *03* folder in your working directory.

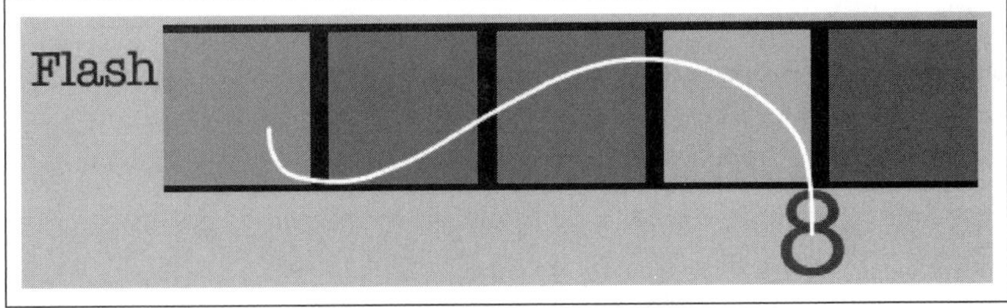

Figure 3-12. The motion guide for the eight layer

5. Switch to the *eight* layer, and select the second keyframe. You will see an outline of the currently invisible *eight* symbol instance. Single-click on the *eight* symbol instance and look for the centered crosshair. Grab the symbol by this crosshair and snap it to the below-Stage right end of the motion guide. If it doesn't snap, be sure View→Snapping→Snap to Objects is enabled. (If it helps, you can disable the alpha color effect you applied earlier. The sample file is configured this way to make it easier for you to see the symbol instance.)
6. Do the same thing in the last keyframe of the *eight* layer. Snap the symbol instance to the left, on-Stage end of the motion guide.
7. Play the animation. The *eight* symbol instance should follow the path of the motion guide from start to finish, as seen in *animation_10.fla*.
8. You can make it look even better with one simple enhancement. Click on the first keyframe in the motion tween you created for the *eight* symbol. In the Properties panel, beneath the Tween menu, enable the Orient to Path option. This will cause the 8 to rotate automatically along the path of the motion guide. Sometimes it helps to rotate the symbol instance a bit at the start and end points of the motion guide, to align its direction with the path.
9. Test your file and save your work. It should look like *animation_11.fla*.

NOTE

Guide layers not used for motion tweens are not exported when you publish a movie; therefore, content on an otherwise unused guide layer does not affect the file size of a movie. You can use guide layers to store design notes—text or graphics to help describe how a file works—to document the process or specify future enhancements under consideration. You can also temporarily convert a normal layer into a guide layer to hide its contents during testing.

You're now almost done with your first animation, but there's one final touch you can add to enhance its realism and style.

Realistic Motion

Beginner animators logically don't have the experience to know what makes an animation pop. Most linear animations are fairly flat and uniform, but there are a few simple tricks that can make your tweens come to life.

One shortcut to relatively realistic motion is to use *easing*. Easing refers to when you slowly ease out of, or into, a keyframe. Think of a bouncing ball example. When you throw a ball up in the air, gravity causes it to slow down and eventually stop at the top of its travels. It then accelerates up to a point, bounces on the floor, and begins the trip all over again. A flat animation would show the ball moving at a constant rate through all the frames. However, with the help of easing (and a few other tricks), you can more closely simulate the way the ball might move in the real world.

Bouncing ball

To experience this firsthand, take a look at the *bouncing_ball* files in the *03* folder of your working directory. This is not an accurate simulation, because the ball will continue to bounce infinitely. However, this simplified example will allow you to focus on the issues at hand.

The first file, *bouncing_ball_01.fla*, shows a straightforward bouncing ball animation. The ball moves at a continuous pace, and no keyframes have been edited.

The second file illustrates the first trick for more realistic motion. In a repeating sequence, the animation will look smoother if keyframes are not duplicated back to back. For example, look at the ball bounce in the first file. The ending keyframe of the down sequence is the same as the beginning keyframe of the up sequence. This causes a "stutter" at the point of the bounce. (In a down/up animation like this it is common to just use three keyframes, so the middle keyframe can be shared by both sequences, preventing this duplication. However, another trick is on the way, so unique keyframes are preferred.) In *bouncing_ball_02.fla*, the y-coordinate of the bouncing ball in the ending keyframe of the sequence has been moved up slightly to avoid the visual duplication.

The third file adds a little nicety that is specific to this type of animation. Inserting another keyframe between the two sequences enables you to squash the ball down a little bit, as it would deform during the bounce. These types of extra touches are not universally implemented, but they can really sell an animation.

Finally, *bouncing_ball_04.fla* introduces easing. The first sequence accelerates before the bounce and decelerates after the bounce. If you compare this file to the first animation, the difference is fairly amazing considering the simplicity of the enhancements.

Realistic motion isn't just handy for a bouncing ball, though. The effect can be applied in many situations. A sliding panel in an interface, for example, could be designed to slide quickly at first and slow gradually to a stop, helping to make the interface more elegant: instead of just plopping into position, it comes to rest gracefully.

Custom easing

Flash 8 makes graceful transitions easier than ever to achieve. The custom easing dialog, shown in Figure 3-13, allows you to draw a simple graph that will dictate the change in your animation over time. To get to the dialog, select the first keyframe of a motion tween, like you would when invoking the tween. Beneath the Tween menu, where you previously selected Motion, there is a button marked Edit. Clicking this button will open the Custom Ease In / Ease Out dialog and allow you to add easing to the tween you are manipulating.

Figure 3-13. The Custom Ease In / Ease Out dialog

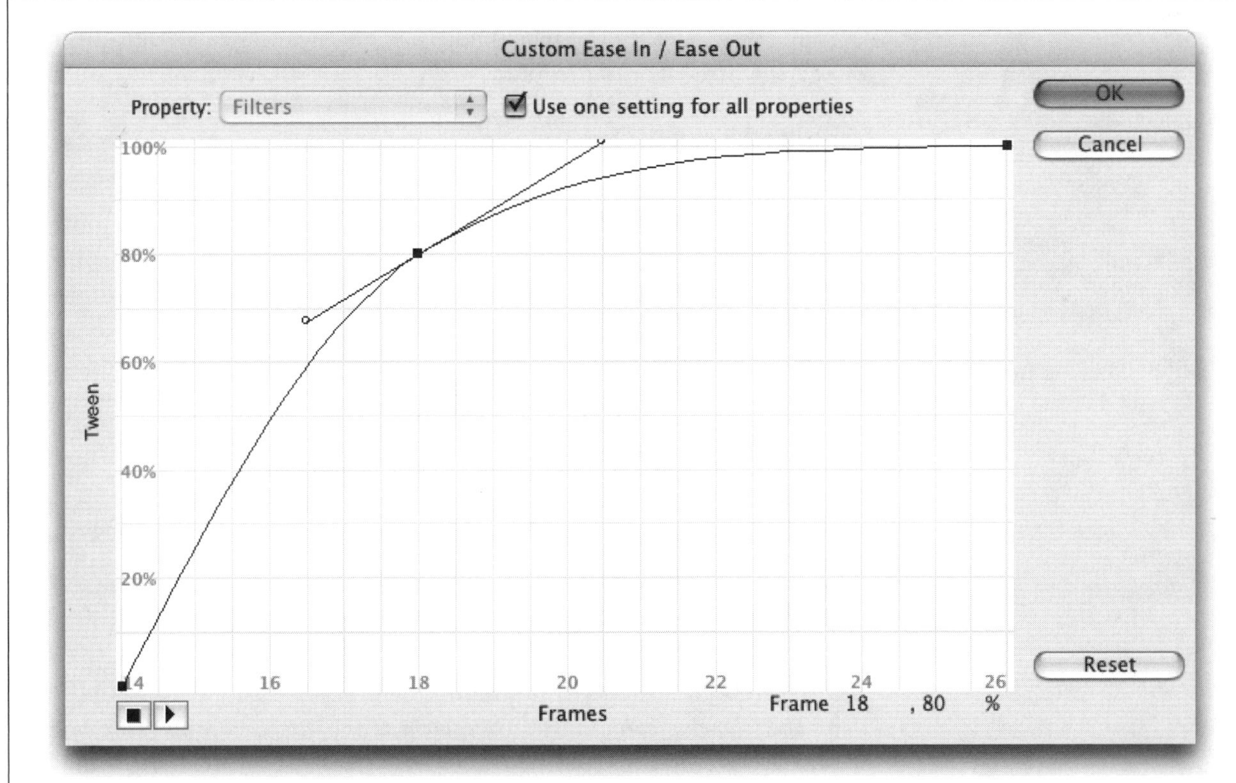

You can adjust the Position, Scale, Rotation, Color, and Filter effects independently by drawing separate graphs, or manipulate all five effects at once with the same graph. In this example, you will focus on position, so no change to the dialog menu will be required.

The custom easing graph represents the length of your animation in frames along the horizontal axis and the percentage of your animation that is complete along the vertical axis. The default straight line means that your animation will complete itself consistently across the span of frames used to create it.

You can add control points by clicking on the graph's line, and then you can drag a point to add acceleration or deceleration. Look at the easing graph in the second span of frames in *bouncing_ball_04.fla*, for example, pictured in Figure 3-13. This 12-frame segment of the animation begins at frame 14 and concludes at frame 26. From a visual standpoint, it starts immediately after the ball bounces on the floor and stops when the ball slows to a stop at the top of its bounce, due to gravity.

Because the ball rebounds from the bounce quickly and slowly comes to a stop, the new control point (selected) is positioned so that 80% of the tweened animation takes place in only the first third of the allocated frames. This means that the ball moves very quickly during the first four frames and then slowly finishes the remaining 20% of the distance it needs to travel over the final eight frames of the span.

Easing the number 8

The *eight* movie clip in your first animation currently follows something akin to the track of a virtual roller coaster, but unfortunately it moves at a constant rate, so it doesn't look very exciting. If you add easing, you can make it look even more like a car on a roller coaster. Try to make it climb the first hill slowly, rush down the slope, and then slow again at the last upturn before coming to a halt:

1. If you're not already there, pick up where you left off in the last step in your *animation* series. If you prefer, open *animation_11.fla* and start from there.
2. Expand the *eight* layer folder and select the first keyframe of its tween.
3. In the Properties panel, click the Edit button to open the Custom Ease In / Ease Out dialog.

NOTE

The following easing values correspond to the sample file, but your motion guide may be different. The idea is just to match the animation speed with the curves of the guide. Experiment until you are happy, or try working with the sample file, animation_complete.fla. You can reset the graph and use the following matching values, if you prefer.

4. Add a new control point by clicking on the straight line. Drag it to approximately frame 21 along the bottom of the graph and approximately 40% along the left of the graph.

5. Add another new control point and drag this one to the approximate intersection of frame 27 and 90%.
6. You've now created a segment that will move slowly for the first 40% of the animation, slightly faster than normal for the next 50% of the animation, and then slowly again for the last 10% of the span. Click on each control point and adjust the handles to smooth out the curve. Your custom easing graph should look like Figure 3-14.

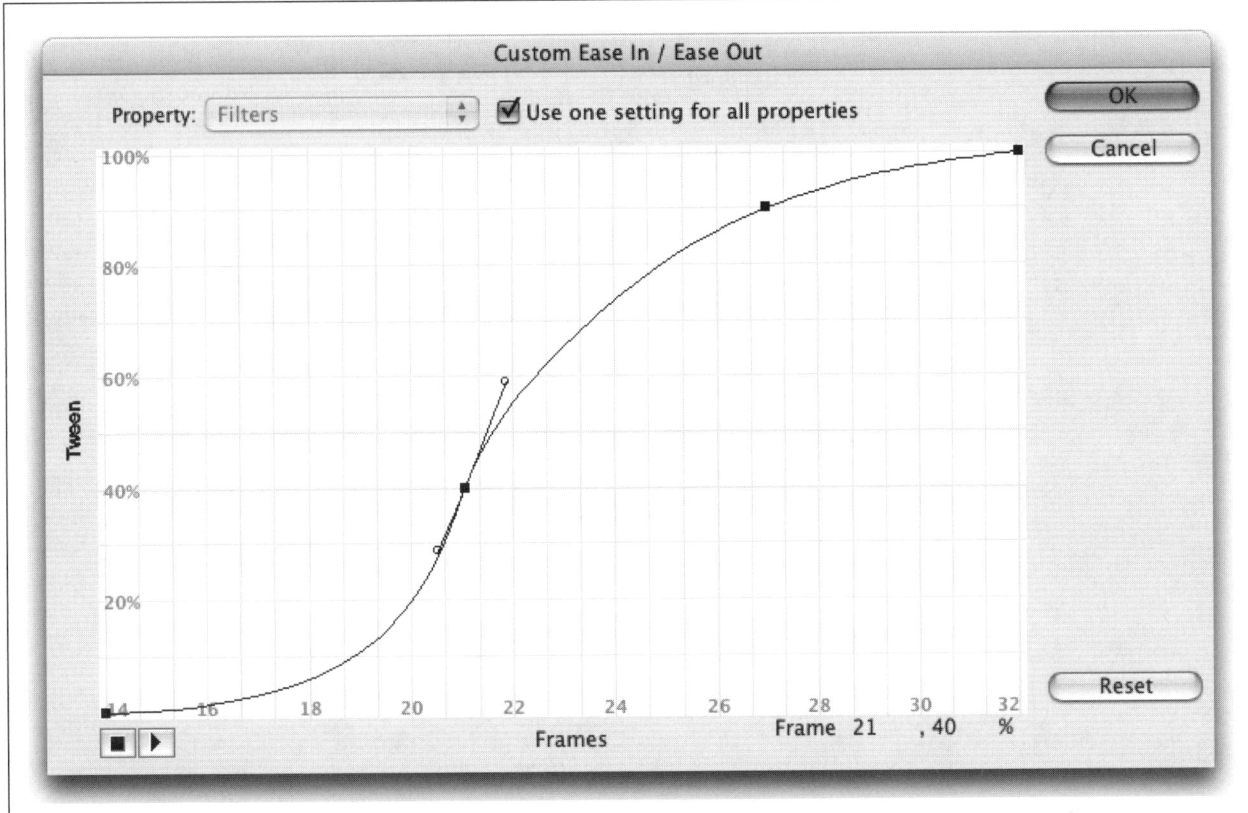

Figure 3-14. The custom easing graph for your final animation

7. Use the Play button in the dialog to preview your animation. When you are happy, click the OK button to dismiss the dialog.
8. Save your work and test your file. The animation should be a bit livelier.

Your First Script

To prevent the movie from looping, you need to add an ActionScript *method* (also sometimes called a *command* or *action*). You'll use more ActionScript later, but for now, just add a simple *stop()* method and publish the movie again.

1. In the timeline for *animation.fla*, add a new layer and drag it above the *text* and *boxes* layer folders.
2. Rename the new layer *actions*. It is a good practice to keep the *actions* layer above all others in the timeline.

NOTE

Placing your ActionScript on the top layer and naming the layer actions is a convention often used by Flash developers to make it easier to find the ActionScript in a movie (some developers name the layer "scripts" instead of "actions"). To follow best practices, don't put any content other than scripts in this layer.

3. To prevent graphics from being added accidentally to the *actions* layer, lock the layer by clicking the second dot to the right of the layer name, under the lock icon.
4. In the last frame of the timeline, insert a keyframe in the *actions* layer. (Locking the layer prevents you from adding graphics to the Stage for that layer, but you can still add keyframes and ActionScript to the layer.)
5. With the last frame still selected, open the Actions panel by choosing Window→Development Panels→Actions, or by pressing F9.
6. Type **`stop();`** into the Script pane of the Actions panel, as shown in Figure 3-15. The *stop()* method tells the playhead to stop when it reaches this frame, instead of looping. A frame script is often used to execute instructions without having to rely on user input (such as pressing a key or clicking a button). See the "Frame Scripts" sidebar for more information.

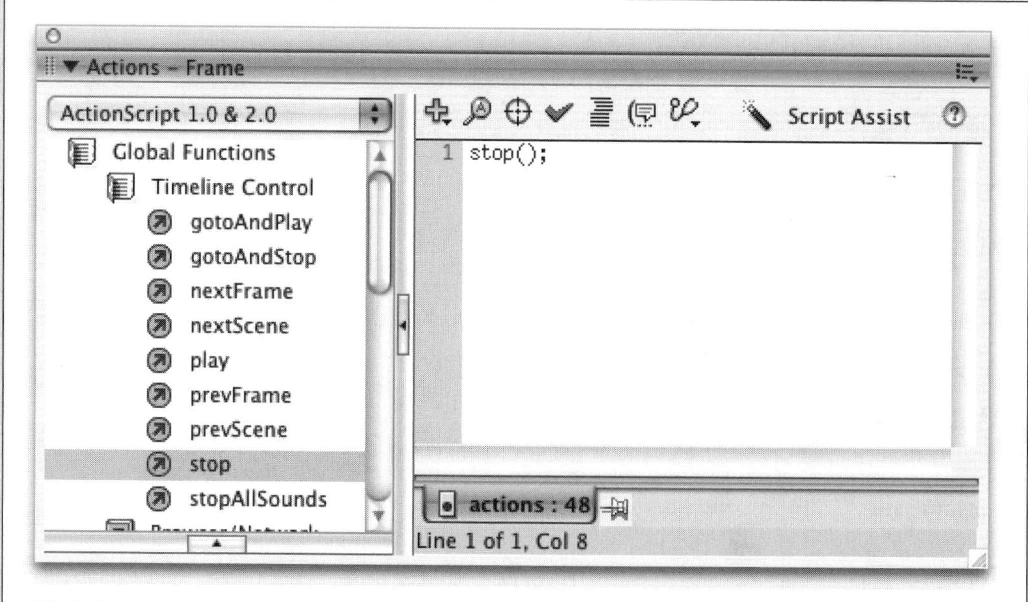

Figure 3-15. The Actions panel with a stop() method added to the Script panel

7. Save your work and test your movie again.
8. If you haven't created the *.fla* yourself or are having trouble doing so, open the *animation_complete.swf* file in the *03* folder of your working directory and watch the final result.

Publishing Your Movie

The animation is done, but your work cannot be shown outside the Flash authoring environment until you *publish* the movie.

Publishing a Flash movie is the act of exporting the completed version of a *.fla* file as another file type. The *.fla* format is used only for editing within the Flash application; it is too bloated with excess information (and too unprotected) to be appropriate for distribution. When you publish Flash content for the Web (for use with the Flash Player browser plug-in), the *.fla* file is compiled into the aforementioned self-contained *.swf* file format. You can publish other file formats too, some of which will be discussed later in this book.

Flash can also automatically create an HTML page in which to display your SWF file. Users don't ordinarily browse directly to the URL of a SWF file. Instead, developers typically publish an HTML file in which the SWF file is embedded (using the HTML `<object>` and `<embed>` tags).

Publish your movie and see how it performs:

1. With the Stage selected, choose the Settings button in the Properties panel. The Publish Settings dialog box opens to the Flash tab, as shown in Figure 3-16.
2. Your current movie will play in older versions of the Flash Player, but realistically, most people use at least Flash Player 5 or 6. In fact, as of June 2005, Macromedia doesn't even track installed versions prior to v5 (see *http://www.macromedia.com/software/player_census/flashplayer/version_penetration.html* for more information). Publishing using the minimum required version helps improve compatibility for your files, but there's no compelling reason to date back prior to Flash 5. Therefore, under the Flash tab, choose Flash Player 5 from the Version drop-down list. Be sure to set the version back to a more current player, though, when creating Flash movies that use features not supported in earlier versions.
3. Once you've specified the desired publishing settings, click Publish to publish your movie. This generates the SWF and HTML files, but doesn't literally publish the file on the Web. (In this case, "publish your movie" effectively means "generate a file," rather than the more traditional meaning of "make the file publicly available.") Both files will

Frame Scripts

The *frame script* is the first of three main script types that you will learn about in the introductory ActionScript overviews herein. A simplified account of the frame script might describe it as serving two primary purposes.

First, it is used to perform administrative tasks such as defining information that you may need later in other scripts, including *variables* that store data and *functions* that collect instructions that should be executed only when called upon.

Second, a frame script is used to execute tasks *passively*. That is, rather than requiring active participation from the user, such as clicking a button or pressing a key, the script is executed during normal movie playback when the playhead reaches the frame in which the script resides. This is particularly useful for simple navigation methods, such as the *stop()* method used in this chapter.

Semicolon;

If you've been investigating Flash scripting on your own, you may have noticed that some scripts include a semicolon at the end of each line, and some don't. This is because the current version of ActionScript does not technically require the semicolon at the end of each line, and will compile correctly without it. Officially, the semicolon is required only when including more than one consecutive instruction in a single line, but that won't be covered in this book.

However, as a best practice, you should include the semicolon at the end of each instruction line of ActionScript. Although not required, it makes the code easier to read and will help establish good habits. This will make it much easier for you to migrate to other circumstances and languages where an ending semicolon is required, such as Cascading Style Sheets (CSS) and PHP.

automatically be placed in the same folder as the *.fla* file, unless you specify otherwise in the Publish settings.

4. In a web browser, try the HTML file you just created. If you have the Flash plug-in installed, you should have no problem enjoying the results of your work.

5. Save your work. You're all done for now.

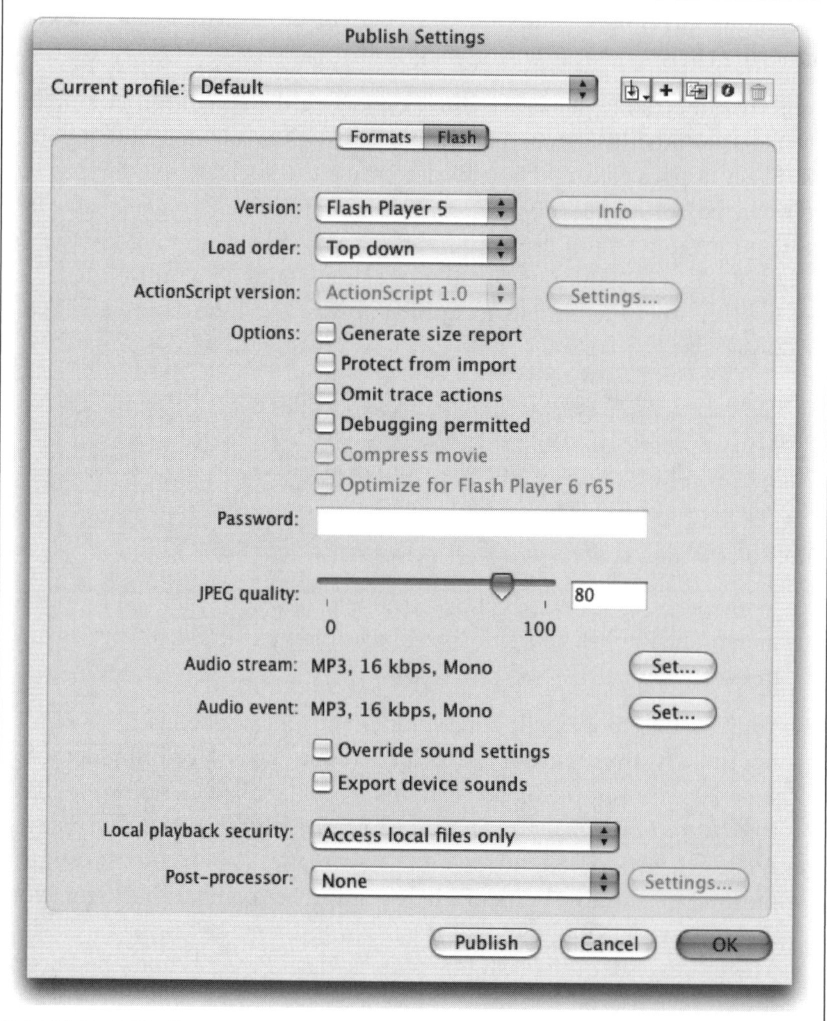

Figure 3-16. The Publish Settings dialog box

What's Next?

Mission accomplished! You now have an animation in SWF format ready to be posted on the Web.

You've already learned the basics of controlling the speed of an animation (by adjusting the frame rate or the number of frames over which the animation occurs). The pacing of an animation is key to its success, so keep that in mind as you begin new projects. A slow-paced ad for a high-speed Internet connection service, for example, would not convey the desired message to the user. Subconsciously, the user would associate a slow ad with a slow Internet connection. Therefore, you'd want to use a slow-paced animation when discussing the competing products (such as dial-up connections), and use a fast-paced animation to dramatize the speed of the high-speed Internet connection.

To practice what you've learned, try modifying other properties of the animation you created. Can you start with invisible boxes and fade them in? Can you animate the text using different starting points, so the text moves in different directions? Finally, try changing the pace of the animation.

Motion effects can convey a sense of depth in Flash animations—something you may want to strive for in your own work. In the real world, objects close to the viewer appear to move more quickly than objects that are far away. How might you use this fact to make, say, an animation of falling snow appear more realistic?

If you want the user to be able to replay your animation, you can add a button to the end that will restart the file from frame 1, as you'll soon see.

In the next chapter, you'll take a look at several types of buttons and simple interactivity. You'll learn:

- How to pick up ActionScript quickly with the Script Assist mode
- A little more about basic ActionScript structure
- How to use components and behaviors
- How to use buttons for navigation

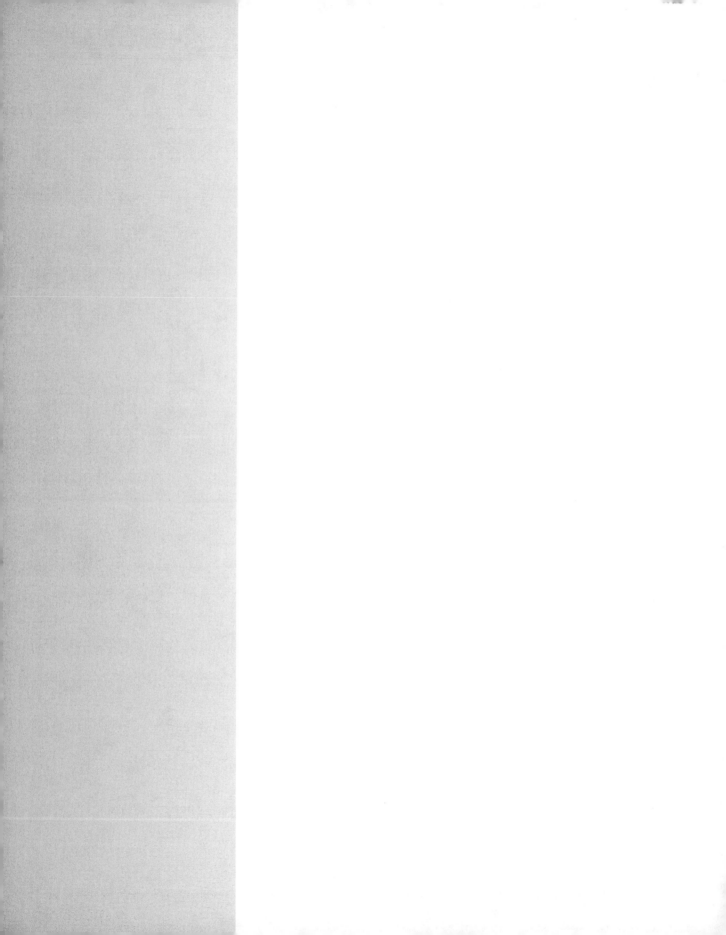

Buttons and Interactivity

4

It's time to get interactive! Flash can be a rewarding design and animation tool, but you won't be using the application to its fullest potential unless you include elements of interactivity. In Chapter 3, you wrote your first script, to prevent your animation from looping by default. In this chapter, you'll give your audience some control through the use of buttons and ActionScript.

In this chapter

The easiest way to add interactivity to Flash is to use a button to run ActionScript. The projects featured in this chapter will all focus on button use. One project, for example, will be to modify the animation you created in Chapter 3, adding one button to replay the animation and another to open a web page.

You may be thinking, "Big deal, I can do those things with HTML." True, but Flash buttons can be more powerful, and sometimes even easier to create, than their HTML counterparts. With Flash, it's easier for buttons to contain animations and sound, to be activated or dimmed dynamically, and to be repositioned automatically when, say, the browser window is resized.

Of course, buttons are just the beginning. ActionScript is a powerful scripting language, and it can be implemented in a variety of ways. Fortunately, the Flash development community is one of the most generous collectives on the Web, and there are many resources available to help you learn more about ActionScript when you are ready. Appendix A contains a very brief list of such resources to get you started, but half the fun is exploring.

Buttons as Symbols

In earlier chapters, you learned about graphic symbols and movie clip symbols. Next, you'll see how to create the third type of symbol, a button. Buttons are similar in many respects to other symbols, but there are two important differences.

The main difference is that, by default, a button doesn't have a full timeline, like a graphic or a movie clip. Instead, it has four distinct frames in which you can place the various button "states" (the default appearance of the button, as well as the way it looks when the mouse is hovered over and clicked down on the button).

The second difference is that a button will automatically update its appearance upon user interaction. That is, the button will automatically change its state, and switch the system cursor between the default selection arrow and a "pointing finger," to respond to corresponding mouse movements. Although the button must still be programmed with ActionScript to affect your movie, the button state and cursor feedback are handled for you.

Simple Buttons

Multiple button states are not required, and sometimes you just need a quick "hot spot." Soon, you'll see how to create more complex buttons (and even an invisible button), but your first project is to start with a basic button symbol.

To create a button with the word *Button* on it:

1. Create a new Flash document to experiment with and save the file as *simple_button.fla* in the *04* folder.
2. Draw a rectangle (choose any color you like) and resize it to 100 × 50.
3. Use the Text tool to create the word *Button*. Center-justify the text using the Properties panel, and center the text object itself within the rectangle. (Hint: Try using the Align panel.)
4. Click and drag to select everything on the Stage, and then press F8 to convert the image to a symbol.

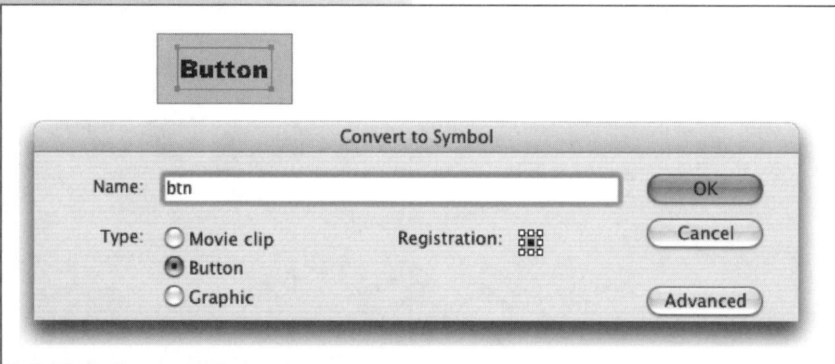

Figure 4-1. Converting the content to a button symbol

5. In the Convert to Symbol dialog box, name the symbol **btn** and choose Button as the Behavior type, as shown in Figure 4-1. Click OK to close the dialog box.
6. Test the movie.

The Preview window opens, and when you move your cursor over the instance of the *btn* symbol, the cursor displays as a hand, just as it does when you roll over a link on a web page. Why didn't the button's appearance change? You've created a default, or "Up," button state, but you haven't yet created new artwork to display when the mouse rolls over and clicks on the button. You'll do that next.

Button States

When you look inside a button symbol, the timeline appears unique because of the aforementioned four predefined frames. The first three are button states. The *Up* state represents the button's appearance when the mouse cursor is not over the button, the *Over* state is displayed when the mouse is rolled over the button, and the *Down* state displays when the user clicks on the button. You'll take a look at the fourth state, the *Hit* state, in a moment.

For the next project, make your button more complex by creating the Over and Down states for your button symbol:

1. In your existing *simple_button.fla* file, double-click the *btn* symbol to edit it in place.
2. Add a new empty layer and call it **`text`**. Name the previous layer **`art`**.
3. Be careful to select only the *Button* text in the original *art* layer, and cut it to your clipboard. Then select the new *text* layer, and use the Edit→ Paste in Place menu command (Ctrl/Cmd-Shift-V). This will paste any clipboard object into the same place on the Stage that it occupied when it was placed on the clipboard (it works for multiple objects as well). The result will be that *Button* now resides in the new layer.

WARNING

The Paste in Place command is relative to the timeline you are editing, and locations and sizes can affect the registration point of each timeline. So, if you cut or copy from inside one symbol and then paste in place outside that symbol (for example, in the root scene or inside another symbol), you may not get the same results.

4. Select the Over and Down frames in the *art* layer, and press F6 to add keyframes. The rectangle in your button is re-created in these frames.
5. Select the same frames in the *text* layer, but this time press F5 to add frames, not keyframes.
6. Click on the Over frame in the *art* layer. This will let you work only on this state.
7. In order to visually distinguish the button's Over state from its Up state, while in the Over frame, change the fill color for the rectangle in the Properties panel.
8. Repeat this process for the Down state, choosing another unique color.
9. Save and test the movie. It should resemble *simple_button_02.fla*, and your timeline should look like Figure 4-2.

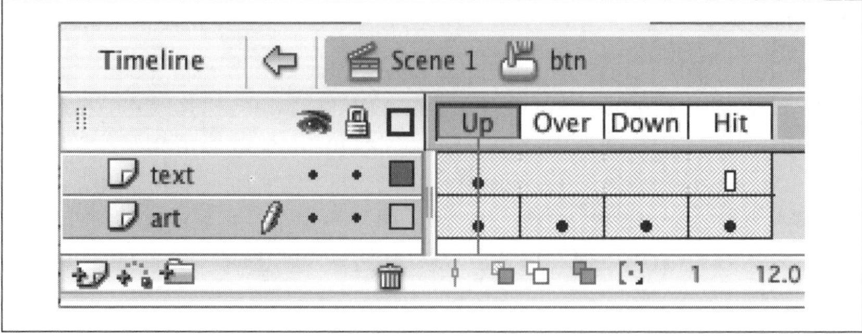

Figure 4-2. Timeline for a button symbol

When you roll over it, the button displays its Over state, which in this case changes the button's color. When you click the button, it displays its Down state, which causes it to change colors again.

You've now seen Flash's ability to automatically switch between the three primary button states and update the cursor, but what does the fourth state do? The Hit state allows you to customize the areas of the button that will respond to the cursor. By default, the button will react to the Up state. However, if the Hit frame is populated, any content in this frame, and only content in this frame, will trigger the mouse and allow the button to work. This makes it very easy to make buttons of irregular shapes, and since the Hit state content is invisible to the user, it means you can really get creative.

For example, think of a button that you might find in a Flash file about *The Simpsons*—a button that looks like a donut, say. You certainly want the button to function when you click on the creamy pink frosting with sprinkles on top, but you may not want the button to work when the mouse is over the inner hole of the donut. To see an example of this setup, open the *donut_button.fla* file in the *04* folder of your working directory.

Just as you can customize the Hit state to exclude a particular area, you can add content to a Hit state to make the button react to more than just what is visible. For instance, if you want to create a slide show, you can place previous/next buttons in the bottom center of the Stage, but also add a thin vertical ribbon, the height of the Stage, on the extreme left and right sides of the viewable area. This way, both the button art and the invisible areas at the sides will trigger the buttons. An example, *slide_show_buttons.fla*, is also included in the *04* folder.

To experiment with modifying a Hit state yourself, consider an old arcade-style button. This traditional push button has a plastic bevel surrounding the button itself. It's easy to understand that the button should work as advertised, but should the bevel also be active?

1. Open *bevel_button.fla* in the *04* folder.
2. Test the movie to try both buttons. The button on the left represents the default scenario, with a Hit state derived directly from the Up state. Look at the button in action and get a feel for the interactive areas.
3. Next, try the button on the right and see how it differs. When you're through, close the test movie and go back to the Stage.
4. To improve the first button, double-click the button to edit it in place. In the mini-timeline, click in the Hit frame in the *bevel* layer, and delete its contents. You've removed the bevel, but not the button. Now only the button itself will respond to the mouse, which is the correct behavior. Figure 4-3 shows the visible button on the left, and the Hit state on the right.
5. Test your movie to try it out. Once you're satisfied, close the SWF and FLA files. You're finished with this segment.

Figure 4-3. Visible button (left) compared with final Hit state (right)

WARNING

Keep an eye on this issue when creating buttons made from text. Remember that only non-transparent pixels will respond to the mouse. Therefore, if you create a Hit state from the word "FOO," the button will respond when the mouse is over the solid areas of the letters, but not when it's between the letters or inside the "O" characters. To improve on this, simply draw a rectangle in addition to the word. The Hit state is invisible, so it doesn't matter what it looks like.

Scripting Your Button

Now that you know how to make a button, you have to learn what to do with it. Remember, Flash will take care of the visual feedback, including cursor and state switching, but the button won't otherwise be functional. Don't worry, though. You can start scripting with a little assist.

Easy Scripting with Script Assist

If you prefer to write your own HTML rather than using a GUI editor, you may want to skip this section and move on to "Hand-Coding." However, sometimes assisted scripting can help even veterans remember a bit of seldom-used syntax, or the specific parts required to complete a line of code. For this reason, giving this section a quick look won't hurt.

If you're not yet comfortable with writing code, Flash 8's *Script Assist* can help you find your way. It's a guided method of shaping your script into its final form. While it would not be possible to create an unknown variety and complexity of code with a wizard-like linear interface, Script Assist is the next best thing.

You start by browsing a nested menu of available ActionScript entries and double-clicking on something you would like to add to your script. Flash does its best to determine where to add the code and to start the script with the appropriate syntax. It then presents a series of user interface (UI) elements, such as text boxes, menus, and radio buttons, to help you finish the code. All you have to do is fill in the appropriate values, and a script is born.

Now modify Chapter 3's project by scripting a button that will open a web page:

1. Open the file *animation_buttons.fla* in the *04* folder. This is the animation you completed in the last chapter, but a new layer called *buttons* has been added. In the last frame of this layer, two new buttons exist in a keyframe. The arrow button will eventually play the animation again, and you'll code the globe now to launch the web site. These buttons have been created for you to allow you to focus on the scripting in this chapter, but if you want to practice creating your own buttons, that's a good idea, too.
2. Select the globe button and open the Actions panel using the Window→Actions menu command.
3. In the Actions panel, make sure that the button is selected and that the title bar says "Actions – Button." (It's easy to put a script in the wrong place if the wrong thing is initially selected.) In this exercise, you want to create a button script rather than a frame script.
4. If you've been following along, or the default setup is still intact, your Actions panel should look the same as it did in Chapter 3: a vertical menu area on the left, and a text editor on the right (see Figure 3-15). This is the configuration used by most Flash coders with some scripting experience. It allows you to type in the script as you might in any text editor, but with additional features such as syntax coloring, code hinting, and similar benefits. This is the setup you used to enter the *stop()* action to prevent your last animation from looping.
5. You'll return to the hand-coding method after this demonstration, but for now you should see Script Assist at work. If the left side is not visible, drag the vertical bar on the left edge of the window to the right, exposing the menu. If the right half of the window has a shorter text area beneath a reserved area, you're probably already in Script Assist

NOTE

In this project, you will add a script directly to the button. This is not the optimal way of creating a button script, but it is the most direct way to demonstrate some of the purposes of, and differences between, script types. You'll learn about the preferred way of scripting buttons later in this chapter.

mode. In any case, enabling the Script Assist button in the right portion of your Actions panel should make it match Figure 4-4.

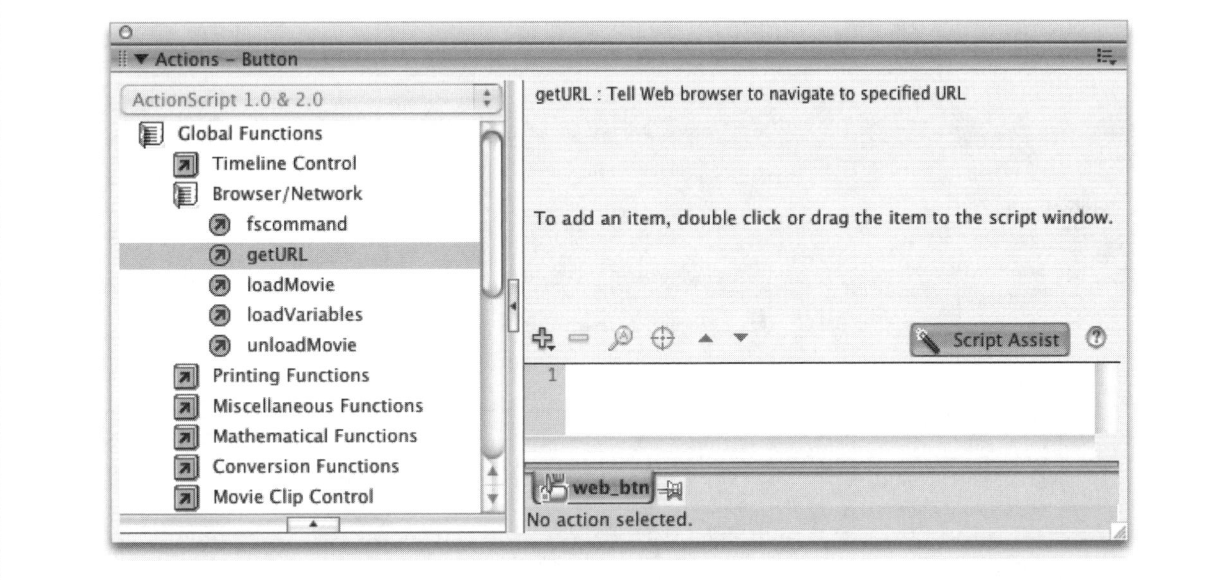

Figure 4-4. The Actions panel, with Script Assist enabled, ready for input

6. Before you populate your script, remember that you want to go to a URL for the book content, and that you are using a button to get there. In the lefthand menu, scroll to the top, open the *Global Functions* category with a single click, and then open the *Browser/Network* subcategory with another single click.

7. In this latter category, you will find a small collection of related actions. (Can you guess which action you want to work with? Whenever possible, Flash uses intuitively named actions.) Double-click on the *getURL* action.

8. You should see that Flash has written much of your script for you. In addition to adding the *getURL()* command, it has also added two lines of code, beginning with *on (release)*, to contain the command. This is called an *event handler*, because it "handles" events—that is, it reacts to events caused by Flash or the user. In this case, it is a button event handler, and it is designed to react when the user releases the mouse button after clicking on this button symbol instance. See the "Event Handlers" sidebar for more information.

9. All you have to do now is let Script Assist help you configure the unfinished *getURL()* action. If the *getURL* line in the script you are writing isn't still selected, select it now. The reserved area above the script will display some text input boxes and menus. In the URL text field, type **http://www.flash8outofthebox.com**. In the Window text field, type **_blank**. Don't worry about the other settings, as they are optional.

10. Notice down below that the script has been completed by the Script Assist mode. You may prefer to type this syntax from memory when you become more comfortable with ActionScript. Your script should now look like Figure 4-5.

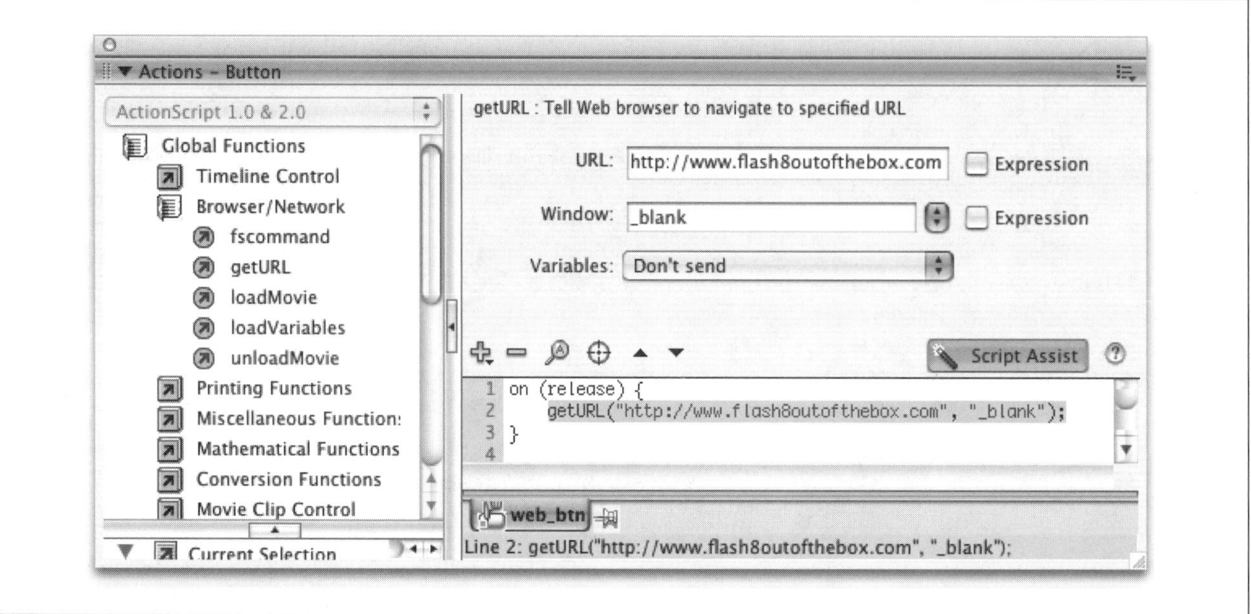

Figure 4-5. Completing the getURL() method with Script Assist

11. Save your work. For optimal results when testing, publish your movie using File→Publish Preview→Default - (HTML). This will display your SWF within an HTML page, so that you don't have to worry about your Flash authoring environment knowing how to talk to your browser.

Hand-Coding

Script Assist can be helpful when you're just starting out, or when you need a quick syntax clarification. However, as you become more familiar with ActionScript, you'll likely find yourself wanting to have more intimate control over your code, and wanting to take fewer steps when writing your scripts.

In the previous project, you used Script Assist to apply an instruction directly to a button. However, code can be more efficient and productivity can be improved if you consolidate your ActionScript in as few locations as possible. One way of doing this is to place much of your code in frame scripts but refer to, or *target*, a desired button when writing code for that button.

To do this, you must give a unique name to each button instance that you intend to script in this fashion. Try to use this approach to add a script to the remaining button in your animation. Make the left arrow go back to frame 1 and play the animation again:

1. Single-click on the button that looks like a left-facing arrow to select it. In the Properties panel, locate the <*instance name*> field in the lower-left corner, and type **`replay_btn`** to name the button.
2. Next, select the last frame in the *actions* layer, where you previously placed your *stop()* script.

Event Handlers

A typical Flash experience may include a variety of *events* that cause other actions to occur. Some of these events may be passive, such as when the playhead enters a frame. Others may be interactive, because they are created by a user activity of some kind, such as pressing a mouse button or key.

When these events occur, they will go unnoticed unless a script is in place to react to, or "handle," them. For example, you could click your mouse forever on a button with no script attached, and no interaction would result. Events would certainly be occurring—the mouse would be pressed and released, for instance—but unless one or more *event handlers* were in place to trap those events, your movie would not respond and your scripts would not be executed.

Different kinds of scriptable Flash elements can be instructed to react to different kinds of events. For example, a particular set of event handlers is most commonly used to handle button events such as mouse press and mouse release. Although they can be triggered again and again by the user, these are typically thought of as single events. Another set of event handlers is used to trap movie clip events, such as when the playhead enters the frame or when data is loaded into the movie clip.

There are also a few ways to write event handlers, depending on how and where they are used. A very basic way to write an event handler is when the script is applied directly to the asset in question. For example, consider a button that is designed to stop playback when the user clicks on the button and releases his or her mouse. If that script is applied directly to the button, the event handler will read this way:

```
on (release) {
    stop();
```

The above format is useful in that it is very direct, but it can also make your code more difficult to follow, edit, debug, and reuse, because your scripts are scattered across many symbols in many places.

The preferred way of addressing this is to consolidate your scripts into fewer locations, such as a few necessary frame scripts, and assign each script to a button's instance name. If the same button above, with an instance name of *stop_btn*, had the same script applied using this method, it would read:

```
stop_btn.onRelease = function(){
  stop();
};
```

This syntax is a bit different from the first example, in that you are setting the event handler equal to something called a *function*. A function is nothing more than a way of writing a part of your script so that the instructions you include therein are executed only when the function is called. In this case, the button is calling the function, but you can call functions yourself, too. This prevents Flash from acting on these instructions automatically, as the *stop()* action you used in your first frame script in Chapter 3 did.

Writing scripts this way is considered an optimal way of coding, or "best practice," but don't be concerned if it seems confusing. You'll learn more about writing functions later; the most important thing at this point is your growing confidence. Just be comfortable with the fact that, in both forms of this script, the event handler is trapping the mouse release event, and reacting by executing the instructions within that handler.

3. Use its instance name, and an event handler, to add a script to this button. If Script Assist is still on, turn it off and practice writing the script yourself. Use the same event handler as you did with the Web button to trap the mouse release event:

```
replay_btn.onRelease = function() {
};
```

4. When you type the dot after *replay_btn*, a code hint appears. These are context-sensitive options that Flash will auto-complete for you, if desired. Instead of typing the needed phrase in its entirety, you can choose *onRelease* from the code hint menu. See the "Code Hints" sidebar for more information.

5. Add a method that will tell Flash to send the playhead to a certain point and then begin playing. Type **gotoAndPlay** and the first of the two parentheses typically required by methods (as discussed in the last chapter):

```
replay_btn.onRelease = function() {
    gotoAndPlay(
};
```

Notice that as soon as you type the opening parenthesis after *gotoAndPlay*, another code hint appears. This code hint initially informs you that you must enter a frame as the needed parameter. If you click on the right arrow, it then tells you that an optional *scene* can be included. A scene is a way of splitting long timelines into more manageable chunks, like stringing together multiple smaller timelines. Scenes are discussed later.

Code Hints

You may have noticed that when you type **_btn** followed by a dot (period) into the Script pane of the Actions panel, a drop-down list appears. This feature is called *code hinting*. Flash recognizes the *_btn* suffix as indicating a button instance and therefore prompts you with a handy list of button-related methods, commands, and properties.

Although entering much of the ActionScript syntax will eventually become second nature, this is a wonderful feature if you're just starting out. It can be difficult to memorize proper syntax for every keyword, and code hinting can help you recall things like case sensitivity, required parameters, and even the correct pairing of keywords and objects.

When prompted with the code hint, you can scroll through the drop-down list with the arrow keys to locate the item you need. You can even start typing, if you know the first letter or two, to jump directly to the nearest item in the list. Once you've found what you're looking for, press Enter/Return to add the item to the script automatically.

Other suffixes, such as *_mc* for movie clip, will prompt code hints as well. The examples in this book will usually include these suffixes to get you started.

In ActionScript 2.0, you can specify the type of an object without using a specific suffix. You'll learn more about this later, but as a short example, you can declare a variable that refers to a movie clip instance as follows:

```
var myClip:MovieClip;
```

The *var* keyword and the `:MovieClip` data type tell ActionScript that `myClip` is a movie clip instance, thus providing code hints without requiring the *_mc* suffix.

The two things the code hint asks for are called *parameters*. Together, they give the Flash Player the information needed to execute the method you are using. In this case, a simple *play()* command would also work, because Flash loops automatically and you want to go back to the first frame. However, in addition to briefly demonstrating parameters, it's good to know about this option because it will let you jump to a frame other than frame 1 and begin playing. For example, if you use frame 14 as the parameter for your *gotoAndPlay()* method, you can replay your animation from the point at which the boxes are in their final locations and the text begins to appear.

6. Finish the script to launch the desired URL when the user clicks the button. Type **1** (or **14**, if you like), close the parentheses, and add a closing semicolon for good form. (If you haven't already, read the "Semicolon;" sidebar in Chapter 3.)

```
replay_btn.onRelease = function() {
    gotoAndPlay(1);
}
```

7. Save your work and test your file. In addition to the globe button launching this book's web site, the left-arrow button will now replay the animation (either from the first frame, as in the example file, or from the point at which the text begins to animate, if you used frame 14 in your script).

Components and Behaviors

Before you're comfortable with ActionScript, another way to jump-start the interactivity in your projects is by using components and behaviors. A *component* is a pre-created "widget" that typically contains both assets and much of the coding necessary to make it work. You need only add a small number of custom parameters to most components to make them do your bidding. In limited cases, even this customization can be automated with *behaviors*, or pre-written scripts that are usually configured using simple UI dialogs.

You will use both components and behaviors in several later chapters, so this introduction will be brief. You will use the simplest of each in this project, and delve deeper when working with audio, video, and similar tasks later.

The Button Component

Occasionally, you won't want to spend time creating standardized assets if you can use substitutes that have been created for you. The Flash UI components are a good place to start for interface development, because you can use a similarly designed family of interface elements for a professional look.

In this project, try replicating the previous web-launch example using the Push Button component:

1. Start a new movie to experiment with and save it as *components_and_behaviors.fla* in your *04* folder.
2. Open the Components panel using the Window→Components menu command, and expand the User Interface category (as shown in Figure 4-6).

Figure 4-6. The Components panel

3. Drag the Button component to the Stage. It will appear with the default word "Button" as its label, and it will respond with the appropriate Up, Over, and Down states, as well as cursor feedback, when tested.
4. Normally, you would configure a small handful of parameters and then write a script, as you did previously. However, in this case you will use a behavior to accomplish most of that, so you need only change the label.
5. With the button selected, open the Component Inspector panel (Window→Component Inspector).

NOTE

In some cases, the Parameters tab of the Properties panel will allow you to change simple component parameters. However, more complex components require the Component Inspector to provide enough room to adjust values. For consistency, you'll use this panel throughout.

6. Make sure the Parameters options are displayed, and click on the *label* row in the *value* column. Replace the word *Button* with **`Book Web Site`** (see Figure 4-7).
7. Save your work.

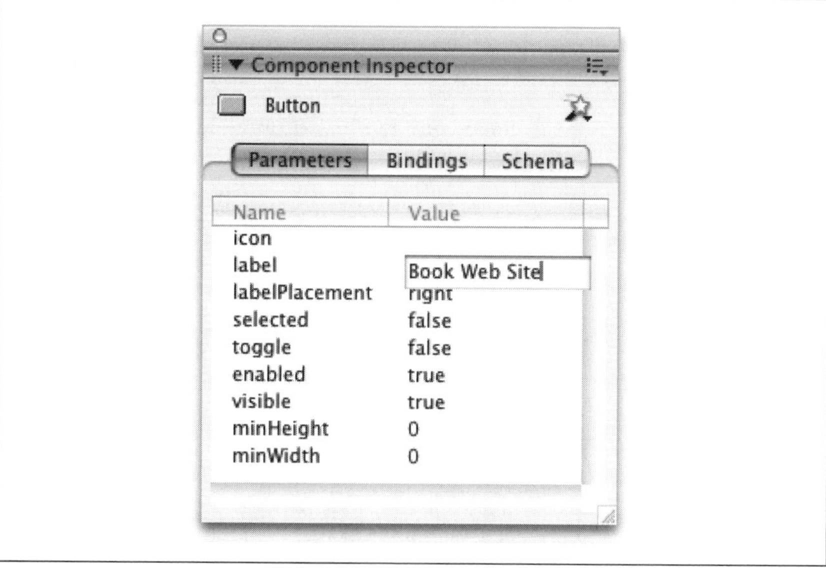

Figure 4-7. Changing the button label in the Component Inspector panel

The Go to Web Page Behavior

You should now have a button that says "Book Web Site" but doesn't yet function. Use a behavior to add the necessary ActionScript to this component:

1. Make sure the button component is selected and open the Behaviors panel (Window→Behaviors).
2. In the upper-left corner of the panel, click on the plus sign (+) to open the Add Behavior menu. Add the Web→Go to Web Page behavior (see Figure 4-8).
3. The dialog shown in Figure 4-9 will appear, allowing you to put in your desired URL and specify in which HTML window or frame the web page should appear. Enter **`http://www.flash8outofthebox.com`** and **`_blank`**, just as before, and dismiss the dialog.

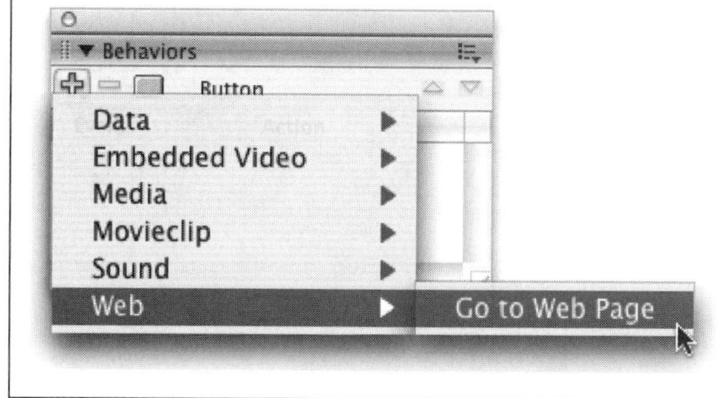

Figure 4-8. Adding a behavior in the Behaviors panel

Figure 4-9. The Go to URL dialog

4. The finished behavior will appear in the Behaviors panel. You can add more behaviors if you wish, but you don't need to for this project, so close this panel.

5. That's all there is to it! Save your work and preview your movie in an HTML page using the File→Publish Preview→Default - (HTML) menu command. The button should function like your previous example, opening the book's web site in a new window.

Behaviors are fine for distilling a complex series of events into a pre-configured script that is designed for a specific task. However, you will find with increasing experience that writing your own code is usually easier and more flexible.

For one thing, the number of available behaviors is fairly limited. Second, behaviors add their scripts directly to the elements being manipulated, making it harder to consolidate code into fewer frame scripts (a coding best practice). Finally, as you become more comfortable with ActionScript, you may find that you can type simple actions faster than you can open and configure dialogs.

However, because you can add multiple behaviors to assets, and you can edit the scripts added by behaviors, they can sometimes be convenient to start with. For example, compare the script added by the behavior to the script you wrote earlier:

```
on (click) {
    //Goto Webpage Behavior
    getURL("http://www.flash8outofthebox.com","_parent");
    //End Behavior
}
```

The *getURL* line is identical, so you've essentially accomplished the same goal in a different way.

You may notice that, just as buttons and movie clips have unique event handlers, so do components. You may also notice that two new lines appear, both preceded by two slashes (//). These are comments that will not be executed. Adding comments to your scripts will help you, and others, understand how you expect the script to work. See the "Comments" sidebar for more information.

WARNING

Look at the file size of the file you just created. The components that ship with Flash are designed to share common elements, which makes using several different kinds of components more economical on file size. The shared assets already in place require fewer additions.

However, compared to creating your own custom buttons, this also means that file size will be significantly increased when using only one or two components. In many cases, you may be better off creating your own assets, or investing in third-party replacements that are designed to have a smaller impact on your file size. See Appendix A for possible resources to find such replacements.

Navigation

The Web wouldn't be what it is today without navigation. The basic ability to link from one page to another is such an essential part of the Internet experience that it's difficult to imagine what the Web would be like without it.

In many Flash projects, the ability for the user to navigate through a series of frames is also essential. Without the ability to jump around between frames, you'd be forced to design every project as a rigid linear path. In this section, you'll create three buttons, each of which will navigate to another part of the movie, displaying different shapes on the Stage.

The first thing you need is a button, so use one from a prior file to speed things along:

1. Create a new Flash document and save it as *navigation.fla* in the *04* folder.
2. Choose File→Import→Open External Library and open the *simple_button.fla* file you created earlier. If you haven't been following along, open the *simple_button_02.fla* file provided in the same directory. This technique is a handy way to make all of the Library assets of one file available to other files during authoring.

Comments

As highlighted in the text, you'll see that lines 2 and 4 of the Go to Web Page behavior include two forward slashes (//) at the beginning. These two slashes indicate a *comment* in ActionScript—a line that is not executed as part of the script. Comments can be used to write notes about your code (so you or someone else can easily discern the operation or purpose of the code). Comments initiated with // are automatically terminated by the next carriage return.

In this case, when Macromedia developed the behavior, they added the two comment lines as notes about how the script was created and where it ends. If you decided to add code to this script, either on your own or with additional behaviors, these comments would help segment the code that came from each behavior.

Since the code is attached directly to the button and the script is brief, a developer could interpret the code easily without the comments. However, as scripts become more numerous and lengthy, comments make the code more discernible.

As a best practice, you should add comments to your code. They not only help others understand your intent, but may even help you remember details if you should revisit the code later.

Comment marks can also be used to temporarily or permanently disable a line of code. Simply precede a line of code with // to "comment out" the line, or remove the slashes to re-enable it. To disable multiple lines of code or write a long comment, start the comment with /* and terminate it with */, like this:

```
/*
This is a
multiline
comment
*/
```

Your comments should always be descriptive and not simply reiterate what is obvious from the code. This comment is not very helpful:

```
// play movie clip from frame 10
myClip_mc.gotoAndPlay(10);
```

This comment explains the code at a higher conceptual level:

```
// play sample animation before asking user to respond
myClip_mc.gotoAndPlay(10);
```

3. Drag an instance of the *btn* symbol to the Stage. It's now a part of your new *navigation.fla* file, so you don't need the external Library anymore.

4. Save your work now, but don't save again until instructed. This will allow you to revert to this previously saved point later and save a step or two.

Now you have a button, but you need to change the text inside it:

5. Double-click the button to edit it in place, and replace the word *Button* on each frame with the word **Box**.

6. Return to Scene 1.

The first button is complete, but you still need two others:

7. Open the Library, double-click on the *btn* symbol name to make it editable, and change the name to **box_btn**.

8. Click on the Options menu in the upper-right corner of the Library panel and choose Duplicate. The Duplicate Symbol dialog box appears.

9. Enter **circle_btn** for the name of the new symbol and click OK to close the dialog box.

10. Drag *circle_btn* to the Stage and double-click on it to edit it in place.

11. On every frame of the *circle_btn* timeline, change the word *Box* to **Circle**.

Reusable Buttons

Before you repeat that last group of steps for the third button, feel free to mutter, "This isn't any fun." It's a lot of redundant work just to make a few buttons this way. There is, however, a better way:

1. Use File→Revert to revert to the last saved state. If you accidentally saved along the way, open the *navigation_01.fla* file and pick up where you left off.

2. Double-click on the *btn* symbol instance to edit it in place, and delete the *text* layer from the button symbol's timeline. This will leave only the multi-state artwork.

Do you see where you're going? Instead of embedding the text within the *btn* symbol, you'll keep it separate, so that the button is unlabeled and can be reused easily. Now you'll add the text separately from the button:

3. Return to Scene 1.

4. Alt-drag (Win) or Option-drag (Mac) the *btn* instance to create a second instance, and align the new instance directly to the right of the first

one. Repeat this process for a third box. There are now three buttons lined up at the top of the Stage, in a horizontal row.

5. To make sure the *btn* instances are aligned perfectly, Shift-select the three boxes and choose Align Top Edge and Distribute Horizontal Center in the Align panel.
6. On *Layer 1*, activate the Text tool and type **Box**. Click elsewhere twice (so you're no longer editing the previous text) to create another text field, and type the word **Circle**. Then click twice again and type the word **Polygon**.
7. Position the word *Box* in the center of the first *btn* instance on the left. Then position *Circle* in the center of the second *btn* instance and *Polygon* in the center of the third, as shown in Figure 4-10.
8. Save your work and test your file.

Figure 4-10. Align the text in front of the btn instances

Now you have three buttons, made from only one button symbol. Not only is this easier than duplicating buttons and changing the text inside them, but using only one symbol decreases the file size for the published movie.

Now create the content for the three screens in the project:

1. Draw a square on the Stage, then draw a circle. Convert both to graphic symbols, naming them **box** and **circle**.
2. Delete them both from the Stage. You will be adding them later, in specific frames, from the Library.
3. In the Tools panel, click on the Rectangle tool, holding down the mouse button until a menu appears, as shown in Figure 4-11. Choose the PolyStar tool from the menu. This tool allows you to draw polygons or stars, and you can configure the number and size of the points. (Later, feel free to explore the tool's options in the Properties panel.)
4. Draw a polygon on the Stage, convert it to a symbol named **polygon**, and delete the instance from the Stage.

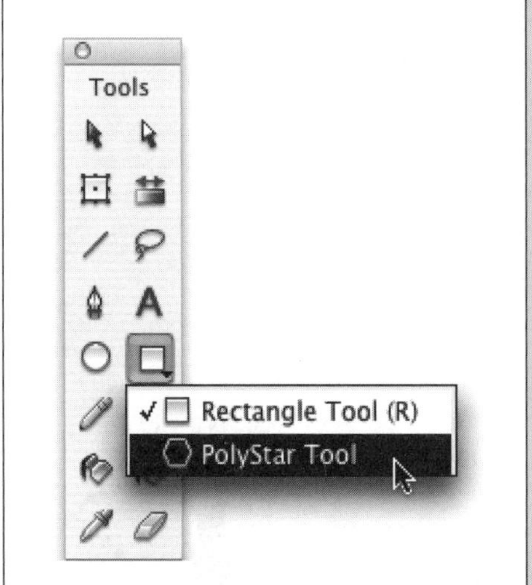

Figure 4-11. Choose the PolyStar tool from the Rectangle tool menu in the Tools panel

Now, you need to divide the movie into three different sections. You'll do this by using *frame labels*. Frame labels allow you to mark a frame with a string that is easy to remember. More importantly, if you add or delete frames before or after a label, the label stays with the frame you marked, making navigation scripts more reliable.

> **NOTE**
>
> *Unlike labels that move with your content, frame numbers are fixed; frame 10 will always be frame 10 even if you add frames before or after. A navigation script that uses frame numbers may work when you write it but cease to work after you've added or deleted frames, because the new frames may have moved your content.*

Start by setting up your layers and labels:

1. Rename *Layer 1* to **`buttons`**.
2. Create a new layer and name it **`content`**.
3. Create another layer named **`labels`** and drag it to the top of the layer stack.
4. Create a final layer named **`actions`** and drag it to the top of the layer stack, so it is above the *labels* layer.
5. Select frame 40 on every layer and press F5 to insert frames.
6. Select frame 1 on the *labels* layer and, in the Frame Label field in the Properties panel, enter **`home`**. Press Enter/Return to commit the name to the selected frame. The frame label *home* now appears in the timeline, as shown in Figure 4-12.

> **NOTE**
>
> *Just as you place all your ActionScript on a layer named actions created for that purpose, you can reserve a layer for frame labels. This is not mandatory, but rather a way to improve the organization and legibility of your timelines.*

7. Choose Anchor from the Label Type drop-down list in the Properties panel. Much like an HTML link anchor, Flash frame anchors allow a browser's Back and Forward buttons to work when navigating through Flash movies, improving usability (currently Windows only).
8. In the *labels* layer, insert keyframes at frames 10, 20, and 30, and add named anchors to these frames, just as you did with frame 1. Name the frame anchors **`box`**, **`circle`**, and **`polygon`**, respectively, as shown in Figure 4-12.

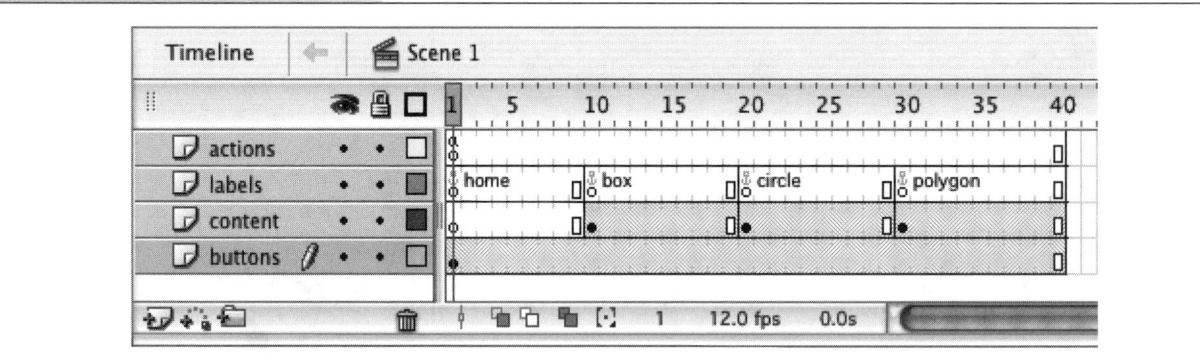

Figure 4-12. The timeline with layers and labels in place

Now you have four discrete frames—*home*, *box*, *circle*, and *polygon*—that will serve as different destinations in the published movie. You can jump to each section using *gotoAndStop()* for a static destination or *gotoAndPlay()* for an animated destination. Add those scripts now:

1. Select the *content* layer and insert keyframes at frames 10, 20, and 30 to correspond with the labels in these frames.
2. At frame 10, drag a *box* instance to the Stage and position it at the center of the Stage (using the Align panel).
3. At frame 20, position a *circle* instance at the center of the Stage. Then, at frame 30, position a *polygon* instance at the center of the Stage. Each labeled frame now contains the shape that corresponds to the label's name.
4. Save and test the movie.

All 40 frames of the movie play without stopping, so each shape flashes by, and the buttons don't control any of it. It's time to write some ActionScript to tame the playhead:

1. Select frame 1 of the *actions* layer and open the Actions panel (F9).
2. Enter a *stop()* command in frame 1 to stop the playhead there:

```
stop();
```

And now it's time to stop and think for a moment. As you saw earlier, there are two different ways to code the buttons. You can either attach ActionScript directly to the buttons, or keep the code separate by putting it in the *actions* layer.

It may be easier to use a behavior and attach the script directly to the button. However, you'll quickly discover that there are too few behaviors to solve all your scripting needs. Also, writing the code yourself allows you to keep it in fewer locations, making it easier to edit later.

NOTE

Remember, any code that accesses movie clips, buttons, or text fields via ActionScript won't work unless you assign the item an instance name. Make sure your instance names are unique so that Flash knows which instance to target when you refer to it from your ActionScript code.

To add the scripts that control the buttons to the *actions* layer:

1. Select each *btn* instance on the *buttons* layer in turn, from left to right, and assign instance names of **`box_btn`**, **`circle_btn`**, and **`polygon_btn`** to them using the Properties panel.
2. Beneath the *stop()* command on frame 1 of the *actions* layer, create an event handler that sends the playhead to the *box* frame label when the user clicks the `box_btn` button:

```
box_btn.onRelease = function() {
  gotoAndStop("box");
};
```

3. Copy and paste this handler below the existing script. You need to alter just two words to make it work with the `circle_btn` clip instance.
4. In the copy of the handler, change `box_btn.onRelease` to `circle_btn.onRelease`.
5. Next, change `gotoAndStop("box")` to `gotoAndStop("circle")`.

6. Repeat this process for the script to react to the `polygon_btn` clip instance.
7. Your code on frame 1 of the Actions panel should now look like this:

```
stop();

box_btn.onRelease = function() {
    gotoAndStop("box");
};
circle_btn.onRelease = function() {
    gotoAndStop("circle");
};
polygon_btn.onRelease = function() {
    gotoAndStop("polygon");
};
```

8. Save and test the movie.

Hooray! You now have a functioning movie. When you click each button, the playhead jumps to the appropriate frame and displays the content on that frame. This is a common way of navigating movie content.

In fact, you can also use this technique to control movie clips. Simply by adding the movie clip instance name before the method, so the method is controlling the movie clip rather than the root movie, you can manipulate the movie clip timeline. You'll do this in Chapter 6, but there are a few more things to accomplish here first.

Improved Usability

Most interactive projects have more than one section, each with different functionality. It's easy for the user to become lost among the many sections, so to remedy this, most developers use visual cues to guide the user. A navigation bar, for example, may show the current section in addition to the available buttons.

In the navigation project you just completed, each button sends the playhead to a different frame in the timeline and displays a shape, but there is no indication of what screen we're currently viewing. It's fairly obvious, because the content resembles the section name, but a real-world project would likely not be this clear.

Improve the usability of your project by adding a generic indicator of which screen the user is on:

1. In the *box* frame in the *content* layer, use the Rectangle tool to draw a small bar, 100 × 5 pixels, directly underneath the *box* button. Make it any color you like, but choose a color that will not blend into the button unseen. A fill with no border is particularly appropriate.
2. Select the bar and convert it to a movie clip called **`active_bar`**.

3. Copy this instance and move to the *circle* content frame. You will see that the *box* bar has disappeared. This is because you placed it in the *box* content keyframe, and this is exactly the behavior you want. Paste the instance into the *circle* keyframe, but this time position it under the *circle* button.

4. Repeat the last step for the *polygon* keyframe.

5. Save and test the movie.

This is a simple solution for creating an "active" state for multi-section projects. Even if the content does not resemble the name of the section, the presence of the *active_bar* instance directly below the relevant button, as seen in Figure 4-13, helps the user remember where he or she is at any time.

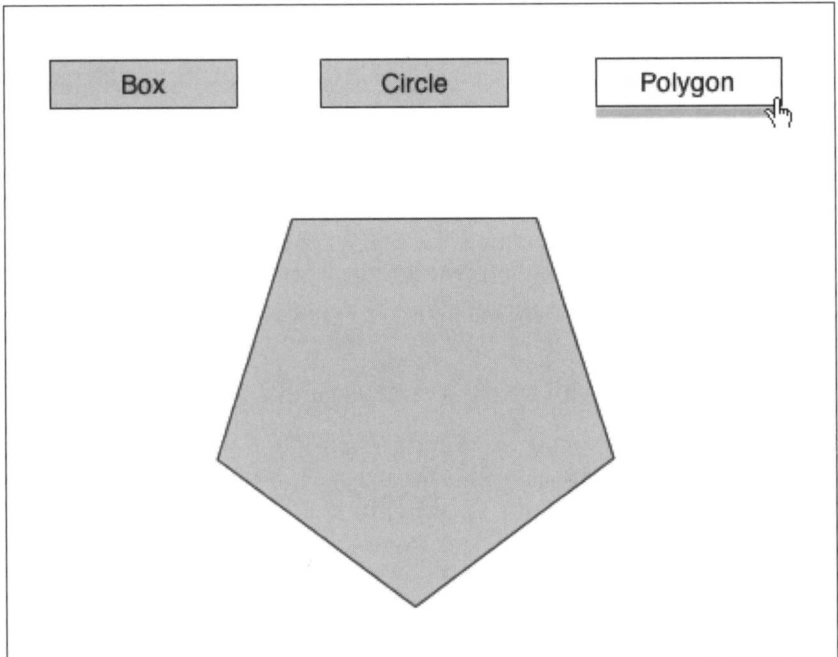

Figure 4-13. Indicators that reveal the user's current location improve usability

For additional advice on how to make your projects more usable, check out the following books:

- *Don't Make Me Think! A Common Sense Approach to Web Usability*, by Steve Krug (New Riders)
- *The Big Red Fez: How to Make Any Web Site Better*, by Seth Godin (Fireside)

These books are both focused around web usability, but the knowledge gained can (and should) be applied to every project you create.

More Fun with Buttons

In the last section, you learned how to create a generic button that promotes reusability. Next, you'll carry that notion forward by creating invisible buttons that can be used to add "hot spots" to just about anything, and by learning how to spice up your buttons with animation.

Invisible Buttons

In some cases, you want the ability to freely place interactive hot spots throughout a project, without having to go to a lot of trouble to create many different buttons. For example, think of a large or complex illustration in which you want to trigger the display of detail views, or a block of text that should display definitions for certain words. Finally, imagine a quiz that requires you to click the correct detail in an image.

In these cases (and many more), it would be difficult to have to create a separate button for every interactive location. However, the generic button you created earlier wouldn't work either, because it would cover the material you want to be visible as a button. This is where *invisible buttons* can be very handy.

Invisible buttons are merely normal buttons with no Up, Over, or Down state. Only a Hit state exists, to define the area that should respond to the mouse. Try to make one now:

1. Create a new file with which to experiment.
2. Draw a rectangle on the Stage and convert it to a button symbol, using any name. The rectangle will serve as a starting point for your invisible button. Double-click on the button to edit it.
3. Select the Hit frame and press F6 to insert a keyframe. You now have Up and Hit states.
4. Select the Up frame and delete its contents. (That's right; delete everything but the Hit state.)
5. Click on Scene 1 to leave Symbol Editing mode.

If the button is invisible, why can you see it? Well, it wouldn't be very convenient if you couldn't *ever* see the button. Flash will automatically create a translucent blue area that represents the button's shape (as defined by the Hit state), which is visible only in authoring mode.

When you test your movie, you will not see the button at runtime, but you will see the requisite cursor feedback to show the button is functioning. If you want to see an example of how invisible buttons work, look at the *invisible_buttons.fla* file in your *04* directory.

Animated Buttons

Animated buttons can be created a number of ways, but in this project you'll look at the simplest. You'll build an animated button by creating an animation sequence within a movie clip and then simply adding that movie clip to a button's timeline:

1. Open *menu_buttons_01.fla*, located in the *04* folder. To skip some of the text-only setup, and to make sure the file matches the following steps exactly (including x- and y-coordinates), this file has been started for you. On the Stage, there is one line of text, in a layer named *txt*. The text has been broken apart, so it is a shape and not editable text, and the layer has been locked. This ensures that this portion of the file will remain intact during this exercise.
2. Create a new layer called **btns**, and drag it to the bottom of the layer stack.
3. Next, create a graphic symbol to use in your animation. Press Ctrl/Cmd-F8 to open the Create New Symbol dialog box. Choose the Graphic symbol type and call it **box**.
4. When you okay the dialog, the symbol will open in Edit mode. Using the Rectangle tool, draw a light-gray-filled rectangle, with no stroke.
5. Use the Properties panel to give it a width of 80 and a height of 25, and position it using an x-value of 0 and a y-value of 0. You are now finished with your box.
6. Press Ctrl/Cmd-F8 again to create another symbol. This time, choose Movie Clip for the symbol type and call it **btn_rollover**. When you OK the dialog, you will again be in Edit mode, but this time you will be editing the movie clip.
7. From your Library, drag the *box* symbol to the Stage. This places an instance of the *box* graphic symbol in your new movie clip.
8. With the box selected, position it at (0, 0).
9. Add a keyframe at frame 5.
10. At frame 1, select the rectangle, and enter **1** into the Height field in the Properties panel. This will reduce only the height to one pixel.
11. Because the entire symbol has been scaled to a new height of one pixel, you will need to reposition it to its former y-coordinate for it to remain centered. With the symbol still selected, enter a value of 12.5 in the Y field of the Properties panel. (Yes, you can use decimal values for pixel positioning. Flash simulates fractional pixels using anti-aliasing.) This value is used because it is one-half of the 25-pixel height of the button.

12. Select the keyframe in frame 1 and, using the Properties panel, apply a motion tween so that frames 1 through 5 are tweened, causing the box to animate to full size.
13. Add a new layer and name it **`actions`**.
14. In the new *actions* layer, insert a keyframe at frame 5, and add a *stop()* command to the Actions panel:

```
stop();
```

15. Press Enter to play the animation. This will allow you to preview the animation of this timeline without having to test your movie.

The rectangle begins short and increases in height from its center point. The *stop()* command stops the animation at frame 5. Figure 4-14 shows the timeline of the animation.

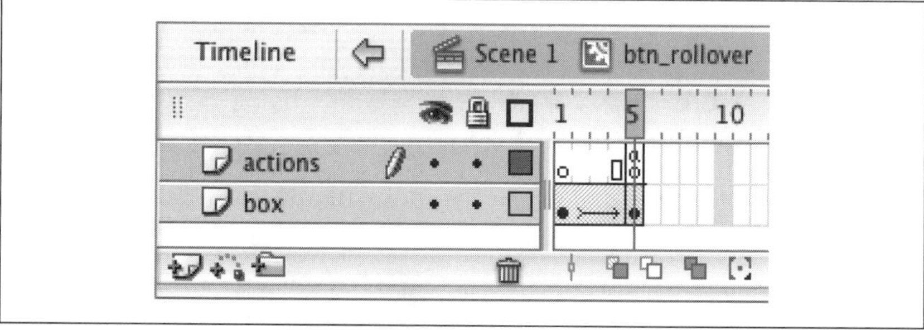

Figure 4-14. The btn_rollover symbol's timeline

Now you will nest the movie clip inside a button:

1. Press Ctrl/Cmd-F8 to create another new symbol. Name the symbol **`btn`** and choose Button as the Behavior type.
2. In Edit mode for the *btn* symbol, select the Over frame and add a keyframe there (by pressing F6). Add another keyframe in the Hit frame.
3. While in the Hit frame, drag the *box* graphic symbol to the Stage and position it at (0, 0).
4. Select the Over state, and drag the *btn_rollover* movie clip symbol from your Library to the Stage. Again, with its current height of 1, you will need to position this symbol at (0, 12.5) for it to remain centered.
5. Leave the Up state empty, just as you did in the invisible buttons project.
6. Return to Scene 1 and drag an instance of the *btn* symbol to the Stage. Position it at (0, 0). As discussed earlier, the Hit state will display a

translucent blue shape that allows you to test your placement. The button should fill the area from the left of the Stage to the first vertical text dividing line, as seen in Figure 4-15.

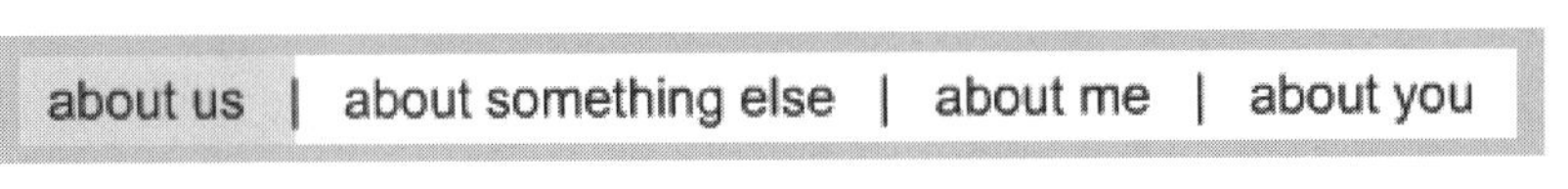

Figure 4-15. The first button of your menu bar in place

7. Add another instance of the *btn* symbol to the Stage, this time positioning it at (80, 0). This button doesn't fill the entire area needed, so that must be corrected.
8. With the button still selected, choose the Free Transform tool. Drag the right edge handle to size the button until you reach the second text divider.
9. Repeat steps 7 and 8 for the last two remaining buttons.
10. Save your work and test the movie. If you want to compare your work with the sample file, open *menu_buttons_02.fla* and see how well you fared.

As planned, when you roll over the "about us" text, the corresponding button's hit area is triggered, its Over state displays, and the animated movie clip on that frame begins to play. When you roll out, the animation disappears.

What's Next?

Finally, your Flash movies are starting to include some interactivity. From here on, you'll build more and more functionality into your movies, and this chapter should better prepare you for what's coming.

To get some practice adding ActionScript to buttons, try coding the buttons in the *animated_buttons.fla* file to go to various web sites. As you gain more experience, you can mimic button behavior using movie clips for even more creative freedom. For more information, check out Sham Bhangal's *Flash Hacks* (O'Reilly)—specifically, Hack #63, "Button Movie Clips."

Also, visit some of your favorite Flash sites to see how other developers design their buttons. Does animation in a button contribute to the overall look of the site, or does it distract you? How do animated buttons integrate with the site's design to blend in with it?

Studying the work of other Flash designers is a wonderful way to get ideas. Learn what you can about how elements in site designs work together to create a cohesive look. Specifically, study when Flash is used and, even more so, when Flash is not used. Many sites benefit from integrating Flash with other HTML content rather than using Flash exclusively.

In the next chapter, you'll begin working with bitmaps. You'll learn how to:

- Import bitmaps
- Use bitmap tiles as fills for shapes
- Trace images to create vector art from bitmaps
- Organize your growing Libraries

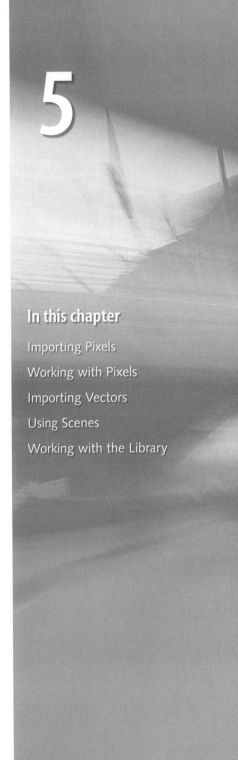

Working with Graphics

5

Flash's drawing tools are primarily vector-based, so they aren't ideal for editing bitmaps. Meaningful bitmap editing requires a program designed for that purpose, such as Adobe Photoshop or Macromedia Fireworks. Similarly, while Flash's drawing methods appeal to many designers, full-powered tools dedicated to this task, such as Adobe Illustrator and Macromedia FreeHand, are often used to create more complex vector-based illustrations. In this chapter, you'll look at how Flash can work with other applications to help you meet your project needs. This chapter includes several mini-projects to get you familiar with working with external graphic assets.

In this chapter

Importing Pixels

Although importing graphic assets is a basic task, there are a few subtleties when dealing with specific file formats and specific applications. To help you take advantage of the full range of features Flash has to offer, and to give you a complete design palette to work with, this section will briefly explain some of the ins and outs of importing pixel-based graphics.

NOTE

The graphics discussed herein are generically referred to as pixel-based or raster graphics, both as a means of categorizing topics and because that is the most common format for these types of graphics. However, you will soon see (especially when discussing Fireworks files) that some formats can contain both pixels and vectors.

A Few Words About File Formats

Many applications can create and edit pixel-based graphics. Adobe Photoshop will occasionally be referenced in this book, as it's the most common example. However, many (if not all) of the points discussed in this segment will apply to most pixel-editing programs.

> **NOTE**
> *The term bitmap is often used to refer to a variety of similar, but not identical, items. The generic use of the term refers to pixel-based graphics, and a more specific usage can refer to the Windows file format BMP. Henceforth, the latter will be specified by the acronym, and "bitmap" will refer to a pixel-based graphic.*

While Flash supports several bitmap file formats, including platform-specific formats such as Windows *BMP* and Macintosh *PICT*, here you will learn how to use the three most commonly used formats: *JPEG*, *GIF*, and *PNG*. It is outside the scope of this book to go into detail about these specific formats, but here is a very brief summary of the high points for each:

- JPEG is most often used for images that have continuous tones, such as photographs or gradients. JPEGs have a 24-bit color depth and can be compressed using a varying degree of quality settings. New to Flash 8, files using the *progressive* JPEG compression format can be imported, in addition to the more commonly used *baseline* JPEG format.
- GIF is usually used when an image has large areas of solid colors, or when a crisper look (possibly even at the expense of some anti-aliasing) is desired. GIFs can contain areas of 100% transparency, but not varying levels of transparency. GIFs can support up to 8 bits of color and can be compressed to varying degrees by limiting the number of colors available to an image. Figure 5-1 shows a continuous gradient, compressed in both JPEG and GIF. Note the banding in the GIF.

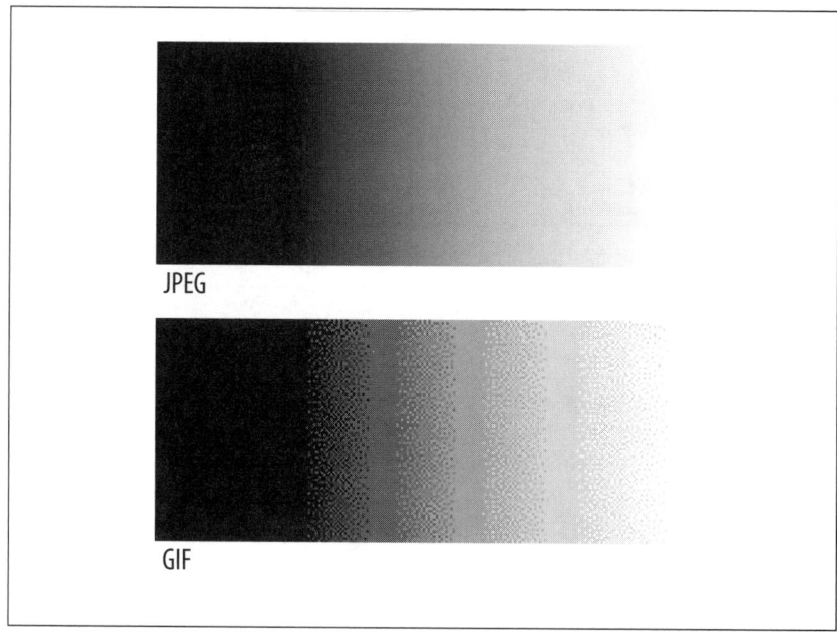

Figure 5-1. The JPEG file format is best suited to continuous-tone images. Note the banding of the gradient in the GIF at right.

- PNG is a lossless format for high-quality images that can support up to 48-bit color and 16-bit grayscale. It is primarily used when support for alpha data is required, as varying levels of transparency are possible. Figure 5-2 shows what the same image in both GIF and PNG formats looks like on a background. The Stage color is medium gray, and the GIF and PNG files have an identical appearance: a black circle on a transparent background. When the graphics are placed on the Stage, the PNG edge between art and transparency is smooth. However, note the halo in the GIF. This is caused by the semi-transparent pixels of the anti-aliased edge of the circle. Since only 100% transparency is supported, partially transparent pixels are converted to solid pixels with partial color.

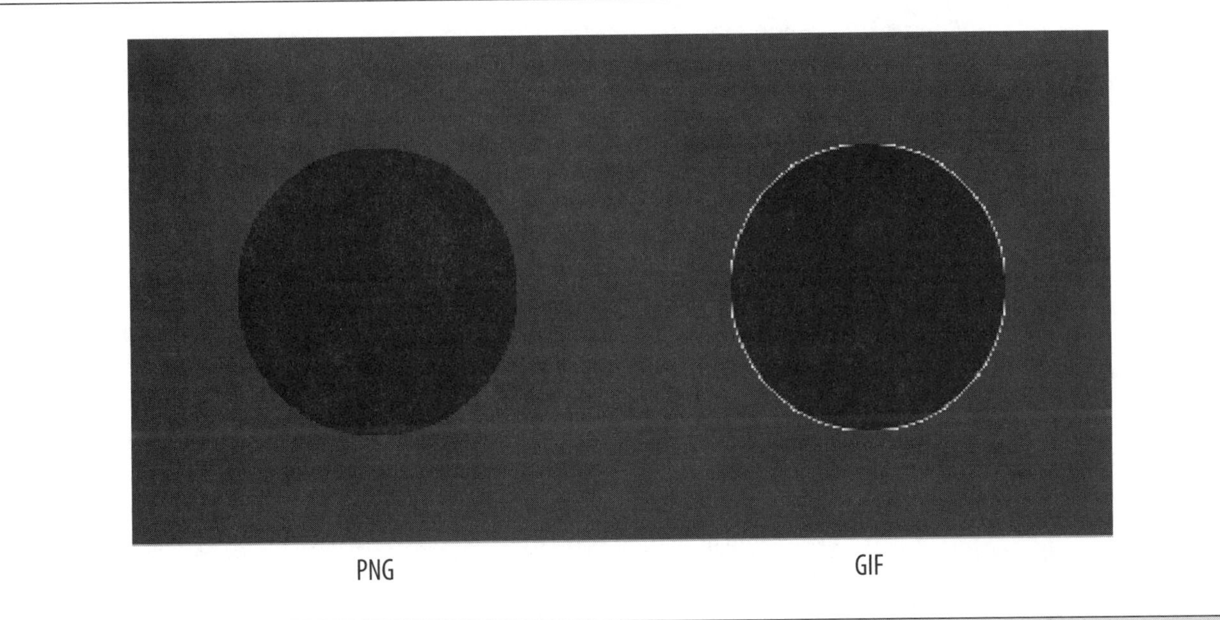

Figure 5-2. The PNG file format is optimal for varying levels of transparency. Note the halo in the GIF at right, caused by semi-transparent pixels.

Importing Standard Formats

When importing the standard versions of these file formats, as you are likely to do most often, Flash will automatically handle the file for you and import a single bitmap image. At the outset of the process, you can decide to import directly to the Stage, or to the Library. The latter is handy when you want to import many images at the same time.

Using the File→Import→Import to Stage menu command, for example, will prompt you with a standard operating system dialog that will allow you to find the file you want to import. Alternately, you can paste a bitmap into Flash from the clipboard, or drag an image in from your desktop.

NOTE

When you import or drag a bitmap into Flash, the filename, path, and certain properties of the external file are maintained, allowing you to update the file from within the Flash Library. This is convenient when you need to make changes to the external file. However, when you paste in a bitmap from the clipboard, Flash has no such information to maintain. A generic name of "Bitmap," followed by a sequential integer to avoid overwriting, will be applied.

When you import a bitmap, whether to the Stage or the Library, a Library item is automatically created. This is because bitmaps are typically large, and Flash wants to make working with them as efficient as possible. The item it creates acts like a symbol, in that you can drag multiple instances of the bitmap to the Stage, and any permanent edits made to that image will be reflected in the instances.

It will not be a symbol in every sense of the term, however, in that you cannot apply color effects and you cannot take advantage of some of the features built into graphic, button, and movie clip symbols. To gain these benefits, simply convert the bitmap to a symbol, the way you would any other relevant asset type.

WARNING

It's important to remember that if you create a symbol from a bitmap, the bitmap must remain in the Library. Do not delete the bitmap, thinking that it has been transformed into the symbol. Instead, think of a bitmap inside a symbol the way you'd think of a movie clip inside another movie clip. In both cases, if you delete the nested item, it will disappear from its related container.

Take a few moments to import the *cheesecake.jpg*, *black_circle_1.gif*, and *black_circle_2.png* sample files provided in the *05* folder of your working directory. (You'll find these files in a subdirectory called *Importing Pixels*.) Experiment with how they do and do not behave like symbols. Compare the transparency levels of the PNG and GIF files on a dark Stage color or background shape. In general, get a feel for working with bitmaps, and then save your file as *bitmaps.fla* in your *05* folder. You won't be using this file again for future exercises, but it will give you something to look at when learning about compression settings later.

Importing from Fireworks

NOTE

If you don't have it, you can install a trial version of Fireworks from this book's CD-ROM. If you don't want to install Fireworks, assets created in the program have been provided for you.

While Photoshop has earned the lion's share of the pixel-based graphics editing market, Macromedia has done a lot to ensure that Flash integrates tightly with its own products, such as Fireworks. This will be particularly pleasing to those who have purchased Studio 8, as Fireworks is part of the Studio suite.

If you use Fireworks, or are interested in trying it, you will likely find that its mixture of pixel-based and vector-based objects can be very useful. It likely won't serve as a substitute for Photoshop, but you may be willing to part company with ImageReady and use Fireworks in its place. Take a moment to open the *navigation.png* and *walk_cycle.png* files in the */05/Importing Pixels* folder. Poke around and see how pixels and vectors are used in the files.

Once you're ready to move on, import a Fireworks file into Flash to see how some of its unique features can be beneficial to Flash users:

1. Create a new, blank document and save it as *fw_navigation.fla* in the */05/Importing Pixels* folder.
2. Import the *navigation.png* file found in the same folder. You will see the dialog pictured in Figure 5-3.

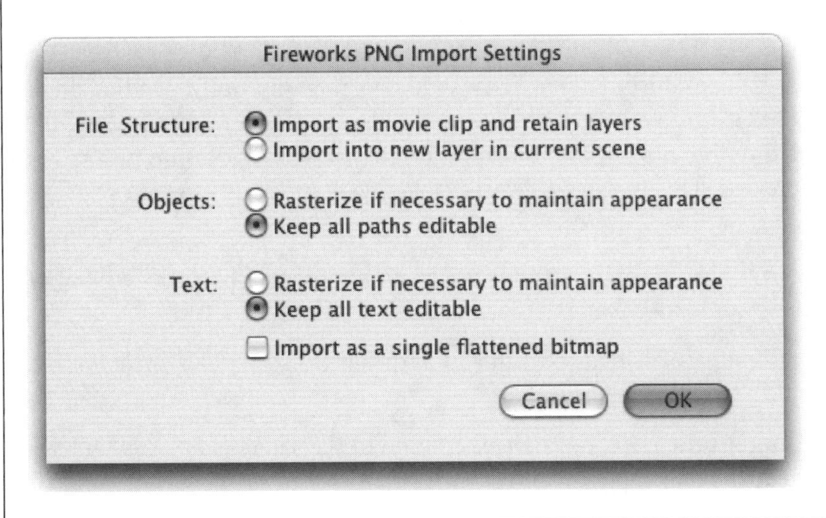

Figure 5-3. The Fireworks PNG Import Settings dialog allows you to choose to what degree the PNG will be preserved upon import

3. Match your settings to those pictured. The first setting will create a self-contained movie clip that contains everything imported from the *.png*. The second will keep vector shapes editable rather than converting them to pixels, and the third will do the same with text elements. As an alternative, you can always import a Fireworks file as a flattened bitmap, but you will lose the ability to edit the mentioned features.
4. OK the dialog and look at the result. In one fell swoop, you've got a navigation system fully contained in its own movie clip, complete with functioning buttons. Test your movie and roll over the navigation column. Once you see the buttons working, close the *.swf* and return to your *.fla* file.
5. Double-click on the movie clip and look within it. You will find several instances of a button, as well as three movie clip symbols. In the next chapter, you'll learn more about movie clips and buttons nested within other movie clips, and how to control them with ActionScript. For now, however, concentrate on how your file has changed upon importing this *.png* file.

6. Open the Library and see what you find. You will notice that it contains two bitmaps and a folder called *Fireworks Objects*. The bitmaps are the two graphics found at the top and middle of the navigation column—as you'll recall, bitmaps are automatically added to a file's Library for improved efficiency. Opening the folder reveals the three movie clips and the button you saw on the Stage earlier.
7. When you are finished experimenting, save your work and close the file. You won't need it again.

When you create a file in Fireworks, whenever possible, symbols you create there will be converted into Flash symbols upon import. Depending on how carefully you maintain your Fireworks files, these and other assets will be added to the Library, and the appropriately named folder you just saw will be created. This is a step toward organizing your Library, which you'll read more about later.

You will have a similar experience when importing Fireworks animations. Open your next Fireworks file to see the result:

1. Create a new, blank document and save it as *fw_walk_cycle.fla* in the */05/Importing Pixels* folder.
2. Import the *walk_cycle.png* file found in the same folder. You will again see the dialog pictured in Figure 5-3. Apply the same settings and click the OK button.
3. This time, you have a walk cycle. Test your movie and watch him walk.
4. You'll learn more about walk cycles in the next chapter, but for now, move on to working with the files you just imported. Save your work and close the file. You won't need it anymore.

Properties

An ActionScript *property* is a way of describing an object, much like an adjective. These descriptions can be obvious, like a movie clip's *_width*, *_height*, and *_rotation* properties, or they can be a bit subtler, like a movie clip's *menu* property, which helps you add a custom menu item to the contextual menu that pops up in the Flash Player when you right/Ctrl-click on the movie clip.

You may notice that some property names begin with an underscore, and others do not. The underscore is meant to indicate that the keyword is a property at first glance, and it was more commonly used in earlier versions of Flash. Knowing when to use the underscore and when not to use it can take a little practice, but it will become second nature after a short time.

At runtime, you can always get the value of a property, such as when checking to see how wide a movie clip is; you can usually set the value of a property, too, such as when setting the rotation of a movie clip to 90 degrees. Some properties, however, are read-only, such as the *_totalframes* property, which tells you how many frames a movie clip has. Since you cannot add frames to a movie clip at runtime, this property cannot be set.

Working with Pixels

While major pixel pushing is reserved for other applications, such as Photoshop or Fireworks, Flash still offers a few ways to edit bitmaps to creative effect.

Breaking Apart a Bitmap

In one way, breaking apart a Flash asset is equivalent to sending it one rung down the Flash evolutionary ladder. Depending on how you created your assets, a symbol can be broken into a group, which can be broken into a shape. The same is true of text: a word can be broken into letters, which can then be broken into shapes.

NOTE

If you haven't already read about the Modify→Break Apart command in Chapter 1, you may want to do so now.

In the case of bitmaps, breaking them apart lets you work with them in non-traditional ways. For example, you can select a portion with the Selection or Lasso tool and remove it, or you can use the Bush tool and paint a new color into it. These are behaviors commonly associated with shapes, but a bitmap that has been broken apart doesn't exactly behave like a shape. For instance, if you click a color hoping to select it, you will find that the entire bitmap is selected.

This is because the bitmap is still behaving as if it were intact, as though you simply modified the container in which it resides. This can be demonstrated using the *bitmap_break_apart.fla* file in the */05/Working with Pixels* folder, as shown in Figure 5-4. After breaking apart the bitmap, step 1 shows the upper-right corner of the bitmap selected by the Selection tool. Step 2 shows that selection deleted, seemingly removing that portion of the bitmap. Step 3 shows the lower-right corner being moved like a traditional shape. Finally, step 4 reveals that the bitmap is still seen in the previously deleted area. What's more, the bitmap continues in areas previously never occupied by its container. This demonstrates what is commonly called *bitmap tiling*.

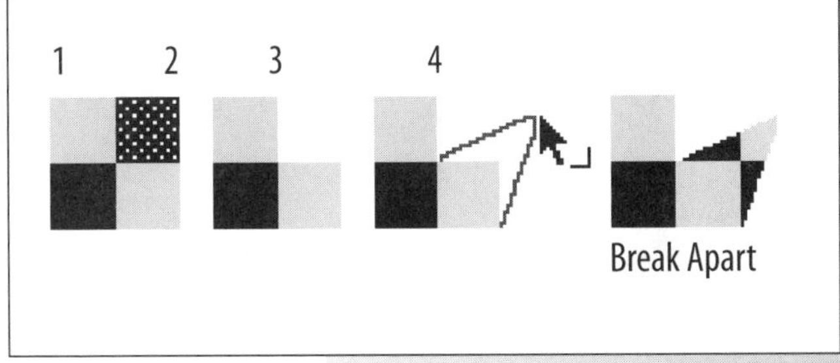

Figure 5-4. As seen in step 4 of this figure, when a bitmap is merely broken apart, a single newly created shape is filled with the tiling bitmap. When a bitmap is traced, it is replaced with multiple newly created shapes that contain normal vector fills.

Using Bitmap Fills

Once you break apart a bitmap, it is possible to eyedrop its image into a fill pattern. That pattern can then be used as a fill for a larger shape, creating a seamless tile, as seen in Figure 5-5.

Figure 5-5. When a larger shape is filled with a bitmap, the bitmap tiles seamlessly

Once you have a bitmap fill, you can do some creative things with it. For example, you can cover large backgrounds with a sacrifice in file size that pales in comparison to a full bitmap of the same dimensions. In the next project, you will try something a little less intuitive. You can apply tweens to the fill itself:

1. Create a new, blank document and save it as *bitmap_tile_tween.fla* in the */05/Working with Pixels* folder.
2. Import the *bitmap_tile.png* file found in the same folder.
3. Break apart the bitmap using Modify→Break Apart (Ctrl/Cmd-B).
4. Select the Eyedropper tool and click on the bitmap. Your fill chip will switch to the new pattern.
5. Delete the bitmap, select the Rectangle tool, and fill the Stage with a new shape. You will see that the fill is a repeating pattern created by the bitmap you broke apart.
6. In the timeline, select frame 24 and add a keyframe. This will create a 2-second animation using Flash's default 24 fps.
7. Still in frame 24, select the Gradient Transform tool and click on the shape. You will see the same tools you used to manipulate the color background in your Jimi Hendrix poster in Chapter 1. Grab the upper-right corner of this tool grid with your mouse, and drag down and to the right a bit. This will rotate the fill.
8. Grab what was the lower-left corner of the square, and scale the fill. Hold down the Shift key to scale the fill proportionally, if you prefer. Your fill should look somewhat similar to Figure 5-6.
9. Next, click in the keyframe in frame 1, and select Shape from the Tween menu in the Properties panel. (If your Properties panel is not visible, show it from the Window menu.)

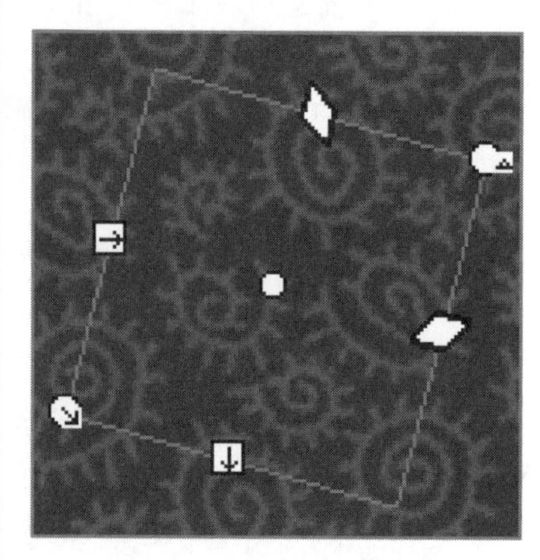

Figure 5-6. Using the Gradient Transform tool, you can scale, rotate, and skew tiled fills for interesting effects

10. Test your file. Your bitmap fill will scale and rotate to the extent that you changed it. If you want to check your work, open the *bitmap_fill_animation.fla* file in the */05/Working with Pixels* folder.

Tracing Bitmaps

In the previous project, you saw that a bitmap behaves as a fill when broken apart. However, you can also convert bitmaps into shapes that respond the way you've come to expect shapes to respond. This is accomplished by tracing the bitmap into a collection of vectors.

Using this technique, Flash will analyze a picture and attempt to outline discrete areas of color, based on tolerance settings you provide. The result can be clarified by comparing the process to breaking apart a bitmap, described earlier. Once traced, the first difference is that you can now select an area of vector with one click. After removing that area, pulling away the lower-right corner will effectively increase the size of the self-contained shape manipulated (Figure 5-7). This is just how the shapes you are familiar with would behave if a bitmap was never involved.

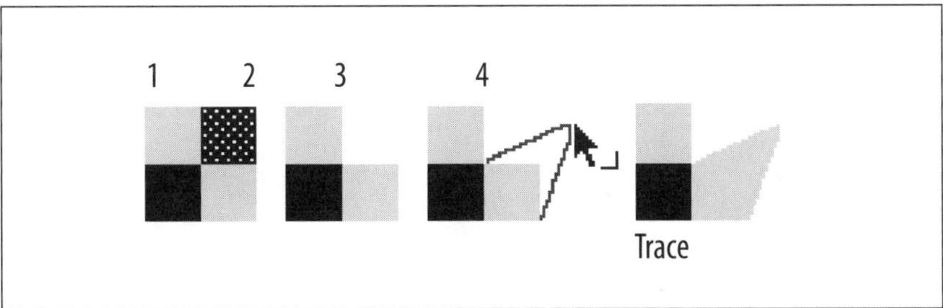

Figure 5-7. A traced bitmap behaves just like a collection of simple Flash shapes

For your next project, trace a bitmap to gain some experience with the dialog settings:

1. Create a new, blank document and save it as *bitmap_trace.fla* in the */05/Importing Pixels* folder.
2. Import the *cheesecake.jpg* file found in the */05/Importing Pixels* folder.
3. Select the bitmap, but do not break it apart. Instead, choose the Modify→Bitmap→Trace Bitmap menu command. The dialog seen in Figure 5-8 will appear. The Color Threshold setting allows you to adjust how clearly Flash separates similar colors. This is similar to Photoshop's Tolerance setting. A higher number means that more hues will be included in any given selection. The Minimum Area setting dictates the minimum number of adjacent pixels that must be included in any single shape. This allows you to set the granularity of the vectors, preventing too many from being created. (This is somewhat akin to using fewer polygons to make a 3D model more efficient.) The Curve Fit

and Corner Threshold settings both contribute to how curvy, or blocky, each vector shape is.

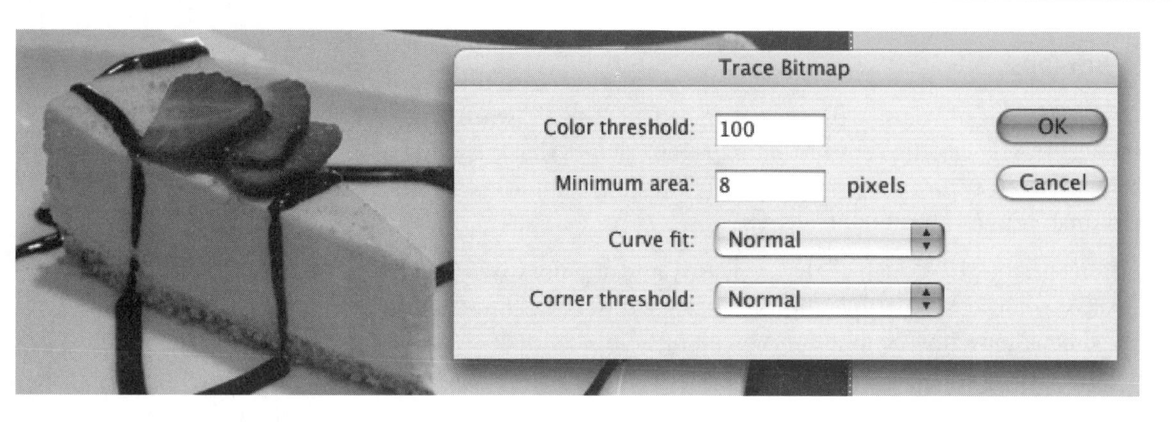

Figure 5-8. Adjust the settings in the Trace Bitmap dialog box

4. Start with the default values and see what you get. Next, try higher and lower color thresholds, and experiment with the other settings. Figure 5-9 shows three such settings groups and their results. When you're done experimenting, save your work.

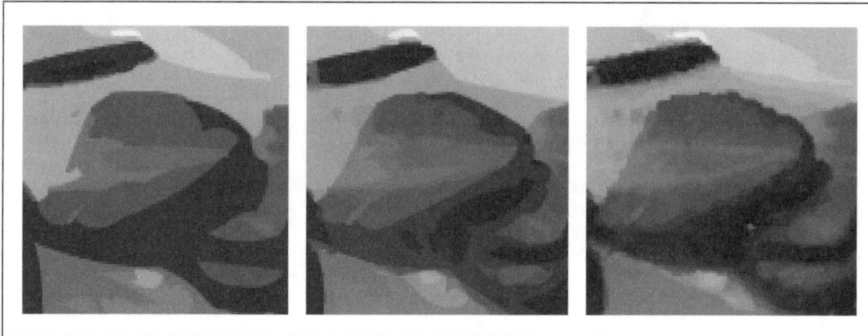

Figure 5-9. These three tracings show the successive result of decreasing Color Threshold, Minimum Area, and Curve Fit/Corner Threshold settings. For example, the Color Threshold settings were 100, 50, and 25, from left to right.

NOTE

If your results are not similar, test your movie. If you then see noticeably different results, you may have your Preview Mode set to a speedier, but rougher, setting. Try changing your View→Preview Mode setting to a higher value. If your Flash authoring doesn't slow down significantly, this will enable you to preview your files more accurately as you work.

Comparing your file size before and after the tracing usually results in a file size drop, although that's not always true. Sometimes trace tolerances can be set too strictly, and a highly compressed image can be converted into many small vectors, which actually increases file size. One way of getting the most file size economy following a bitmap trace is to optimize your curves:

1. With the bitmap tracing still visible, select all the vectors in the tracing using Edit→Select All.
2. Choose the Modify→Shape→Optimize menu command. This will bring up the Optimize Curves dialog shown in Figure 5-10.
3. Experiment with the Smoothing setting, being sure to enable the "Use multiple passes" and "Show totals message" options. The former, although slower, will be more accurate and will usually result in a slightly better looking optimization. The latter will show you the amount of reduction in total curves accomplished by the process.

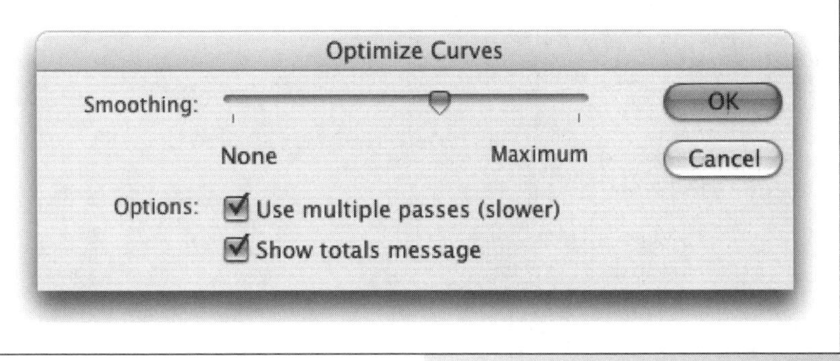

Figure 5-10. Bitmap tracings, as well as any other vectors, can be made more efficient by removing unneeded curves

As a comparative example, *bitmap_trace_02.fla*, found in the */05/Working with Pixels* folder, is an interactive look at different trace settings, complete with possible shape optimization data. Open and test the movie to see the difference a setting can make.

Methods

When reading a text that includes discussions about ActionScript, you will frequently run across the term *method*. A method is an action that is taken by an object, akin to the way a verb and a noun work together. For example, just as a DVD can play, so can a movie clip.

You have already seen several uses of methods. For example, in Chapter 3, you used the *stop()* method in the main timeline of your animation project, and in Chapter 4, you used methods such as *gotoAndPlay()* and *getURL()* for part 2 of the same project.

There are two common structures for methods. The first is when a method affects any timeline (or other object) in which the method call itself resides. In this usage, the method is sometimes included without additional syntax. For example, in Chapter 4, your replay button used the *gotoAndPlay()* method to control the main timeline, which is where the *replay_btn* was placed:

```
replay_btn.onRelease = function() {
    gotoAndPlay(1);
};
```

Another example usage is when you want a method to affect a specifically referenced object, such as a different movie clip. For example, the following line instructs a movie clip called *legs_mc* to stop:

```
stop_btn.onRelease = function() {
    legs_mc.stop();
};
```

Here you see that the method is attached to the specific object in question with the dot syntax you've used in previous projects. You will use this approach in the next chapter, as you expand the interactivity used with movie clips. In both cases, it is helpful to recall the aforementioned mnemonic device: the relationship between object and method is very similar to the relationship between noun and verb.

Importing Vectors

As is true with raster graphics, Flash can import vector assets from a variety of external applications, and in a variety of formats. Here, we'll look at how to import Adobe Illustrator, Macromedia FreeHand, and Adobe PDF assets, and even other SWF files.

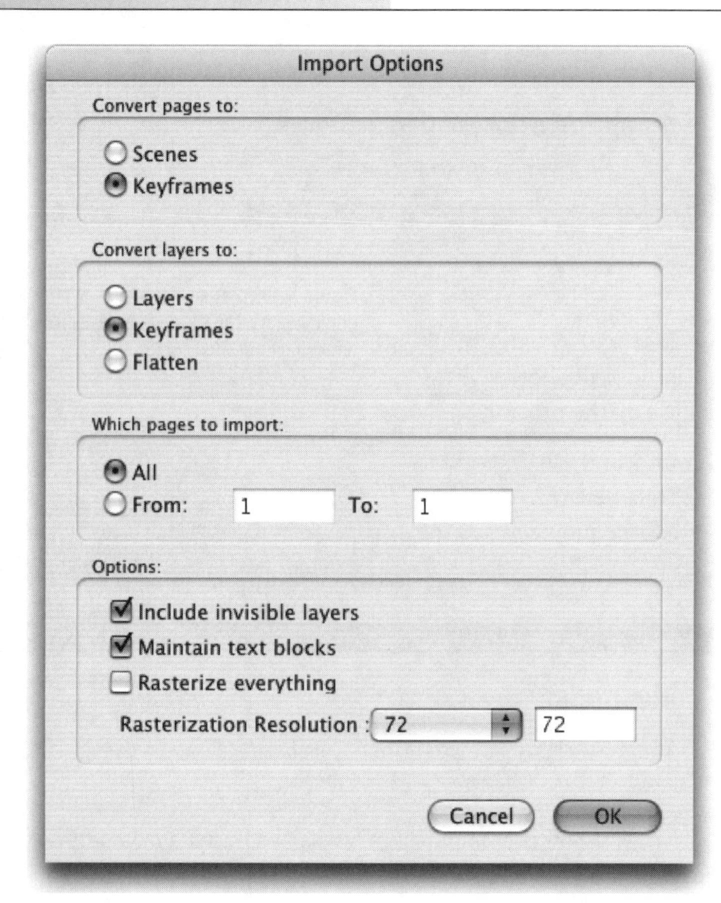

Figure 5-11. Standard vector asset import settings

Importing from Illustrator or FreeHand

Both Illustrator and FreeHand support enhanced importing options, as seen in Figure 5-11. Both will allow you to convert drawing layers to Flash layers or keyframes, as well as flatten the drawing into one layer and keyframe of vectors. They also both allow you to optionally import hidden layers and maintain text blocks. Finally, Illustrator allows you to rasterize the entire drawing into a bitmap of almost any resolution. (You will learn more about pages in the section "Importing from PDF.")

If you have Illustrator, you can open the *tabbed.ai* file (found in the */05/Importing Vectors* folder) in Illustrator and the companion *ai_keyframes_01.fla* file in Flash. You will see the beginnings of an interface, as layers are converted to keyframes upon import. In the next step of the process, shown in *ai_keyframes_02.fla*, simple scripts have been added directly to the buttons to mock up the tabs in action. Although a very simple example, this is an excellent way to get an interface working quickly in Flash if you are comfortable with a particular drawing program.

Special features in drawing programs can also be used to great advantage. For example, FreeHand's Xtra, Animate→Release to Layers, can be used to turn shape tweens (called *blends* in the FreeHand vernacular) and groups into multi-layered files. Using the "Convert Layers to Keyframes" option in the vector import dialog discussed previously, you can then create an instant animation when importing the file into Flash.

If you have a recent copy of FreeHand, begin by opening *flower_01.fh11*, found in the */05/Importing Vectors* folder. Using the aforementioned Xtra, this single-layer file is turned into *flower_02.fh11*. Each element is repeated on a new layer, adding a new element each time. The result is an animation build that can be immediately translated into Flash.

If you don't have FreeHand, or you want to move on, import the result that has already been prepared for you:

1. Create a new, blank document and save it as *fh_flower.fla* in the */05/Importing Vectors* folder.
2. Import the *flower_02.fh11* file found in the same folder.
3. Match your settings to those found in Figure 5-11.
4. Once the import is finished, save your work and test your movie. The flower animation will build over time.

When you are finished viewing the animation, close the *.swf* and return to your *.fla*. Open the Library and notice that six new symbols have been added to the file. These were originally FreeHand symbols, but they have been conveniently converted to Flash symbols for you. With a little advanced planning, FreeHand economies can make your Flash files more efficient, too.

Functions

As discussed briefly in Chapter 4, a *function* is a set of actions that Flash can perform only when called upon to do so. This is useful for preventing the actions from executing automatically, as would be the case in a simple frame script.

If you've been following along with the projects in this book, you've already been exposed to functions a few times. Although not too much attention was focused on functions themselves, you've seen them used with button and movie clip event handlers, like so:

```
start_btn.onRelease = function() {
    myClip1.play();
};
```

This type of function is called an *anonymous function* because it has no name. Instead, it is directly associated with an event handler, and the function is called by the event in question. In the above case, the function is called when the mouse is clicked on the button named *start_btn* and then released.

Custom functions can also be named and called any time, not just when associated with a specific event handler. For example, the following function will set the location of two movie clips and play them both:

```
function playAllClips() {
    myClip1._x = 20;
    myClip1._y = 20;
    myClip1_mc.play();
    myClip1._x = 60;
    myClip1._y = 20;
    myClip3_mc.play();
}
```

Once defined, you can then call this function by name from another script:

```
playallClips();
```

A few simple rules must be followed when working with functions, but they're easy to understand and remember. You'll learn more about their use when you work with functions in several other chapters, and during the discussion of scope in Chapter 7. You won't need to grapple with all of this now—for now, it's helpful merely to understand the purpose and structure of a function so you'll know what it is when you see it.

Importing a SWF

In most cases, you can even import a *.swf* into your *.fla* file. (In a later chapter, you will learn how to protect your *.swf* files from importing, but for now, you will work with the default setting where protection is not enabled.)

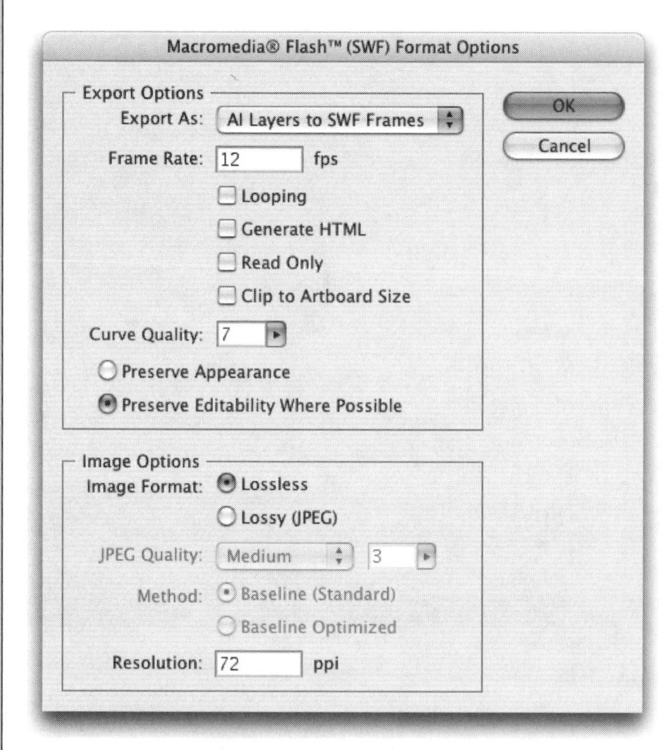

Figure 5-12. The export features in FreeHand and Illustrator (shown here) allow you to create SWF files directly from within these programs

When importing SWF files, you will not be able to import much more than graphics. However, this is still useful if you want to bring a SWF created by another program into a Flash file that you're working on.

Many third-party programs, including FreeHand and Illustrator, can create *.swf* files. These export options can even be used to create simple animations without ever opening Flash. Illustrator, in particular, can often provide better results in color and shape translations (especially from a CMYK original) by exporting a *.swf* that you then import into Flash, rather than importing the Illustrator or *.swf* document directly.

Exporting a *.swf* from a third-party tool is usually straightforward. Figure 5-12 shows the Illustrator options, as an example. Note that you can convert layers to keyframes (or files, or create one composite file). You can also apply a small selection of settings for direct export to animation, preserve appearance or editability, and set bitmap compression settings for converting embedded bitmaps.

Importing from PDF

Flash 8 can import PDF documents, using the same vector import dialog discussed previously. Depending on how complex the PDF is, Flash usually does a pretty good job of reproducing the original content.

In basic terms, importing a PDF is no different from importing an Illustrator or FreeHand file. However, the following project will give you a chance to experiment with Flash's Convert Pages to Scenes option. Although pages are supported in other applications, the idea of pages in a PDF is very intuitive and common, so you'll run with that idea now:

1. Create a new, blank document and save it as *pdf_scenes.fla* in the */05/Importing Vectors* folder.
2. Change the dimensions to 640 × 480, using the Modify→Document menu command.

3. Double-click the *editorial.pdf* file to open it, and click through its two pages. It is a simple two-page mock magazine article about a car, with an image and a pull-quote.
4. Import the *.pdf* into Flash. When the import dialog appears, match your settings to those seen in Figure 5-11, *except* for the first option. For this project, change the "Convert Pages to" option to Scenes instead of Keyframes.
5. Save your file and look at the result of the import.

You will probably notice right away that only one page of the PDF is visible. This is because the two pages have been separated into two discrete segments, called *scenes*.

Using Scenes

Scenes provide a way to organize large files or animations into multiple timelines. This makes it easier to view smaller sections at a time, without having to scroll endlessly. For example, you may have a large linear animation that is organized into chapters. Such a file may be easier to work with if you separate each chapter into its own scene. Similarly, you may have a story-driven game with levels that are separated by animations that further the story. In this case, each level and animation might be placed into its own scene.

To add Scenes, use the Insert→Scene menu command. Scenes can be given descriptive names to make it easier for you to distinguish one from another. To switch between scenes in authoring mode, use the Edit Scene menu in the upper-right corner of the main document window, as seen in Figure 5-13.

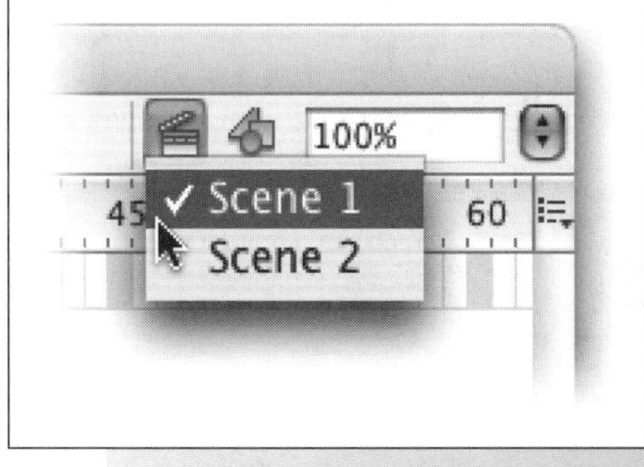

Figure 5-13. Use the Edit Scene menu to switch scenes and timelines.

Alternately, you may use the Scene panel (Window→Other Panels→Scene) to accomplish all of these tasks. It lists all current scenes, allowing you to click once to switch scenes, or double-click to rename a scene. In addition to adding scenes in this window, you can also delete and even duplicate scenes—handy when the bulk of a timeline remains intact and only subtle changes are required in the new scene.

Scripting Scene Changes

At runtime, a movie with multiple scenes behaves just like a movie with one long timeline. For example, if you test the movie you just created, you will see the two pages from the PDF flashing back and forth, just as if they were side by side in keyframes.

Adding scene navigation is as simple as adding frame navigation:

1. Continue with the file you created earlier, when importing the *editorial.pdf* file.

2. Create a button in the lower-right corner of each scene that you can use to switch between them. If you prefer, open the provided *pdf_scenes_01.fla* in the */05/Importing Vectors* folder, which already has buttons included.

3. In Scene 1, give the button an instance name of **next_btn** using the Properties panel. In Scene 2, name the button **prev_btn**.

4. Remember that the playhead will automatically move between scenes by default, so you need a script to prevent this from happening. In the first and only frame of each scene, add a *stop()* action.

5. Now you must script the button. In the first frame of Scene 1, add an *onRelease* event handler to the `next_btn` instance with a *nextScene* action. Your frame script should now look like this:

```
stop();
next_btn.onRelease = function() {
    nextScene();
};
```

6. Follow a similar course in the first frame of Scene 2, this time adding the *prevScene* action to the `prev_btn` instance:

```
stop();
prev_btn.onRelease = function() {
    prevScene();
};
```

7. Save your work and test your movie. You will see that the movie does not automatically switch scenes, and now does so only when you click on the buttons you created. If you want to check your work, *pdf_scenes_02.fla*, found in the same folder, is the complete file.

Working with the Library

Importing many graphics, and perhaps creating symbols along the way, can leave your Library a bit of a mess. To begin with, since bitmaps can be large, Flash automatically places a copy of each one in your Library. You will soon find out that the same is true for sounds and videos. Much like with symbols, you can drag these elements to the Stage, making multiple instances without noticeably increasing file size.

Furthermore, importing some types of assets will result in your Library filling up with additional objects. As you read earlier, FreeHand and Fireworks both translate their symbols into Flash symbols whenever possible. Sometimes, as you saw when working with the Fireworks file, additional folders are created in the process. Keeping the Library tidy is important if you want to keep your files manageable.

Organizing Your Library

There are many ways to organize a Library. Some developers like to use folders for each type of asset, while others organize assets according to their function. Still others prefer to organize Libraries based on the order of use. For example, in a Flash file for a cartoon, the Library might be organized so that each character's assets are in one place, and are further divided into subfolders to keep animated and inanimate symbols separate. A movie clip for a walking sequence could be in a folder with blinking eyes, for instance, while the hair and nose might be in another folder.

To create a folder in a Library, use the New Folder button in the lower-left corner of the Library panel, which looks like a folder with a plus sign (+). You can also create a new symbol using the New Symbol button to the left, and delete an element using the Delete button, which looks like a trash can.

You can add as many folders to the Library as you want, and inside each folder, you can nest other folders. How you organize the Library does not affect the movie at runtime at all. The important thing is just to stay organized, so assets are always easy to find. Large projects can contain hundreds of assets, and keeping them organized is key to maintaining a good workflow—including working with multiple files.

NOTE

Be aware that deleting a folder also deletes all of its contents. If you want to keep certain assets from a folder you plan to delete or want to reorganize your Library, simply drag assets from one folder to another. Although deletions can be undone, it is a good idea to make a backup copy of your .fla before doing anything major.

Sharing Libraries During Authoring

Your organization can have far-reaching effects, because Flash 8's new Library enhancements make it easier than ever to share assets between multiple files. As discussed briefly in Chapter 1, you can now show the Libraries for all open documents in one Library panel, using a menu to choose the current Library (see Figure 5-14). This simplifies dragging an asset you want to reuse from one document to another, or from a common Library to the document of your choice. If you prefer, you can spawn a new Library panel to drag symbols between them.

Even with these features, working with multiple documents can still get confusing. If desired, you can "pin" a Library to a specific document. This way, you can still select any open Library, but each time you switch between documents, any Library pinned to the active document will be displayed.

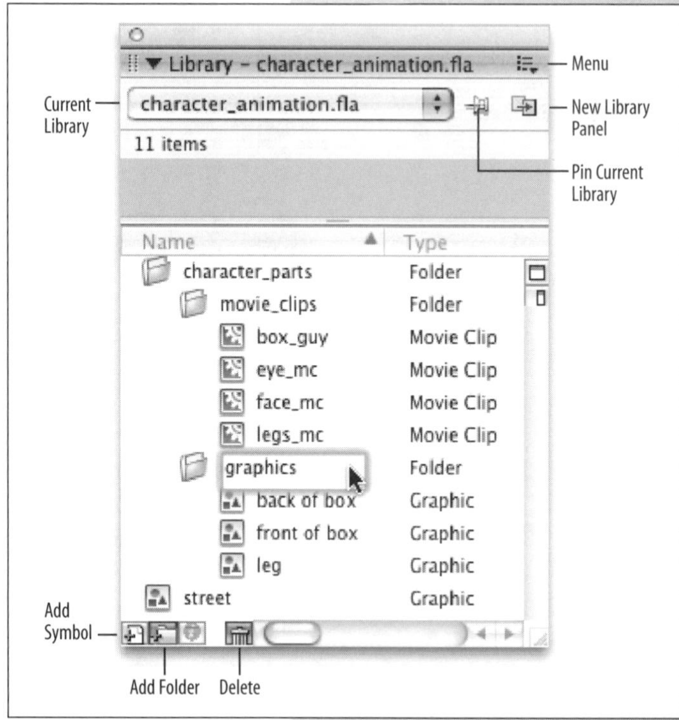

Figure 5-14. An organized Library, with key features highlighted

The Library is also a central location for modifying many properties for symbols and imported assets. A context-sensitive Properties button will show the properties of most selected Library items. It looks like an *i* and can be found between the New Folder and Delete buttons in the Library panel's lower-left corner. (The menu in the upper-right corner of the Library panel is also handy for exposing these properties.) You'll look at several properties in upcoming chapters, but for now you'll concentrate on two that are specific to images.

Compression Settings

Flash allows you to compress your graphics in a few different ways. With a JPEG, for example, you can retain the compression setting applied when the JPEG was created, or you can override its compression setting and apply a new one on a case-by-case basis. Figure 5-15 shows the Bitmap Properties about a JPEG, accessible from the Library's Properties button or menu after selecting the JPEG you want to examine.

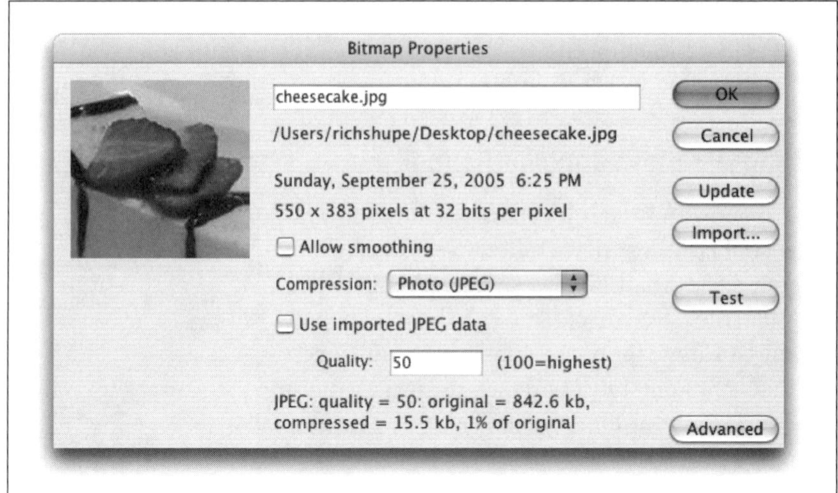

Figure 5-15. A test of the cheesecake.jpg compression settings reveals that, at a quality setting of 50, the compressed image is expected to occupy 15.5 KB of file size

In addition to information such as the import time and the location of the source file, there are a few settings here that you can adjust to optimize the bitmap. You can smooth its edges with anti-aliasing, choose between compression methods of Photo (best for continuous tones) and Lossless (best for larger areas of solids), and set the degree of compression used. In this case, the compression used when the graphic was created is being changed to 50% compression. (Higher values yield better looking, but larger, graphics.) Clicking the Test button will show you the expected size of the graphic at runtime.

Roundtrip Editing

Right/Ctrl-clicking on a bitmap in the Library is another way to quickly access additional features, including *roundtrip editing*. This convenient feature enables the editing of a selected asset in an appropriate external editor, and then automatically updates the embedded asset with the changes. For example, Figure 5-16 shows the launching of Fireworks to edit a *.png* document. This can dramatically speed workflow, because it means that you don't have to reimport assets that require editing.

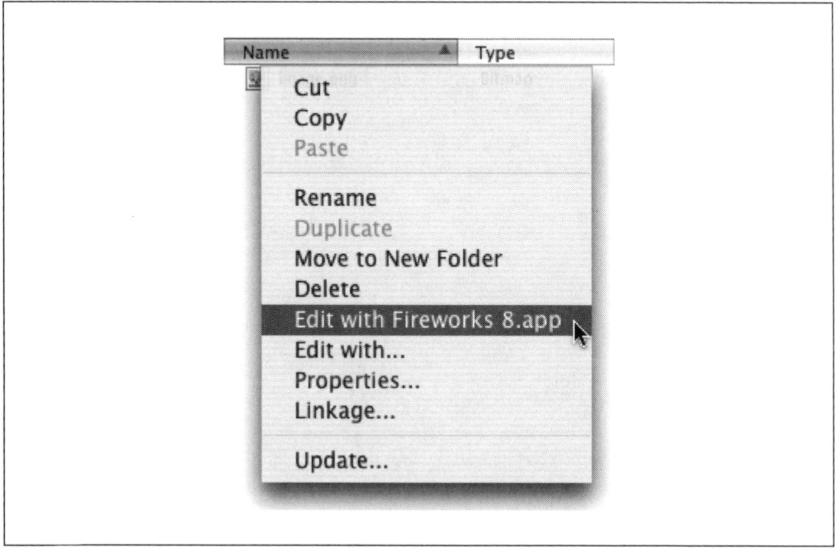

Figure 5-16. Roundtrip editing allows you to edit a Flash asset in a specified application, make changes, and then automatically update the Flash file upon closing the document in the external editor

These Library features, and your growing familiarity with the Libraries, will become very important when you start filling them with assets. In Chapters 8 and 9, you will begin using sound and video, and in the next chapter, you will work with additional symbols, including movie clips.

What's Next?

As you can see, Flash is capable of importing several different kinds of graphic file formats and manipulating those assets in many ways. Now that you know what you can work with, the creative part is up to you. In Chapter 12, you'll learn how to load external graphics files on the fly, but for now try working with the skills you've already acquired.

Toy with bitmaps in clever ways to try to create interesting effects. For example, break one apart and recolor portions of the image for a primitive silk-screened look. Create different kinds of bitmap tile tweens for large but file-size-efficient background effects. Trace different kinds of images with different Color Threshold and Curve Fit settings to achieve a fun, posterized effect. If you end up with something you like, put it aside until Chapter 7, when you can begin morphing the image into new, unimagined artworks.

In the next chapter, you'll work more closely with movie clips and add more interactivity to your files. You'll learn:

- How to create movie clip animations
- How to create, and improve, character walk cycles
- More about symbol instance names
- How to use ActionScript to control one movie clip independently of another
- How to target a symbol using absolute or relative pathnames
- How to make your movie clips respond to user mouse clicks

Movie Clips and Interactivity

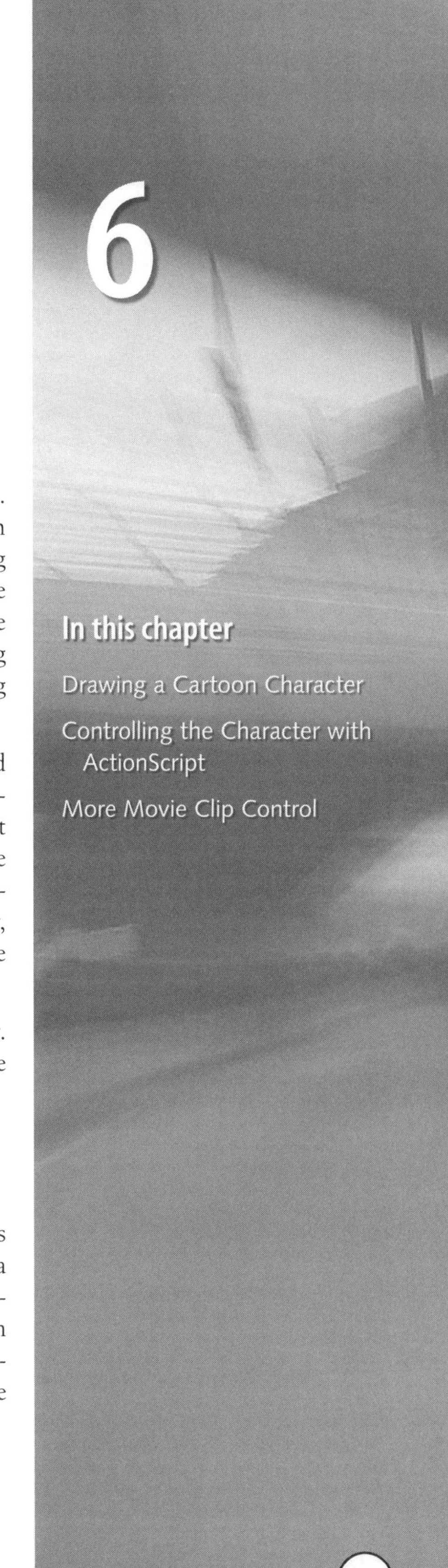

In Chapter 3, you created a simple animation entirely in the main timeline. But what happens when you need to create more complex animations, such as for a cartoon character? A cartoon character usually has several moving parts, such as its mouth, eyes, arms, and legs. If you had to animate the legs every time the character walked and animate the mouth every time the character spoke, it would be very time-consuming. Furthermore, adding variety would require you to create multiple permutations, such as walking while talking versus walking while not talking.

To simplify this process, animators use another type of Flash symbol, called a *movie clip*. In this chapter, you'll look at how movie clips allow you to create animations that play independently of one another. Next, you will revisit the dual "out of the box" themes of this book: thinking in ways that may be atypical or new to you as a Flash user, and accomplishing as much as possible with the tools you began with. Your project will be to create Box Guy, the unofficial mascot for this book, and to learn to control multiple movie clips to animate his eyes and legs.

Before you begin animating, you need to construct your cartoon character. To do this, you'll use a few simple tools, layers, and symbols. Once all the parts are built, you'll bring the character to life through animation.

Drawing a Cartoon Character

The first thing you need for your cartoon character is a body. Since this character will serve as a mascot for this book, you'll make his body from a box and then add a face and legs. In doing so, you'll see how the configuration options for the tools you will use affect the outcome of each drawn part. In more complex situations you might sketch some character prototypes on paper and create a storyboard for the animation, but for this simple task you will focus strictly on how to use Flash.

Starting with the Body

Start by creating the body for the character. Later, you'll add other elements and create a background image for Box Guy to walk in front of for a short distance.

First, you have to create a document and configure your tools:

1. Create a new Flash document and save it as *box_guy.fla* in the *06* folder.
2. Change the Stage dimensions to 550 × 200.
3. Select the Rectangle tool by pressing R (no modifier key necessary). In the Rectangle tool's Options area (in the context-sensitive lower portion of the Tools panel), select Object Drawing mode, as seen in Figure 6-1, if it is not already selected. You will practice with both drawing modes in this exercise.

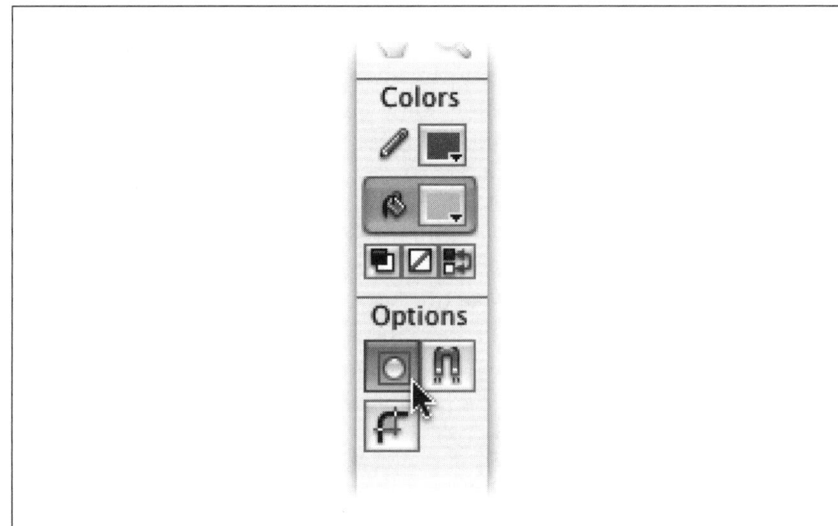

Figure 6-1. The Rectangle tool's Object Drawing mode option

4. In the Properties panel, set the Rectangle tool's stroke color to dark gray, set the stroke weight to 1, and choose Solid for the stroke style. Choose square caps and a miter join, as seen in Figure 6-2. For the fill color, choose a lighter gray.
5. Now that you've got the Rectangle tool configured, draw a box. On the Stage, hold down the Shift key and draw a rectangle. The Shift key helps by constraining your drawing into a perfect square. Because you're in

Object Drawing mode, the square has effectively been "pre-grouped," so it won't interact with any other shapes.

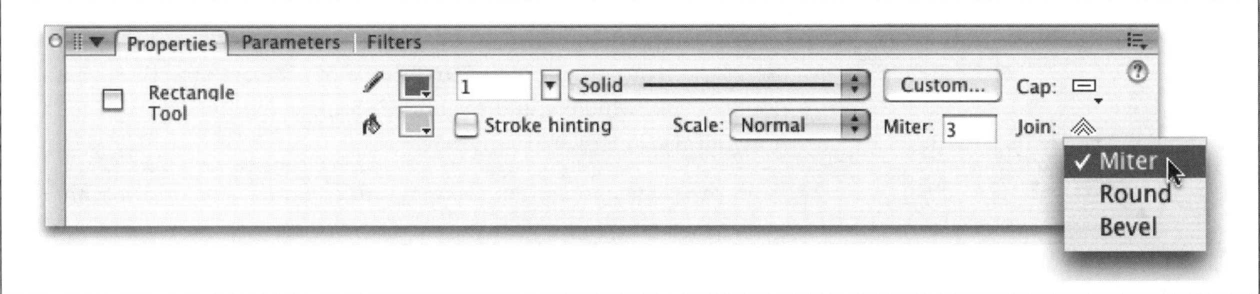

Figure 6-2. The Properties panel, showing the Rectangle tool's Cap and Join settings

6. If the square is not still selected, activate the Selection tool by pressing V. Then resize the square to 80 × 80 pixels using the Properties panel.

Like most men, Box Guy could use some depth if he's going to appeal to the other Box People out there. Draw another square and turn him into a cube, again using Object Drawing mode:

1. Alt-drag (Win) or Option-drag (Mac) the square to duplicate it. Position the copy a little bit above and to the right of the first square but overlapping it, as shown in the first grouping of Figure 6-3. Because you used Object Drawing mode, you are free to move the second square around, deselecting it if necessary, without concern about the two shapes affecting each other.
2. Once you are satisfied with the position of the second square, select both squares and choose Modify→Break Apart (Ctrl/Cmd-B). Now the two shapes will interact and can be connected with additional lines.
3. For the next lines you draw, you will use Merge Drawing mode. Select the Line tool. In the Line tool options in the bottom of the Tools panel, be sure that Object Drawing mode is disabled and Snap to Objects is enabled. Use the Line tool to draw a connecting line from the upper-left corner of the first square to the upper-left corner of the second square. You should see the cursor snap into position at the corner of the underlying square.
4. Next, draw connecting lines from the lower-left and lower-right corners of the top square to their corresponding corners in the lower square. The result is shown in the second grouping of Figure 6-3.

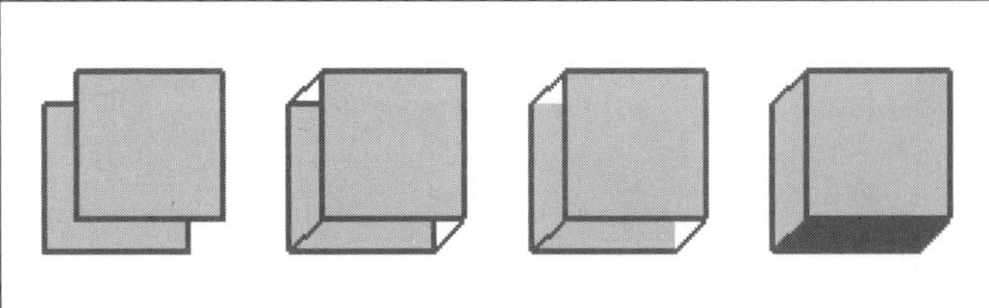

Figure 6-3. Build a box from scratch

Your drawing now looks almost like a cube, but the incomplete left and bottom sides cause this work in progress to fall short of a three-dimensional box. Fortunately, the interaction of the shapes you've drawn will work in your favor and make this easy to correct:

1. Select the remaining top horizontal line of the first box. Be sure not to double-click, which would select the entire stroke. With only the small horizontal segment selected, delete it.
2. With the same care, select the remaining vertical line on the right side of the first box and delete it as well. The result is shown in the third grouping of Figure 6-3.
3. Select the Paint Bucket tool and confirm that the previous light gray fill color is still selected. If not, select it now. (If you don't recall which color you chose, you can use the Eyedropper tool to pick the color from your drawing.)
4. Add the fill color to the white areas that remain in the top left and lower right of the drawing. If the fills don't get applied, choose Close Medium Gaps or Close Large Gaps from the Paint Bucket tool options in the Tools panel and try to apply them again.
5. Select the fill area that represents the bottom of the box and change its color to dark gray. The box now looks as if its bottom is shaded because of overhead lighting, as shown in the last grouping of Figure 6-3.

Now you have a body for your cartoon mascot. Soon, you'll add a face and legs, but the legs should appear to emerge from the bottom of the box. You can place items closer to the foreground or background (called *z-positioning* or the *stacking order*) using layers. Separate the front and back of the box, convert them to symbols, and put them in separate layers:

1. Double-click the fill area of the box in front to select its fill and stroke.
2. Convert it to a graphic symbol by choosing Modify→Convert to Symbol (F8) and setting the Behavior type to Graphic. (You'll use the same procedure for creating other graphic symbols.) Name the symbol **`front of box`**.
3. Shift-select the remaining fills and strokes of the cube and convert them to a graphic symbol called **`back of box`**.
4. Choose Edit→Cut (or press Ctrl/Cmd-X) to cut the *back of box* instance from the Stage.
5. Add a new layer to the timeline and drag it underneath *Layer 1*.
6. Choose Edit→Paste in Place (Ctrl/Cmd-Shift-V) to paste the *back of box* instance in the new layer in the exact location from which it was cut.
7. Rename the top layer **`front of box`** and the bottom layer **`back of box`**.
8. Save your work.

Soon, you'll draw legs in a layer between the *front of box* and *back of box* layers, so that the legs appear to emerge from the bottom of the box. First, however, give the character a face.

Adding a Face

In this section, you'll create a face using several movie clips in separate layers. You'll use separate movie clips for each eye and the mouth.

To add the face to the character:

1. Add a new layer to the timeline, above the others, and name it **face**. Doing this first ensures that when you create the eyes and the mouth, they'll be in the *face* layer.
2. Create an oval for an eye. Select the Oval tool from the Tools panel and position the tool just above and to the left of the center of the box (where an eye might be). Draw a vertical oval about 20 pixels tall, and make sure the fill and stroke colors are both dark gray.

For Instance

You learned earlier how to create instances on the Stage from symbols in the Library. *Symbol names*, which are assigned in the Symbol Properties dialog when creating a symbol, are primarily used to identify items in the Library.

Instance names, which are assigned via the Properties panel, are used to identify symbols on the Stage so they can be controlled via ActionScript. Some Flash elements, such as graphic symbols, can't be given instance names. This is because they cannot be controlled with ActionScript.

Any ActionScript intended to access or control movie clips, buttons, text fields, components, or similar objects won't work unless you first assign the target items instance names. Using the Flash interface, you can easily assign an instance name to an applicable object at authoring time. Select the object on the Stage and enter the instance name on the left side of the Properties panel, where you will typically see the placeholder text "<Instance Name>," or an empty field.

Using ActionScript, names can also be assigned to relevant symbol instances created from a Library symbol at runtime. For example, using ActionScript, you might dynamically create 20 balloon instances from a single *balloon* Library symbol. In this case, the new instance names can be specified at the time the symbol instances are created.

You can use any names you like for instances, as long as they follow a few simple rules. An instance name must be one word, cannot have spaces, should not start with a number, and should not already exist in the ActionScript lexicon. If multiple-word names are desired, it's common to use underscores (_) between words. Another popular alternative is so-called *camelCase*, also known as *mixedCase* or *interCaps*, in which the first word is lowercase and subsequent words are given initial capital letters.

Not all instances must be named. If, for example, ActionScript does not refer to an instance, you might not bother naming it.

It's important to understand the difference between symbol names and instance names, although Flash documentation (including this book) often glosses over this difference in the interest of readability. This book uses font conventions to distinguish between the two types of name: throughout the book, when named objects are discussed, Library symbol names are shown in *italics* and instance names are shown in `fixed-width` text. For example, if the book refers to the *back of box* instance, you should understand that it is technically an unnamed, on-Stage instance of the symbol named *back of box* in the Library. If it refers to `box_guy_mc`, you should know that this refers to a named instance of the *box_guy_mc* move clip symbol.

3. Convert the oval to a symbol and name it **eye_mc**. Instead of creating a graphic symbol, however, choose Movie Clip for the Behavior type in the Convert to Symbol dialog box. In just a minute, you'll enhance the *eye_mc* movie clip symbol to make the eyes blink independently of the animation on the main timeline.
4. Alt-drag (Win) or Option-drag (Mac) the *eye_mc* instance to the right, to create a second instance.
5. Take advantage of Flash's drawing tools to create the smile. Draw a straight line using the Line tool, and then switch to the Selection tool. Click once on an empty area of the Stage to be sure the grim mouth is not selected. Next, click on the middle of the line and drag it down. A natural arc will form to create the smile, as shown in Figure 6-4.
6. Use the same technique to create dimples at each end of the smile. Arrange the finished smile and two eyes to make a face.

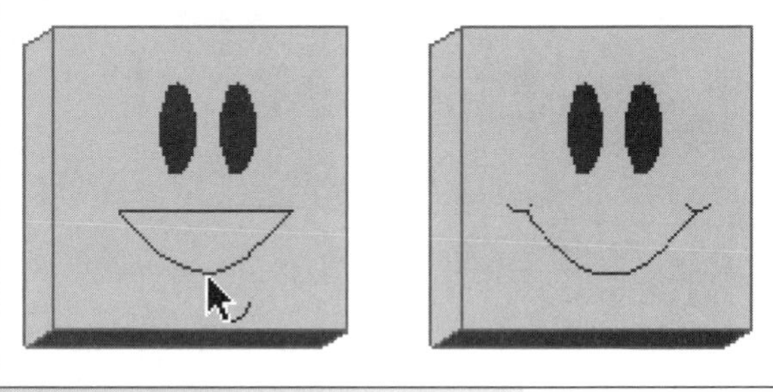

Figure 6-4. Drawing the mouth (left) and the finished face of the box character (right)

7. Select the two eyes and mouth, and position them over the *front of box* instance to give the character its face.
8. With the two eyes and mouth still selected, convert them to a movie clip symbol, and name it **face_mc**. You want to group them together into one symbol so they can be positioned as one entity. (Frankly, you could use Modify→Group instead of creating a symbol if your only goal was to group them together. However, creating a symbol gives you the ability to control the *face_mc* clip and any clips within it in a hierarchy via ActionScript, as described later under "More Movie Clip Control." For example, you could make the eyes blink or wink randomly, or you could change the mouth position.)
9. Save your work.

In order for the eyes to blink, *face_mc* must be a movie clip, not a graphic symbol. Adding the *_mc* suffix to the end of movie clip symbol names makes them easier to identify in the Library; however, the symbol's type is typically determined by the setting in the Symbol Property dialog box at the time of creation, and not by the name's suffix.

Our character is starting to get a personality, but there's still plenty to be done.

Animating the Eyes

To bring your cartoon character to life, you need to give him some human characteristics, such as blinking eyes. As alluded to earlier, movie clips come in handy here because they allow the eyes to move independently of the remainder of the character. Thus, Box Guy can walk and blink at the same time, or he can just blink like a proverbial deer in the headlights.

Using movie clips to create independent animations

A movie clip acts like a movie within a movie. Each movie clip symbol has its own timeline, and movie clip instances play independently of the main timeline. So, if you create a 25-frame animation in a movie clip symbol's timeline and place an instance of the symbol on the Stage, it will play even if the main timeline is stopped.

You need the character's eyes to blink regardless of what is going on in the rest of the animation, so use a movie clip to create a blinking eye animation:

1. Double-click the *face_mc* symbol, and then double-click on one of the *eye_mc* instances. This lets you edit its symbol in place. Make sure you're editing the correct symbol by checking the Edit bar, which should say *Scene 1, face_mc, eye_mc*. (If the Edit bar says *Scene 1, face_mc*, the first double-click opened the *face_mc* symbol for editing; double-click again on an *eye_mc* instance to edit the *eye_mc* symbol.) Notice that the movie clip symbol has its own timeline and can contain one or more layers.
2. Select frame 32 of the *eye_mc* clip's timeline and press F5 to add a frame. (Here, the term "*eye_mc* clip" is used for brevity, but it is technically an on-Stage clip instance of the *eye_mc* movie clip symbol from the Library. Did you notice the difference, and were you able to discern its meaning in context?)

Movie Clips

Movie clip symbols are the worker bees of the Flash world. You'll use them in almost every Flash project. A *movie clip instance* (or simply *clip* for short) is typically derived from a movie clip symbol in the Library. The symbol can be created from something already on the Stage, using the Modify→Convert to Symbol command, or created from scratch, using Insert→New Symbol (Ctrl/Cmd-F8). A movie clip symbol has its own layers and timeline, just like the main movie. It can contain vectors, bitmaps, sounds, or even other symbols, including button, graphic, and other movie clip symbols. The term *movie clip* is used informally to mean either a movie clip symbol in the Library or an instance of that symbol on the Stage. Most Flash documentation doesn't make the distinction explicit in all cases, but the difference should be clear from context.

Placing multiple elements within a movie clip is not the same as *grouping* (which can be achieved by selecting multiple objects on the Stage and choosing Modify→Group). Grouped objects—such as multiple shapes or the fill and stroke for a single shape—do not have their own timelines, and they cannot be targeted through ActionScript. This distinction will become clearer as you learn more about movie clips, but for now, assume that for maximum efficiency, any asset you expect to reuse should be converted to a symbol.

Items nested within a movie clip behave similarly to items placed in the main timeline. The primary differences are in how they are accessed via ActionScript and how they are positioned in the movie's coordinate space. You'll see shortly how to access *nested clips* (i.e., clips arranged within other clips, creating a hierarchy) via ActionScript.

3. Add a new keyframe at frame 30.
4. At frame 30, select and delete the fill within the oval. Then, select and delete most of the stroke, leaving only a curved line at the bottom, as shown in Figure 6-5. This makes the eye appear closed, which is part of the blink sequence.

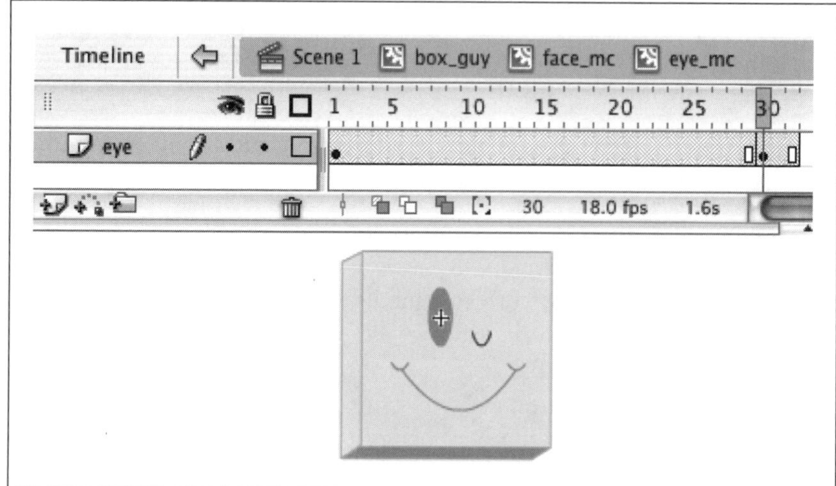

Figure 6-5. The closed eye for the blinking animation

5. Press Enter/Return to watch the animation. When the playhead reaches frame 30, the eye animation closes for two frames, then stops.
6. Return to Scene 1 by clicking *Scene 1* in the Edit bar, and choose Control→Test Movie or press Ctrl-Enter (Win) or Cmd-Return (Mac) to see the animation.
7. Save your work.

There is only one frame in the main timeline, but the blinking eye animation takes place in the *eye_mc* clip's timeline. The *eye_mc* clips—remember, there are two instances of the *eye_mc* clip symbol in *Layer 1* of the *face_mc* symbol's timeline—play in their entirety and then loop. So, no matter what the rest of the character is doing in the animation, the eyes continue to blink. This separation of character parts makes movie clips very useful for animators. Once the parts of a character have been created, they can be reused whenever necessary, and they can be manipulated independently, so the eyes or mouth can animate independently of the legs. This allows you to combine them in different ways, for much more variation without a lot of extra work. For example, if animating a dog, you might use one movie clip to create a wagging tail and a second clip for the dog's legs moving. You might then turn the whole dog into a movie clip that can be controlled independently of the dog's owner (another clip) on the Stage.

Next, you'll draw legs for your character and animate them so you can make him walk across the Stage.

Drawing the Legs

So far, Box Guy is a bit of a bore. All he does is sit there and blink. You want him to walk across the Stage, so you need to give him some legs. Here, you'll create a *walk cycle* (i.e., a series of character positions that, when played in sequence, makes the character appear to walk):

1. Insert a layer between the *front of box* and *back of box* layers, and name the new layer **legs**.
2. Activate the Pencil tool, and choose Smooth in the Tools panel's Options section. Instead of the default behavior of straightening the lines you draw, Flash will now smooth them.

Walk Cycles

This exercise demonstrates a very simple walk cycle in which Box Guy's legs move in two successive positions. A more realistic walk cycle might include swinging a character's arms or adding a bounce to its steps. Other animation cycles could be developed to show the character moving at different speeds. A horse's run, for example, is not simply a faster version of its walk. Also, consider these cycles from different angles, allowing the character to walk or run to the left, right, foreground, and background. As a character moves from the foreground to the background, its size should change relative to its distance from the viewer. Observe both the physical world and existing cartoons to find animation cycles to imitate.

An important part of creating cartoons is making sure a character walks and moves in a way that is appropriate. For example, a giraffe, which generally has very long legs, covers much more ground in a single walk cycle than a squirrel, so if using the two side by side, you might animate the squirrel running as fast as it can while the giraffe walks slowly beside the squirrel. The important part is that you don't have the character covering too much (or too little) ground in each part of its walk cycle. If the walk cycle covers too little ground compared to how far you move the character across the Stage, the character appears to slide across the Stage instead of walking. Likewise, if the walk cycle covers too much ground, the character appears to slip in place, like an ice skater with no traction.

Another thing to watch for is walk cycle "stutter." When the first and last frames of a walk cycle are identical, the cycle can appear to stutter, or stall, for a fraction of a second. This is demonstrated in the *bouncing ball* files in the "Realistic Motion" discussion in Chapter 3, and it's something you'll practice avoiding with Box Guy later on.

As a simple example, think of a cycle of letters: "a, b, c, b, a." If you looped this sequence, like a walk cycle, the last "a" would be followed by the first "a," and it would read "a, b, c, b, a, a, b, c, b, a."

To avoid this, make sure the last keyframe of a walk cycle doesn't match the first. If you've tweened the animation, it is common to delete the last keyframe or alter it a bit so animation appears to be just short of completion in its final frame. The loop will then look more natural. Using the letter metaphor again, the new sequence would be: "a, b, c, b." When looped, the sequence would read: "a, b, c, b, a, b, c, b."

After a little experimentation, you'll see that creating good-looking walk cycles can be difficult and time-consuming. There are lots of tricks to reduce the number of positions in a walk cycle, which reduces both the time required of the animator and the movie's download size. For example, you can flip the character (by selecting the object and choosing Modify→Transform→Flip Horizontal) to create a walk cycle in the opposite direction. You can also make the character hop slightly so that it doesn't appear to slide across the floor inappropriately. For details on these and additional animation tips, pick up a copy of Sham Bhangal's *Flash Hacks* (O'Reilly).

3. Somewhere on the Stage, in the *legs* layer, draw a leg with a foot similar to what you see in Figure 6-6, and convert it to a graphic symbol. If you prefer, you can open *box_guy_complete.fla*, located in the *06* folder, and copy and paste the drawing inside the *leg* symbol. (To enter Edit mode for the symbol, double-click on the symbol icon in the Library.)

Figure 6-6. Box Guy's legs appear to emerge from the bottom of the cube

4. Alt-drag (Win) or Option-drag (Mac) to duplicate the leg (we want him to walk, not hop, so he'll need two legs).
5. Shift-select both legs and convert them to a graphic symbol named **`legs`**. Then position the *legs* instance underneath the *front of box* instance so the legs appear to emerge from the bottom of the cube, as shown in Figure 6-6.
6. Save your work.

To see your mascot in action, you'll make him move from one spot on the Stage to another and stop. Start by turning him into a movie clip symbol, which makes it easier to control him using the timeline or ActionScript:

1. If you wish, save a backup of your file.
2. Select all the parts of the character and convert them into a movie clip symbol named **box_guy_mc**. Three of the four layers in the timeline are now empty, because all of the parts contained in those layers are now part of a single symbol in one layer.
3. Delete the empty layers and rename the remaining layer **box_guy**.
4. Soon, you'll use ActionScript to control the instance of the *box_guy_mc* symbol, so you must give it an instance name. Assign this clip the instance name **box_guy_mc** in the Properties panel.

NOTE

ActionScript can't control a movie clip instance unless it is first given an instance name, as discussed in the "For Instance" sidebar, earlier in this chapter.

You want the character to move across the Stage from left to right. You do this by placing him at different positions in the starting and ending keyframes and then tweening the animation:

1. There is always a keyframe in frame 1, so you'll use that as the starting point for the animation. Select frame 1 and then drag the *box_guy_mc* clip off the Stage to the left.
2. Insert a keyframe at frame 60.
3. In frame 60, drag *box_guy_mc* to the right side of the Stage.
4. Select any frame in the *box_guy* layer, before the keyframe at frame 60, and choose Motion from the Tween drop-down list in the Properties panel. This causes Flash to tween the character from the starting position to the ending position.
5. Save your work and test the movie (Control→Test Movie).

Making Him Walk

Okay—so you saw that coming, right? The character blinks and slides from the left side of the Stage to the right, but his legs don't move and the animation loops back to the beginning. It's easy to fix both problems:

1. Close the Test Movie mode's Preview window and double-click on the `box_guy_mc` clip to edit the *box_guy_mc* symbol in place.
2. Select the instance of the *legs* symbol, which is nested inside the *box_guy_mc* symbol.
3. You converted the legs to a graphic symbol earlier, but now you want to animate them, so you need to change the symbol type of *legs* to Movie Clip. You could break apart the symbol and create a new one, but there is an easier way to accomplish your goal that also won't contribute to file size by creating a new symbol. In the Properties panel, choose Movie Clip from the Symbol Behavior drop-down list. This allows the symbol instance to behave as a movie clip. Assign **`legs_mc`** as the instance name for the *legs* symbol.
4. Open the Library (Ctrl/Cmd-L or F11), select the *legs* symbol, and click the Information icon in the lower-left corner, shown in Figure 6-7, to open the Symbol Properties dialog box.

NOTE

Even though you changed the Behavior type of the instance on the Stage in step 3, you must also change the original symbol's Behavior type for it to truly become a movie clip. Setting different Behavior types for Library symbols and their on-Stage instances can become confusing, but it can also be very handy. For example, if you have a graphic instance on the Stage that you'd like to reposition via ActionScript, you can simply change the Behavior type of the instance to Movie Clip and assign it an instance name.

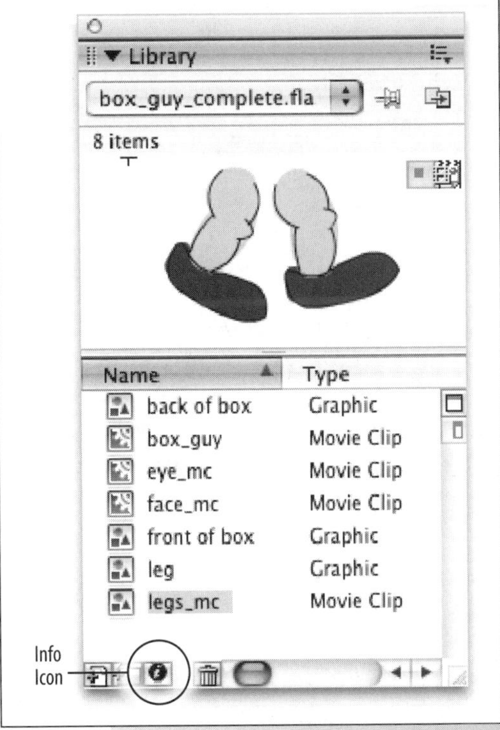

Figure 6-7. Click the Information icon in the Library to open the Symbol Properties dialog box

5. In the dialog box, change the *legs* symbol's Behavior type from Graphic to Movie Clip, rename the symbol **`legs_mc`** (to help identify it as a movie clip in the Library and to keep names consistent for easy cross-referencing), and click OK to close the dialog box. The symbol is now a movie clip.

To finish up, you must animate the legs in their own timeline to create the walking action:

1. Double-click on the `legs_mc` instance to edit the *legs_mc* symbol in place. The Edit bar indicates you are now editing *Scene 1, box_guy, legs_mc*. In other words, you are editing the *legs_mc* movie clip symbol, an instance of which is located inside the *box_guy_mc* movie clip symbol, an instance of which is, in turn, located in the main timeline.

That is, editing a movie clip in place edits the original symbol, not the on-Stage instance of the clip.

> **NOTE**
>
> *Remember, when a symbol is placed on the Stage, Flash creates a reference, called an instance, to its Library counterpart. However, double-clicking the instance edits the original symbol from which it is derived. Therefore, every other instance derived from this symbol will also reflect any changes you make.*

2. Shift-select both legs and choose Modify→Timeline→Distribute to Layers to place the legs in individual layers. Delete *Layer 1*, which is now empty, and rename the two remaining layers **back_leg** and **front_leg**, with the back leg in the top layer ("back leg," in this case, refers to the character's right leg, which starts in the back position).

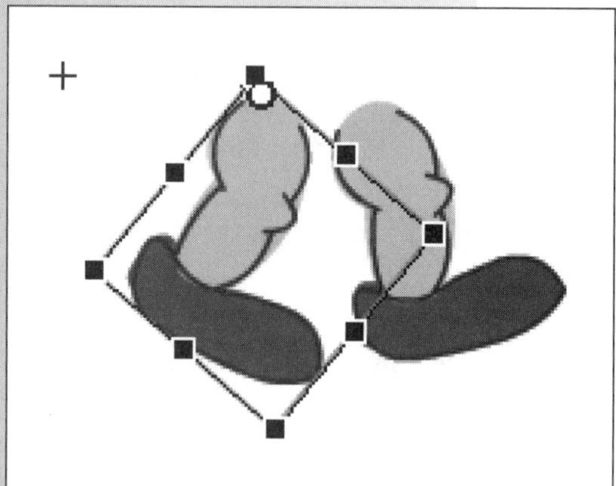

Figure 6-8. The Free Transform tool displays handles used to rotate, skew, or resize an object on the Stage

3. Activate the Free Transform tool from the Tools panel, and select the back leg. Eight handles appear around the bounding box of the leg, as shown in Figure 6-8. Move the cursor over the top corner handle and, when the cursor appears as a rotating arrow, click and drag to rotate the leg until it's in a starting position that looks natural for walking. The Free Transform tool can also be used to skew and resize an object on the Stage, which you'll read more about later.
4. With the back leg still selected with the Free Transform tool, move the center circle, or *anchor point*, to the top of the leg. When you rotate the leg again in a moment, it will rotate around its anchor point, like a construction-paper puppet with limbs held together by brass connectors at the joints.

5. Repeat steps 3 and 4 for the front leg.
6. Insert keyframes in both layers at frame 5 and frame 10. The legs need to rotate from frame 1 to frame 5, and then return to their starting position at frame 10. Adding the ending keyframe ensures that the leg positions at frames 1 and 10 match, because a new keyframe always inherits what is in the previous keyframe. Leaving frames 1 and 10 as they are makes your animation loop seamlessly.
7. Select frame 5 in the *back_leg* layer and use the Free Transform tool to rotate the leg again. (You may need to first reposition the anchor point in the leg graphic, because you've added keyframes since you first set the anchor point.) This time, rotate it so it appears to move from being the trailing foot to the lead foot.
8. Conversely, rotate the front leg in the *front_leg* layer so the foot goes from being the lead foot to the trailing foot (again, you may need to first reposition the anchor point). This alternation of the feet will provide the illusion of walking.

9. Create a motion tween in both layers, from frame 1 to frame 5 and then from frame 5 to frame 10. To select multiple frame spans, select a frame in one of the frame spans, then press Ctrl (Win) or Cmd (Mac) and select a frame in each of the other frame spans. Then choose Motion from the Tween drop-down list in the Properties panel to apply a motion tween to every frame span at once. The timeline should match Figure 6-9.

Save your work and test the movie.

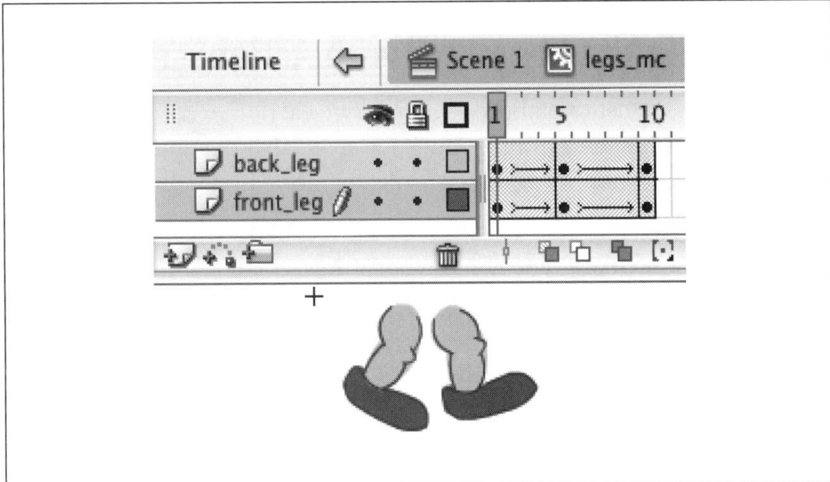

Figure 6-9. The timeline for legs_mc

> **NOTE**
>
> *As discussed in the "Walk Cycles" sidebar, when the first and last frames of a walk cycle are identical, the cycle can appear to "stutter" for a fraction of a second. To avoid this stutter effect, alter the last keyframe of a walk cycle so it appears to be just short of completion. In the previous exercise, add a new keyframe in frame 9 of each of the legs, and delete each frame 10. Alternately, you could rotate the leg in keyframe 10 back a smidge in the direction it was swinging from, to give the character a stylish gait.*

Making Him Stop

Things are starting to look good, but the animation in the main timeline is automatically looping, causing Box Guy to suddenly jump from the right side of the Stage back to the left side, where he started. Just like in Chapter 3, you need to add a *stop()* action to stop the main timeline:

1. Close the Preview window and return to Scene 1 (using the Edit bar).
2. Add a new layer to the main timeline and name it **`actions`**. Remember, it's a good practice to keep all ActionScript in its own layer so it's easy to find.
3. Add a keyframe to frame 60 in the *actions* layer.
4. Open the Actions panel (Window→Development Panels→Actions or F9). In the Script pane of the Actions panel, add the command **`stop();`** in frame 60. This causes the main timeline to stop animating once frame 60 is reached.
5. Save your work and test the movie.

Now the character walks his way from the left side of the Stage to the right side in a fluid motion, and then stops. However, even though Box Guy stops, his legs seem to have minds of their own. In fact, the movie clip for the blinking eyes and the clip for the legs both continue to play even though the main timeline is stopped. This reveals an important fact: when you stop or play a clip via ActionScript, nested clips do not automatically stop or play at the same time. That is, a parent clip and its nested clip have timelines that play independently.

Next, you'll use ActionScript to stop Box Guy's legs from moving. You'll leave the eyes blinking periodically, for realism.

Controlling the Character with ActionScript

As you saw previously, you need to add a *stop()* action to the main timeline to prevent an animation from looping automatically. In addition, you need to tell the legs to stop moving when the character is standing still. To do this:

1. Close the Preview window and reopen the Actions panel.
2. Go back to the script in frame 60 in the *actions* layer. Press Enter/Return to add a blank line at the end of the script, and type **`box_guy_mc.legs_mc.stop();`** to make the legs stop moving in this frame as well.
3. Save your work and test the movie.

This last line of code, added to the main timeline, is simply another *stop()* command, but it's targeted at the `legs_mc` instance located inside the `box_guy_mc` instance. Remember that clips exist in a nested hierarchy, starting from the main timeline. The dot operator (a period) is used to build the path to the intended target clip, much like slashes are used to separate folders in a directory path. In this case, `box_guy_mc.legs_mc.stop();` tells the Flash Player to look inside the `box_guy_mc` clip in the main timeline and tell the `legs_mc` clip to stop its playback.

Now Box Guy walks across the Stage and stops—and his legs stop too.

Creating the Background

Before publishing the movie, create a background graphic like the one in Figure 6-10, so the character appears to be walking down a street:

1. Add a new layer, name it **bg** (short for background), and drag it beneath the other two layers.
2. Drag the playhead to frame 1, so the character isn't in the way as you draw the street.
3. On the Stage, draw a gray rectangle that occupies the bottom half of the Stage. Delete the right, left, and bottom lines of the stroke. You don't need them.

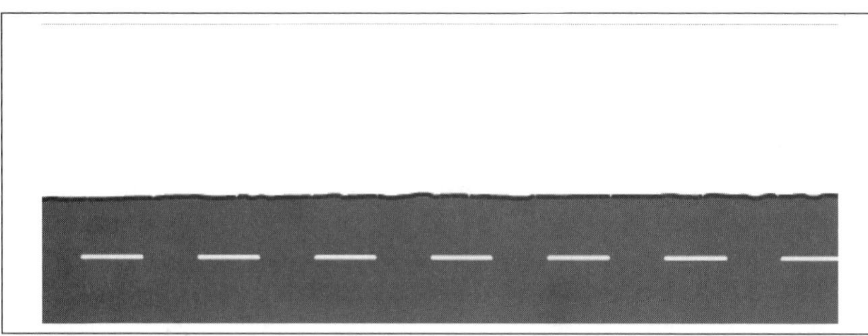

Figure 6-10. The completed street background

Absolute and Relative Target Paths

The main timeline in a Flash movie is metaphorically referred to as the "root directory" of the file. This is based on familiar analogies, such as the way your computer's hard drive directories or an HTML web site's directories are organized.

When navigating to a file on your computer or a web site, you often need to traverse directories. Using pathnames allows you to point to a file from another location. The equivalent of pathnames are also used in Flash to refer to other objects ActionScript can control. Unlike in a web site URL, however, you do not use slashes (/) to describe the structure of objects you are traversing. You still form a path referring to a nested structure by stringing together nested objects, but in ActionScript, you join these objects with periods (.). This is called "dot syntax."

Just like when writing HTML, in ActionScript you can refer to an object you wish to target with an *absolute path* or a *relative path*. An absolute path points to a target starting from the root directory of the movie. In fact, the main timeline in a Flash movie is also referred to as `_root` in dot syntax. This would be similar to a file path on your computer that started with the name of your hard drive, or an HTML link that started with your domain name.

Absolute paths are easy to use because they never change, but they are also quite rigid. If you moved the aforementioned computer file to another hard drive but didn't change the path you were using, the file wouldn't be found. Similarly, if you moved a web site to another domain but used absolute paths in all of your links, your site would cease to work.

The same is true with absolute paths to ActionScript targets. Say you referred to the legs that are currently nested inside the movie clip that is your Box Guy using an absolute path. To do this, you would write `_root.box_guy_mc.legs_mc`. If you later put Box Guy inside another movie clip, or even loaded your main file into another Flash movie (such as a preloader), the path would no longer reach the desired target.

An ActionScript relative path is more flexible. This type of path points to a target relative to the timeline in which the path is used. For example, your original path, `box_guy_mc.legs_mc`, is relative to the main timeline. However, even if the main file is loaded into another Flash file preloader, the path will still work. The target clip will not have the same relationship to the `_root` any longer, because the new preloader is now the `_root`. However, the clip's relationship to the previous main timeline is the same.

A couple of keywords are very useful when writing relative paths. The `_parent` keyword means the timeline in which the "current" timeline (the timeline from which the path is used) resides. In other words, the `_parent` is one level up. This is similar to writing `../` in an HTML link to go up one directory. The `this` keyword refers to the "current" timeline (the timeline from which the path is used). For example, if you wanted to refer to `legs_mc` from the main timeline, you could use `this.box_guy_mc.legs_mc` for the relative path. If you wanted to target `legs_mc` from `box_guy_mc`, you would use `this.legs_mc` for the relative path.

You'll learn more about paths in the next chapter, when reading about scope.

4. Select the remaining stroke, along the top edge of the rectangle, and change its stroke style to Ragged (the third choice in the Stroke Style drop-down list in the Properties panel). Set the stroke color to dark gray.
5. Next, you need to add yellow lane-divider markings to make it look like a street. Activate the Line tool, set the stroke color to yellow, and set the stroke style to Dashed. Set the line thickness to 5.
6. Click the Custom button in the Properties panel to open the Stroke Style dialog box. Beneath the Type drop-down list, enter **40** into the fields that set the length of each dashed line and the distance between the lines. Click OK to close the dialog box.
7. Draw a line from one side of the Stage to the other, in the center of the rectangle. Now you have a lane divider such as you see on a typical street, as shown in Figure 6-10.
8. Shift-select all the parts of the street graphic and convert them to a graphic symbol named *street*.
9. Save your work.

Finally, you need a blue sky. In some cases, it's easiest just to change the color of the Stage. To do so, click once on the Stage and then click on the Background color swatch in the Properties panel.

However, you will find that this approach can be problematic. For example, later in this book, you'll learn how to load one Flash movie into another. When you do this, the Stage of the loaded movie becomes invisible and your blue sky disappears. Also, when creating a self-running projector, you may want the rest of the monitor blocked off to focus on your content. The Flash Stage color is used for this purpose, so you might end up with a big blue background behind your file—including under the street.

To get around these issues, it's a good practice to use a color shape in the lowest possible layer:

1. Create a new layer and drag it beneath all the other layers. Name it **sky**.
2. Use the Rectangle tool to fill the Stage with a sky-blue box. Delete the box's stroke if it has one. (If you need many colored backgrounds in a file, you can make this a graphic symbol and reuse it to keep the file size down. Change the color of each use in the Properties panel using the Color menu's Tint option.)
3. Save your work.

4. Choose File→Publish to generate a completed SWF file.
5. If you have been following along, *box_guy.swf*, located in the *06* folder, shows what your completed movie should look like.

Our movie is complete. The character walks from one side of the Stage to the other, blinking the whole time, and stops. When he stops walking, his legs stop moving but he continues blinking, giving the character a lifelike quality.

Nesting movie clips within other clips is common in Flash development, as is using multiple clips within one project. Clips can be nested multiple levels deep (a clip within a clip within a clip), as we've done here. A movie clip can be used for an animated logo in a Flash web site, as a container for video in an interface (which you'll construct later), and even as a menu system, similar to those made with JavaScript in traditional HTML-based design.

More Movie Clip Control

In addition to using a simple *stop()* command, you can also allow the user to control Box Guy if you implement the necessary functionality. For example, you can tell Flash to restart the animation when the user clicks on the character. To accomplish this, add an *event handler* to your ActionScript. An event handler tells the Flash Player, "When an event—such as the user clicking on the character—occurs, perform the following action(s)." In this case, the desired action is to replay the animation. How do you do this?

Whenever the user clicks on Box Guy, you'll tell the main timeline to play again, and send the same instructions to the legs. Since timelines automatically loop by default, this will keep both timelines playing until the next stop instruction is received. Here's how it's done:

1. In frame 60 of the *actions* layer, add the event handler code below, using the Actions panel. You will probably quickly grasp the *onRelease* event handler, as a variant of *on (release)* from your work with buttons in Chapter 4. The *onRelease* event handler allows the movie clip to react to a user's mouse input just like a button. It tells Flash to perform this action when the user clicks the mouse on the specified clip (in this case, `box_guy_mc`). Movie clips also have their own unique event handlers, which you'll learn about in the next chapter. For now, use *onRelease* to make your movie clip behave like a button:

   ```
   box_guy_mc.onRelease = function() {
       play();
   };
   ```

2. Test your movie to see the main timeline play from the beginning. Notice that the legs remain stopped.

NOTE

Note that, as is a best practice, you placed this code in the main timeline, not the clip's timeline. Because the script is written in the main timeline, the clip paths are relative to the main timeline. This means that the play() command instructs the main timeline to play. (If you haven't read the "Absolute and Relative Target Paths" sidebar, you may want to do so now.)

3. Edit the script to add the same *play()* action to the legs (changes shown in bold):

```
box_guy_mc.onRelease = function() {
    play();
    this.legs_mc.play();
};
```

4. Remember, the `this` keyword refers to the timeline in which the path is used. Here, that's `box_guy_mc`. Since the script is written in the main timeline, all paths need to be relative to that timeline. Your desired target, `legs_mc`, is not in the main timeline, but rather inside `box_guy_mc`. Therefore, you need to begin the relative path with `this`. Save your work and test the movie.

5. When the character stops walking, click on it to replay the animation.

The script you wrote sets up a function that runs when you click on the `box_guy_mc` clip in the movie. In the previous chapter, we briefly discussed how to write and call a function. If you look closely, this format is a bit different. These functions do not have names, and are on the right side of an equation. In this format, the function is directly assigned to the event handler.

Movie Clip Event Handlers

To keep things simple, you used familiar button event handlers with your movie clips, which is appropriate within the context of these exercises. (If you need to refresh your memory on event handlers, see the sidebar of the same name in Chapter 4.) Movie clips also have their own special event handlers designed for specific purposes.

One such purpose is to trap repeating events that occur within a frame. For example, frame scripts execute only once when the playback enters the frame. By contrast, the movie clip event *onEnterFrame* can cause a script to execute multiple times within a frame—as many times as your movie's frame rate allows.

To see this in action, create a new movie and place this action in frame 1:

```
trace("frame event");
```

Test your movie and notice that "frame event" is placed in the Output panel only once.

Next, draw a shape on the Stage, and convert it to a movie clip symbol using Modify→Convert to Symbol (F8). Give the symbol an instance name of **`myClip_mc`**, and add this code to frame 1:

```
myClip_mc.onEnterFrame = function() {
    trace("enterFrame movie clip event");
};
```

Test your movie again and notice that, while you still see the single trace of "frame event" in the Output panel, you also see many occurrences of your movie clip trace.

This separation of functionality between frame, button, and movie clip events allows you to pick the right tool for the job when you write your scripts. You might use a frame script to perform an action once in a frame, a button event handler to easily respond to user interaction, or a movie clip event handler to respond to universal or repeating events.

There are additional movie clip event handlers with their own specific purposes, and you'll learn about some of them later in this book. If you're anxious to explore, testing their functionality is a great way to learn more about them.

These are called *anonymous functions*, and because they don't have names, they can't be called in the traditional sense. In this case, they are assigned directly to an event handler and are automatically called when the event in question (here, a mouse press) occurs.

In future chapters, you will see that event handlers can also call named functions. This is convenient when the function must be called from other locations as well, or when two different event handlers must call the function.

What's Next?

Before moving on to the next chapter, try using your new ActionScript knowledge to make the character's eyes stop blinking. (Hint: You'll need to give instance names to the on-Stage instances of the *face_mc* and *eye_mc* movie clip symbols so you can target them from ActionScript, and you'll need to stop each *eye_mc* instance separately.)

If you feel inspired, try to improve Box Guy's walk cycle by making sure the first and last frames of the movie clip do not appear to be identical. See the last Note in "Making Him Walk" for tips on how to do so.

Finally, flip the character horizontally (by selecting the movie clip instance and choosing Modify→Transform→Flip Horizontal), and make him walk from right to left. Can you make him walk back and forth?

Movie clips are arguably the most powerful objects in Flash. They can be used for independent animations, such as the one you created in this chapter, or as self-contained pieces of functionality and logic for a movie. For example, later in this book, you'll use a movie clip to create a preloader for external assets that load into a Flash movie while it's running. (A preloader gives users a visual progress update when an external asset is being loaded.) The preloader clip contains nothing but ActionScript and a text field.

Another great benefit of using movie clips instead of animating everything in the main timeline is that clips can be used in more than one project. If you plan to create an entire series of cartoons using the same characters, for example, you can create walk cycles for each character and simply import them into each new movie.

In the next chapter, you'll use what you've learned to build an animated ad. You'll focus on:

- How to reveal content over time in your next look at animating text
- How to hide and reveal content with masks
- How to morph shapes with shape tweening
- Basic ActionScript movement
- More about variables and conditional scripting

More Animation Techniques

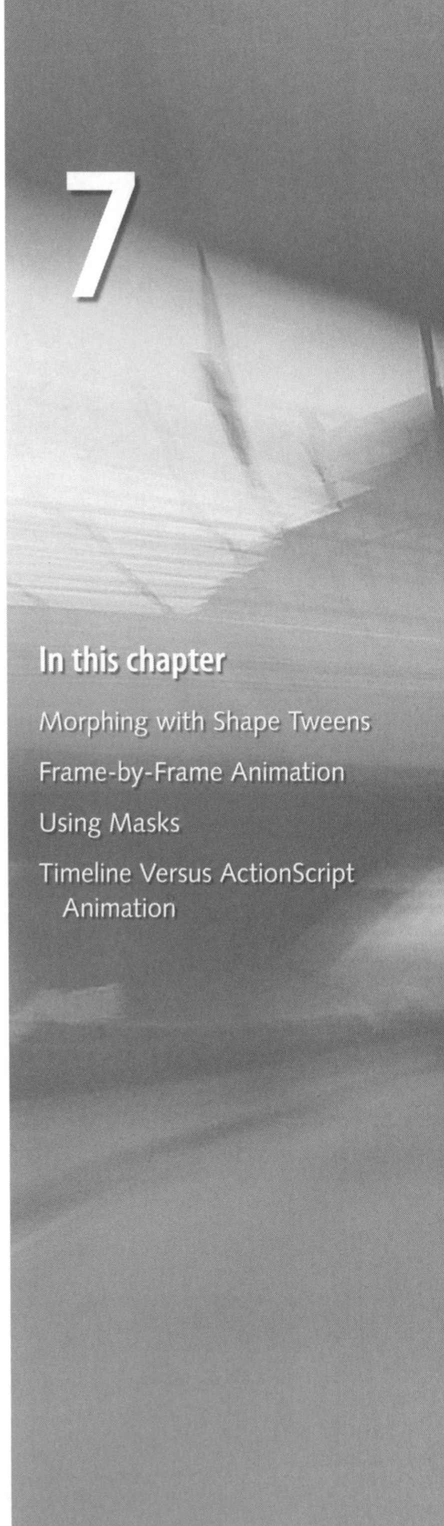

Although motion tweening will likely be the most common animation technique you use in the timeline, there are several other techniques and tools that can help you animate in Flash. This chapter's project calls for you to create an animated advertisement for the sale of a home, and it will give you experience with some of these techniques.

Morphing with Shape Tweens

As you've seen in prior chapters, motion tweens are typically used when you want to move or manipulate a symbol over time. You can change many properties of a symbol instance during a motion tween, but by the very nature of symbols, you can't radically alter their... shapes.

If a bell is ringing in your head, you're on the right track. Shapes are not instances or references to other objects, and they can be altered. Shape tweens, similar in creation to motion tweens, allow you to do so over time. Here's a simple example:

1. Create a new Flash document and save it as *shape_tween.fla* in the *07* folder.
2. Select the Rectangle tool, pick a fill color, and draw a square of approximately 90 × 90 pixels near the left center of the Stage.
3. Add a blank keyframe to frame 12 using the F7 key.
4. Select the Oval tool, pick a contrasting fill color, and draw a circle of approximately 90 × 90 pixels near the right center of the Stage.
5. As you would with a motion tween, select the first keyframe and pick a tween from the Tween menu in the Properties panel. This time, however, pick *Shape*.

6. Save your work and test your movie. The result, over time, looks something like Figure 7-1, seen here in outline view. If you want to check your work, look at *shape_tween_01.fla* in the *07* folder.

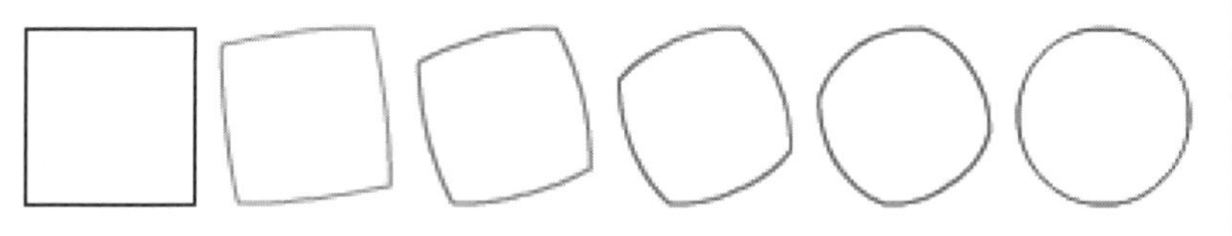

Figure 7-1. A shape tween as it appears over time

The square morphs into a circle over the duration of the tween. Any shape can morph into any other shape, provided there are nothing but shapes in the layer. However, the complexity of vectors can lead to unpredictable results. Look carefully, for example, at the morph you created. It looks as if the square is rotating as it becomes a circle.

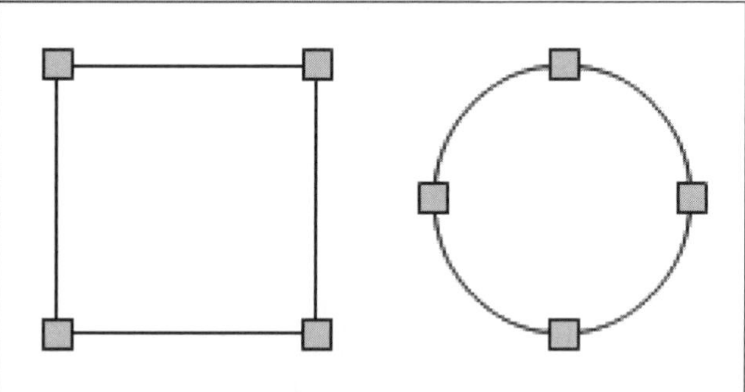

Figure 7-2. The main anchor points of a square and circle, as seen by Flash

This is because Flash is doing its best to figure out how to change one vector into another, and the main anchor points of a square and a circle aren't matching up perfectly. Flash sees the main anchor points of the square in its four corners and the main anchor points of the circle at left, top, right, and bottom, as seen in Figure 7-2. It is matching the anchors of the square and circle, respectively, in pairs: upper-left to left, upper-right to top, lower-right to right, and lower-left to bottom. Therefore, the shape appears to rotate during the tween, even though it's just morphing.

Shape Hints

To improve the quality of the morph, you can add *shape hints* to each keyframe. Shape hints let you tell Flash precisely which points in each vector to match up during the tween. So, if you add shape hints matching the corners of the square with the secondary anchor points of the circle, the morph will no longer appear to rotate. Here's how:

1. Select the first keyframe and choose Modify→Shape→Add Shape Hint (Ctrl/Cmd-Shift-H).
2. A small circle with an *a* inside will appear in the center of your shape. Drag it to the upper-left corner of the square.
3. Select the last keyframe, and you will see a corresponding *a* shape hint. Drag it to the upper-left arc of the circle. (A peek at the final result in Figure 7-3 may help guide the positioning of the shape hints.) These two points will now match up during the tween.

4. Continue the process until you have four matching shape hints. (Often, just one or two hints are enough for Flash to catch on, but sometimes many are required.) The result can be seen in Figure 7-3.
5. Save your work and test your movie. The result will be a cleaner morph from square to circle. If you want to check your work against the sample files, look at *shape_tween_02.fla* in the *07* folder.

> **NOTE**
> *There is a limit of 26 shape hints for each shape tween.*

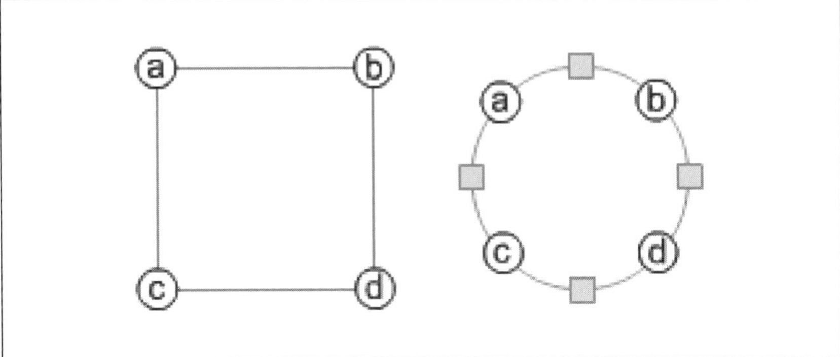

Figure 7-3. Shape hints tell Flash which part of each vector to match up during the tween

The rotation that occurs when the square is morphed into the circle without shape hints is a relatively subtle distortion compared to some of the more severely confused morphs that can occur. A very simple example can be found in the *07* folder of your working directory. Compare *eye_to_i_before.fla* with *eye_to_i_after.fla* to see how shape hints can improve a morph. You can try something like this on your own by morphing one word into another. Flash can't be expected to create the morph the way you want it with so many vectors and without any additional guidance. Shape hints provide the assistance needed in these situations and can really be worth the labor it takes to add them.

Using Shape Tweens in Animations

An oft-seen transition technique is one in which an interface appears to draw itself, line by line, until it is complete and filled with content. This can be accomplished a number of ways in Flash, but one easy way is by shape tweening lines from one size to another. You'll use this method now to draw the outline of a house:

1. Create a new Flash document and save it as *animated_ad.fla* in the *07* folder. Change the document background color to light yellow.
2. Activate the Line tool, and set the stroke color to black with a stroke weight of 1.
3. Draw a very short and straight vertical line at the bottom of the Stage, about one-quarter from the right of the Stage.

4. Convert frame 5 to a keyframe (F6).
5. At frame 5, activate the Selection tool and move the cursor over the top end of the line you drew in step 3. The cursor displays a small right angle icon next to it. This means you are hovering over the end point of a line.
6. Click and drag upward to extend the length of the line to the vertical center of the Stage.
7. Select the first keyframe and apply a shape tween.
8. Press Enter/Return to play the animation.

The line starts short and gets longer, ending at frame 5. The shape tween has effectively drawn the line for you. Continue with the rest of your animation, and draw the remainder of the house outline (it will help, during the descriptions of how to draw each line, to take a look at the finished product in Figure 7-4):

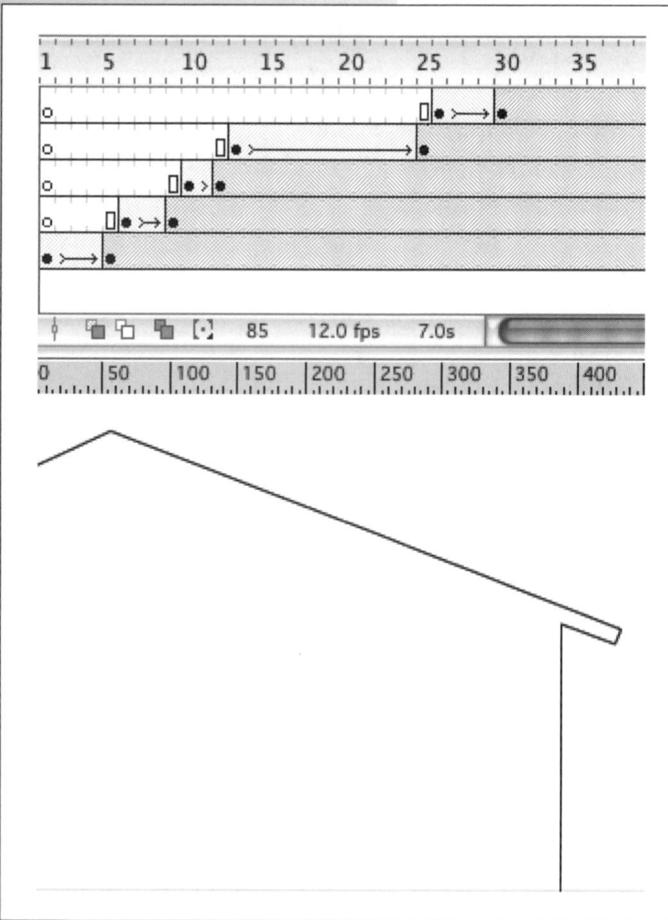

Figure 7-4. The finished shape tween

1. Insert a new layer, and add a keyframe to frame 6 of the new layer. Adding a new layer makes it easier to keep the shape tweens discrete and makes it possible to adjust timing later, if you don't want your animation to be sequential.
2. Add frames, through to frame 85, in your first layer so you can see the previously drawn line to know where to continue drawing. Starting in frame 6 of the new layer, draw a short diagonal line from the top end of the first line down and to the right about 5 pixels.
3. Add a keyframe to frame 9 of *Layer 2* and, in that keyframe, stretch the new line so it's about half an inch long.
4. Add a shape tween to the frame span between frames 6 and 9.
5. Add a new layer, insert a keyframe at frame 10, and draw another short diagonal line up and to the right approximately 5 pixels.
6. Add a keyframe at frame 12, stretch the line, and add a shape tween to the frame span.
7. Repeat steps 5 and 6, drawing short lines in the direction indicated in Figure 7-4 and then tweening them until your timeline and Stage match *animated_ad_01.fla*, located in the *07 folder.*

8. After each shape tween, add frames to the layer until you reach frame 85.
9. Finally, in a new layer called **`actions`**, add a *stop()* action in frame 85.
10. Save your work and test the movie to see the animation.

Frame-by-Frame Animation

Typically, frame-by-frame animation techniques are reserved for things like precise positioning and character animation. However, you can also use frame-by-frame techniques for quick and simple animations, including text effects.

The Cascading Text Effect

In this segment of the project, you'll make the ad headline appear one character at a time, fading in and zooming from 200% to actual size. Done quickly, this is a simple but eye-catching effect:

1. Add a layer above the shape tweens and below the actions, and call it **`headline`**.
2. In frame 30, add a keyframe. Use the Text tool to create a headline centered within the space above the house outline: **`3 BEDROOM, 2-1/2 BATH: $450K`**.
3. Be sure the text is selected, and convert it to a movie clip using F8. Call the movie clip **`headline`**.
4. Double-click the movie clip to edit its contents.

Inside your movie clip, you have one line of text on one layer in a single frame. To generate the cascading text effect, the characters need to tween in, so each one needs to be on its own layer. Use Flash's Break Apart command to split the text into individual characters that can be manipulated as separate elements:

1. With the text selected, choose Modify→Break Apart to separate the characters in the text. Each character now has its own bounding box and can be treated as an individual graphic, as shown in detail view in Figure 7-5.
2. With all the characters selected, use the Modify→Timeline→Distribute to Layers menu command. This will create a new layer for each character.
3. To tween the characters and fade them in, they must be symbols. Select each in turn and convert them to movie clip symbols, naming them clearly as you go. When you reach the first duplicated character, however, name that symbol

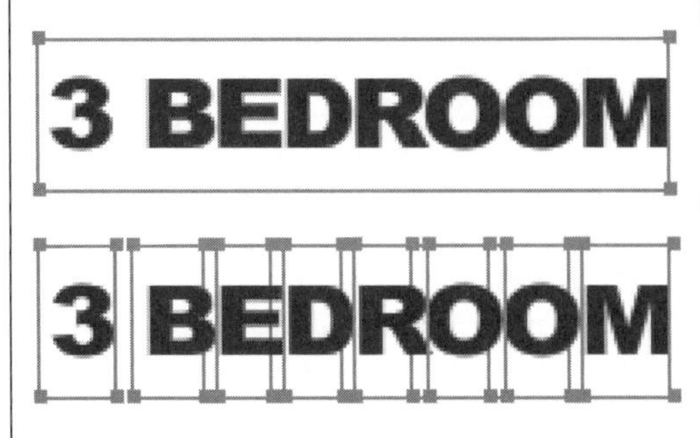

Figure 7-5. Before (above) and after (below) breaking apart the line of text

Delete1. Thus, in *BEDROOM*, the first *O* should be named **o**, but the second should be called **Delete1**. You will also find a repeated *2* and *B* in the headline. Name these **Delete2** and **Delete3**, respectively. This handy trick will allow you to optimize your file by taking advantage of the reuse of symbols.

4. After you're done, swap out the duplicate characters with the first symbols. Select the second *O* in *BEDROOM* and click the Swap button in the Properties panel. The other symbols you've created will be visible. Select the *O* symbol. It will replace the duplicate in the exact same position, and you will have eliminated one unnecessary symbol from your timeline.
5. Repeat step 4 for the duplicated *2* and *B*.
6. Now that you've removed the unneeded symbols from the timeline, you can remove them from the Library. To be sure you haven't made a mistake, select Update Use Counts from the Library's Options menu. (Alternatively, Keep Use Count Updated can be enabled to always show the usage of each Library element.) In the Library column marked Use Count (you may have to widen your Library panel to see it), you should see a zero. If not, check to make sure you've correctly swapped your symbol instances. When the unwanted symbols all show zero use counts, you can delete them.
7. As a last step, name your layers to match the symbol names.
8. Save your work. Your file should now look like *animated_ad_02.fla*.

Now that you have symbols in discrete layers, you can finish the tweens:

1. Reopen the *headline* movie clip and select frame 5 in all the layers by clicking and dragging vertically down the layers. Press F6 to create a keyframe.
2. Move the playhead to the first frame. You want to select the first frame only, in all the layers. In one motion, starting with the top layer, click and drag down through all the layers to select all the characters on the Stage. You will know if you did this correctly because only the first keyframe will appear selected in the timeline, in all the layers.
3. Since you want to scale and fade in each character, you need to give the first keyframe of each letter an alpha of 0 and a scale of 200. While all the characters remain selected, use the Window→Transform command to open the Transform panel. In the first two fields, for horizontal and vertical scale, enter a value of **200%**.
4. In this case, you don't want characters scaling in from off-Stage extreme left or right, because you won't see most of the tween. So, using the Align panel, enable the Align to Stage option and horizontally center the characters. This will pile them all up in the center of the clip.

NOTE

Like most programs, Flash allows you to scale horizontally (also known as _xscale) and vertically (otherwise known as _yscale). In the Transform panel, these properties are set using the first two fields. Double-headed arrows indicate which field is horizontal and which is vertical. You can manipulate each value independently or, with the Constrain option, together.

5. The last thing to do while the characters are still selected is to choose the Alpha color effect from the Color menu in the Properties panel and change the setting to **0**. This will make it look like all the characters have disappeared. However, you can see that they are still selected, so you know only the alpha value for each has changed.
6. Finally, select the first frame in all the layers by again clicking and dragging vertically down the layers. With all the frames selected, choose Motion from the Tween menu in the Properties panel.
7. Add an **actions** layer and place a *stop()* action in the last frame.
8. Save your work and compare your file with *animated_ad_04.fla*.

In just a few steps, you've created a motion tween that fades and scales each of the 24 characters. However, the animation is so quick that it doesn't look very impressive. The characters aren't coming in one at a time, as intended. To accomplish this, stagger the tweens like you did in your first animation in Chapter 3:

1. Reopen the *headline* movie clip.
2. Shift-select all of the frames in the second letter layer (the *B* in *BEDROOM*). Once they're selected, click and drag them two frames to the right with your mouse.
3. Do the same thing with the second letter in *BEDROOM* (*E*), dragging the frames of that layer four frames to the right. The idea is that each successive layer will be staggered two frames to the right, as seen in the detail in Figure 7-6.

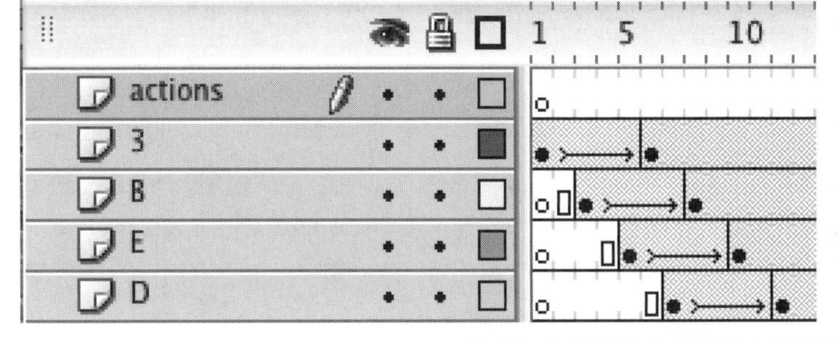

Figure 7-6. A timeline detail for the cascading text effect

4. When you are finished, add frames to all but the last layer, making the frame count consistent for all the layers.
5. Finally, move the *stop()* action in the *actions* layer to the last frame.
6. Save your work and test your movie. Compare your file to *animation_ad_05.fla*.

Text effects with dynamic text

To perform certain text effects, such as rotating text, the outline of the font must be available at runtime. Static text will be converted to vectors for you, so you don't have to worry about it. However, in the future you will want to use ActionScript to control text or allow the user to type in text. In these cases, fonts must be embedded to maintain their visual appearance. This will increase *.swf* download size, but you can try to minimize this effect. (Device fonts—those available on the system at runtime—won't work because the outline information for these fonts isn't available to Flash at runtime.) Here's how to embed a font:

NOTE

Static text and embedded fonts maintain font appearance at runtime, but not during authoring. Temporary font substitution will occur if you try to edit a file without the needed fonts. Since you must be able to edit the sample code provided on the CD, the text has been broken apart into shapes for consistency. However, this is not necessary in your own development.

1. Start with a dynamic or input text field, and use any font you like, including bold or italic, if required.
2. Click the Embed button in the Properties panel to open the Character Embedding dialog. (If you don't see the Embed button, make sure your text field's type is set to Dynamic Text, not Static Text.)
3. In the dialog, multiple-select the ranges of characters you want to embed.

Try to resist embedding the entire font, as this dramatically increases file size. If you know for sure that only a few characters will be used, such as in a headline that reads "FLASH!," you can even embed only those characters using the field at the bottom of the dialog.

Onion Skinning

When using frame-by-frame animation, particularly if you are positioning items by hand in each frame, it can really help to enable *onion skinning*. Onion skinning is a term that describes the ability to see frames before and after the current frame, in varying degrees of opacity, as if each frame had been drawn on the translucent skin of an onion.

Onion skinning is most useful when you are looking at an animation of sequential frames where only the current frame is visible and must be aligned to adjacent frames. Seeing translucent frames before and after the current frame allows you to manipulate art placement to your liking. If you also enable the Edit Multiple Frames option, you'll even be able to adjust more than one frame at a time.

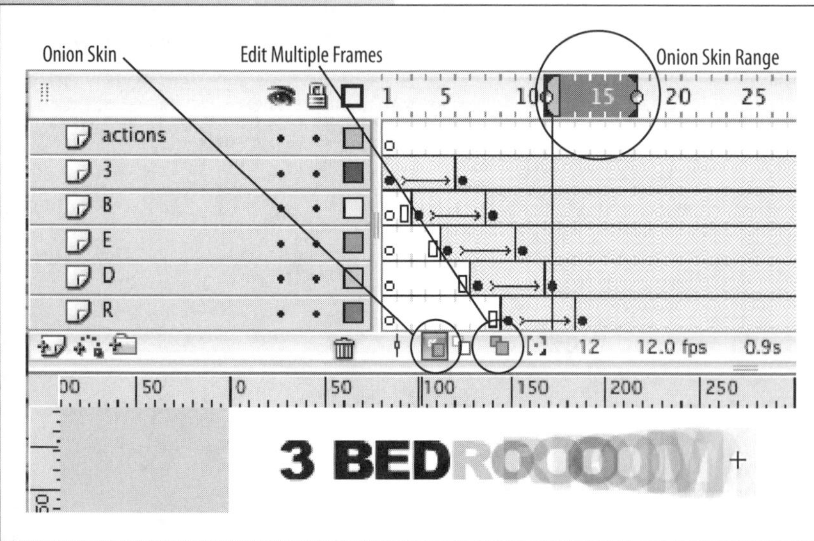

Figure 7-7. A timeline detail illustrating onion skinning

In the context of this project, Figure 7-7 shows five future frames at one particular point in the animation. The Onion Skin option is enabled at the bottom of the timeline. The onion skin range of frames, displayed before and after the current playhead position, is adjusted in the numbered frame bar above the timeline.

Using Masks

Up to this point, you have been working with assets in their entirety. However, it is often desirable to show only a portion of an asset. In some cases, you can simply edit the asset to show only a segment thereof. But if you need to reuse that asset (either in its entirety or a different part of it), you will need to create a copy, increasing file size. *Masks* provide the solution, allowing you to temporarily mask out parts of an asset and reveal only the desired area.

Flash masks simplify the masking process because they actually represent the hole through which you are looking. That is, if you wanted to see a small circular area of an image, you would only have to draw the circle; you wouldn't have to cover up all the unwanted areas of the image. For a more detailed explanation, see the "Masks" sidebar.

In this project, you'll learn how to use timeline mask layers and how to control dynamic masks with ActionScript.

Mask Layers

Your advertisement won't be very successful without a photo, so it's time to add one. Use a mask layer to show a portion of a photo in the area described by your shape-tweened outline:

1. Create a new layer and drag it to the bottom of the timeline so it is beneath the first shape tween layer. Call this layer **house**.
2. Import the *house.jpg* photo and place the photo in the *house* layer. Select the photo and convert it to a movie clip symbol named **houseMC**.
3. Move the playhead to frame 30 so you can see the finished house outline. Position the photo movie clip so that most of the house and a bit of lawn are visible within the area described by the outline and the left and bottom edges of the Stage.
4. The house is also visible outside the outline, so add a mask layer to fix that. With the *house* layer selected, add another layer immediately above it and name it **house_mask**.
5. Double-click the *house_mask* layer icon to open the Layer Properties dialog, and select *Mask* from the available options.
6. Repeat step 5 using the *house* layer, but in this case select *Masked*.
7. You now need to fill in the outlined area with a solid shape to use as the mask for the *house* layer. To speed things along, you can use the mask already provided to you in the source files. As you read briefly in Chapter 5, a file can be opened as an external Library, making it easy to copy assets from that file into your current document. Use the

File→Import→Open External Library menu command to open the *animated_ad_library.fla* file.

8. Drag the *maskGraphic* symbol from the external Library to your main movie and place it in the *house_mask* layer, carefully positioned so the top and right edges butt the outline. It should be placed at approximately (0, 75).

9. To see the effect during authoring, lock both the masking and masked layers. You should now only see the house photo inside the outlined area.

10. Save your work and test your movie.

Your ad is taking shape, but the masked photo detracts somewhat from the impact of the shape tween. Add one final touch by fading in the photo after the shape tween has made its best impression:

1. Click and drag the first keyframe, in both the *house_mask* and *house* layers, to frame 13. Moving the photo to this point lets your shape tweens animate all on their own for the first second.

Masks

You have seen that Flash files are typically created by compositing one or more layers in a file. You've also seen how both the main timeline and movie clip timelines organize the layers and display their contents over time. *Masks* are often used to create traditional visual effects in Flash, such as a spotlight effect in which one layer is viewed through the "hole" created by the masking layer. That is, as shown in Figure 7-8, the *masking layer* defines the area of the underlying *masked layer* that remains visible (the remainder is "masked off" and therefore invisible).

Think of masks as "viewing windows." The graphical shape you place on a masking layer acts as a window, allowing a partial view of the layer beneath it. This is similar to how you can look through a window in your house to see the front yard, but you can't see through the walls, which mask the view of the neighbor's house.

The masking layer masks only the content of a masked layer; it does not affect content on normal layers. If you wish to mask more than one adjacent layer with the same mask, double-click on each and change their layer types to Masked. You can also drag a layer beneath a masked layer (or anywhere in a group of masked layers) to convert it automatically.

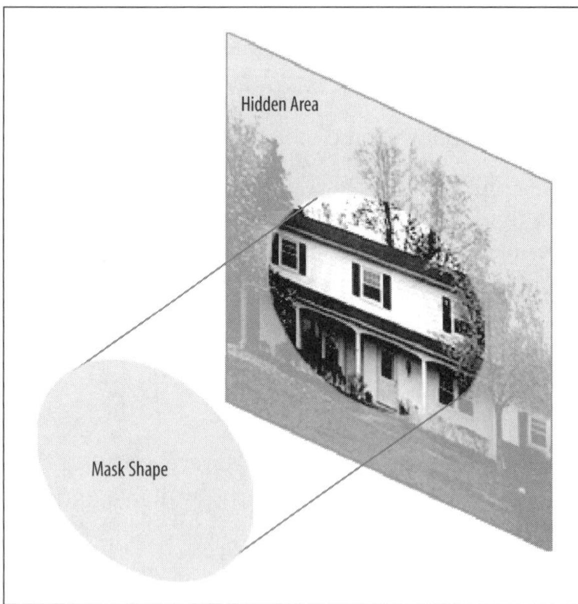

Figure 7-8. The mask area controls what portions of the masked asset are visible

2. One second isn't enough, however, so let the image fade up slowly while the animation finishes. Select frame 48 in the *house* layer, and make it a keyframe.

3. Move the playhead to the first keyframe (frame 13) in the same layer, select the *houseMC* movie clip, and give it an Alpha setting of **0** in the Properties panel.

4. Finally, select the keyframe in the *house* layer in frame 13, and add a motion tween using the Properties panel.

5. Lock the *house* layer again and test your work. Your timeline should now resemble the detail view shown in Figure 7-9. If you wish, compare your progress with *animated_ad_06.fla* in the *07* folder.

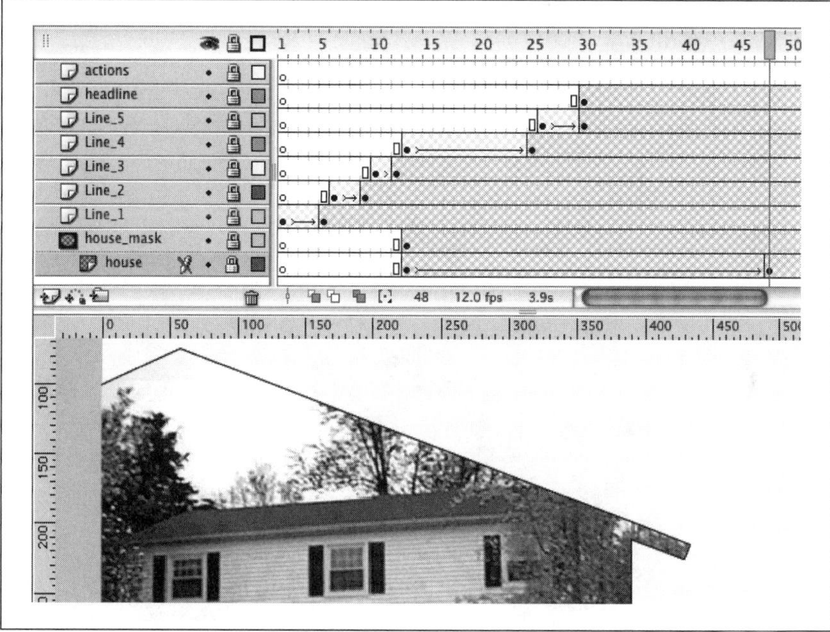

Figure 7-9. The masked layer appears indented beneath the masking layer in the timeline

Scriptable Masks

Mask layers add flexibility when it comes to working with portions of assets, but, as you will read repeatedly in this book, more creative options are possible with the aid of ActionScript. One simple ActionScript method allows you to assign one movie clip to mask another. This means that you can script interactive masks and turn masking on and off.

In this next segment of the project, you'll add representative homeowners to bring a human touch to your ad:

1. Add a new layer named **couple** above the shape tween layers and below the *headline* layer.

> **NOTE**
>
> *Keeping layer names short and descriptive makes it much easier to work with the timeline.*

> **NOTE**
>
> *Symbol names should also be descriptive, but they can be a little bit longer without being cropped by the Library panel. Short and descriptive is also the rule of thumb for instance names, because you will be writing scripts that refer to them. You want to be sure the name is clear, but not hard to type.*

2. Import the *couple.png* file and position the couple on the lawn as if they are about to enter their new home.
3. Convert the photo to a movie clip called **coupleMC**, and give it an instance name of **couple_mc** using the Properties panel.
4. Add another layer directly above the *couple* layer and call it **scr_mask**, short for "scriptable mask."
5. Switch to the Rectangle tool (R) and, in the *scr_mask* layer, draw a rectangle on the Stage with a solid fill and no stroke. Make it tall enough to cover the couple and wide enough to cover a bit of extra space on either side. Don't forget their shadow on the left. The rectangle should be approximately 250 × 115 pixels.
6. Convert the rectangle to a movie clip symbol called **scriptableMask** and give it an instance name of **scrMask_mc**.
7. Position the scriptable mask symbol just to the right of the couple, at approximately (180, 285). When you're finished, the relative positioning should look something like Figure 7-10.

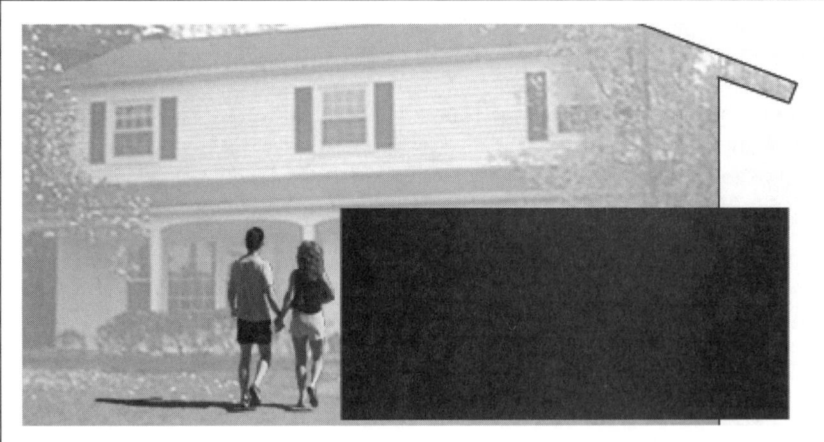

Figure 7-10. The scriptable mask symbol appears just to the right of the couple—the item to be masked.

8. In frame 1 of the *actions* layer, add this script:

```
couple_mc.setMask(scrMask_mc);
```

9. This turns the rectangle into a mask for the couple. Test your movie to make sure that neither is visible. Remember that a mask is a hole through which you see. Since the rectangle is not on top of the couple, you can't see them.
10. Next, make the mask follow your mouse. In frame 1 of the *actions* layer, add to your script by setting up an event handler for the *scriptableMask*

movie clip. Within the event handler, use the self-referential keyword `this` to set the x-coordinate of the movie clip to the x-coordinate of the mouse. The code should look like this:

```
scrMask_mc.onEnterFrame = function() {
    this._x = _xmouse;
};
```

11. Save your work and test your movie. Depending on where your mouse is, you still may not see the couple. Move your mouse over the lawn, however, and the couple should wipe in and out of view. If you like, compare your movie with *animated_ad_07.fla*.

Alpha Masks

The reveal is a nice surprise, but thanks to a new feature in Flash 8, you can make it look even nicer. At long last, Flash 8 can now use alpha data in a mask. This means that your mask can contain a gradient with a color that has, for example, 100% alpha fading to a color that has 0% alpha, giving it soft edges.

Unfortunately, you still can't do this quickly in a mask layer, but accomplishing it with ActionScript is very easy. First, change your scriptable mask by replacing its content with an alpha gradient:

1. Double-click the mask symbol to edit it, and select the solid color you used.
2. Open the Color Mixer. You will create a custom gradient, much the same way you did in Chapter 1.
3. This time, instead of using a radial gradient, switch the gradient type to *Linear*.
4. The color bar at the bottom of the panel should default to solid black fading to solid white. If it doesn't, don't worry. It doesn't matter what color is used in a mask. Click the lefthand gradient color chip and give that color an alpha value of **0**. You should see the grid background in the gradient bar to indicate transparency.
5. You don't have a lot of room to move your mouse and fade in the couple, so make the gradient narrower. Drag the right-hand color chip to the left until it is about a quarter of an inch from the left.
6. Optional: If you want to fade out the couple if you move your mouse too far to the left, you can duplicate steps 3 and 4 with two new color chips in the right half of your gradient. Just like the prior steps, but mirrored horizontally, the extreme right should have an alpha of 0, and another alpha of 100 should be a quarter of an inch from the right edge of the gradient.

7. Your finished gradient should look like Figure 7-11. (If you opted not to use step 6, your gradient will be solid on the right.)

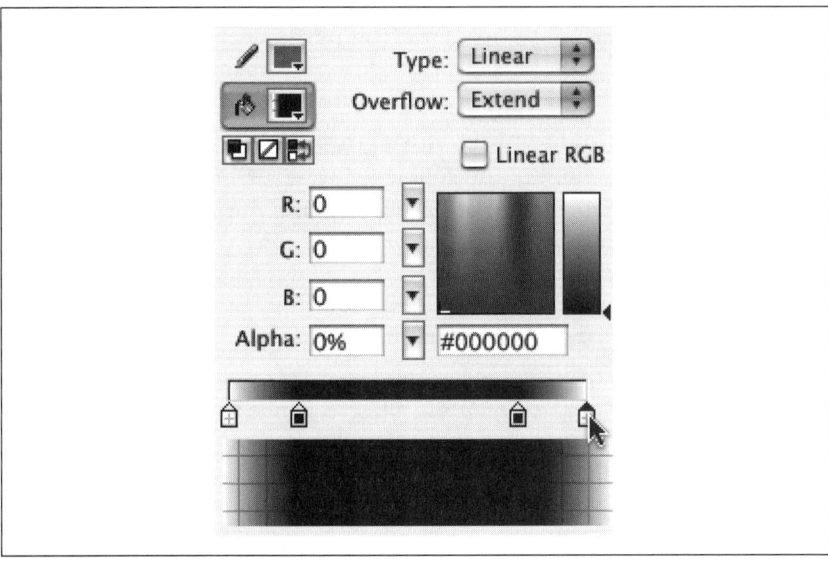

Figure 7-11. The alpha gradient for the scriptable mask—this figure includes the optional gradient on the right

NOTE

If you want to store the gradient for later use, open the Color Swatches panel and click in an empty area to add a swatch. It will appear at the bottom, in the strip of gradient swatches.

8. Because you started by selecting the mask shape before making your gradient, it should not have the gradient applied. If this is not the case, switch to the Paint Bucket tool and apply the gradient to the shape in the mask symbol, *scriptableMask*.

9. Save your work.

If you test your movie now, you may be surprised to see that the mask wipe still uses a hard edge. This is because one final step is required. For the alpha gradient to have an effect, Flash must composite the mask clip and masked movie clip together. For increased efficiency, Flash 8 makes this possible by treating them both as bitmaps.

So, you must select each movie clip and enable runtime bitmap caching. You'll learn more about that in Chapter 10, but for now you should know that, when caching is enabled, Flash caches a bitmap version of a movie clip whenever any major changes are made to it. This allows bitmap transformations, which are often more efficient than vector transformations, to be applied to the clips.

You can enable this property by selecting each bitmap and clicking "Use runtime bitmap caching" in the Properties panel. Or, in your goal to use more and more ActionScript as your comfort level increases, add this to your frame 1 script:

```
couple_mc.cacheAsBitmap = true;
scrMask_mc.cacheAsBitmap = true;
```

Now when you test your movie, you should see the couple fade in with a soft wipe. Your file should now resemble *animated_ad_08.fla*.

Variables and Scope

If you need Flash to remember something for later reuse, you often need to define a variable and populate it with a value. This is similar to how you use the equivalent of variables in your day-to-day life. Every time you make an effort to remember something, you are, metaphorically speaking, using variables. When you commit a phone number to memory, you store that information in a way that allows you to recall it as a phone number, not as something else. For example, you don't try to recall that information by searching your memory for an address.

Storing data in a variable can be as simple as writing:

```
myNumber = 1;
```

Recalling that information only requires that you refer to the variable by name to retrieve its data. For example, the following line will display the value of the variable in the Output panel:

```
trace(myNumber);
```

The Output panel is a text-only window that allows you to display information during authoring as a debugging technique. (It's not available when you view your files in a browser.) It is also used to show you any errors that you may have in your scripts. The *trace()* command simply tells Flash to display something in the Output panel. In this case, testing your movie would display the number `1`.

While putting information into and getting information out of variables is straightforward, being sure to work with the variable you want is important. In most cases, the *scope* of a variable is limited to the timeline in which it is defined.

Consider a file that has a movie clip called *myMovieClip* in the main timeline. A variable defined in the main timeline has a value only in that timeline, and a variable defined in the movie clip will be valid only in the context of that movie clip.

For example, if you wrote the following in frame 1 of the main timeline:

```
myNumber = 1;
myNumber = 2;
trace(myNumber);
```

you would see *2* in the Output panel. The *myNumber* variable is defined in the main timeline, and its value is changed with the second line of the script. However, if you wrote the following:

```
myNumber = 1;
myMovieClip.myNumber = 2;
trace(myNumber);
```

you would see *1* in the Output panel. This is because, although the second line gives *myNumber* a value of 2, it is a different *myNumber*—this variable is a new *myNumber* stored in the movie clip, not the same *myNumber* used in the main timeline. The example above uses the familiar *dot syntax* you've been using for a few chapters, but in this case you are working with a variable, rather than a method or a property. Just as when you started writing event handlers this way, this prevents the need to apply the script directly to the movie clip, so your code is more centralized.

You are not likely to arbitrarily use the same variable name in multiple locations, so that will not often cause confusion. However, sometimes this is good practice, as in the case of multiple movie clips that all share similar functionality but retain some unique variable values that set them apart. For this reason, whether you use the same variable names or not, it helps to understand that even though the same variable name may be used in more than one timeline, scope will affect the population and retrieval of any variable.

Over the next several chapters, you will use variables for a variety of purposes, so you'll have plenty of chances to work with them and understand scope in practice. In the next chapter, you'll also learn about static data typing, which allows you to tell Flash what types of data you will be storing in a variable. This helps Flash warn you when you try to do something unexpected with the data of a specific variable.

For now, however, it's just important that you understand what variables are, and that they are necessary when you need to remember something from one situation to another. You will practice with this concept in the "A Conditional Surprise" section of this chapter.

A Conditional Surprise

You've taken the time to add a sneaky reveal to your ad, to make it more interesting. However, there's still a chance that the surprise can be ruined. If your mouse happens to be near the couple during the opening tweens, the couple may even appear before the house does! To prevent this from happening, you'll need to use a *conditional statement* and a *variable*.

You'll use conditional statements throughout the remainder of this book, and in much of your own scripting. A more in-depth look at these logical structures can be found in the sidebar "Conditional Statements," but, briefly, they are designed to execute instructions only if something else is true. For this reason, they are often referred to as *if statements*. A simple example is: if the light is green, you may drive through the intersection. This type of logical thinking prevents accidents from happening, because the relevant instructions (driving, or showing the homeowners in your file) are executed only when the required conditions are met.

To make a conditional statement work, you need a condition to satisfy. Here, you'll use a variable to store an on/off state for the conditional to check (variables are discussed in greater depth in the sidebar "Variables and Scope"). Much like a light switch, when you set the variable to "on," or "true" in the Flash vernacular, the conditional will work; in this case, your scriptable mask will move with the mouse. When the variable is "off," or "false," the mask will not move and your homeowners will not be visible prematurely.

In the context of your file, if the variable *showCouple* is true, the scriptable mask will follow the mouse. If not, the mask will not be able to move. Here's how to set it up:

1. If you haven't already done so, get out of your scriptable mask and back to the main timeline.

2. In frame 1, change your script a little by using the following *if* statement to surround the line about moving your scriptable mask. The edited section of the script follows, with changes in bold:

```
scrMask_mc.onEnterFrame = function() {
    if (showCouple == true) {
        this._x = _xmouse;
    }
};
```

You will learn about the syntax in an upcoming section of this chapter, so don't worry. The odd repetition of equals signs will be explained!

Adding this code ensures that the mask won't move unless the *showCouple* variable is true. If you test your movie, you will see that the couple never appears. But how can you set the variable to true? One way to accomplish that is to add a button to your ad:

1. Add a new layer above your shape tweens and below the couple, and call it **buy_button**.
2. You don't want the couple to be visible until after your animation is over, so add a keyframe to the last frame, frame 85.
3. In that keyframe, in the *buy_button* layer, create a button in the lower-right corner of the main timeline. The sample file uses a "For Sale" sign, so if you want to use that, take it from the external Library you used when working on your mask layer. See "Mask Layers" for review, if needed.
4. Give your button an instance name of **buy_btn**.
5. In the *actions* layer, in frame 85, add the following button event handler to the existing script:

```
buy_btn.onRelease = function() {
    showCouple = true;
};
```

This script sets the variable *showCouple* to true, and the file now works the way you want it to. However, by using a nice scriptable mask reveal, you've taken the chance that your users may not ever know the couple is there. As an additional measure, add some instructions to encourage them to explore.

Placing the instructions in a keyframe in frame 85 would be adequate, since they won't appear until you are ready for them. However, that doesn't teach you anything new, so you'll put the instructions there but also use another movie clip property to make them invisible until the button you made is clicked:

1. Create a layer called **instructions** above the *buy_button* layer and put a keyframe in frame 85.
2. Select the Text tool and, to the right of the house, add the following text:

   YOU could own this home. (Explore the photo with your mouse.)

   Feel free to be less explicit if you want to leave more to the imagination of the user.
3. Convert the text to a movie clip, call it **instructions**, and give the clip an instance name of **instructions_mc**.
4. Finally, in frame 85, change your frame script to control the visibility of the *instructions_mc* movie clip. When the playhead first enters the frame, the *_visible* property will be set to false. Only when the *buy_btn*

is used is the property set to true. The final frame script looks like this:

```
stop();
instructions_mc._visible = false;
buy_btn.onRelease = function() {
    instructions_mc._visible = true;
    showCouple = true;
};
```

5. Save your work and test your movie. If desired, compare your file with *animated_ad_09.fla*.

Your file should now outline the house that starts to fade in during the outline animation, cascade the headline character by character, and then display a For Sale sign. When you click on the sign the instruction should pop in, and you will be able to see your virtual homeowners when you move your mouse left over the lawn.

NOTE

Adding a new layer for each discrete element is not always necessary. In many cases, it makes your file easier to work with, but adding too many layers can require unwanted scrolling in your timeline. Feel free to combine more than one element in one layer, as long at that layer isn't being used for a tween. Also, don't forget what you learned in Chapter 3: you can group layers into folders in the timeline. The final source file in this project has been reduced to fewer layers using both of these measures, so you can compare timelines and see which approach works better for you.

Conditional Statements

It is not always preferable for all ActionScript instructions to execute right away. You already have experience with triggering scripts only when a user event occurs, such as the press of a button. It's also sometimes desirable to execute portions of code only when certain circumstances are true. This is possible with the use of *conditional statements*.

A conditional, or *if*, statement always tests for truth. You can use a special symbol to test if something is false, but even in that case, you are effectively asking, "Is it true that this is false?" Remembering that you are always testing for truth will get you fewer unexpected results from your code.

Conditional statements can be written with varying degrees of complexity. You can start with a simple test, add alternative actions in case of failure, and even combine more than one evaluation in a single test. You will see examples of all of these scenarios in this sidebar, making the concepts clearer. If any of the symbols used here are unclear, see the "Operators" sidebar.

For all of the examples herein, the following given truths will be used when evaluating each conditional:

```
//givens
x = 2;
y = 3;
myVar = true;
```

The most basic structure of a conditional is a single *if* statement:

```
if (x > 1) {
  stop();
}
```

In this example, the timeline in which this code appeared would be stopped because x, with a value of 2, is indeed

— continued—

Conditional Statements (*continued*)

greater than 1. In addition to a single test, you can also provide an alternative course of action. Consider the following example:

```
if (x > 20) {
    myClip.gotoAndPlay(1);
} else {
    myClip.gotoAndPlay(10);
}
```

Here, because *x* is not greater than 20, the evaluation fails and the second instruction is executed, sending the movie clip *myClip* to play from frame 10. More than one evaluation can be used, too. You must have only one *if* and only one optional *else*, but you can have any number of optional *else if* structures. Here is an example:

```
if (x < 0) {
    trace("x is negative");
} else if (x == 0) {
    trace("x is zero");
} else {
    trace("x is positive");
}
```

In this situation, since *x* is 2, the first two tests will fail and the alternative will execute, placing "x is positive" in the Output panel.

Note the double equals sign in the second (*else if*) test. This is a required comparison operator. The single equals sign you are used to seeing is an *assignment* operator. If the *else if* statement had accidentally been written with a single equals sign, the value of zero would have been assigned to *x*. This event would, of course, always make that test true, since you just made the assignment. Therefore, the result would incorrectly trace "x is zero" in the Output panel, even though *x* is really 2.

In a single *if* structure, however, only one evaluation can be true. If more than one test can evaluate to true, only the first will be executed, and the script will then continue on with any code that follows the conditional. Here's an example:

```
if (x > 0) {
    trace("x is positive");
} else if (y > 0) {
    trace("y is positive");
} else if (myVar == true) {
    trace("myVar is true");
}
```

In this case, all three evaluations are true, but only "x is positive" will appear in the Output panel. All other tests will be skipped, since the first test evaluated successfully.

Note that in the case of variables that have a value of true or false (called *Booleans*), it is possible to condense the test statement by dropping the operator. Remember that an *if* statement tests for truth. Therefore, it is possible to say:

```
if (myVar) {
    trace("myVar is true");
}
```

When greater complexity is required, it is sometimes convenient to use more than one test in an *if* structure. This is possible if you use the *and* logical operator, represented by a double ampersand (&&), or the *or* logical operator, represented by a double pipe (||). They require that *all* or *any* of the tests be true, respectively. For example:

```
if (x > 0 && x < 5) {
    trace("success");
}
```

Since *x* is both greater than zero and less than five, this statement would evaluate successfully. Now consider this:

```
if (x == 2 || y == 10) {
    trace("success");
}
```

Although *y* is not 10, *x* is 2. Using the *or* operator means that one successful evaluation is a successful test, so "success" will still appear in the Output panel.

Finally, if you want to test if something is *not* true, you can use the *not* logical operator. The exclamation point (!) is used to test if something is false. Therefore, looking back on your Boolean test, consider the following change:

```
if (!myVar) {
    trace("myVar is true");
}
```

Using the *not* operator means this would fail, because *myVar* is true.

You've just been exposed to the majority of the possible conditional statement scenarios in one relatively brief assault, so don't feel bad if it takes a while to sink in. This book is designed to revisit these topics in multiple projects, so you'll use conditionals a few more times throughout the book. If any such example remains unclear, refer back to this passage for help.

Operators

An essential element of virtually all ActionScript is the *operator*. A generic description of an operator is a symbol that represents a function already built into the language that acts on an object. In more basic terms, operators typically calculate a new value from one or more existing values. The equals sign (=) is an example of an operator, and it is used to assign a new value to a variable.

For space reasons, this cannot be an exhaustive look at operators of all kinds. Basic operators, such as the arithmetic operators used for addition (+), subtraction (-), multiplication (*), and division (/), will be omitted. Similarly, not every operator in every category will be discussed here, and operators used for more advanced purposes are outside the scope of this text. However, all operators are clearly explained in the help system built right into Flash, as well as numerous online resources. So, if you are ever uncertain about a specific use of an operator, you are never far from a more detailed explanation.

In this sidebar, you will learn about some of the less obvious operators that are used frequently in basic contexts and that may appear in this book. The lines starting with // are comments to help you understand the code, as described in the "Comments" sidebar in Chapter 4.

The most common operator is the aforementioned *assignment* operator, which you have used many times. It is only mentioned in this list to allow you to contrast its look and functionality with the *comparison equals* operator (==) that you will see in just a moment.

```
// assignment operator, single equals sign:
x = 1;
```

The next most common group of operators is the *arithmetic* operators. You no doubt have experience adding two numbers using the plus sign (+). However, you may not have seen the following *shortcut* operators before. These are just pairs of symbols that represent a longer structure used when changing a value by a specific factor. Examples include adding 1 to something, multiplying something by 2, and so on. You will frequently see the first and second examples in loops, as a variable is incremented (or decremented) as the loop progresses.

```
// add one, as in:
// x = x + 1
x++;

// subract one, as in:
// x = x - 1
x--;

// add, subtract, multiply, divide by any number n,
as in:
// x = x + n
x += n;
x -= n;
x *= n;
x /= n;

// example:
// x = x + 10
x += 10;
```

Comparison operators are used in conditional statements. (For more information, see the "Conditional Statements" sidebar.) These operators are used to compare two values. Take special note that when comparing a variable to a value to test if they are equal, two equals signs are required. Also, the exclamation point (!), when combined with the equals sign, means *not equal to*.

```
// less than (or greater than), as in:
if (x > 1) {
}

// less than (or greater than) or equal to, as in:
if (x <= 1) {
}

// is equal to?, as in (note DOUBLE equals sign):
if (x == 1) {
}

// is not equal to?, as in (note DOUBLE equals sign):
if (x != 1) {
}
```

If the double equals sign is not used when required, the familiar functionality of the single equals sign will apply. This is an assignment operator, which is not what you would want to use in this context. See the "Conditional Statements" sidebar for a demonstration of this situation.

—continued—

Operators (*continued*)

The final group of operators discussed here is *logical* operators, which are also used in conditional statements. The first is the *not* operator, which is used to test if something is false. The second two are the *and* and *or* operators, which are used when testing multiple conditions in a single statement.

```
// NOT (!, is movie clip not visible?), as in:
if (! myClip._visible) {
}

// AND (&&, where BOTH must be true), as in:
if (x == 1 && y == 2) {
}

// AND (||, where EITHER can be true), as in:
if (x == 1 || y == 2) {
}
```

If these samples don't all make sense immediately, don't worry. You will use operators in most scripts that you write, and using them will rapidly become second nature. In the upcoming section on ActionScript animation, for example, you will practice with a variety of shortcut operators, and in upcoming chapters you will also use comparison and logical operators. For now, as long as you understand what operators are, you can always look them up to confirm the purpose or syntax of any one.

Timeline Versus ActionScript Animation

Throughout the remainder of this book, you'll use ActionScript more and more to add interactivity and logic to your Flash content. For now, however, start by creating a simple animation once with the timeline and once with ActionScript. Comparing the two processes will help you identify which is most suitable for each situation you encounter.

Many of the same effects that are achieved using motion tweens can also be created using ActionScript. Simple animations may be quick and easy with the timeline, but speed isn't always the only thing to consider. When animating an object on the Stage, for example, ActionScript is smoother. Occasional pauses due to timeline looping can be eliminated with this approach, as can hiccups caused by duplicated frames.

Scripted motion also allows for many (even random) runtime variations, whereas timeline-only motion can't be changed at all. Similarly, scripted animations can respond to user actions (such as following the mouse) in ways that timeline-based animations cannot. This opens up new possibilities for games, physics simulations, and animations that are impractical to create by hand. Therefore, scripted animation can be used when timeline-based animation is not possible or is prohibitively difficult or time-consuming.

Motion Tweens Revisited

As the first step in this part of the project, you'll animate a clock strictly with the timeline. Since you want to concentrate on the pros and cons of timeline tweening and ActionScript animation, it's best to start out with the same conditions in both situations. For this reason, you'll start with a basic clock ready to animate:

1. Using the same file you've been working on, add a new layer above the headline and name it **`clock`**.
2. In frame 85, add a keyframe.
3. Open the *animated_ad_library.fla* using the File→Import→Open External Library menu option.
4. Drag the *clock* movie clip from the external Library into your file, dropping it in the new keyframe (frame 85) of the *clock* layer. Position it at approximately (420, 80).

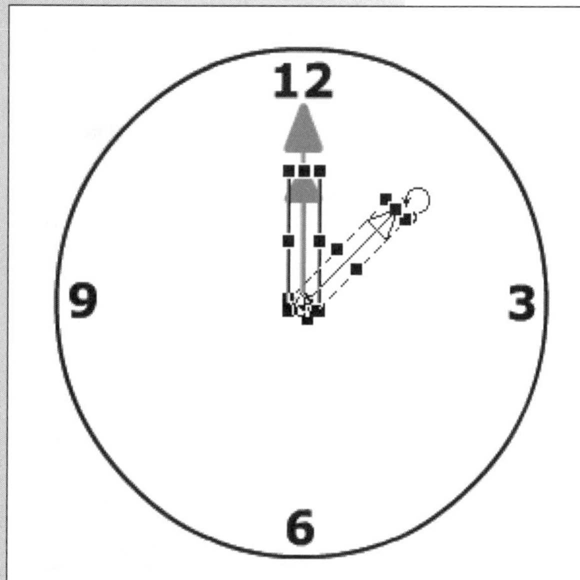

Figure 7-12. Moving the transform point to the base of the clock hand symbol allows for easier rotation

5. Double-click the clock to edit it. You will see that the bottom layer consists of the clock face, the middle layer contains the minute hand, and the top layer contains the hour hand.
6. Zoom in until you can see the hour hand quite clearly. Click on it and notice where the *transform point* is. You will probably recall that the crosshairs are the *registration point*. This is usually the point used to position symbols on the Stage. The small white circle is the point around which transformations (scaling, rotation, skewing, etc.) occur. Choosing the Free Transform tool and selecting any symbol instance adds handles around all sides of the symbol and allows the transform point to be moved. By default, the transform point is the geographical center of a symbol. You will notice in each of the clock hands that the transform point has been moved down to the bottom of the hand, as seen in Figure 7-12. This makes it possible to rotate the symbol instance not around its center point, but around the base of the hand, just like on a real clock.
7. Move the playhead to frame 96. Select frame 96 in all three layers, and add frames (F5). This ensures that each layer's content is visible through to frame 96.
8. Select the first keyframe, at frame 1, of the *hour_hand* layer and create a motion tween. Rather than rotating the hour hand manually, however, look below the Tween menu at the controls that have just been enabled. Select CW from the Rotate drop-down menu and enter **`1`** for the times value, as shown in Figure 7-13. This causes the clock hand to automatically rotate clockwise once throughout the course of the tween.

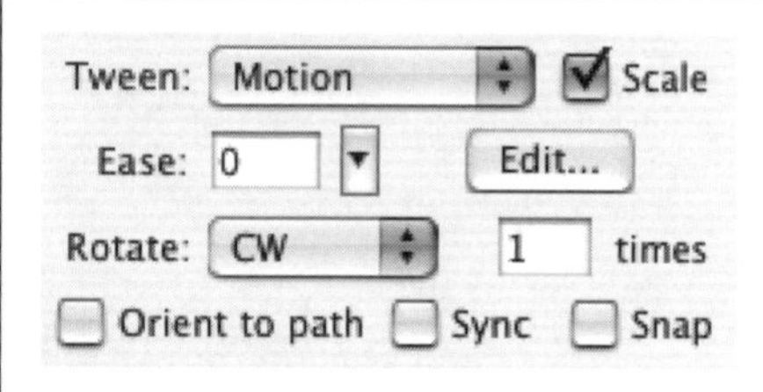

Figure 7-13. Set the clockwise rotation of the hour hand

9. Repeat the process for the *minute_hand* layer, this time entering a value of **8** in the times field. This causes the minute hand to rotate eight times during the tween, causing it to appear as though it's moving much faster than the hour hand as time flies by.
10. Test the movie. The clock pops in at the end of the ad like it should (so it won't detract from the house animation), but it looks a little funny there without anything to tie it to the ad. Place a static text box next to the clock that says:

    ```
    Time is Short. Act Now!
    ```

    Right-justify the text to make it fit nicely with the clock and the slope of the house outline's roof.
11. Save your work and test the movie again. Compare your work with *animated_ad_10.fla*.

Getting the clock hands to rotate around the face of the clock was definitely quick and easy. For simple animations that never change, timeline tweens can be very useful. However, your animation is now set. Although you can certainly make changes to the timeline, the animation cannot vary at runtime. In the next section, you'll replace your clock tweens with an ActionScript solution.

ActionScript Alternative

When animations are created strictly using the timeline, there is little or nothing the user, or you as a programmer, can do to influence those animations at runtime. However, if the movement is controlled with ActionScript, the options available to you and your users are vast. Start by removing the tweens from your timeline-based clock and converting to a simple rotation script:

1. In frame 85, double-click your clock to edit it in place. Delete all frames, except for the last keyframes, in all layers. To do this, select all frames in all layers (except the last keyframes) and press Shift-F5.
2. If you click on each of the hands, you will notice they already have instance names. If this is no longer true, name the smaller hand **hour_mc** and the longer hand **minute_mc**.
3. Above the timeline, click *Scene 1* to get back to your root movie. Still in frame 85, select the *clock* movie clip and give it an instance name of **clock_mc**.
4. In frame 85, add to the frame script in the *actions* layer. Add the following movie clip event handler to control the clock:

    ```
    clock_mc.onEnterFrame = function() {
            this.hour_mc._rotation ++;
            this.minute_mc._rotation += 12;
    };
    ```

5. Save your work and test your movie. With the previous simple script, you have achieved the same kind of animation that you previously did with the timeline with less work, and the result is not only smoother but, as you will soon find out, can be changed at runtime.

Before continuing, review your operators by looking at the functionality of the previous script. Every *enterFrame* handler updates the *rotation* property of each hand. Because the event handler is applied to the *clock_mc* movie clip, the `this` keyword in the handler refers to the clock itself. Within the handler, you see the *hour_mc* and *minute_mc* movie clips inside *clock_mc* targeted. The hour hand should move slowly, so the `++` mathematical shortcut is used to add one degree of rotation to the existing rotation. This is just a shorter way of writing:

```
this.hour_mc._rotation = this.hour_mc._rotation + 1;
```

The minute hand moves 12 times as fast because the `+=` shortcut adds 12 degrees of rotation. Again, this is a shorter way of writing:

```
this.minute_mc._rotation = this.minute_mc._rotation + 12;
```

Now it's time to learn how to change the animation on the fly. You are going to write a very simple routine that doesn't even require conditionals to change the rotation direction of the clock hands. To do this, you need to first create a variable that will be used as a multiplying factor.

If you multiply the degrees you're adding to the rotation of each hand by 1, nothing will change: 1 multiplied by 1 is still 1, and 12 multiplied by 1 is still 12. However, if you multiply 1 and 12 by –1, you will get –1 and –12, respectively. When you add a negative rotation, the hands will rotate backwards!

1. In the same script, replace the existing *clock_mc* event handler with the following script:

```
speedFactor = 1;
//
clock_mc.onEnterFrame = function() {
        this.hour_mc._rotation += 1 * speedFactor;
        this.minute_mc._rotation += 12 * speedFactor;
};
//
clock_mc.onRelease = function() {
        speedFactor *= -1;
};
```

2. Save your work and test your movie. The clock will now rotate backwards if you click on it. Better yet, if you click on it again, it will rotate forwards again. Why? Because, as you saw previously, if you multiply 1 by –1, you will get –1, causing a backward rotation. However, if you multiply –1 by –1, you will get 1 again, causing a forward rotation. Again, a simple script makes your file much more dynamic and fun for the user. But you're not finished yet...

3. Add the following two event handlers, save your work, and test your movie:

```
clock_mc.onRollOver = function() {
        speedFactor *= 4;
};
clock_mc.onRollOut = function() {
        speedFactor *= .25;
};
```

The first event handler adds a new change when you roll your mouse over the clock. It takes whatever the existing *speedFactor* variable is (either 1 or –1) and multiplies it by 4. This makes the hour hand rotate at 4 or –4 degrees per *enterFrame* while the minute hand rotates at 48 or –48 degrees per *enterFrame*, making the rotation four times as fast.

The second event handler changes the variable again when your mouse is moved off the clock. In this case, it multiplies the *speedFactor* value by one-quarter, restoring it to its previous speed. Now the clock can be changed with three different event handlers, moving smoothly in two directions at two different speeds.

Your ad is finished. If you want to compare your work to the source files provided, your movie should now be very similar to *animated_ad_complete.fla*.

What's Next?

As you can see, Flash provides a wide array of animation tools and techniques for you to use. Making the most of Flash often comes down to choosing the right tool for the job.

Before moving on, practice with some of the skills you've learned in this chapter. Try to create some interesting shape tweens, morphing words into drawings and drawings into words. You'll probably need to use shape hints for more complex images, but the review may help develop your tweening skills. Try a hand-drawn animation and see if the Onion Skin feature, perhaps in concert with the Edit Multiple Frames option, helps you perfect the final sequence.

You will likely find yourself using masks more often than you think, so brush up on their use. Don't think of masks strictly as an animation technique. They can be useful in animations and as transitions, but they are also useful in experimental art and even in more static application interfaces. Try creating something new with a scriptable mask, and adding alpha transparency to the effect.

Finally, take a moment to review the previous in-depth looks at ActionScript—not only in this chapter, but in previous chapters as well. Remember that the sidebars in this book are not meant to be casual supplemental references.

Rather, they are meant to be isolated explorations that have been separated from the main text to allow a smoother flow of the step-by-step projects. You'll be using a lot more ActionScript from here on out, so this extra effort will serve you well.

In the next chapter, you'll learn how to work with sound. You'll see:

- How to import audio files for use in the timeline
- How to make basic edits to embedded sound files
- How to encode sounds for use when loading them externally
- How to use components to control external sounds
- How to write your own sound control scripts when component use is not preferred

Using Sound

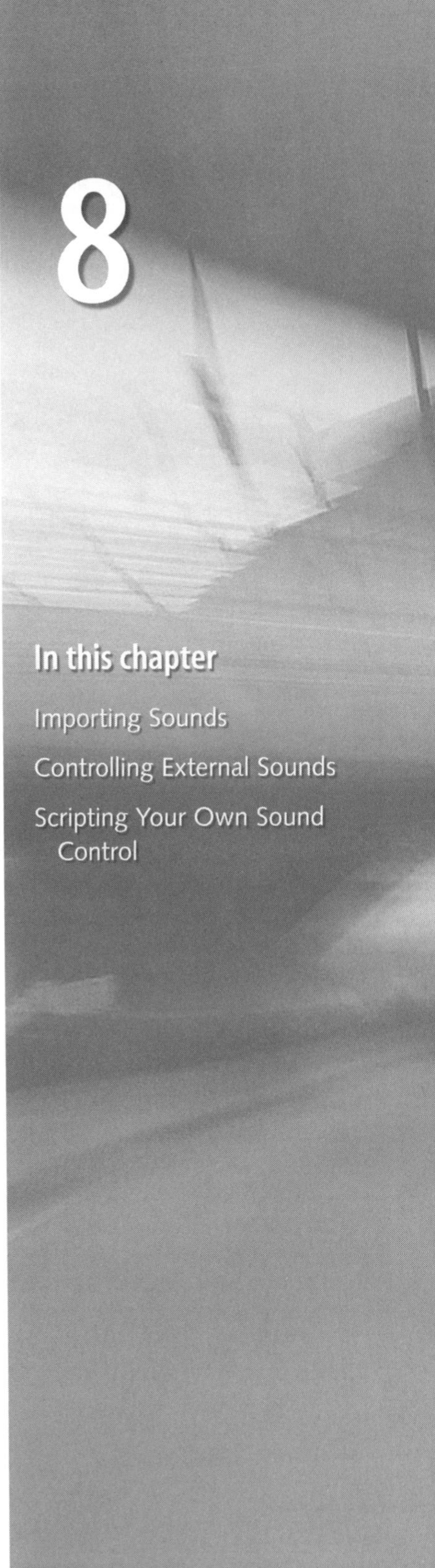

Used carefully, sound can dramatically enhance an animation or interactive experience. Music can be used for animation soundtracks, and sound effects can add a touch of realism to an animation or a bit of life to an interface. However, it's important to remember that sound doesn't usually come without a price. Sound files can contribute significantly to the size of a SWF, and sound can be overused or used gratuitously, detracting from the overall effect. The task, therefore, is to know how and when to use sound for maximum impact.

Importing Sounds

There are two primary ways to use sound in Flash. The first is by importing a sound into Flash so that it is distributed as part of the compiled *.swf* file. The second is by loading an external sound at runtime using ActionScript. In most cases, your project will be better served by loading external sounds during playback. This helps keep the size of your main *.swf* down and makes it easier to update your project.

However, there are some cases where internal sound is preferred. Perhaps the most common need for internal sound is when you want to try to synchronize audio and visual assets. Another example is when you don't know enough ActionScript to load the sounds yourself and you are not satisfied with using a Flash component. Finally, you may need to confine your project to a single *.swf* for use in content management systems that don't play nice with external assets.

Preparing Sound for Import into Flash

Flash can import a variety of standard file formats, including AIFF (Mac only), WAV (Windows only), and MP3 (both platforms). If you have QuickTime installed, it can act as a conduit to allow AIFF and WAV to become cross-platform file formats, importable into Flash on both Macintosh and Windows machines.

Many developers say that importing uncompressed AIFF or WAV files will give you the best sound quality. This is because Flash will compress the files when publishing to *.swf*. When uncompressed sounds are used, Flash will not be compressing an already compressed sound and, therefore, will not contribute to further sound quality degradation.

Other developers argue that using uncompressed sound makes the *.fla* file too large and unwieldy and dramatically increases publishing time. It becomes time-consuming to test your movie during development, and harder to open and store each file.

As is often the case, you will need to do what you find to be best for you. Try working with your preferred higher-quality format, WAV or AIFF, and then contrast that same working experience with using MP3 files. For the import examples in this book, all three file formats have been provided.

Sync Type

For imported sound files, Flash offers a few basic ways of dealing with the audio. To see them in action, first import two sounds to work with and place one in your timeline:

1. Create a new file and save it as *stream_sound.fla* in the *08* folder of your working directory.
2. Import the *Nero* file from the *08* folder, selecting the compression format of your choice.
3. For consistency, open the Library panel and rename the file to *Nero*, removing the file extension from the original name if necessary. You won't have to do this in your day-to-day work, but keeping the name consistent with this text will make the projects easier to follow.
4. To examine basic timeline sound options, add a sound to frame 1. To do this, select frame 1 of *Layer 1* and, in the Properties panel, pull down *Nero* from the Sound menu. Finally, choose *Stream* from the Sync menu. Your Properties panel should now look like Figure 8-1.
5. Save your file.

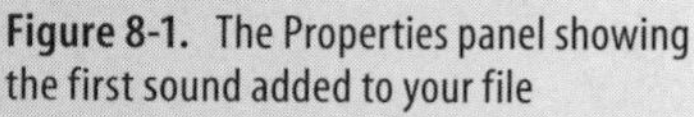

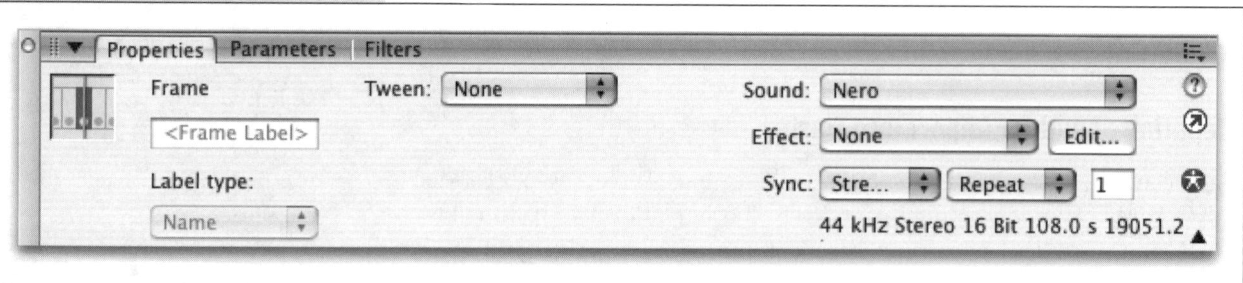

Figure 8-1. The Properties panel showing the first sound added to your file

The Sync menu, as seen in Figure 8-1, is where you choose how Flash handles your timeline sound. Choosing the appropriate sync type can significantly improve the user's experience when viewing your file. Here is a brief overview of each type:

Event
: Plays sounds beginning when the playhead first enters the starting keyframe and lasting until the sound is finished, independently of the timeline. This is an important factor to consider. It means that, for example, the sound will continue to play even if the *.swf* stops playing, and if the sound is triggered again, another instance of the sound will play even if the previous instance is not finished. Also, event sounds must be fully downloaded before they can play. For these reasons, event sounds should be limited to very short sounds placed in the timeline, such as a sound meant to simulate a user's mouse click. In these cases, it is unlikely that multiple occurrences of the sound will overlap or linger beyond their intended playback duration.

Start
: As with the Event sync type, plays sounds until they are finished, independently of the timeline. However, if the sound is already playing, no new instance of the sound plays.

Stop
: Takes the Start sync type one step further, preventing multiple instances of the sound from playing, but also stopping the sound when the last keyframe of the frame span in which it resides is reached.

Stream
: Attempts to synchronize the sound with the timeline in which it resides. The Stream sync type does its best to force the timeline animation to keep pace with stream sound. As with most video technologies, if the animation cannot keep pace with the sound, Flash will skip frames in the timeline tray to sync them up. Stream sounds stop when their frame spans elapse or when the *.swf* stops playing. Most importantly, stream sounds, like the timeline itself, can begin to play even while the remainder of the *.swf* is downloading. For all of these reasons, stream sounds are best for long audio files, such as soundtracks and ambient sounds.

Sounds can be repeated or looped, and the number of times this occurs can be specified in the field provided. It's not a good idea to loop streaming sounds, though, because Flash will expand the file size by the number of loops. If looping is desired, Stop is typically the recommended sync type.

To get a feel for how this works in practice, try working with a few examples of the Stream and Event sync types.

Using stream sounds

The *Nero* sound you placed in frame 1 is a long music file suitable as a soundtrack for an animation. In fact, you will see this file in use as a video soundtrack in Chapter 9. In your current setup, however, the sound will play for only one-twelfth of a second (assuming Flash's default frame rate of 12 frames per second), because the sound currently spans only one frame.

Add the required frames and listen to the sound:

1. To allow the sound to play through to its end, add 1300 frames to *Layer 1*. You may need to add them in two or three steps, as Flash optimizes its interface by displaying only a minimal number of frames until you need more.

> **NOTE**
>
> *You may notice the waveform visible in the layer as you add frames. This can be handy when trying to match animation events to portions of the audio. You can increase the size of timeline layers to better see the waveform by using the menu at the end of the frame number bar, located directly above the timeline's vertical scrollbar. If Large isn't big enough, you can select Preview. This adds the benefit of placing thumbnail previews of each layer's content in the timeline. It can take a while to generate the thumbnails, though, so use this view only when needed.*

2. Save and test your movie. It will take a little more time than usual because the sound is being compressed.
3. You will hear the sound play until the end (approximately 1 minute and 48 seconds), and then it will loop. This looping is not part of the sound itself; it occurs because the end of the file was reached and, without an ActionScript command to the contrary, Flash loops the *.swf* by default.

Using event sounds

As described earlier, for small, short sounds, one of the other sync types is preferable to Stream. Take a look at how the Event sync type can be used to play a short sound effect when you click a button:

1. Open the *alert_example.fla* file in your *08* folder and save it as *button_sound.fla* in the same folder.

   This file has been set up with two keyframes with simple stop actions, and a button script in each keyframe that sends the playhead to the other keyframe. It's a simple simulation of an alert dialog. In frame 1, pressing the button to continue your way through the program causes a warning to be displayed. You then continue past the warning—in this case, cycling through the process again for tutorial purposes.

2. Test the movie to try it out. There's no sound, but you will add that next. When you understand the simple file structure, continue on.
3. Import the *bip* audio file. Again, use the file format of your choice and rename the sound to *bip*, removing the file extension if necessary, just for consistency.
4. Double-click the button to edit it. Add a new layer called **sound** and put keyframes in the Down and Hit state frames.
5. Select the Down state frame and add the *bip* sound via the Sound menu in the Properties panel. Select Event from the Sync menu. Your edited button should now look like Figure 8-2.
6. Save your work and test the movie. You should now hear a sound each time the button is pressed. If you want to compare your file with the source file provided, it should now resemble *button_sound_01.fla*.

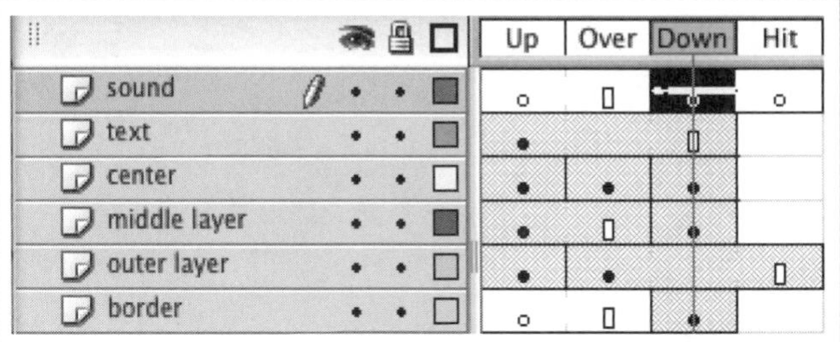

Figure 8-2. The edited button with the sound in the Down state frame

In this example, notice that the sound occurs both when the alert is displayed and when you continue past the alert. This is because the sound is in the button, and the button is used in both places.

However, you can reconfigure the file structure slightly so the sound is heard only when the alert is displayed:

1. Open the *alert_example.fla* file in the *08* folder again. This time, save it as *frame_sound.fla* in the same folder. In this example, instead of placing the sound inside the button, you will place it in the frame in which the alert is displayed.
2. Create a new layer called **sounds** in the main timeline, and create a keyframe in frame 2.
3. Using the same procedure you've used the last couple of times, use the Properties panel to add the *bip* sound to frame 2 in the *sounds* layer. Your edited timeline should now look like Figure 8-3.
4. Save your work and test the movie. You should now hear the sound when the alert is displayed, but not when you continue on afterward. Placing the sound in the frame with the alert, and not within the button, localizes it to the alert. This allows you to reuse the continue button when it suits you. If you want to compare your file with the source provided, it should now resemble *frame_sound_01.fla*.

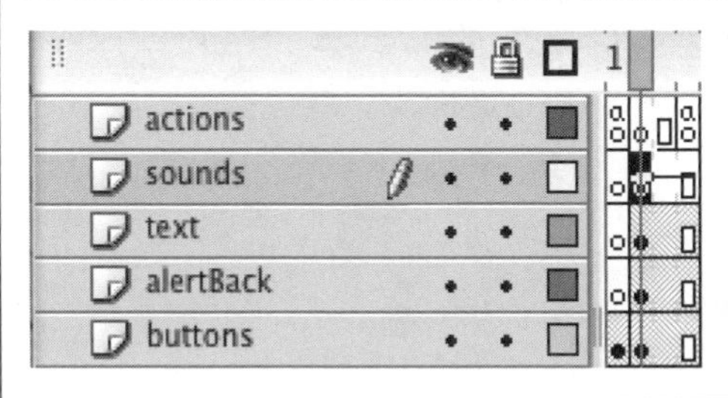

Figure 8-3. The edited timeline with the new sound in the new sounds layer

Compression Settings

Regardless of which sync type suits your specific situation, you can apply one of many compression algorithms to the sound when publishing to *.swf*. Whether you like it or not, compression is a battle between quality and file size. The trick is to determine which setting gives you the lowest possible file size without ruining fidelity.

Detailing the various compression options available is outside the scope of this text, but here are some basic guidelines to get you started:

- When delivering your content via a network (either the Internet or a local network such as an intranet), it is usually a good idea to choose MP3 as your compression scheme. This is Flash's default option.
- Whenever possible, use 16-bit sounds. 8-bit sounds are too hissy and degraded, and thanks to advancements in compression technology, they yield few benefits over 16-bit files.
- Use the lowest sample rate you can without compromising quality beyond acceptable standards. Typically, you will use 22.050 kHz for network delivery. You may use 11.025 kHz for speech only, and you may use 44.100 kHz for disc-based delivery (as in kiosk use or CD-ROM delivery).
- Taking the previous tip further, when working with Flash, always make sure you use a sample rate that is derived from 44.1 kHz. Otherwise, Flash will resample the audio, altering its pitch. This is really important in the world of MP3 compression, because many software packages offer sample rates of 32, 24, and 16 kHz, among others. This is a common problem, so watch for it.
- Use mono when you can, to keep file size smaller. You can still pan and fade mono sounds using in-Flash editing techniques and ActionScript, both of which you will learn about in upcoming sections of this chapter.
- When your chosen compression option offers a quality setting (such as the MP3 option), you can save development time by using the fastest option during development and switching to the best option for final output.

There are many more subtleties you may wish to consider, as these brief tips cover only the simple settings that you have direct control over in the Flash interface. Also, these tips do not cover basic optimization efforts, such as using loops instead of longer files when possible and trimming any unwanted leading or trailing segments of your sound. The Flash Help system, as well as numerous online resources, can provide additional information.

In Flash, you can apply these settings in two ways. In File→Publish Settings, in the Flash section, you can select global compression settings that will apply to the entire file by default. However, as you saw with graphics compression in Chapter 5, you can also set the compression settings on a case-by-case basis in the Library. Right/Ctrl-click on any sound in the Library, and the Sound Properties dialog will appear. Here, you can change the settings for each individual sound.

Simple Edits

In addition to basic playback options, Flash provides simple sound editing capabilities. With a sound in a frame selected in the Properties panel, clicking the Edit button will open the Edit Envelope dialog, seen in Figure 8-4. In this rudimentary editing environment, you can use volume markers to create fades, pans, and segments marked by in and out points.

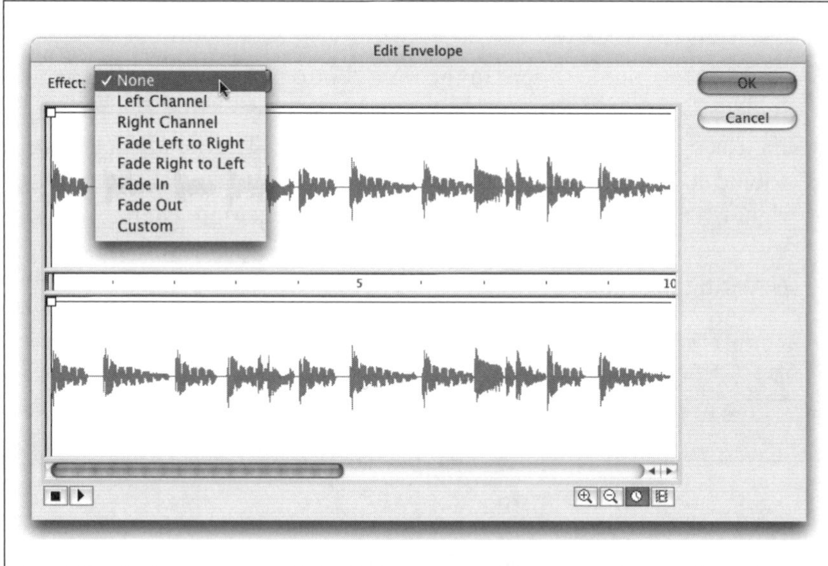

Figure 8-4. The Edit Envelope dialog, with the Effect menu displayed

The Effect menu in the upper-left corner of the dialog allows you to choose from preset effects, but you can also create your own:

1. Reopen the *stream_sound.fla* file you created earlier.
2. Select frame 1 of *Layer 1*, where you placed the *Nero* sound clip. In the Properties panel, click the Edit button next to the Effect drop-down list.

   For a stereo sound such as this one, you will see two sound waves. (A mono sound will display only one sound wave.) They represent the sound data in the left (top sound wave) and right (bottom sound wave) stereo channels. The horizontal bar in the center of the panel displays the time of the sound clip. Using the bottom-right buttons, this time can be displayed in seconds or frames, and the magnifying glass can be used to show more or less of the sound wave at once.

3. Click the Zoom Out magnifying glass three times, until your sound wave resembles Figure 8-4.
4. In the upper-left corner of each channel, you'll see a small square resting on a horizontal line that spans the length of the sound. This is a *volume control handle*. Using as many handles as necessary, you can change the volume of a sound over time, allowing for fades and pans.
5. At frame 8, click the volume line in the left (top) channel. A handle will be added to both channels at this point.
6. Repeat this process at frame 4.
7. In the left (top) channel, drag the handle you just created (at frame 4) down to the bottom of the channel. This causes the volume to drop to zero in this channel only, over four seconds.
8. Reduce the volume to zero in the right (bottom) channel, using the first handle. This causes the volume to start at zero in this channel only, increasing to full volume over four seconds. The handle placement should look like Figure 8-5. The resulting effect is a pan from left to right over the first four seconds, and then, as the right channel stays at full volume, an increase in the left channel over the next four seconds, centering the sound.

Figure 8-5. Using volume control handles to create a pan over the first four seconds and a center over the next four seconds

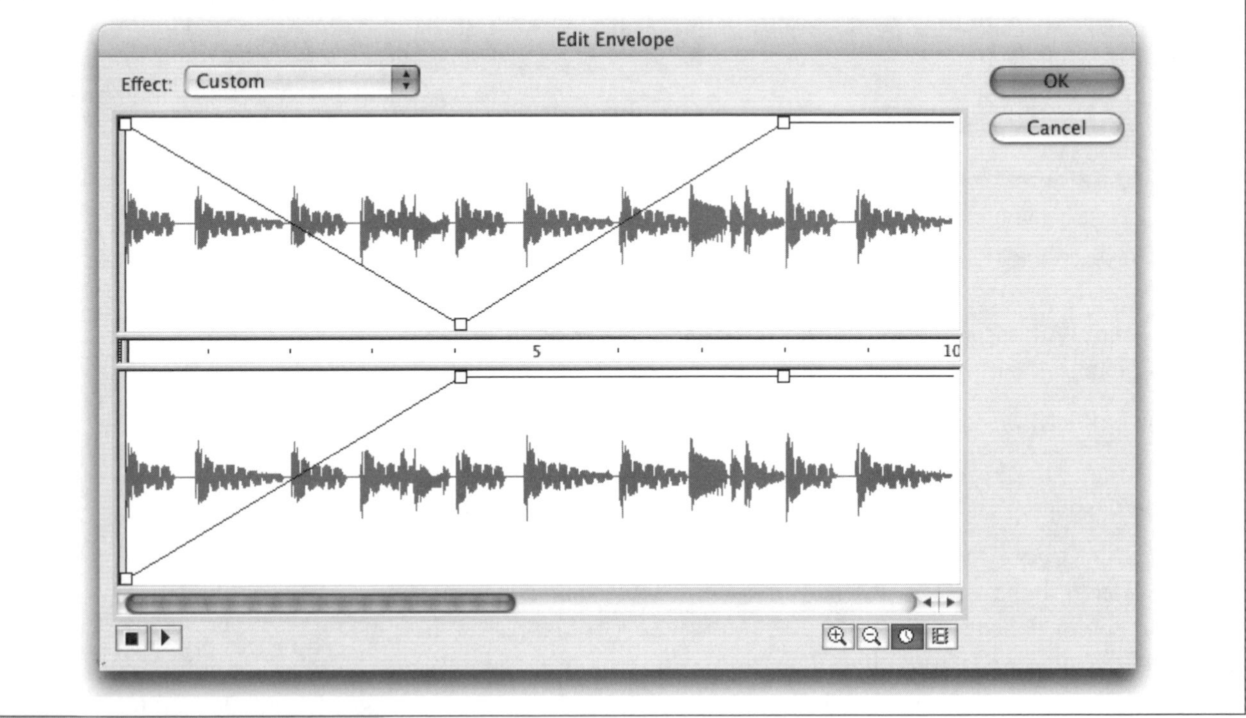

9. Use the play button in the lower-left corner of the dialog to make sure you're happy with the results of your edits.
10. Click OK to close the dialog box, then save your work and close your file.

This technique not only lets you make changes to the sound, but it does so on an instance basis. This means that you can create an envelope for a sound in frame 1, and then a different envelope for the same sound used in another part of the timeline. By positioning two volume control handles atop each other in one channel, you can get an immediate muting of a sound, allowing for in and out points without the need for fades.

While handy for quick edits, these tools are understandably crude. If you need more exacting edits or audio processing effects, or if you do not need the entire audio clip, it is usually best to use an external sound editor. You'll look at that next.

NOTE

If you do not already have a favorite sound editor, the free, open source, cross-platform Audacity (http://audacity.sourceforge.net) is a good place to start.

Controlling External Sounds

One of the best ways to keep file size, and therefore download time, to a minimum is by keeping as many assets as possible external to your main file. You will look at this extensively in Chapter 12, but you will focus exclusively on sound in this chapter. Loading and playing external sounds makes the playback experience fast and efficient, and makes it easier to work on the project as a whole. Publishing your files will be faster because you won't have to compress internal sounds each time, and it's easier to update external files because editing the main *.fla* is usually not required.

There are a few ways to work with external sounds. Here, you will look at how to use components to load and control the audio files with a little scripting, and then you will see how do similar things by writing code of your own.

Encoding

You read earlier in this chapter that Flash can import a variety of sound formats. When it comes to loading external sounds, however, MP3 is the only encoding option. The same guidelines that applied to encoding imported sounds also apply to encoding external sounds—particularly making your sample rate a derivative of 44.1 kHz.

Media Components

In some projects, all you need or want is a simple controller that will load your file and play it. In other cases, a simple controller is needed to allow the user to play back the sounds as desired.

Your next mini-project is to whip up a controller in just a few seconds, to show you how easy it can be:

1. Create a new Flash file, and save it as *media_components_mp3.fla* in your *08* folder. Give it dimensions of 320 × 90 pixels.
2. Name the first layer **`components`**, and create a new layer called **`actions`**.
3. Open the Components panel and drag the *MediaDisplay* component to the Stage in the *components* layer. It can be found in the *Media Player 6 – 7* components category. (Despite the category name, these components also work in Flash Player 8.) This will specify the source file to play—in this case, an MP3.

NOTE

When working with video files, the MediaPlayback component contains everything you need. However, this is awkward when using MP3 files because they have no visual data. The separate MediaDisplay and MediaController components are an alternative to the integrated MediaPlayback. They allow you to target a source in the display component but tuck it away by positioning it off-Stage or making it small. The controller can then appear self-contained.

4. Using the Properties panel, size the *MediaDisplay* component to 10 × 10 pixels, position it at (0, 0), and give it an instance name of **`my_display`**.

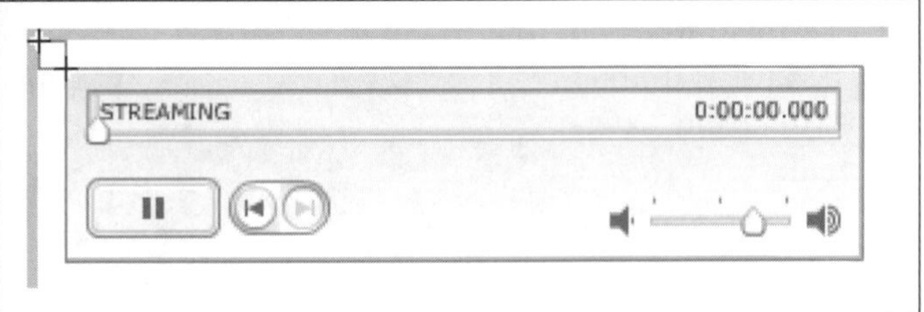

Figure 8-6. The MediaController component controls the MediaDisplay component, minimized but visible in the extreme upper left of the Stage

5. From the same category in the Components panel, drag the *MediaController* component to the Stage in the *components* layer. This will control the MP3 file specified in the *MediaDisplay* component. Position it at (10, 10), and give it an instance name of **`my_controller`**. Your Stage should now look like Figure 8-6.
6. As you have seen before, one way to set the component parameters is by using the Component Inspector. Select the controller and open the Component Inspector (Window→Component Inspector). The default display behavior of the controller is to show a progress bar continuously, but to automatically show the controller elements only when rolling over the controller. In the Component Inspector, change the *controllerPolicy* parameter from *auto* to *on*. This setting always shows the controller. For this mini-project, this is the only setting you need to configure in the controller.

All that remains is to identify which MP3 to play—in this case, the *Nero* music track you used earlier—and to associate the controller with the display. This specifies which display, and therefore which MP3, to control. Using the Component Inspector to configure parameters is great for anyone who doesn't know ActionScript, but you are reading to learn, so you'll set the remaining minimal parameters using code. Even though you already set the controller display mode using the Component Inspector, the ActionScript to accomplish this has been included here for the sake of completeness:

7. Add the following script to frame 1 in the *actions* layer:

```
my_display.contentPath = "nero.mp3";
my_display.associateController(my_controller);
my_controller.controllerPolicy = "on";
```

8. Save your work and test the movie. Your file should now resemble *media_components_mp3.fla*. The sound file should begin playing immediately, which is the default behavior, and you should be able to control its playback with the controller.

Data Types

Data types, by themselves, are exactly what their name implies: types of data. For many reasons, it is helpful to be able to distinguish one kind of data from another when running a script. For example, to avoid errors, it would be helpful to know that you were performing a mathematical operation on a string if you thought the data you were manipulating was really a number.

Flash recognizes many data types. Some are quite general programming types, such as *Number* (a numeric value), *String* (text, or a string of characters), and *Boolean* (a true or false value, which you read about when learning about conditionals in Chapter 7). Still others are very Flash-specific. For example, when you refer to a movie clip in a script, it too has a data type: *MovieClip*. There are also data types such as *Sound* and *Video*. Many ActionScript classes, including *MovieClipLoader* and *LoadVars* (both of which you will use in this book), have associated data types, too.

If most of the focus on data types is behind the scenes, as it has been so far in this book, you don't have to worry about it. The original version of ActionScript, now referred to as ActionScript 1.0, automatically *cast* data into the correct type whenever possible. This is known as *dynamic typing* because the data types are dynamically reassigned.

The downside to this approach, however, is that you aren't warned when this occurs, so you have no way of knowing it's happened. Consequently, it's harder to know how to find a bug in your code.

ActionScript 2.0, first introduced in Flash MX 2004, brought true object-oriented programming to Flash. ActionScript 2.0 is not an entirely new language, but it is much more mature and capable than its predecessor. In some ways, it is more similar to robust low-level languages such as Java. The object-oriented aspects of ActionScript 2.0 are beyond the scope of this text. However, you will look at another important concept ActionScript 2.0 introduced, which does not rely on object-oriented techniques: *static typing*.

Unlike the dynamic typing of ActionScript 1.0, static typing requires that you declare what kind of data will be stored in a variable, for example, and will not automatically cast to another type. This means an extra step or two when writing your scripts, but it has the huge advantage of warning you about data type mismatches when you compile your code. Right away, you know there is an error and where it is. If you can determine why a mathematical operation is being applied to a string, for example, you will be able to squash your bugs faster and more effectively.

The data type of a variable is specified using *post-colon syntax*. That is, the *var* keyword begins a variable declaration statement, and the data type immediately follows a colon after the variable name. This can be done without any further assignment, as a way of declaring your variables and data types before scripting, or along with an assignment for brevity. Examples of both techniques follow:

```
var myNum:Number;
var myString:String = "Flash";
```

—continued—

Data Types *(continued)*

When this syntax is used, the ActionScript 2.0 compiler can warn you if you make a mistake related to data types. For instance, it can display a type mismatch error warning when data isn't of the expected type. If you try the following, you will be warned of a type mismatch because you are trying to assign a string to a number:

```
var myNum:Number = "Flash";
```

Similarly, the compiler can warn you when you try to use an unsupported method or property. For example, it should make sense that you can't specify an x-coordinate for a sound. Without visual data, you can't position a sound on the Stage. Therefore, if you try to set the *_x* movie clip property for the *Sound* class (which you'll learn about in the section "Scripting Your Own Sound Control"), you will get a warning that no such property exists:

```
var mySound:Sound;
mySound._x = 10;
```

It's also a good idea to type the data passed into a function and returned from a function. Argument typing is similar to variable typing, but the *var* keyword is not required. Typing a value returned by a function is a bit different. This typing statement is placed just after the function constructor. The following example tells the compiler that a number should be passed into the argument, and that a number should also be returned by the function:

```
function timesThree(whichNum:Number):Number {
    return whichNum * 3;
}
```

When a value is not returned by the function, using a data type of *void* is recommended. This tells the compiler to alert you if anything unexpected is returned:

```
function timesThree(whichNum:Number):Void {
    trace(whichNum * 3);
}
```

Finally, for completeness's sake, it is usually recommended that anonymous functions, even without arguments, declare no return by using the *void* data type:

```
my_btn.onRelease = function():Void {
    my_mc.play();
};
```

You will find that this is frequently omitted, simply because the scripter knows no value is returned. However, it is still recommended. Type checking is meant to help you with compile-time error reports. Omitting type declarations in ActionScript 2.0 will not prevent your file from compiling, but you won't receive any notifications of possible errors, either.

You may be asking yourself why, when you didn't make type declarations in the prior chapter examples, you didn't receive errors. There are two reasons. First, when you're learning a new topic, it's helpful to learn it in digestible pieces. This is another example of *chunking* information. Second, and more importantly, current Flash Players must remain compatible with older projects. If a data type is not specified for a variable or object, the compiler won't perform type checking. This allows older code to go through the ActionScript 2.0 compiler without generating errors.

Although backward compatibility allows untyped objects to be compiled without error, it is considered a best practice to use static typing. All of the examples in the last half of this book will follow this guideline.

Information about additional issues relevant to static typing, such as using the Object data type when more than one kind of data may pass through an object and circumventing type checking altogether, can be found in Colin Moock's *ActionScript: The Definitive Guide* (O'Reilly).

Scripting Your Own Sound Control

There will undoubtedly be instances when you don't want to rely on components, or you want to script specific features for your sound player. For these reasons, it's a good idea to have at least a minimal understanding of the *Sound* class, so you can create sound objects and control them with code. Fortunately, it's very easy.

Creating a Sound Object

All you have to do to play an MP3 using your own script is create a sound object, load the sound, and, once the sound is finished loading, play it. This next mini-project starts by doing just that, using the *Nero* sound you've been working with:

1. Create a new file and save it as *mouse_sound.fla* in your *08* folder.
2. In frame 1, add the following script:

```
var my_sound:Sound = new Sound();
my_sound.loadSound("nero.mp3");
my_sound.onLoad = function():Void {
    my_sound.start();
};
```

3. Save your work and test your movie. The sound should begin playing automatically.

That was quick and painless, but there's more you can do with sound than just playing it.

Volume

Controlling the volume of a sound is as easy as setting it to a value from 0 to 100, inclusive:

1. Continuing with the current movie, add the following line to the end of your frame 1 script:

```
my_sound.setVolume(50);
```

2. Save your work and test your movie. The sound should now play at half volume.

Hard-coding a volume like that is useful for an initialization routine but isn't very practical for ongoing use. However, if you could vary the value used for *setVolume()*, instead of restricting your use to a value of 50, you would be able to change the volume at will. You could, for example, create a volume slider that matched the vertical (or horizontal, if you prefer) position of a slider button movie clip. You'll do just that in a moment, but first you'll look at the pan property.

Pan

The *pan* property defines what amount of the sound is in each of the left and right channels (for stereo sound). Setting the pan of a sound is as easy as setting the volume, with one wrinkle: you need to be able to specify any pan between all left channel and all right channel. Therefore, a range of 0 to 100 is insufficient.

Instead, the range of a pan is from –100 (all left) to 100 (all right), with a value of 0 being equal amounts of sound in both channels. To see how it works, try this:

1. Continuing with the current movie, add the following line to the end of your frame 1 script:

   ```
   my_sound.setPan(100);
   ```

2. Save your work and test your movie. The sound should now play only in the right channel.

Again, hard-coding a pan value would not be as useful as allowing the user to change the value. If desired, you could take the same approach with pan as discussed in the "Volume" section. You might use a slider with a center point or, more intuitively, a knob that would allow you to use a rotation value.

The Whole Works

Next, you'll create two different projects to see these principles at work. First, you'll create a mouse toy that controls volume and pan with mouse position, and then you'll script a pre-configured interface to make an MP3 player of your own. Both require a bit more ActionScript labor than you've had to do up to this point, but it will be worth it.

Mouse sound

For this project, you'll let the x-coordinate of the mouse control the pan and the y-coordinate of the mouse control the volume. Before you can continue, however, there are two small user interface issues that you'll need to consider.

First, the Flash coordinate system begins with (0, 0) in the upper-left corner of the Stage, and the x and y values increase moving to the right and down. Therefore, a span of y values starts at zero and increases as you move the mouse *down*. This is not very intuitive for the average user, so you'll use a little math to flip these values, allowing the volume of the sound to start at zero at the bottom of the Stage and increase as you move the mouse up.

Second, if the x values start at 0 on the far left, it will not be very intuitive for the user to get values between –100 and 100 while keeping his or her mouse on the Stage. Thus, you will adjust the *_xmouse* value to assume a position of zero in the horizontal center of the screen:

1. Start with almost the same code you've been using, but with one exception. Instead of playing the sound when it's loaded, play it when the user clicks the mouse anywhere in the main timeline. Entirely replace your existing frame 1 script with the following:

```
var my_sound:Sound = new Sound();
my_sound.loadSound("nero.mp3");
this.onMouseDown = function():Void {
    my_sound.start();
};
```

2. Next, make your file run more efficiently by performing two simple calculations and storing them in variables that can be recalled later. This prevents your file from having to repeat these calculations at every enter frame. The first gives you the horizontal center point of the Stage, and the second gives you the height of the Stage:

```
var centerStage:Number = Stage.width / 2;
var sh:Number = Stage.height;
```

3. Then add an *enterFrame* event handler for the main timeline with the following code:

```
this.onEnterFrame = function():Void {
    my_sound.setVolume(Math.abs(100 - (_ymouse / sh) * 100));
};
```

This code will set the volume of the sound based on how far the mouse has moved up the Stage vertically. Remember that you want a value from 0–100 for volume. If you divide *_ymouse* by the Stage height, you will get a percentage of vertical Stage distance traveled by the mouse. You can then multiply that by 100 to get a value between 0 and 100, rather than between 0 and 1.

However, that's not all. That will work with the default y value of 0 at the top. Therefore, the values will only increase when moving the mouse down, which is the opposite of what you want. To offset this, you can subtract the value you get from 100. Therefore, where the value at the bottom used to be 100, it is now 0. The problem is, a value of 0 at the top is now *negative* 100.

The final step is to take the *absolute value* of the number you've calculated. This will make a positive number from a positive number or a negative number. The *Math* class takes care of that for you automatically by simply invoking the built-in *Math.abs()* method. Now, at last, you will get values from 0 to 100 by moving the mouse up the Stage, vertically.

4. Add a second and final line to the same *enterFrame* handler (the new line is indicated in bold):

```
this.onEnterFrame = function():Void {
    my_sound.setVolume(Math.abs(100 - (_ymouse / sh) * 100));
    my_sound.setPan(((_xmouse - centerStage) / centerStage) * 100);
};
```

This line sets the pan based on the horizontal mouse value, or *_xmouse*. The twist is that it needs to calibrate zero at the center of the Stage. It uses the same method of distance traveled divided by total distance times 100, but it offsets the distance traveled by accounting for the center of the Stage. Therefore, using your 550-pixel-wide Stage as an example, and a mouse value of 0, you get:

Far left:	(0 – 275) / 275 = –1 * 100	= –100
Center:	(275 – 275) / 275 = 0 * 100	= 0
Far right:	(550 – 275) / 275 = 1 * 100	= 100

5. Save your work and test your movie.

You should now be able to move your mouse to the right of center Stage to pan the sound to the right, and to the left of center Stage to pan the sound to the left. Also, your sound should be at full volume at the top of the Stage, and muted at the bottom of the Stage.

MP3 player

This project calls for you to create a basic sound player. The player will include track selection, play, pause, stop, and song loop features; a volume slider; and a pan knob. This is an intermediate project, and the step-by-step walk-through will be just a bit sparser than usual as a challenge to push you forward. Everything you need has been provided, though, so with a bit of effort you should be just fine.

For brevity, the code for the slider and knob will be skipped in the following steps. However, the code is not complicated and uses the basic principles discussed in the "Mouse sound" section. When you feel comfortable with this project, you can double-click on the volume slider and pan knob and look at the code in each to see how they were scripted.

NOTE

If you plan to use the template file provided, you can disregard this note. However, if you decide to reconstruct the file for yourself at a later time, you should be aware of five things. In the provided source file:

1. *The slider and knob were updated to use static data typing.*
2. *The sound object referenced by both the slider and knob scripts is now my_sound in the parent of both movie clips (which is, in this case, the main timeline).*
3. *Both the slider and knob scripts now update their respective properties only during dragging.*
4. *The knob was simplified a bit to remove a key-based auto twist feature.*
5. *The first field, used for track name, was copied from the inside of either the slider or the knob.*

Again, for brevity, you will start with a file that has already been assembled, with instance names applied to the various pieces. However, all of the pieces for your player were taken from a button library that has been a part of Flash for several versions. The assets can be found in the Library spawned by the Window→Common Libraries→Buttons menu command. Within the opened Library, the buttons can be found in the *Classic Buttons→Playback* folder, and the volume slider and pan knob can be found in the *Classic Buttons→Knobs and Faders* folder.

Here's how to implement your player:

1. Open the *mp3_player_manual_01.fla* file in the *08* folder. Remember, the interface elements and instance names are all in place, and the slider and knob have been scripted to work on their own. However, you have to script the sound object and all the buttons. The interface should look like Figure 8-7.

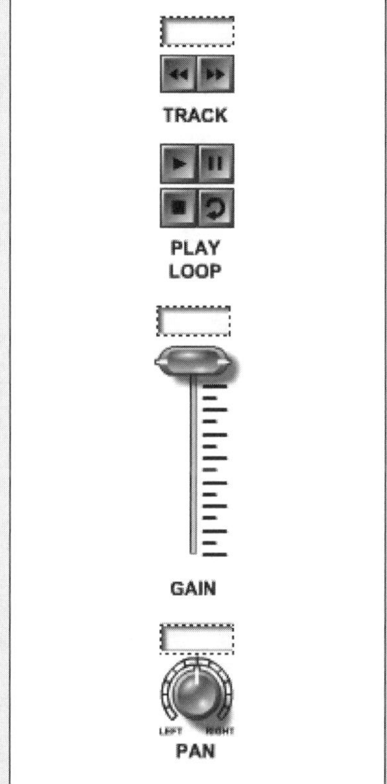

Figure 8-7. The MP3 player interface

2. Start by initializing variables and setting the visibility of the loop indicator to false:

```
var my_sound:Sound = new Sound();
var whichTrack:String = "GB1.mp3";
var trackNum:Number = 1;
var trackPos:Number = 0;
var trackLoop:Boolean = false;
var trackPlaying:Boolean = false;
loopLabel_mc._visible = false;
```

3. Next, define the function used to switch tracks:

```
function switchTrack(incr:Number):Void {
    trackNum += incr;
    if (trackNum > 3) {
        trackNum = 1;
    } else if (trackNum == 0) {
        trackNum = 3;
    }
    track_mc.value.text = "GB" + trackNum;
    whichTrack = track_mc.value.text + ".mp3";
    trackPos = 0;
    my_sound.loadSound(whichTrack);
    my_sound.stop();
}
switchTrack(0);
```

This function accepts an integer and returns nothing. When called, the *trackNum* variable is incremented with 1 or –1, increasing or decreasing the track number. The conditional makes sure that only the numbers 1, 2, and 3 are used. The track name is then assembled ("GB" + 2 + ".mp3," for example), its position is reset to zero, the sound is loaded, and then it's stopped awaiting playback. Finally, the function is called once as an initialization step, loading the first track.

4. An *onSoundComplete* event handler is created to restart the sound when it's finished playing. However, this occurs only if the *trackLoop* variable is true:

```
my_sound.onSoundComplete = function():Void {
    if (trackLoop) {
        my_sound.start(0);
    }
};
```

5. Next and previous buttons are scripted to call the function defined earlier. The next button sends a positive increment (1), increasing the track number, while the previous button sends a negative increment (–1), decreasing the track number:

```
next_btn.onRelease = function():Void {
    switchTrack(1);
};
prev_btn.onRelease = function():Void {
    switchTrack(-1);
};
```

6. If the track is not already playing, the play button starts the sound. However, it accounts for the current position of the sound:

```
play_btn.onRelease = function():Void {
    if (!trackPlaying) {
        trackPlaying = true;
            my_sound.start(trackPos / 1000);
    }
};
```

   The track position is normally zero when the sound is stopped, but the pause feature will record the sound playback position when the pause button is clicked. Starting the sound from that position will cause it to pick up where the pause left off. Note that the sound position property is measured in milliseconds, but the offset parameter of the *start* method is measured in seconds. Therefore, the position value stored in the pause button must be divided by 1000 to get the right units.

7. Pause and stop buttons set the *trackPlaying* variable to false, store the track position in the *trackPos* variable, and stop the sound:

```
pause_btn.onRelease = function():Void {
    trackPlaying = false;
    trackPos = my_sound.position;
    my_sound.stop();
};
stop_btn.onRelease = function():Void {
    trackPlaying = false;
    trackPos = 0;
    my_sound.stop();
};
```

   The only difference between the pause and stop buttons is that the stop button hard-codes a value of zero for track position to reset the sound for subsequent playback from the beginning.

8. Finally, the loop button turns the looping feature on and off:

```
loop_btn.onRelease = function():Void {
    trackLoop = !trackLoop;
    if (trackLoop) {
        loopLabel_mc._visible = true;
    } else {
        loopLabel_mc._visible = false;
    }
};
```

All this button really does is reverse the *trackLoop* variable. If it was true it is changed to false, and vice versa. This variable is checked when the *onSoundComplete* handler is called, as seen in step 4. However, as an interface consideration, the *loopLabel_mc* movie clip that says "LOOP" is shown or hidden, accordingly.

That's it! Not only have you gotten through quite a bit of ActionScript in this chapter, but you're using strict data typing and really making progress. Congratulations.

What's Next?

As you complete each new chapter, you're learning new ActionScript skills. If your confidence is growing, try using some of the other properties and methods of the *Sound* object before moving on.

For example, try to create a pair of buttons that let you mute and unmute your sounds instantly. Make a mute button that uses *getVolume()* to store the current volume setting in a variable and then uses *setVolume()* to set the volume to zero. Then make an unmute button that retrieves the old volume level from the variable you used previously and uses *setVolume()* again to restore the previous setting.

If you're not yet ready to try this experiment on your own, don't worry. By the time you're finished with this book you'll be able to tackle this task, and more. If you want to see how it could be done, or check your work, look at *mute_01.fla* in the *08* folder.

In the next chapter, you'll take a similar look at how to add video to your projects, with and without ActionScript. You'll learn how to:

- Embed video in your SWF files
- Encode video using the Flash 8 Video Encoder
- Load external videos using additional media components
- Script your own video control using ActionScript

Using Video

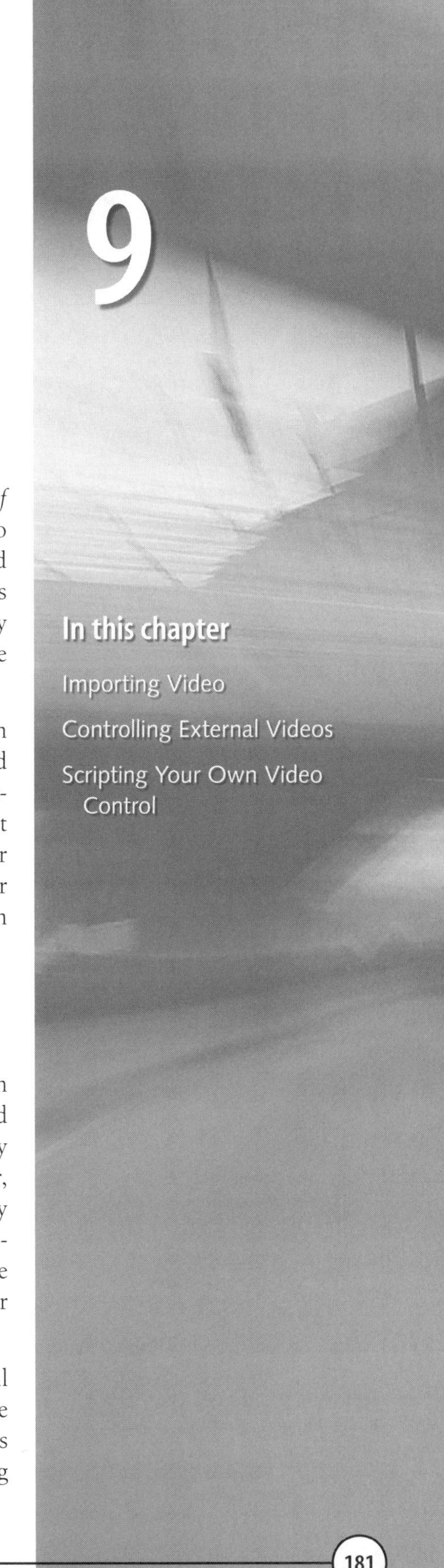

Flash video has come a long way since videos were first delivered via *.swf* several years ago. In fact, although this is still rare, it has matured to the point that some developers choose the Flash Player as their preferred method to deliver standalone videos (without any interactive content). This is largely because of the ubiquitousness of the Flash Player, and is usually coupled with a companion streaming server, but it does say a lot about the quality of today's Flash video options.

Using video in Flash has many parallels with using sound in Flash. You can import video into a *.fla* (although it is not recommended), and you can load and play external videos, either with components or with your own scripting. The similarities between using sound and video in Flash are significant enough that you may find yourself understanding Flash video even quicker than you embraced Flash sound. To reinforce this familiarity, this chapter has been organized using a structure similar to that of Chapter 8. Repetition of applicable points will be emphasized, rather than avoided.

Importing Video

As with sound, there are two primary ways to use video in Flash. Videos can be imported into Flash and embedded in the *.swf* file, or they can be loaded as external assets at runtime using ActionScript. Originally, the only way to deliver video via Flash was to embed the video in a *.swf* file. However, technology has improved to the point that this is now recommended only for extreme circumstances. Several reasons account for this recommendation, and they are, essentially, the same reasons used to argue for the use of external sound: embedding video dramatically increases the size of your *.swf*, and it makes updating your project more difficult.

In most situations, your project will be better served by loading external videos during playback. However, as with sound, internal video may be preferred for a few reasons (synchronization of video with other Flash assets chief among them). The quality and performance differences between using internal and external video are great enough that embedded video is becoming increasingly rare. Still, it is good to understand both processes, so you can compare the results yourself.

Preparing Video for Import into Flash

Flash can import a variety of standard video formats, including MOV, AVI, MPEG, and DV. Essentially, Flash can import any standard format supported by QuickTime (Mac and Windows) or DirectShow (Windows only).

Contrary to sound, video must be compressed during the import process, so using a higher-quality source will yield better results. Remember, though, that working with large embedded videos makes your *.fla* file size larger and your work slower. So, some developers argue that it's easier to start with a low-quality video and then replace it with a high-quality version when nearing project completion. Ultimately, however, you are likely to only embed short videos, so the savings probably won't warrant the effort.

In the first mini-project of this chapter, you will import a small video to use as a button for viewing extreme sports content:

1. Create a new file and save it as *embedded_vid.fla* in your *09* folder. Using the Modify→Document menu option, change the file's frame rate to 15 fps. For embedded video, the frame rate of the Flash file must match the frame rate of the video, or the playback will be affected.
2. Select the File→Import→Import Video menu option.
3. A wizard will appear. The first screen, Select Video, requires only that you find the video you wish to import. Choose the default option, "On your computer," find the *extreme_sports_loop.mov* video in your *09* folder, and press the Continue button.
4. On the Deployment screen, select "Embed video in SWF and play in timeline."
5. The Embedding screen then displays. Configure your settings to match Figure 9-1, and then press Continue.

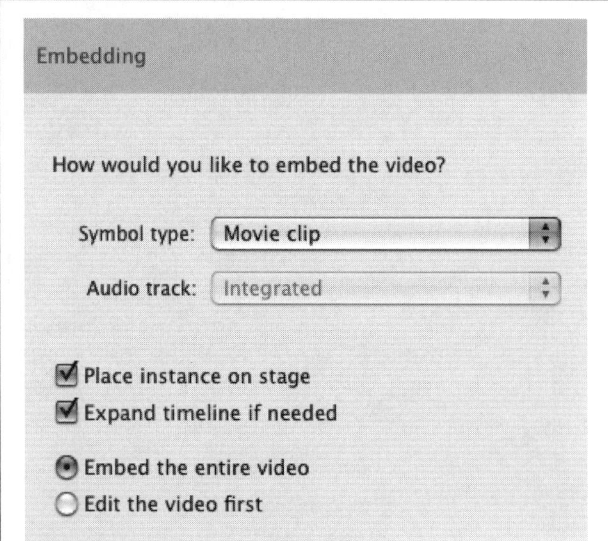

Figure 9-1. The Advanced Settings screen of the Video Import Wizard

NOTE

Unlike sounds, videos cannot be edited after being imported. During the import process, however, simple in-out edits can be made to identify sections of a larger video that you may want to import. This is editing at its most basic and is not a substitute for a video editor. However, it can be handy for pulling in a small segment from a pre-existing video without having to use a video editing application.

6. The next screen is the Encoding screen. This project calls for a simple embedded file. You want to reach the widest possible user base you can, and with the smallest possible file size. For this reason, choose "Flash 7 - Low Quality (150 kbps)." (The poor source quality of this nostalgic video would render the modem quality setting unwatchable.) This option uses the Sorenson Spark codec and will actually play in Versions 6 through 8. You will use the Flash 8–specific settings in an upcoming project.
7. Continue on to the summary screen and press Finish to start the import process.
8. Flash will import the video and, because of the settings you chose on the Embedding screen, place the video into a movie clip on the Stage in frame 1.

NOTE

Based on the "Expand timeline if needed" option on the Embedding screen, if you had chosen to place your video into a graphic symbol or embedded video object, Flash would have expanded your timeline with enough frames to accommodate the length of the video. This is a bit more cumbersome to work with, but necessary if you want to export your Flash project for broadcast video. You'll learn more about that in Chapter 15.

9. Save your work and test your movie.

NOTE

Although you won't use them now, take a quick peek at the Advanced settings. Here, you can customize compression settings (rather than using a preset), crop the source video for smaller imported dimensions, and more accurately specify in and out points to import segments of a longer video. Cue points (discussed briefly in "What's Next?") are available only for external videos.

In Figure 9-2, you should see a public domain video of a film shot by none other than Thomas Alva Edison in 1899. The original film is called "Bicycle Trick Riding, no. 2" and is documentation of the slammin' extreme sports of the day. Although the 37-second film shows additional tricks, such as balancing and backwards riding, this segment has been trimmed down to a neat 4-second loop that can be used as a button.

Figure 9-2. The embedded video

To quickly demonstrate the use of imported video as a movie clip button, do the following:

1. Give the movie clip an instance name of **`extremeSports_mc`**.
2. Add the following script to frame 1:

```
var extremeSports_mc:MovieClip;
extremeSports_mc.stop();
extremeSports_mc.onRollOver = function():Void {
        this.play();
};
extremeSports_mc.onRollOut = function():Void {
        this.stop();
};
```

3. Save your work and test your movie.

The first line of this script tells the ActionScript compiler that *extremeSports_mc* is a movie clip. This static data typing will help you spot errors, as you learned in Chapter 8. The second line stops your movie clip from playing initially, and the two event handlers play and stop the clip on rollover and rollout. The effect is an interactive video that is relatively small (so it doesn't contribute mightily to file size) and tightly integrated into your *.swf*.

To Embed or Not to Embed?

Considering the technological advances that have been made in the area of Flash video, embedding clips in *.swf* files is largely discouraged. You've heard repeatedly in this book that file size is a major factor, but it's an even bigger issue with embedded video. For example, when a video is embedded, the entire *.swf* must be downloaded before the video will play. Also, the entire movie must fit into the end user's available RAM for the file to play.

There are other problems with embedded video, too. External videos look and perform better than embedded videos. Embedded videos really slow down production and have to be recompressed upon every import. Also, sync between the embedded clip's audio and video tracks can start to drift after two minutes or so.

The rule of thumb here is to use external video whenever possible. When internal video is absolutely required, add time to your production and testing schedules. Finally, if internal video is required because you ultimately want to export to video, Chapter 15 discusses possible additional options, including using linked videos that remain in QuickTime format.

Controlling External Videos

In this section, you will learn how to use components to control external video, and how to write your own control scripts. Using external video in Flash is very similar to using external sound. The major difference between external video and external sound is that FLV video files are only used by the Flash platform, making them a bit harder to create and repurpose than MP3 audio files. Fortunately, a variety of tools exist to create FLV files, including two that ship with Flash.

Encoding

The most rudimentary way to encode videos into FLV format is to use the Import Video Wizard, just as you did during the "Preparing Video for Import into Flash" section of this chapter. This may not make sense given the name of the wizard, but the same process you used earlier can also create external FLV files. Instead of embedding the video, the wizard will create an external FLV and configure your new file with the new *FLVPlayback* component.

NOTE

Depending on the source material, the speed of your computer, and the software you are using, it can take a long time to encode a video into FLV format. If you are most interested in the step-by-step process of this project and wish to leave the long encoding process until later, you have two options. First, you can use the small video you imported in the previous section, extreme_sports_loop.mov, instead of the suggested nero.mov. Second, you can read this section without following the steps and use the nero_01.flv file provided on the CD-ROM in the 09 folder.

Flash's Import Video Wizard saves external video files in the same location as the currently active document. Therefore, you must have a recently saved file open for the wizard to determine an export path. Here's how it works:

1. Create a new document called *nero1.fla* and save it in your *09* folder. Use Modify→Document to give it dimensions of 320 × 280.
2. Select the File→Import→Import Video menu option to show the Import Video Wizard again. On the Select Video screen, choose the default option, "On your computer," and find the *nero.mov* video in your *09* folder. When you're ready, press the Continue button.
3. On the Deployment screen, select "Progressive download from a web server." This format will also work locally, for testing and disc-based distribution (e.g., for kiosks and CD-ROMs).
4. Because you are not embedding this video, the next screen is the Encoding screen. This time, choose "Flash 8 - Medium Quality (400 kbps)." This option uses On2's VP6 codec, new to Flash 8. The Flash 8 Player is required to play back this FLV file. When you're ready, press Continue.

NOTE

Although the Flash 8 Player is required to display FLV files compressed with On2's VP6 codec, you do not have to update Flash 6 or 7 .swf files to load the external video assets. As long as the end user has the Flash 8 Player, the FLV will also work when loaded into Flash 6 or 7 .swf files.

On2's VP6 provides superior quality at smaller data rates than Sorenson Spark, and also supports alpha channels. This means you can reproduce things like fire, smoke, fog, and similar effects that require alpha data, compositing the video with your other Flash assets live at runtime.

However, VP6 is more processor-intensive than Spark, so performance may be an issue on older machines. This is especially true when playing videos with alpha data. Therefore, it's a good idea to test your files on a machine that is as close as possible to your intended lowest common denominator.

5. A new screen called Skinning will appear. Choose "SteelExternalAll.swf" for the skin. Your screen should look like Figure 9-3.

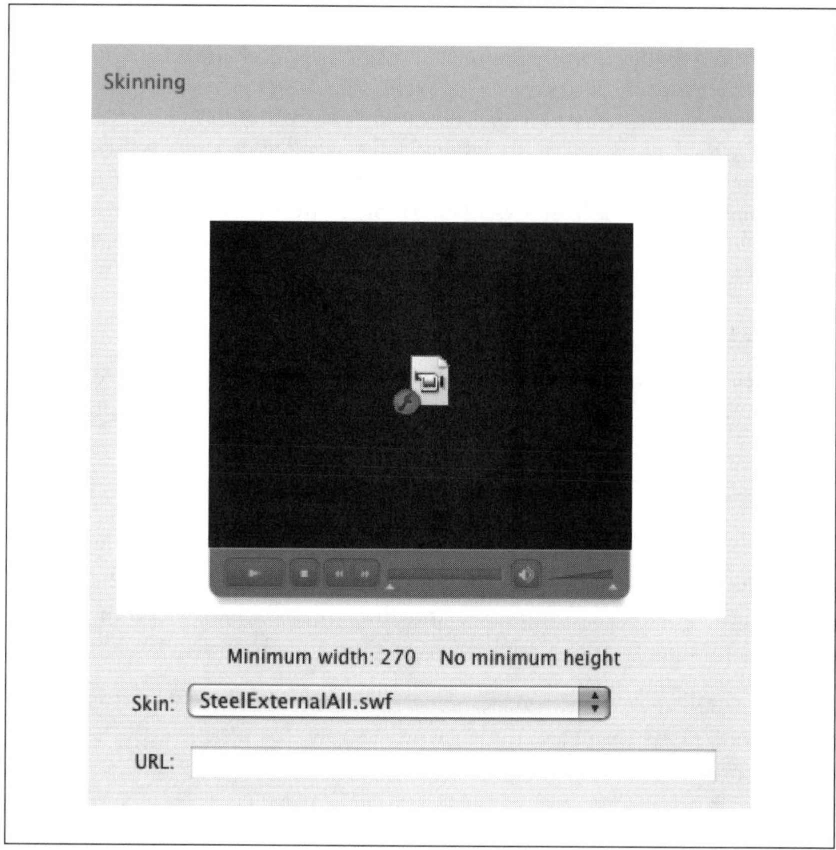

Figure 9-3. The Skinning screen of the Video Import Wizard

The built-in Video Import Wizard provides a shortcut: it will set up the active *.fla* with the new *FLVPlayback* component and automatically link to your newly compressed FLV file. The "SteelExternalAll.swf" option provides a full-function controller that is external to your FLV. Other colors and partial feature sets are also available, including versions that appear above and inside the bounding area of your video. (You can also use your own custom skin, if you've already created one.) You will look at this component again later, so when you're finished previewing the presets in the menu, press Continue.

After presenting a summary screen, Flash will compress the video into FLV format and save it in the same directory as your active document. When the process is complete, it will return you to your main document, having added the *FLVPlayback* component and preselected the controller you chose earlier. To finish:

6. Click the display area of the component and, using the Properties panel, position it at (0, 0).
7. Save your work and test your movie.

Your file should publish very quickly (because all assets are external) and show the video, complete with controller, for you to use. You will learn how to configure options of the controller in an upcoming section of this chapter.

Standalone encoding applications

While it's convenient to encode FLV files from within Flash, doing so can take longer and yield poorer results than encoding with a dedicated FLV compression tool. Fortunately, two additional pieces of software ship with Flash 8 Professional.

The first is the Flash 8 Video Encoder. Essentially, this is a standalone version of the encoder built into Flash. However, it appears to produce better results faster, and it offers the huge benefit of supporting batch processing. The interface, beyond the batch-processing window, is the same for the most part.

The second piece of software is the Flash 8 Video Exporter. During the installation of Flash 8 Professional, the Exporter is installed and made available to any QuickTime-savvy application. Although, as a codec, it can't offer batch processing, it can be handy to export to FLV from within your favorite video editing application. The Exporter, too, shares essentially the same interface as Flash's Video Import Wizard and the Flash 8 Video Encoder.

Third-party tools are also available. Although requiring an additional purchase, they typically offer better, faster results than the aforementioned solutions that ship with Flash. There are two major tools in this market, but others exist. The companion web site to this book, *http://www.flash8projects.com*, will host a regularly updated list of Flash resources that will include additional information about encoders.

The first major third-party tool is Sorenson Squeeze. As the developers of the original Flash video codec, Sorenson Spark, they have experience compressing for Flash and have created a sturdy tool that is also easy to use. At the time of this writing, Sorenson had announced support not only for their own Spark codec, but for On2's VP6 codec, making it possible for Squeeze to compress FLV files that take full advantage of Flash 8's features. See Appendix A for more information about Squeeze.

The second major third-party FLV compression application is the Flix Flash 8 Video Encoder, by the makers of the Flash 8 video VP6 codec, On2. Flix is a powerful, feature-rich tool that offers a host of features, including expanded file support and the ability to vectorize video for interesting effects. Most notable, however, is the fact that the version of Flix that was current as of this writing compressed files that were as much as 25% to 30% smaller than those produced by any other exporter. See Appendix A for more information about Flix.

Streaming Versus Progressive Download

Talk about streaming video abounds, but unless you're using dedicated streaming server software, you're probably not working with streaming video. Instead, you are probably working with a pseudo-streaming technology sometimes called *fast start* or *quick start*. These technologies effectively pre-fetch or *buffer* a portion of the video and then allow playback while downloading the remaining content.

This approach is also commonly called *progressive download*, because the asset is downloaded in progressive stages without affecting playback too much. FLV files encoded for progressive download can also be used locally, and these will be the focus of the video projects in this book.

The Flash platform includes a streaming server, currently called Flash Media Server 2. (Until recently, it was called the Flash Communication Server.) Use of this server is outside the scope of this text, but additional information is available online, including at Macromedia's web site (*http://www.macromedia.com/software/flashmediaserver/*).

FLV Components

The *FLVPlayback* component is the new Flash 8 version of the media components you used in Chapter 8. It only works with FLV files, not MP3 files. Even if you ended up with a working component after the in-Flash video encoding example, start from scratch now to see how easy the *FLVPlayback* component is to use:

1. Create a new file and save it as *nero2.fla* in your *09* folder. (Don't worry if you don't have a *nero1.fla*. That just means you chose not to encode the sample video in the previous project.) Set the stage dimensions to 320 × 280.
2. Drag the *FLVPlayback* component to the Stage and position it at (0, 0).
3. With the *FLVPlayback* component on the Stage selected, open the Component Inspector, click on the *contentPath* parameter field or its associated magnifying glass button, and find the *nero_01.flv* file in the *09* folder. Repeat this process for the *skin* parameter, and choose the controller you prefer. (If you want to match the sample file provided, choose an External All option, such as "ArcticExternalAll.swf.")
4. Save and test your movie. If you want to compare your file to the provided source, it should match *nero_01.fla*. Don't close your file, however, as you can jump-start the next project with it.

That's all there is to it. You should now be able to control your external video with the controller, as seen in Figure 9-4. There's one important thing to know about the *FLVPlayback* component, though. The controller is an external *.swf* file that is automatically loaded by the component. Look in the *09* directory after testing your movie, and you will see that the controller skin you chose has been copied to this directory. This file is also required when distributing your files.

Figure 9-4. The FLVPlayback component, with full controller, playing an external FLV file

You're not stuck with the preset controllers when using the *FLVPlayback* component. When you are experienced enough to create your own custom skin, you can select that file instead. That requires a bit of ActionScript, some of which you will learn in this chapter, but some that you'll have to become comfortable with on your own.

However, in the meantime, you can build your own controller, piece by piece:

1. Use the File→Save As command to save your current file as *nero3.fla* in your *09* folder.
2. Select the *FLVPlayback* component and open the Component Inspector. Click on the *skin* parameter field and select "none." You still have the *FLVPlayback* component configured to show the *nero_01.flv* file, but it will not display a controller.
3. Open the Components panel and look inside the *FLV Playback Custom UI* component category. You can use these pieces to build a controller any way you want, with very little scripting. All of the components will function the way you expect them to, and all you'll have to do is associate them with the *FLVPlayback* component.

4. For brevity, drag just the *PlayPauseButton* and *StopButton* components to the Stage, and position them anywhere beneath the *FLVPlayback* component.

5. Select the display playback component and give it an instance name of **flvplayer**. Then select the two buttons and give them instance names of **playPause_btn** and **stop_btn**, respectively.

NOTE

These components are not really buttons, but the _btn suffix will not alter their functionality and may help you remember what each object is at a glance. If you want to be strict about your naming conventions, you can change these names, as long as you do so again in the following script.

6. Finally, add the following script to frame 1:

```
flvplayer.autoPlay = false;
flvplayer.playPauseButton = playPause_btn;
flvplayer.stopButton = stop_btn;
```

The first line prevents the video from playing automatically, as a change from your prior projects. The second and third lines use the *playPauseButton* and *stopButton* properties to identify the component instance names of the components that serve these purposes. Just by making this assignment, you'll enable the buttons to control your video. Think of the button components as already scripted but with nothing to control. Once you pair them with an *FLVPlayback* display, they will work together.

Scripting Your Own Video Control

If you're not using Flash 8 Pro or don't want to weigh down your Flash movie by using components, ActionScript will give you full control over external FLV files. A few lines of code accomplish the same thing the components did, with a smaller file size. You will lose the graphical interface provided by the components, but you can create your own or do without.

Sometimes you just want a video to begin playing automatically and to present required information to the user without a controller, but for this project, you will create simple play and stop buttons. Don't use components for this, however. Instead, roll your own buttons.

Creating a Video Object

To load an external FLV into your file, either from a server stream or a local file, you need to have a video object on the Stage:

1. Create a new file and save it as *nero4.fla* in your *09* folder. Set the document dimensions to 320 × 280.

2. Open the Options menu in the Library and choose New Video. The Video Properties dialog will display, asking you to name the symbol and choose the type of video you intend to create. Name the symbol **Video 1** and select the "Video (ActionScript-controlled)" option.

3. Rename *Layer 1* in your timeline **video**, and drag an instance of *Video 1* to the Stage. Resize it to 320 × 240 pixels, and position it at (0, 0).

4. Assign the video object an instance name of **my_video** and lock the *video* layer.

In a few minutes, you'll reference my_video in the ActionScript for the project. First, however, you need to connect to the video source and stream it.

Making a Connection

Remember from the earlier discussion on "Streaming Versus Progressive Download" that the term *stream* is most accurately used when referring to data being transmitted by streaming server software, such as the Flash Media Server 2. When scripting your own video interface, you will use the ActionScript necessary to receive a stream, but change one parameter if you wish to load a file via progressive download.

Null

A *null* value is a way to specifically say that there is no value at all. This is better than using 0, for example, because 0 is actually a value: it is an integer and it has a *Number* data type, and therefore it cannot stand in for the equivalent of *no value*.

Using *null*, instead of using nothing at all, tells the ActionScript compiler that the value required has not been accidentally omitted. Consider an example explained earlier in this chapter (repeated here for context).

When working with external Flash video files, or FLV files, you can literally connect to a streaming server and receive the FLV via streamed data, or you can download the FLV, either from a remote location or locally, until it is on your local system and ready to play.

The latter file may appear to stream, because Flash can buffer a portion of this type of FLV and then continue to download the file in progressive stages even while the video is playing. However, this method of delivery, known appropriately as "progressive download," is not really streaming.

So, if connecting to a server is expected in the first part of the process of playing an FLV, you must tell the ActionScript compiler that you will not be taking that step. For example, assume the syntax for connecting to an actual server is:

```
var connection_nc:NetConnection = new
NetConnection();
connection_nc.connect("URI_to_server_here");
```

If you wanted to use a progressive download FLV, and therefore didn't want to connect to a server, you might think of omitting the URI value, like this:

```
var connection_nc:NetConnection = new
NetConnection();
connection_nc.connect();
```

However, the ActionScript compiler would interpret that as an omission by mistake. Instead, you need to send a *null* value in the place of the URI, indicating to the compiler that you don't want to connect and want to work with a progressive download FLV instead.

It is not always possible to replace an undesired value with *null*, but it a useful tool when this option is understood by the syntax with which you're working.

The first step is to create a *NetConnection* object. In simple terms, this is the part of the process needed to connect to a specific server. This is also where the aforementioned parameter change will allow you work with a non-streaming file. The second step is to create a *NetStream* object. This is the actual stream that you will receive from the connection established earlier.

Although it's an imperfect analogy, it may help to think of the *NetConnection* as the phone call you make to a company switchboard, and the *NetStream* as the conversation you have via one of the extensions at the company. That is, the main phone line is the server to which you connect. You then specify which extension you want to talk to, and that data is delivered.

The complete process is not difficult. Here, you will add a simple button control to create a working file that is similar to the previous component examples, but much smaller:

1. Add a new layer called **actions**. In frame 1 of the *actions* layer, build a script over the following five steps.

2. First, create a *NetConnection* object and give it the name **connection_nc**:

   ```
   var connection_nc:NetConnection = new NetConnection();
   ```

3. Next, use that object to connect to a Flash Media Server by passing the URI of the server to the object. Or, in this case, specify that the object should *not* make a connection by passing a *null* value in for the server URI. (See the "Null" sidebar for more information about *null* values.) This tells the connection object that you will be working with a progressive download rather than a stream, so the object will not actually expect to communicate with a server:

   ```
   connection_nc.connect(null);
   ```

4. Next, you want to create a *NetStream* object that will hold the specific stream from the server connection or, in this case, the progressive download file. Call it **stream_ns**:

   ```
   var stream_ns:NetStream = new NetStream(connection_nc);
   ```

5. Now that the stream has been created, tell it to buffer five seconds of the file before allowing playback to begin. This helps keep the download process ahead of the playback:

   ```
   stream_ns.setBufferTime (5);
   ```

   If you are working with very limited or overtaxed bandwidth, the playback may catch up to the download, and the video will stutter or stop. In that case, you may need to increase the buffer amount to give the download process a bigger head start.

6. Finally, attach the video delivered by the *stream_ns* object (whether it is an actual stream or a download) to the video object you created on the Stage:

```
my_video.attachVideo(stream_ns);
```

7. Save your movie.

This part of the script is done. Now you just have to wire up the buttons to control the objects you just created.

Wiring a Simple Interface

While the previous examples had full-featured controllers, this project will be brief and simple. Once you've had success with three simple buttons, you can move on to adding additional elements to the interface:

1. Add two layers below your *actions* layer. Name the lower of the two **buttons**, and give the name **buttons text** to the layer immediately below *actions*.

2. In the *buttons text* layer, create three static text elements that say **Play**, **Pause/Resume**, and **Stop**.

3. In the *buttons* layer, create an invisible button that can easily be reused for all three playback control purposes. (If you need a refresher on invisible buttons, see the similarly named section in Chapter 4.) Give them instance names of **play_btn**, **pause_btn**, and **stop_btn**, and match them with the appropriate text in the *buttons text* layer.

4. Now move on to the scripting. Create an *onRelease* event handler and instruct the *stream_ns* object to play the *nero_01.flv* file:

```
play_btn.onRelease = function():Void {
    stream_ns.play("nero_01.flv");
};
```

5. For the Pause/Resume button, create a simple toggle. This is inadequate in the long run, because it provides no visual feedback, but it will serve its purpose here, keeping the code simple and easy to understand. Create a Boolean (true/false) variable and start it off with a value of false. Your video will not begin in the paused state:

```
var pausedState:Boolean = false;
```

6. Next, create an *onRelease* event handler for the Pause/Resume button. Every click must reverse the true/false value of the variable you just created. When the value starts as false, make it true. Conversely, if it's true, make it false. Do this by using the *not* operator. (For more information, see the sidebars on conditionals and operators in Chapter 7.) Finally,

NOTE

For an example of a toggle with visual feedback, see the bonus mute_01.fla file in the 08 folder. Be sure to read Chapter 8 first, for any necessary background.

use the *pause* property of the stream object, sending in the true or false value you just modified:

```
pause_btn.onRelease = function():Void {
    pausedState = !pausedState;
    stream_ns.pause(pausedState);
};
```

7. The last step is to create your Stop button. As far as the streaming process goes, all that remains is to close the connection. However, this will leave the asset visible in the on-Stage video object, so you need to clear that so it will disappear:

```
stop_btn.onRelease = function():Void {
    stream_ns.close();
    my_video.clear();
};
```

8. Save your work and test your movie.

NOTE

Closing down the stream object is just like hanging up a phone at the end of a conversation. It signals the end of communication with the party on the other line (equivalent to the stream or progressive download asset), and it frees up the line for another conversation later (akin to freeing the memory used by the now-terminated stream and allowing future streams).

Your file should now play and stop when you click the Play and Stop buttons and pause and resume with each successive click of the Pause/Resume button, as seen in Figure 9-5. If you have any problems, check your work against the *nero_04.fla* file in your *09* folder.

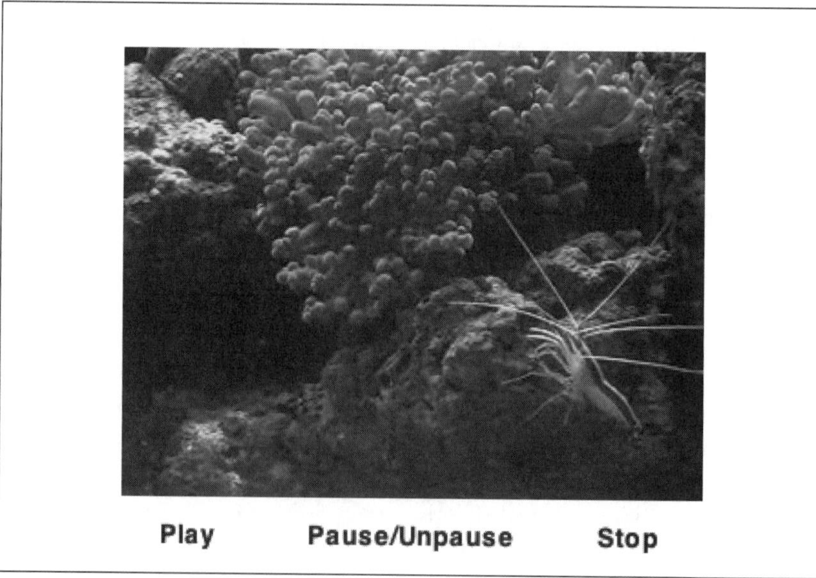

Figure 9-5. The completed custom player

Ideally, this chapter has given you an overview of video use in Flash, without being too difficult. You've covered a lot of ground here, including embedded and external video assets, using components, and scripting your own video controls.

The only significant remaining asset type is text, which will be discussed in Chapter 11. First, however, you'll take one last look at visual assets.

What's Next?

Before you continue, try to expand on what you've learned in this chapter.

Practice compressing video files using Flash, the Flash 8 Video Encoder, and the Flash 8 Video Exporter, if you can install it in a video editing application. Compare and contrast the quality and compression speeds of each tool.

Investigate some of the video features not covered in the limited space of this text. Look into *cue points* and how to embed them in FLV files and make use of them. Cue points are like frame labels, in that they are markers that are added to FLV files prior to, or during, compression, and they can be recognized by ActionScript and used as navigation points when seeking through the video. They can also be used for synchronizing video events with other parts of your Flash file.

Finally, build more robust custom controllers. Start with the remainder of the *FLV Playback Custom UI* components, and then move on to expand on your simple hand-scripted interface.

In the next chapter, you will discover a number of ways to composite bitmap and vector assets on the fly and learn how to inject a heightened sense of expression into your files with real-time filter effects. You will:

- Learn how to increase the performance of movie clips by caching them as bitmaps at runtime
- Apply bitmap effects to movie clips, including custom filters such as Drop Shadow, Bevel, and Glow, which have long been popular in bitmap editing applications such as Photoshop
- Composite bitmaps and movie clips at runtime using blend modes such as Darken, Screen, and Multiply (also long-time features of many bitmap editors)
- Come to understand the core ActionScript structures *arrays* and *loops*

Compositing and Bitmap Effects

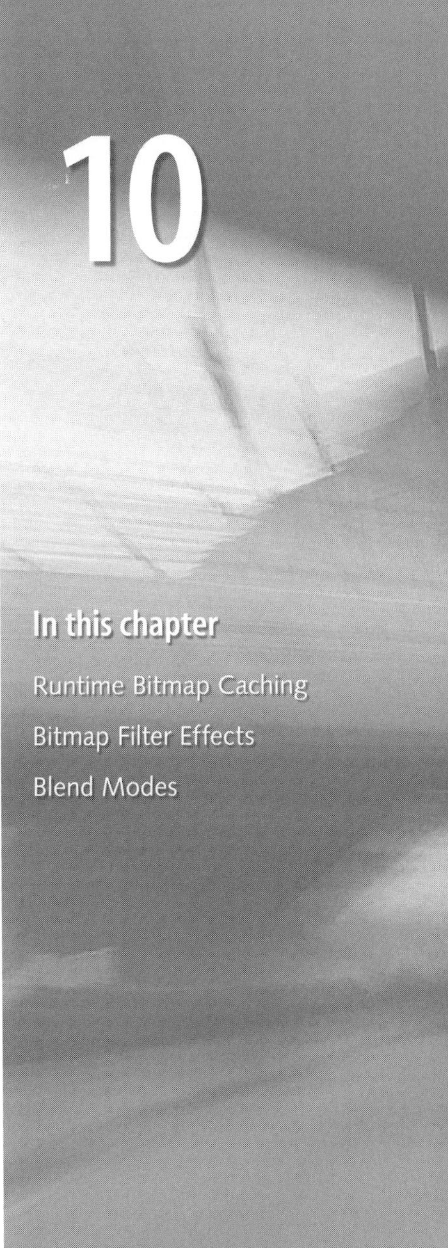

Flash 8 introduced an entirely new approach to compositing visual assets at runtime that has dramatically increased artistic options available to Flash users. Traditional techniques (such as manipulating movie clip opacity, using the PNG file format for bitmap transparency, and pre-creating graphic, movie clip, and button states) are frequently still useful and even preferred. However, new bitmap rendering routines now offer new ways of accomplishing similar goals, often yielding better results.

Runtime Bitmap Caching

Many people, when hearing Flash 8's new compositing features described as bitmap rendering techniques, have a similar reaction: understandably, they think that these features are applicable only to imported JPEG, PNG, GIF, or other bitmap file formats. However, one of the best overall features of Flash 8 is its ability to treat movie clips—including vector-only movie clips—like bitmaps, for the purposes of compositing. This is a feature known as *runtime bitmap caching.*

You may be asking yourself why you would want to convert your beautifully sharp vectors into pixels. Fortunately, that's not exactly what's happening. It's true that the Flash Player will handle the movie clip as if it were a bitmap, but only when instructed to do so. Any vectors remain editable, and their appearance remains crisp and clean. Also, it's an automatic process that typically gives your file a significant performance boost.

Ideally, you should never have to think about what goes on behind the scenes in the Flash Player, but sometimes understanding a few basics helps you optimize your projects. The vector processing that makes Flash unique does not come without a price. Recalculating all of the vector math necessary to render shapes, colors, opacities, and more requires quite a bit of computer power. Moving pixels around the screen, however, is easier to achieve.

Accordingly, the Flash engineering team came up with a way for you to continue authoring with vectors as usual but, during runtime, have the player cache a bitmap version of your movie clip for compositing. For example, say your file contained a relatively complex vector-based movie clip that filled the Stage in layer 1, and additional complex movie clips that moved across this background. For every frame update, the Flash Player would have to factor in how all these vectors interacted, requiring a lot of energy.

But what if Flash took a temporary snapshot of these movie clips as it started rendering? In this case, the player would only have to move bitmaps across another bitmap, requiring a lot less work from your computer.

This simplified example demonstrates the principle behind runtime bitmap caching. Obviously, not all Flash projects will be as limited as the file described in this scenario. However, with this feature enabled, each time a movie clip experiences a major update, the bitmap will be re-cached and performance will again improve. Most movie clips will benefit from bitmap caching, and the cumulative effect can be substantial.

There are, of course, exceptions, the most notable of which are rotation and scaling. The interactions between movie clips and other elements in a Flash file require significant recalculating during rotation and scaling, so in these situations little boost will be experienced as a result of bitmap caching. However, when these operations conclude, performance will increase. Plus, the feature can be enabled and disabled with ActionScript, allowing you to use it when it is most suitable to do so.

An even bigger improvement can be seen when you tell Flash not to worry about transparencies within the movie clip. This is achieved by specifying an opaque background for any relevant clip. Clearly, not all clips can take advantage of this option, yet even when a movie clip contains areas of transparency (such as an irregular shape or an alpha value of less than 100%), this feature can be exploited temporarily. This feature, too, can be controlled with ActionScript. Therefore, you can give a movie clip an opaque background when it rests on a clear Stage, for example, but still see through the clip in situations when it is layered atop other elements.

Enabling Caching via the Interface and ActionScript

The runtime bitmap caching option of any movie clip can be enabled or disabled in the Properties panel with the click of a button. With a movie clip selected, you need only toggle the checkbox labeled "Use runtime bitmap caching," as seen in Figure 10-1.

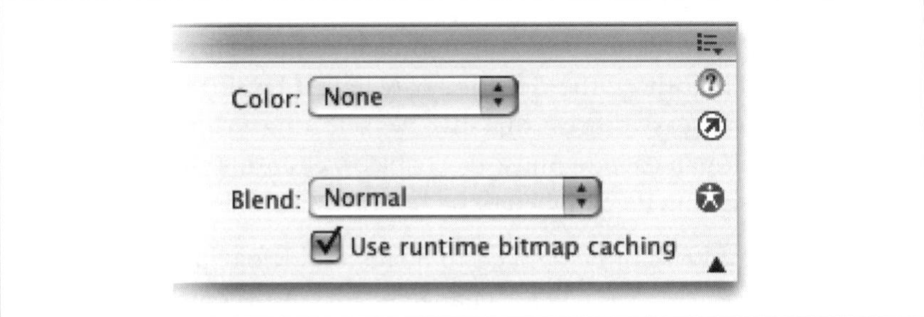

Figure 10-1. Runtime bitmap caching can be enabled in the Properties panel with a movie clip selected

You can also do this using ActionScript. The syntax is as follows:

```
myClip_mc.cacheAsBitmap = true;
myClip_mc.opaqueBackground = 0xFFFFFF;
```

The optional *opaqueBackground* property requires a color value for the solid background you wish to add. This sample code creates a white background for the movie clip.

NOTE

The value for the color is in hexadecimal notation, as used when specifying web colors. The syntax is very similar, but the typical number sign, or hash (#), is replaced by the prefix `0x`. *This is true when creating colors for many purposes in ActionScript.*

Bitmap Filter Effects

Although the performance bump you gain from using bitmap caching would be enough for many to justify the feature, there are additional benefits that stem from its use. For example, once you start treating your movie clips like bitmaps, it's possible to apply real bitmap effects to those movie clips.

Flash 8 contains seven bitmap filter effects:

- Drop Shadow
- Blur
- Glow
- Bevel
- Gradient Glow
- Gradient Bevel
- Adjust Color

If you have a reasonable amount of experience with bitmap-editing applications, such as Adobe Photoshop, you will likely be familiar with these types of effects. (In Photoshop, these features are called Layer Styles.) Applying them in Flash is an easy process that involves selecting an appropriate movie clip (runtime bitmap caching must be enabled), choosing the effect of your choice, and assigning its parameters.

More than one filter can be applied to a single movie clip. For maximum flexibility, filters can be created, changed, or removed at runtime using ActionScript. If preferred, filter parameters can also be assigned without any scripting using the Filters tab of the Properties panel.

Using the Properties Panel

Start out by adding a drop shadow to the Box Guy animation you created in Chapter 6:

1. Open *box_guy_complete.fla*, located in the *06* folder of your working directory. To keep your files separate and grouped by topic, save the open file as *box_guy_shadow.fla* in the *10* folder.
2. In frame 1 of the *box_guy* layer, select the Box Guy movie clip.
3. In the Properties panel, enable runtime bitmap caching. This is not strictly necessary, because adding a filter to a movie clip automatically enables this feature. However, it is not reflected in the interface, and this step may help you remember that, although you're working with a movie clip, this is still a bitmap rendering process.
4. Select the Filters tab in the Properties panel. In the upper-left corner, click and hold the plus sign (+) to open the Add Filter menu. Select Drop Shadow from the menu.

   The editable area of the Filters tab will refresh to show you the parameters available to the Drop Shadow filter, as seen in Figure 10-2. The standard *Color* chip allows you to set the color of the shadow. *Distance* represents the number of pixels the shadow will be from the movie clip. The *Angle* parameter dictates the angle at which a virtual light source will shine, thereby casting the shadow. *Blur X* and *Blur Y* are the amount of spread, or blurriness, of the shadow along each axis. *Strength* is similar to alpha opacity, and determines how dark the shadow will be. Finally, in simple terms, *Quality* determines how accurately the shadow will render. (Don't worry about the three checkbox settings on the right. You'll learn about those in a moment.)
5. Configure your settings to match Figure 10-2.
6. Save your work and test your movie.

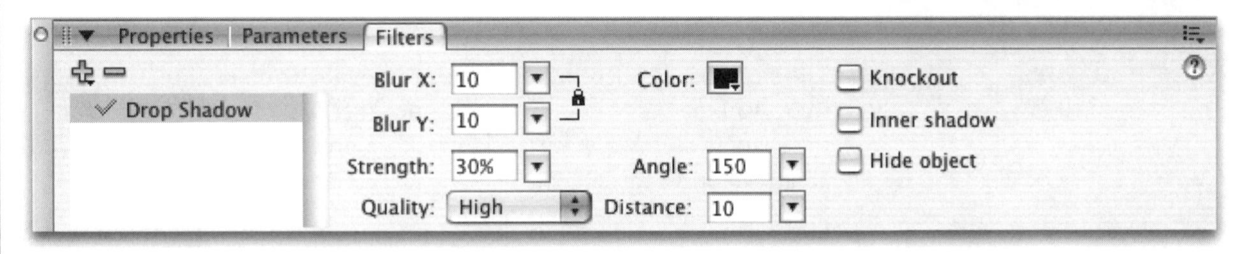

Figure 10-2. The Filters tab of the Properties panel, showing the parameters of a Drop Shadow filter

When previewing your movie, the first thing you should notice is that Box Guy not only has a shadow, as seen in Figure 10-3, but it animates right along with him. The filter is rendered every step of the way, making the shadow appear accurate in each frame of the movie clip.

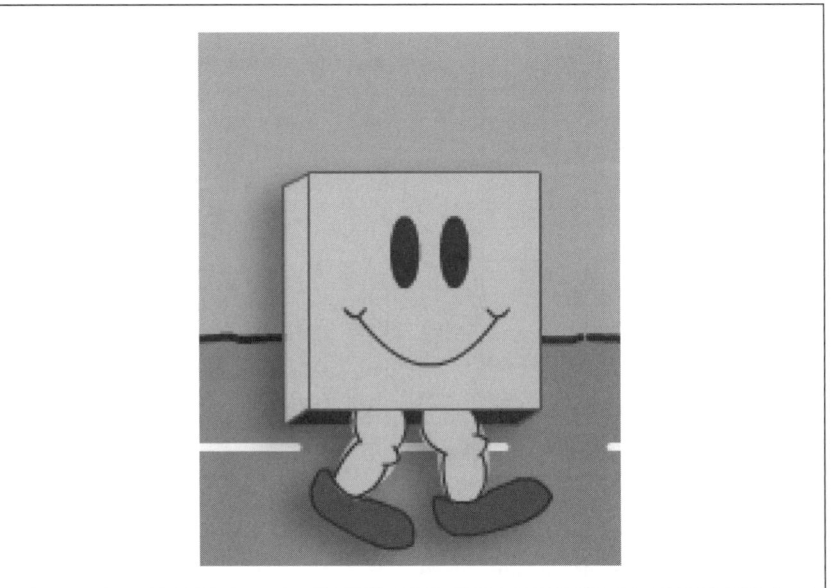

Figure 10-3. Box Guy with a standard drop shadow applied

If you followed the prior steps exactly, you may also notice an unexpected occurrence: the shadow disappears over the duration of the animation. This is because filter effects themselves can also be tweened. This feature makes it possible to create interesting, more realistic effects with moving light sources, distance, and so on.

In this example, make sure the filter stays consistent:

1. Select Box Guy in the last keyframe of the tween and again match the Drop Shadow settings to those seen in Figure 10-2.
2. Save your work and test your movie.

Now Box Guy's shadow should remain consistent throughout the animation.

The shadow adds depth, but it's not very realistic unless Box Guy happens to be walking very close to a wall. Since there's no wall in your animation, the shadow seems unnatural. However, a great filter option allows you to greatly improve this effect.

Previously, you temporarily disregarded a trio of additional features of the Drop Shadow filter. These three features, indicated by the checkboxes on the right in Figure 10-2, allow you to create additional special effects using Drop Shadow, as well as a few other filters.

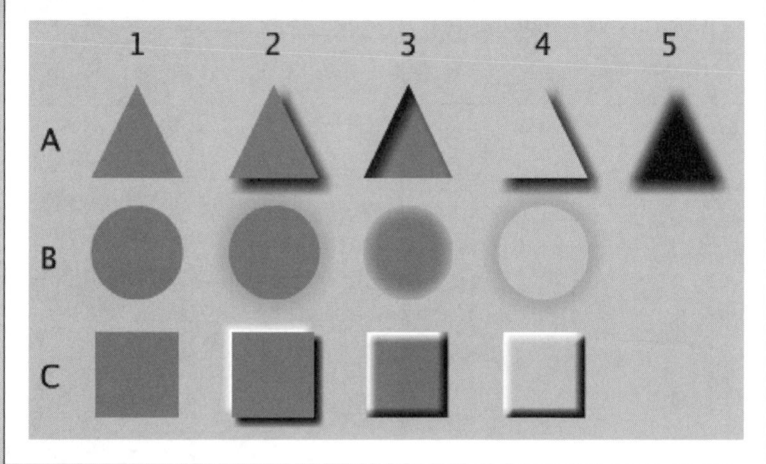

Figure 10-4. Examples of common options available to three filters

Figure 10-4 shows examples of the use of three filters and their special features. Rows A, B, and C show the Drop Shadow, Glow, and Bevel filters, respectively.

Here are the effects applied in each column of Figure 10-4:

- Column 1 shows the original, unaffected movie clips.
- Column 2 shows the basic *Outer* effect: shadow, glow, and bevel are applied outside the original clip. This is the default behavior for the Drop Shadow and Glow filters.
- Column 3 shows the *Inner* effect, where the filter treatment is applied inside the movie clip dimensions.
- Column 4 shows the *Knockout* effect. In this case, the filter is rendered using your *Inner* or *Outer* effect preference, but the original movie clip is removed, knocking out any underlying effect. This is best illustrated by the partial shadow in row A. The angle setting of the filter displays the shadow down and to the right. The *Knockout* effect removes any shadow that would have been hidden beneath the original clip.

  This effect is great for creating instant accents from bitmaps. A knockout drop shadow atop a bitmap would make it appear as though a portion of the bitmap had been extruded. A knockout glow could be used to highlight an area of an image or interface. A knockout inner bevel creates an instant button when placed on top of a bitmap, making it possible to reuse the shape over and over without any additional bitmap overhead.
- Finally, column 5 shows the *Hide Object* effect, unique to the Drop Shadow filter. Similar to the aforementioned *Knockout* effect, *Hide Object* hides the original movie clip, but it does not further affect the shadow. This makes it possible to create standalone shadows from any movie clip, as you'll see in the next part of this project.

Shadows with perspective

In the previous exercise, a standard filter application gave Box Guy a distinct 2D shadow appearance. In the next exercise, you will duplicate Box Guy and apply filter effects to the duplicate. In this way, you can make the character and his shadow independent of each other and distort the shadow to give the appearance of perspective.

In just a few steps, you will skew a copy of the movie clip, give the copy a drop shadow, and then hide the object in the copy, leaving only the shadow behind. These steps are illustrated in Figure 10-5. You can then create a new symbol from the two copies of Box Guy and tween it as before. Within the new symbol, both copies of Box Guy—the traditional movie clip and its shadow-only counterpart—will move, creating a more realistic synchronized shadow animation.

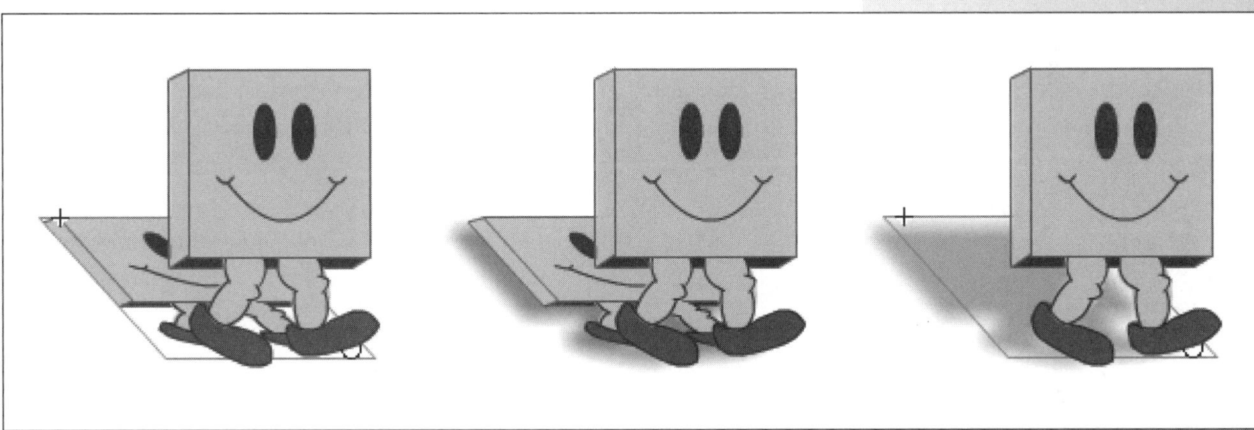

Figure 10-5. Three stages of Box Guy's improved shadow: after skewing and positioning (left), with drop shadow enabled (middle), and with the Hide Object option enabled (right)

Here's how to create the effect shown in Figure 10-5:

1. Begin by closing any previous files and opening *box_guy_shadow_p_01.fla*, located in the *10* folder. The *p* stands for perspective, and by starting this project anew, you will be able to compare the two shadow techniques. As you can see, this file is the same as the previous files, except that there is no motion tween. Save this file as *box_guy_shadow_p.fla* in the *10* folder.
2. Select the Box Guy movie clip in the first frame and duplicate it using Ctrl/Cmd-D.
3. Using the Free Transform tool, select the duplicate and skew it. (You can skip ahead and do this numerically in step 6 if you wish, but it helps to practice with the tools until you feel very comfortable with them.) Position your cursor near the top center handle. You will see the *skew* cursor feedback, in the form of two parallel horizontal arrows, as seen in Figure 10-6. Position your cursor just to one side of the top center handle to avoid the familiar *scale* cursor of two vertical end-to-end

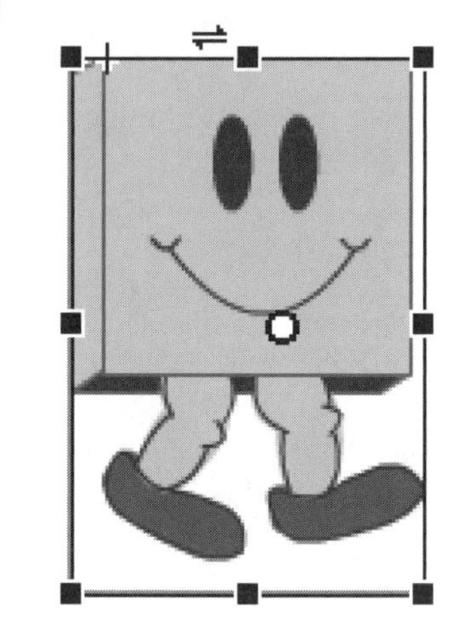

Figure 10-6. Using the Free Transform tool to skew the duplicate of Box Guy that will eventually become his shadow

arrows. Similarly, avoid the cursor feedback of the circular rotation arrow, which means you've strayed too near a corner handle. Once you're satisfied with your cursor position, drag the cursor to the left until your mouse reaches the former position of the left corner handle. (Don't worry; it doesn't have to be exact.)

4. Next, scale the movie clip vertically. This time grab the top center handle closely, being sure you see the vertical end-to-end scale arrows. Scale down the movie clip to approximately two-thirds its prior height.
5. Reposition the duplicate so its feet touch the feet of the unaltered Box Guy. If necessary, use Modify→Arrange→Send Backward to put the skewed copy below the original clip.
6. Your pair of Box Guy movie clips should look like the first stage of Figure 10-5. If you want to check (or make) the transformations numerically, you can select the duplicate clip and show the Window→Transform panel. Uncheck the Constrain option, and enter a vertical scale of approximately 60% and a horizontal skew of approximately –40%.
7. Save your movie. If you want to check your work, your file should now resemble *box_guy_shadow_p_02*. All that remains is to add the shadow effects and tween a new symbol.
8. Select the duplicate clip and the Filters tab in the Properties panel. Match the settings to those in Figure 10-2 again, but this time enable the *Hide Object* feature. Your character and shadow should now look like the final stage in Figure 10-5, and your file should be similar to *box_guy_shadow_p_04*.
9. Select both the original and shadow clips and use Insert→Convert to Symbol to create a new movie clip.
10. Repeat the tweening process you used in Chapter 6 by creating a keyframe in the last frame of the *box_guy* layer, moving the new movie clip in that frame to the right of the Stage, and adding a motion tween to the first frame in the layer. (If you need any review to accomplish this, look back over the step-by-step project in Chapter 6.)
11. When you're finished, save your work and test your movie. It should now resemble *box_guy_shadow_p_complete*. Box Guy will walk down the street again, this time accompanied by his animated shadow in a more realistic perspective.

Now that you know how to add filter effects using the interface, move on to the ActionScript needed to do so on the fly at runtime.

Using ActionScript

Having access to filter effects through the interface is great for non-scripters and rapid prototyping by designers. However, like many other Flash features, manipulating the filters at runtime, using ActionScript, can add a whole new dimension to your projects.

Unlike with anything you've done so far, the first step required when scripting filters is to import the *filters class* you want to work with. A *class* is a way of defining a custom data type—in this case, a filter—with the related functions, properties, variables, and similar code structures that go along with it. Some classes are built into Flash, but others, including all classes you define yourself, exist in external class files or *packages*, which are collections of more than one class.

With a little time, and additional resources, you will soon become comfortable with the object-oriented structure of ActionScript 2.0 and later. A detailed look into ActionScript is beyond the scope of this book, but the newest editions of Colin Moock's *Essential ActionScript* and *ActionScript: The Definitive Guide* (O'Reilly) are highly recommended.

An in-depth look at ActionScript will reveal more about its underpinnings, but for the time being, think of external classes and packages this way: no additional steps are required to use the *MovieClip* class because it's already tightly integrated into the Flash environment in which you're working; however, some features—particularly new and user-defined features—must be loaded before they become available to the programmer.

Arrays

Up to this point, you've only been able to store one value in a given variable. Moreover, if another value was applied to the variable, the previous value was discarded (or overwritten, if you will). Consider this example:

```
var myNum:Number = 1;
myNum = 2;
```

The final value of the *myNum* variable is 2, because its value was reassigned in the second line of the example code.

However, there are many situations in which you would be better off if you could store multiple values in a single variable. Consider lists that you make in everyday life, such as shopping lists. Think of the list—or the paper it's written on, if you prefer—as a variable. The shopping list contains many different items. Now imagine if you had to create a separate variable to hold every item. That is, imagine if you had to write each item that you would otherwise have put in a single list on a separate piece of paper. In one small way, this analogy illustrates the usefulness and efficiency of lists.

In ActionScript, as in most languages, a list is called an *array*. Any time you want to store more than one value in a variable, that variable must be an array. For example, the bitmap filter effects discussed in this chapter are applied in an array. If you only wanted to apply one filter at a time, it might make sense to say something like:

```
myMovieClip.filters = myDropShadow;
```

But this simple syntax would not work if you wanted to apply two filters. For instance, what if you wanted to apply both a drop shadow and a bevel to the same movie clip? To accomplish this, you need to use an array. Using an array allows you to say something like:

```
myMovieClip.filters = [myDropShadow, myBevel];
```

—continued—

Arrays (*continued*)

The brackets in this syntax enclose the array items. Once a variable is defined, you can also use brackets to set or get an array's values, as shown here:

```
var my_array:Array = new Array();
my_array[0] = "Flash";
trace(my_array[0]);
```

The first line creates a new array object using the same static data typing approach that you have used in the last few chapters. The second line sets the first value of the array as the string "Flash." Finally, the third line gets the first value from the array and displays it in the Output window.

You may have noticed the 0 in the brackets in the preceding code example, and wondered why a 1 wasn't used instead. This is because ActionScript arrays are *zero-based*, meaning that the first value is referenced by an array index of 0, not 1. If a 1 were used in the prior example, it would refer to the second item in the array.

Most programming and scripting languages use this approach, including C, C++, C#, Java, JavaScript, Perl, PHP, and more. There are a few benefits of zero-based arrays, but space limitations don't allow a detailed look into the topic. The most common rationale is that an array index describes the number of items offset from the first item in the array. Therefore, the first item must have an index of zero.

This can take a bit getting used to if you have experience in languages that use one-based arrays (such as BASIC, Lingo, or AppleScript), or if you haven't yet thought beyond simple everyday counting, where the "first item" is item one. However, if you embrace zero-based arrays, you will find it much easier to code in languages that you may want to use in conjunction with your Flash projects (such as JavaScript and PHP).

At the time of this writing, one property and a dozen methods were used to work with arrays in ActionScript, in addition to the bracket-index syntax described previously. In the interests of space, only the four most commonly used are discussed here.

The lone property, *length*, is a read-only property used to determine how many items are in an array. Counting the number of items in an array is not affected by the fact that the array is zero-based. For instance, a three-item array would have indices 0, 1, and 2, but it would still have three items. Continuing with the previous code, tracing the length of the array *my_array* would put *1* in the Output window, because the array has one value: the string "Flash."

The following code samples will use comments to indicate Output window results. You can trace the length of an array like this:

```
trace(my_array.length);
//1
```

You can add an item to the end of an array using the *push()* method:

```
my_array.push("ActionScript");
trace(my_array);
//Flash, ActionScript
```

And you can sort an array using the *sort()* method:

```
my_array.sort();
trace(my_array);
//ActionScript, Flash
```

By default, the *sort()* method sorts arrays alphabetically. This can yield unexpected results when sorting numbers. Consider the numbers 3, 20, and 100. Sorted alphabetically, these numbers would be ordered 100, 20, and 3. Case sensitivity can also play a role when sorting strings. For a deeper understanding of these issues, look into array constants such as *Array.NUMERIC* and *Array.CASEINSENSITIVE*.

Finally, you can remove the last item of an array, and return its value, by using the *pop()* method:

```
trace(my_array.pop());
//Flash
trace(my_array);
//ActionScript
```

In this final example, *pop()* removed "Flash" because it was the last item in the sorted, two-item example array, leaving only "ActionScript."

Arrays are very useful and make a powerful addition to your programming skills. If you want to learn ActionScript, take some time to practice with arrays at your earliest convenience.

You can work directly with a specific external class by specifying its fully qualified name, which includes a path to the external file where the class is defined. However, you can simplify this by importing the class, or one or more packages of classes, so that you can thereafter refer to the class only by its class name—just as you would a function. For example:

1. Open *dynamic_filters_01.fla*, located in your *10* folder, and save it as *dynamic_filters.fla* in the same folder. This file contains two copies of a movie clip that will serve as buttons, created dynamically via filters. They each already have instance names.

2. In frame 1 of the *actions* layer, add the following script. This imports the *BevelFilter* class and allows you begin working with it:

   ```
   import flash.filters.BevelFilter;
   ```

3. Next, create a filter object, or instance of the BevelFilter class, by defining its parameters:

   ```
   var bvFilter:BevelFilter = new BevelFilter(5, 135, 0xFFFFFF, .8,
   0x000000, .8, 10, 10, 1, 1, "inner", false);
   ```

   This creates a bevel *distance* (or depth) of 5 pixels, an *angle* of 135 degrees, a *highlight color* of white with an *alpha* of 90%, a *shadow color* of black with an *alpha* of 80%, a *blur x* and *blur y* of 10 (softening the bevel edges a bit), and a *strength* and *quality* of 1 (or 100%). Finally, it specifies a bevel *type* of inner, and no *knockout* effect.

If it were only possible to add one filter to a movie clip, assigning it to the clip would be relatively straightforward. However, it's quite common to use more than one filter. For example, you may want to blur or bevel a clip and still have it cast a shadow.

To accommodate the need to add more than one filter to a clip, you must make use of an *array*. As described in the "Arrays" sidebar, an array is a type of data that can contain more than one value. Think of a database, phone book, or shopping list as an array. These everyday things would be unmanageable if a separate data structure, like a lone variable, was required to store each piece of relevant information. An array lets you store many pieces of information, of many different types, in a single object, like a variable.

For a closer look at this data type, take a look at the sidebar. All you need to know about array syntax for this example is how to store information in an array. There is more than one way to do this, but this project will use arrays that you write out explicitly—multiple items, separated by commas, enclosed in brackets.

Because it's possible to use more than one filter, the array syntax is used even when only one filter is required. This makes the syntax consistent, and makes it is easier to add additional filters later. To see how arrays work, pick up where you left off:

4. Assign the new filter object created in step 3 to the *filters* property of the first button, *filterButton1_mc*:

   ```
   filterButton1_mc.filters = [bvFilter];
   ```

   This starts the button off with the bevel properties you assigned when creating the filter object in step 3.

5. Next, create button event handlers that will trap the mouse press and release events. Within each, change the *angle* property of the Bevel filter. This will cause the highlight and shadow areas to change, making it look like the button has been pushed in from an up bevel state to a down bevel state. In addition, because you are changing a property of the bevel object, be sure to update the *filters* property of the movie clip:

   ```
   filterButton1_mc.onPress = function():Void {
       bvFilter.angle = 270;
       this.filters = [bvFilter];
   };
   filterButton1_mc.onRelease = function():Void {
       bvFilter.angle = 135;
       this.filters = [bvFilter];
   };
   ```

6. Save your work and test your movie. If you want to compare your work to the source provided, your movie should now be similar to *dynamic_filters_02.fla*.

You should see a beveled button on the left, and a normal movie clip on the right. Pressing the button on the left should cause the bevels to invert, making it look like the button is being pressed into the Stage.

Adding a second filter

Now it's time to see what is required to add more than one filter to a movie clip. In the next portion of the project, you will add a shadow and a bevel to the second button. Because you're now also working with the Drop Shadow filter, this, too, will have to be imported.

One of the conveniences of bundling more than one external class in a single package is that you can import the entire package at once. And, since only those classes used in your file will be compiled into your final *.swf*, it's not inefficient to import all the filters even though you're not using Blur, Glow, or the others.

To import all the classes in a single package, use an asterisk (*) in place of a specific class name, as a wildcard. In the first step of this next section, you'll *change* the first line of your existing script. For the remaining steps, add all code to the end of your script:

1. Change line one of your current script to import all filters, rather than just the bevel filter.

   ```
   import flash.filters.*;
   ```

2. Continuing on at the end of the existing script, create a shadow filter object and assign its properties:

   ```
   var dsFilter:DropShadowFilter = new DropShadowFilter(7, 135,
   0x000000, .5, 10, 10, 1, 1, false, false, false);
   ```

   This creates a shadow *distance* of 7 pixels, an *angle* of 135 degrees, a shadow *color* of black with an *alpha* of 50%, a *blur x* and *blur y* of 10 (softening the shadow edges a bit), and a *strength* and *quality* of 1 (or 100%). Finally, it specifies not to use the *inner* type, not to use a *knock-out* effect on the clip, and not to *hide* the clip.

3. Add both filters (using the same array syntax, separating them with commas) to the second button:

   ```
   filterButton2_mc.filters = [dsFilter, bvFilter];
   ```

4. Finally, create the same button event handlers, remembering to reapply the changes to the *filters* property each time. However, this time, change the distance of the shadow:

   ```
   filterButton2_mc.onPress = function():Void {
       dsFilter.distance = 0;
       this.filters = [dsFilter, bvFilter];
   };
   filterButton2_mc.onRelease = function():Void {
       dsFilter.distance = 5;
       this.filters = [dsFilter, bvFilter];
   };
   ```

5. Save your work and test your movie. If you want to compare your work to the source provided, your movie should now be similar to *dynamic_filters_03.fla*.

NOTE

Steps 2–4 are very similar to the previous BevelFilter instructions. In fact, there are only three departures: the variable name and parameters will change, you will be manipulating a different property, and you will be adding two filters instead of one. However, the processes for each of these steps remain the same as in the previous example.

The second button, when pressed, should reduce its shadow distance, making it appear as though the elevated button is being pushed against the flat Stage. Figure 10-7, Figure 10-8, and Figure 10-9 show the successive stages of the buttons. Respectively, they show no effects applied, initial up states, and down states on mousePress.

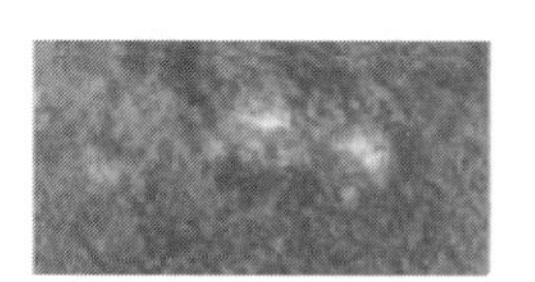
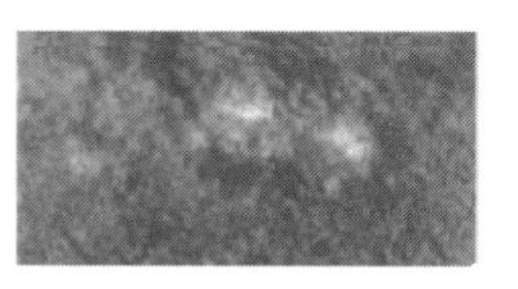

Figure 10-7. Two buttons as they appear in authoring mode with no filter effects applied

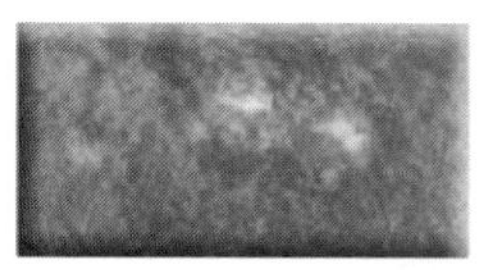
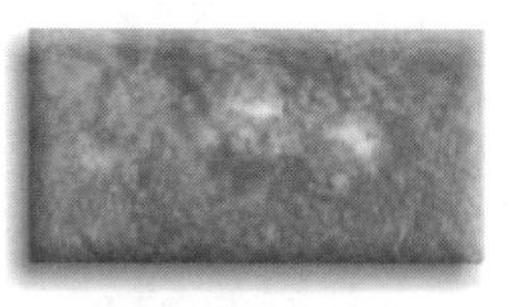

Figure 10-8. The same buttons seen in Figure 10-7, now showing their default states at runtime

The left button has a Bevel filter applied with an angle of 45 degrees, while the right button has the same Bevel filter, but also a Drop Shadow filter applied.

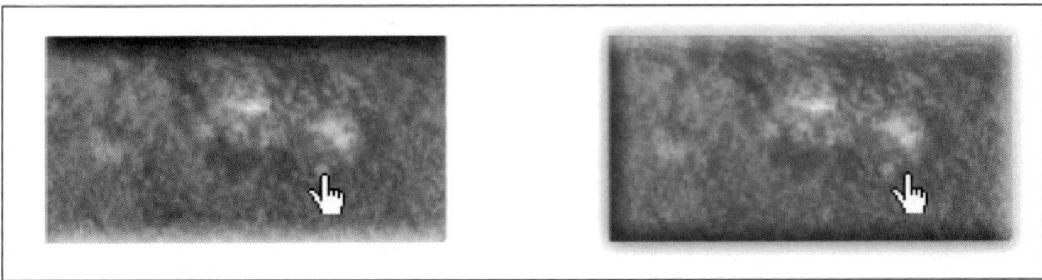

Figure 10-9. The same buttons seen in Figure 10-7 and Figure 10-8, now showing their appearance when clicked by the mouse

Blend Modes

Blend modes, as the name implies, identify different ways that one movie clip blends into everything below it. Although not really a bitmap rendering effect, blend modes are typically discussed alongside the other topics in this chapter because they are deeply rooted in the bitmap-editing world. Flash blend modes are similar in most ways to the blending modes in Photoshop, for example. In reality, the main vector renderer handles Flash blend modes, so they don't require runtime bitmap caching.

There are approximately a dozen blend modes in Flash, including the likely familiar Darken, Multiply, Lighten, Screen, Overlay, and Hard Light, among others. In this project, you'll focus on the Darken blend mode.

Using the Properties Panel

Using the interface to enable a movie clip's blend mode couldn't be simpler. Just select a movie clip and then select a blend mode from the menu in the lower-right corner of the Properties panel, as seen in Figure 10-10.

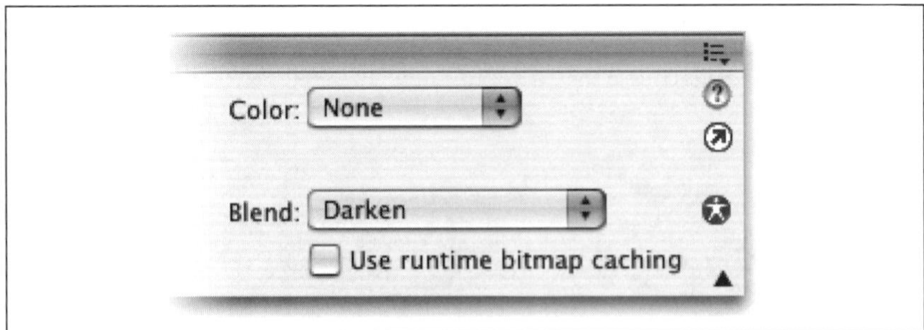

Figure 10-10. Detail of the Properties panel showing the Darken blend mode applied to a movie clip

Here's an example:

1. Create a new movie and save it as *blend_modes.fla* in the *10* folder of your working directory.
2. Import *city.jpg* and position it at (0, 0) on the Stage.
3. Import *hero.jpg* and position it at approximately (50, 20) on the Stage. Your file should now look like Figure 10-11.
4. Select the hero bitmap and convert it to a movie clip. Blend modes cannot be used on bitmaps.
5. With the movie clip still selected, go to the Properties panel and choose the Darken blend mode. Your hero should now look like he's leapt from the top of a skyscraper, as in Figure 10-12.
6. That's it! Save your work.

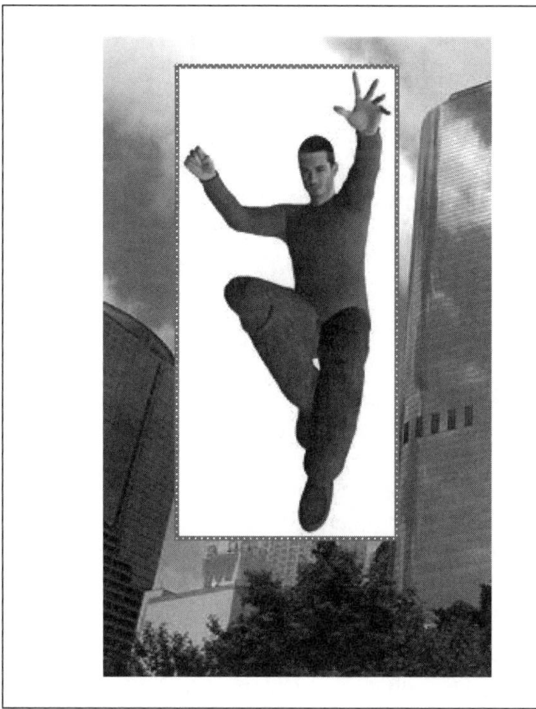

Figure 10-11. The normal state of a JPEG when layered on top of another JPEG

Figure 10-12. The same JPEG as seen in Figure 10-12, but inside a movie clip with the Darken blend mode applied

Loops

Loops are ActionScript structures that make it easy to do things more than once. For example, if you wanted to duplicate a movie clip 10 times, using a brief loop would prevent the need to repeat the necessary code 10 times in a script.

There are a few kinds of looping structures available in Flash, but you will look at two here. The first is a specific part of ActionScript called the *for* loop. The *for* loop just says, "Repeat something a specific number of times." Think of a real-life example: how do you go about saying your name three times?

Most people start by saying their names once. But how do you know you haven't said your name three times already? Obviously, your thinking process tells you that you haven't yet said your name, but cognitive reasoning is not part of computer programming. The computer can't make that kind of determination without information. So, thinking like a computer, how do you do you go about saying your name three times?

To create the loop itself, you first need an initial value, stored in a variable of some kind. *Remember, you have said your name zero times.* Next, you need a test that will tell you, when it fails, that you can stop saying your name. *You must say your name three times. Is zero less than three? Yes, then continue with the loop.* Finally, you need to increment your initial value to count along with your progress. *After you've said your name once, add one to the initial value. Therefore, you've said your name one time.*

Once you have the loop set up, the task you are repeating goes inside the loop structure. You'll see the syntax in a moment, but first, how do you get out of the loop? The looping process continues until you've said your name the third time, right? Not exactly. You actually need to attempt to say your name a fourth time before the aforementioned test will fail. *You've said your name three times. Is three less than three? No. You're now finished with the loop, so stop saying your name.*

The ActionScript for this example looks like this (saying your name will be represented by the *trace* command):

```
for (var i:Number = 0; i < 3; i++) {;
    trace("your name");
}
//your name
//your name
//your name
```

In this syntax:

- *for* tells the ActionScript compiler which kind of loop to use.
- *var i:Number = 0* starts your variable with an initial value of zero.
- The semicolons allow the execution of more than one instruction on a single line.
- *i < 3* is the test that, if passed, allows the loop to continue.
- *i++* is equivalent to *i = i + 1*, which just increments the counter variable until the loop fails.
- The content of the loop structure, the *trace* command, is executed with each successful iteration of the loop.

If you want to use static data typing (almost always a good idea), you can tell the ActionScript compiler that the *i* variable should hold a number. This way, if you choose to use *i* inside the loop, you can be sure your code will complain if you end up with a type mismatch error. For example:

```
for (var i:Number = 0; i < 3; i++) {;
    trace(i * 3);
}
//0
//3
//6
```

Loops are very fast and very powerful—they can even be *too* powerful. A loop is one of the most processor-intensive code structures in ActionScript. Make sure you have a quick way out of a loop, because an *infinite loop* (a loop with no method of exit) can crash your application. (Flash has a nice way of warning you about this possibility, asking you if you want to abort a troublemaking script. If you ever see this warning dialog, always heed its advice. Abort the script and look for your problem.)

While a loop is executing, little can be going on at the same time. Therefore, sometimes you want the effect of a loop, without actually using an ActionScript structure to achieve your goal. Enter the second type of loop you'll look at in this text: the simple *enterFrame* loop.

This is not a part of the ActionScript lexicon, but it is a nice alternative when you don't wish to use the other type of loop, the *for* loop. All you need to do is combine an *enterFrame* event handler with a conditional:

—continued—

Loops (*continued*)

```
var x:Number = 0;
this.onEnterFrame = function():Void {
    if (x < 3) {
        trace("your name");
        x++;
    }
};
//your name
//your name
//your name
```

In this case, *x* starts at zero, and the timeline in which this code appears proceeds with a natural frame advance. The conditional checks if *x* is three yet; if not, Flash traces "your name", increments the value of *x*, and starts the process over again. When *x* becomes three, the conditional fails and the trace ceases.

Unlike with a loop, however, this will continue for as long as the playhead is in this frame. The trace won't occur once *x* becomes three, but the conditional will continue to evaluate and fail. Depending on the complexity of your code, this can affect performance.

However, if this is the only task required of your *enterFrame* event handler, you can use ActionScript to delete it, thereby removing the drain on your resources. To do this, use the *delete* command, which will delete most any object. If you rewrite the code just a bit, the *enterFrame* handler will be deleted when *x* reaches three:

```
var x:Number = 0;
this.onEnterFrame = function():Void {
    if (x == 3) {
        delete this.onEnterFrame;
    } else {
        trace("your name");
        x++;
    }
};
```

If you need additional information on any part of this discussion, reread the following sidebars: "Semicolon;" (Chapter 3); "Event Handlers" (Chapter 4); "Functions" (Chapter 5); "Movie Clip Event Handlers" (Chapter 6); and "Variables and Scope," "Conditional Statements," and "Operators" (all Chapter 7).

Using ActionScript

Hold on to your hats, because using ActionScript to assign blend modes... is as easy as using the interface. One line of ActionScript is all that is required:

1. Select the hero movie clip and use the Properties panel to set the blend mode back to Normal.
2. While in the Properties panel, give the clip an instance name of **hero_mc**.
3. Add a layer at the top of the timeline called **actions**, and add the following script in frame 1 of that layer:

   ```
   hero_mc.blendMode = "darken";
   ```

4. Save your work and test your movie.

Easy, right? You can also specify blend modes using integers. This is less descriptive, but helpful when stepping through a numeric loop or working with existing integers.

A special bonus file called *blend_modes_all.fla* has been included on the CD in the *10* folder. It uses ActionScript to move 12 multicolored stars over a gray gradient background. Each time you click the mouse, it will cycle through, and display, each blend mode. This allows you to see how each blend mode will affect underlying art.

NOTE

It is difficult to represent these effects in black and white screen shots, and without changing the blend modes on the fly. Therefore, this is bound to be confusing without seeing the sample in action. It would be a good idea to run the demo movie before proceeding.

For example, watch how Lighten, Darken, Multiply, and Screen each work when moving from the light gray to dark gray background. Also, watch how Add and Subtract mix star colors, and how Invert affects both the background and other stars.

Some blend modes are Flash-specific and require a little explaining. For instance, the Layer blend mode was created to get around a side effect of applying alpha color transforms to nested bitmaps within a movie clip. Normally, the parent transform is errantly applied to each bitmap individually, despite the fact that you applied the transform to the parent movie clip, not its contents. This causes some unpredictable mixing within the clip. If the new Layer blend mode is applied to the parent clip before the transform, the individual nested bitmaps will be composited first, and the alpha color transform will be applied to the movie clip uniformly.

To see this in action, watch the clips that have three colored child stars. The Layer blend mode is also very valuable when fading in a movie clip that has layered bitmaps and movie clips within it. Using this mode, all elements within the fading clip will be treated as one when it comes to the fade.

Similarly, Alpha and Erase are a bit difficult to see in a simple demo. Again, these effects work only on children with alpha data, within a parent movie clip. In this case, the effect is clearest when applied to bitmaps inside the child movie clips. When the Alpha effect is applied to an interior movie clip, it will attempt to extract the alpha data from that movie clip and apply it to any underlying movie clips. Erase is similar, but it will invert the alpha data first. The trick is, the Stage must remain opaque. So, Alpha and Erase will not work when applied to a movie clip in the root timeline.

To see these effects in action, look at the two stars that appear to be fragmented. Open them up. In reality, there are two stars within these parent clips: *star3* uses Erase on its second star, and *star9* uses Alpha on its second star.

This will be clearer if you watch the demo movie in action. Also, the demo movie combines many skills you've learned throughout this book, and it is heavily commented. Set aside a time to look through the code and understand how it works.

What's Next?

Flash's runtime compositing has never been more powerful. With blend modes and filter effects at your disposal, you can create dynamic visual layouts that would have been very difficult or impossible to create previously.

Remember, however, that these features come at a sacrifice to performance, so don't use them carelessly, or without testing. Think of blend modes and filter effects as having a similar effect as vector scaling and opacity, discussed earlier in this book. All of these features can be taxing on your computer's processor, so look at your files on a variety of machines to make sure you are happy with the playback of your projects.

Before moving on, try a variety of filter effects and blend modes. Look through the code in the bonus *blend_modes_all.fla* file and try to understand how it works. Pay particular attention to the loop code, as you have not focused on that prior to this chapter. Finally, try to create some demanding animations and see how much faster they will play with runtime bitmap caching enabled. Remember to avoid scaling and rotating for a fair comparison, as these transformations largely negate the gains provided by the feature.

Now it's time to move on to text.

In the next chapter, you will:

- Learn about different text element types, including text that is equivalent to graphics, text that can be programmed, and text that can be entered by the user
- Work with fonts resident in your computer's operating system, as well as custom fonts that can be embedded for platform and machine independence
- Learn how to author text in HTML format and which HTML tags are supported by Flash
- Learn how to apply Cascading Style Sheets to HTML text
- Discover how to use Flash 8's new text-rendering engine, including new formatting and anti-aliasing options

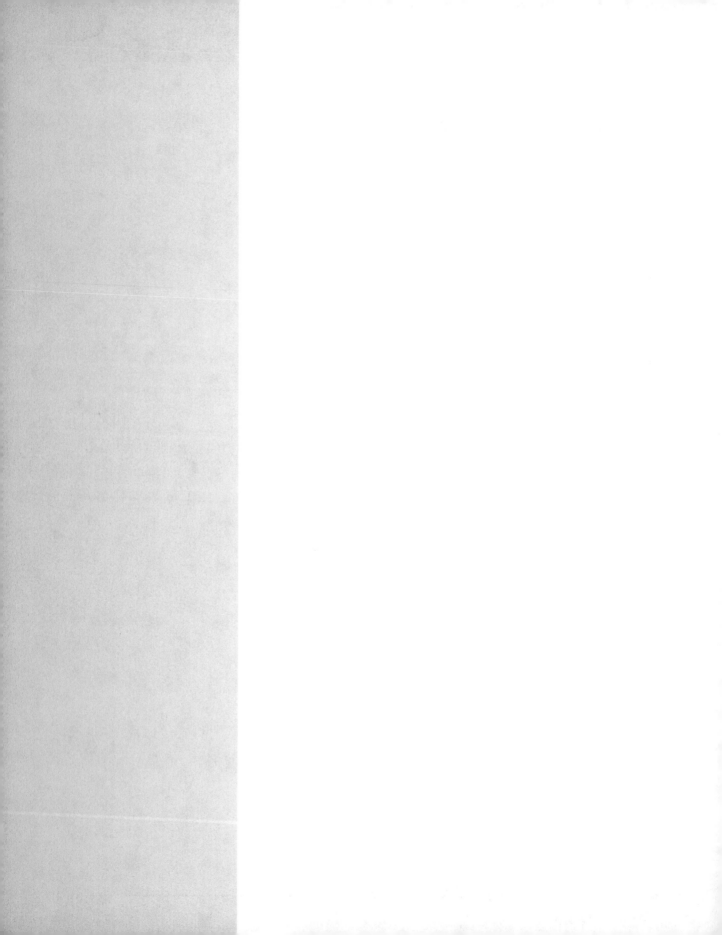

Working with Text

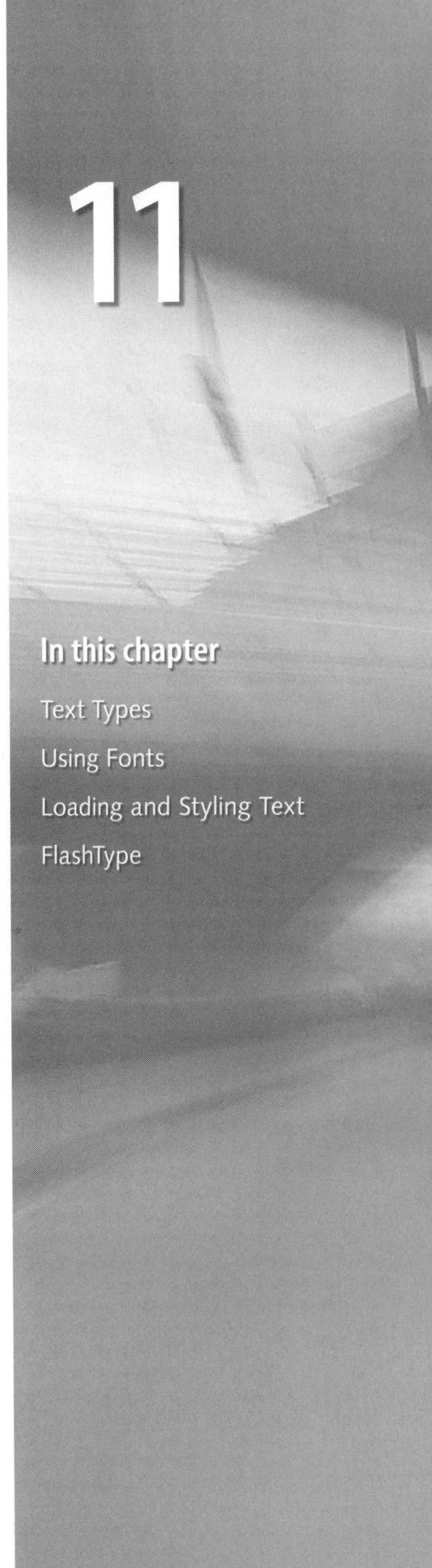

Although Flash is primarily known for its graphics and animation capabilities, text is also a vital part of the Flash environment. Flash is increasingly being used for promotional efforts, distance learning (as you'll see in Chapter 13), and Rich Application development, among other things. Text is possibly the *most* important individual part of any of these types of projects, and using Flash to create them doesn't change that fact.

In some ways, particularly regarding the legibility of small type sizes, text in Flash has been a problem. In fact, this issue created a cottage industry of developers producing bitmap fonts designed especially for use in Flash. Flash 8, with its new *FlashType* text-rendering engine, has gone a long way toward improving this situation.

Text Types

If you've been reading along, you've had plenty of experience using the Text tool to create text elements, but it helps to understand the different *kinds* of text elements available within Flash.

Static

The most basic type of text element is *static* text. This is the kind of text you've been creating throughout the projects in this book. Static text is editable within the authoring environment but is rendered as a graphic when published to *.swf*. This means that you can use custom fonts without concern for how they will look on end users' machines. Typically, you will use static text any time you don't need to program the text content or accept input from the user.

Using the Flash interface, all kinds of text are configured using the Properties panel. Figure 11-1 shows the panel when viewing a static text element. The left quarter of the panel offers the standard numerical input fields for the width, height, and x- and y-coordinates of the text element.

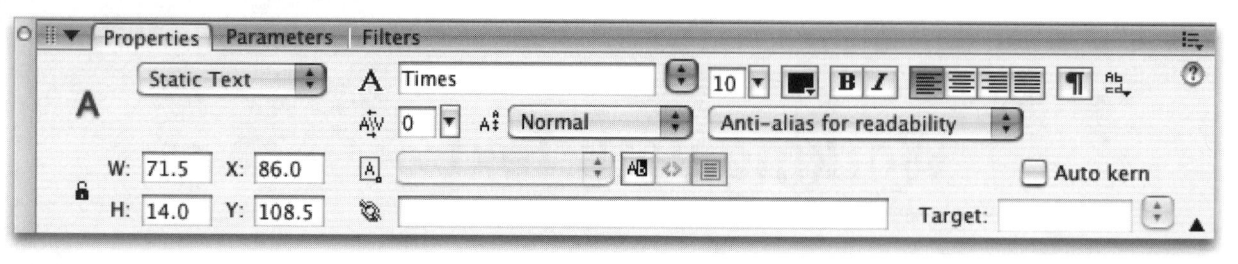

Figure 11-1. Static text options as seen in the Properties panel

The contents of the right three-quarters of the panel are context-sensitive, changing based on the kind of text element selected. The top row contains basic text-formatting controls standard in any application. These include font name, size, color, bold and italic, justification, and simple paragraph formatting options, accessed by the button with the Paragraph symbol (¶). The paragraph options, as seen in Figure 11-2, include first line indent, line spacing (akin to leading), and left and right margins.

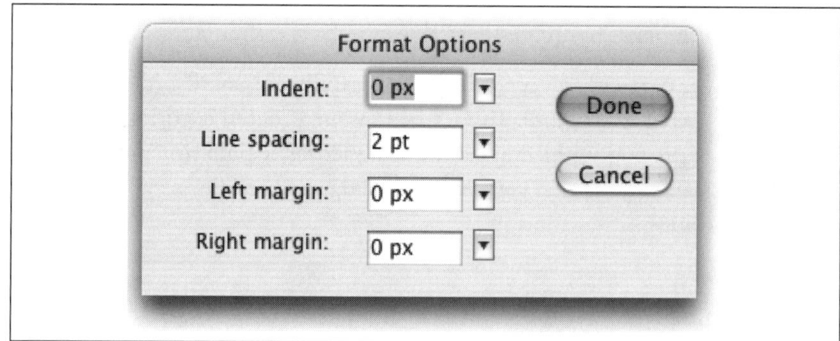

Figure 11-2. Paragraph format options

The last icon in the top-right row of buttons in the Properties panel, indicated by the *Abcd* icon with a drop-down menu, allows you to orient the text vertically, if desired. When this option is enabled, a context-sensitive button will appear allowing you to rotate the text or stack the letters one on top of another.

The second row of controls includes kerning, a subscript/superscript menu (which defaults to Normal), and the anti-aliasing menu. You will look at anti-aliasing options later in this chapter. Briefly, you can choose between using font information provided by the user's operating system, a bitmap version of the font with no anti-aliasing, two preset anti-aliasing options, and a custom anti-aliasing option that you can configure.

When working with static text elements, the third row of properties in the panel allows you to control only two features. The first, indicated by the *Ab* icon under the subscript/superscript menu, allows you to make the static text selectable. The user cannot edit the text, but being able to select it makes it possible to copy it to the clipboard. The second option is the auto-kern feature, to control character kerning automatically.

Finally, the last row of options allows you to associate an HTML link with any selected text, including a target option for opening the link in another window or frame. Using this option, you can open web-enabled assets in a browser and, as explained in the "asfunction: ActionScript via Links" sidebar later in this chapter, even execute ActionScript.

Dynamic

Unlike with static text, you can program the content of dynamic text fields using ActionScript. You'll see how to do this in a moment. First, look over the Properties panel to see how the available options differ from those for static text elements. Figure 11-3 shows the panel as it will appear with a dynamic text element selected.

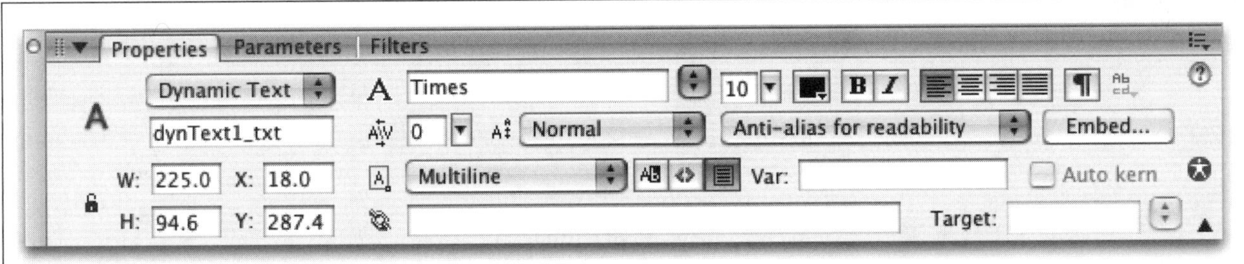

Figure 11-3. Dynamic text options as seen in the Properties panel

The first major difference that can be seen in the panel is that you can assign instance names for dynamic elements. This is usually necessary if you are to control the field with ActionScript—a feature not possible with static elements. This instance name serves the same role as that of all the other instance names you've used in the past: it lets you access the properties and methods of the object in question.

For example, to add to (or retrieve) the text within a dynamic element, you can reference the *text* property this way:

```
myDynamicText_txt.text = "Walter Westinghouse went to town.";
```

Another major difference between dynamic and static elements can be seen at the far right of the second row of options, where an Embed button now appears. The text within dynamic elements is not automatically converted to a graphics format. This means you must manually embed the font outlines for any font you use in a dynamic field, or they may not render properly for other users. The reasons for this will be discussed later in this chapter, but it's important enough to stress here as well, because it's easy to miss. During authoring, any fonts you work with will obviously be on your machine, but they may not be installed on other machines. If you don't know this ahead of time, you may not understand why fonts look good in one place but not another.

Note also in Figure 11-3 that the third row of options is now active for dynamic elements. Skipping over the width and x position discussed earlier, look at the new features from left to right. The first menu allows you to control how text will wrap in the field. Next appears the selectable text button, which can still be enabled or disabled for dynamic fields. Adjacent to this is a button that controls the *html* property of dynamic elements. When activated, the text within will support the basic HTML tags understood by Flash. (You'll read more about those in a minute, too.) The last of these new buttons, if enabled, will simply give the field a black border and a white background.

The last new feature—the field that you see at the end of the active elements in the third row—is the *variable* field. By placing a variable name in this field, you can create a text display for any variable in your project. For example, assume you've been using the variable *myVar* in a frame, and its current value is "Chairs Missing." Placing a dynamic field in this frame with *myVar* in the *var* field will display the "Chairs Missing" text on the Stage.

This is similar in some respects to accessing the *text* property of a dynamic field through its instance name. There are pros and cons to each approach. Using *var* means that, as long as you factor in the scope of your variables, you can always display their values without any further ActionScript. Think of this method as providing a visual representation of a variable's value. However, nothing but the value of the variable can be changed. Using the instance name to get or set a dynamic field's text won't influence any variables, but you will be able to work with any property supported by the field.

Experiment with these features to see their differences and similarities:

1. Create a new file and save it as *instance_and_var.fla* in your *11* folder.
2. Create two dynamic text elements on the Stage, and use the Properties panel to disable the "Show border around text" option for both elements.
3. Still using the Properties panel, give the first element an instance name of **`my_txt`**, but no *var* value.
4. Give the second element a *var* value of **`myVar`**, but no instance name.
5. Add a new layer and, in frame 1 of that layer, add the following script:

```
my_txt.text = "Rattlesnake Insurance";
trace(my_txt);
my_txt.border = true;

var myVar:String = "Finely Honed Machine";
trace(myVar);
myVar.border = true;
```

In the first group of lines, you are working with an instance of a dynamic field. The first line sets the text of the field. If this were a variable, you could display the value of the variable by tracing it, as in line 2. In this case, however, the instance is an object, not a variable. Instead of displaying the text of the variable in the Output window, you will trace a reference to this object. The third line manipulates a property of the field instance, which you will do again later in this chapter.

The second group of code lines refers to the variable to which you have given a visual display, via the other dynamic text element. Think of it first like every variable you've used thus far. You can type and populate it and then trace it, with lines 1 and 2, respectively. However, if you try to set a field property by mistake, you will be alerted to the error.

6. Save your work and test your movie. You will get an error saying that no *border* property exists for the *myVar* variable.
7. Delete or comment out the last line of the script.
8. Save your movie and test it again.

Input

Input text fields are very similar to dynamic elements, but input fields allow the user to enter content. This accounts for the only two significant differences between the properties of input fields and other text elements. Since input fields are designed to accommodate user data, the selectable option cannot be disabled. Similarly, the ability to predefine text-based links is irrelevant, so this feature has been replaced by an option that allows you to limit the number of characters a user can add to a field.

The Properties panel pictured in Figure 11-4 shows these subtle differences.

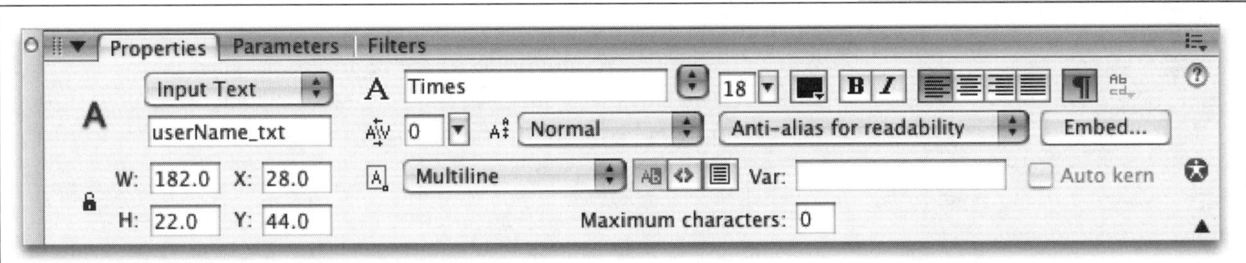

Figure 11-4. Input text elements use the same options as dynamic elements, with the exception of the link fields

Using Fonts

The previous section of this chapter briefly alluded to issues surrounding font use in dynamic and input text elements. (Remember, although you obviously need the relevant font to edit a static text element during authoring, these text types will be converted to graphics for runtime distribution.)

There are two ways to use fonts in dynamic and input text elements. The first is to rely on fonts that you expect to be present on the end user's machine. These are referred to as *device fonts*. The second is to guarantee that any custom fonts will render properly on any machine by embedding the font outlines in your file.

Device Fonts

Device fonts are extremely useful for keeping file size low because they don't require you to embed font outlines in your file. However, this also means that you are restricted to a small list of fonts that you expect to be found on most systems.

NOTE

You should be sure to test your files on as many machines and platforms as possible to verify your font use and expected results. However, this is a liberal list of fonts that may be found on most modern operating systems:

- *Arial, Arial Black, Comic Sans MS, Georgia, Impact, Tahoma, and Verdana are typically found in some like-named variant.*
- *Times and Courier on a Mac are known as Times New Roman and Courier New on Windows, and are usually mapped to one another by the application displaying the font. Helvetica on the Mac is also usually mapped to Arial on Windows.*
- *Other special fonts, such as symbol/dingbat fonts Symbol, Webdings, and Wingdings, are usually found in some similar form but don't always display properly across platforms.*

To use a device font, simply select that option from the anti-aliasing menu in the Properties panel.

Embedding Fonts

When custom or uncommon fonts are required, or when you wish to take advantage of advanced anti-aliasing options or font switching through ActionScript, embedding font outlines is required. Here's how it works:

1. Using your active *instance_and_var.fla* file, select one of your text elements and type a string therein in the font and styles you wish to embed.
2. Click the Embed button in the Properties panel, with any dynamic or input text element selected. (If the option is not selectable, you may have your anti-aliasing option set to "Use device fonts.")
3. You will see a dialog similar to the one pictured in Figure 11-5. Multiple-select any range of character outlines, or glyphs, that you wish to embed (using Shift-click for contiguous selections, or Ctrl/Cmd-click to select separated items).

NOTE

To embed styled font outlines, such as bold and italic, style at least one character of placeholder text in each format. For example, you can routinely add a string like this:

a **b** *c* ***d***

which contains one character in each style.

WARNING

Don't embed the entire font if you don't need to, as it will contribute significantly to file size. For example, if you know you only need uppercase alpha characters for a headline, or only numbers and punctuation for dollar amounts, select only those glyphs that are needed. In fact, if you know the exact string you intend to use, you can embed only specific characters in the field at the bottom of the dialog.

4. Save your work and test your movie.

If any characters don't display, be sure you've styled placeholder text prior to embedding, as discussed in step 1.

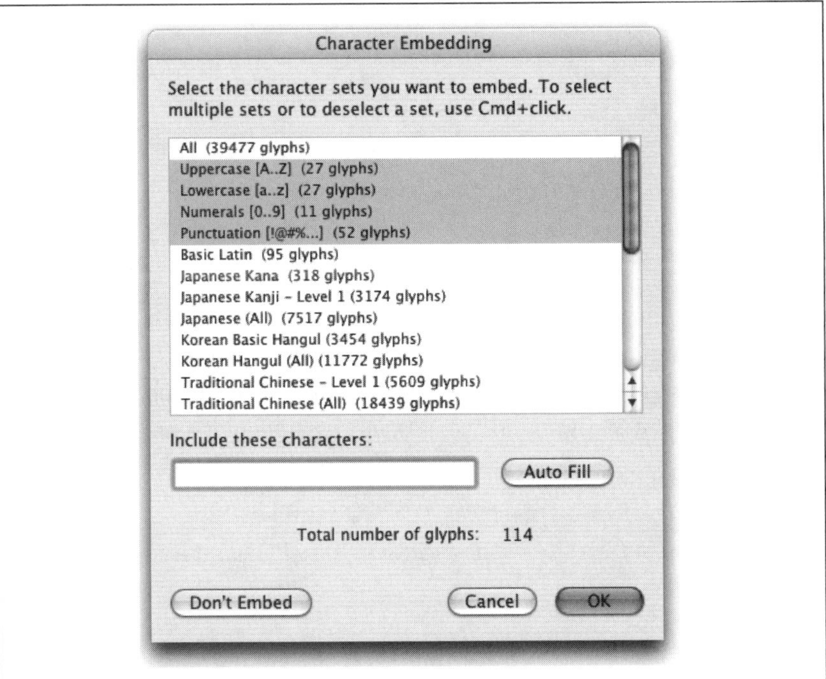

Figure 11-5. The Character Embedding dialog, embedding only basic characters to keep file size as low as possible

Loading and Styling Text

Now that you know how to set up your text elements and use the typeface of your choice, it's time to populate those fields. Typing in straight text and even adding normal strings through ActionScript are both tasks you've accomplished in prior chapters. However, using HTML tags in fields is something new. In this section, you'll see how you can use rudimentary HTML and CSS in Flash.

HTML

First, it's important to realize that Flash's support for HTML tags is very limited. Table 11-1 lists the tags that are supported.

Table 11-1. HTML tags supported by Flash

Tag	Syntax	Attributes
Anchor	`<a></a>`	`href`, `target`
Bold	`<b></b>`	
Break	` `	
Font	`<font></font>`	`face`, `size`, `color`
Image	`<img />`	`src`, `id`, `width`, `height`, `align`, `hspace`, `vspace`
Italic	`<i></i>`	
List item	`<li></li>`	
Paragraph	`<p></p>`	`align`, `class`
Span	`<span></span>`	`class`
Underline	`<u></u>`	

There is also a Flash-specific tag that allows you to take advantage of the *TextFormat* ActionScript class for text formatting in an HTML context. Use of this class will be detailed in a later section of this chapter, but for completeness's sake, the HTML syntax has been included in Table 11-2.

Table 11-2. The Flash-specific HTML tag

Tag	Syntax	Attributes
Text format	`<textformat></textformat>`	`blockindent`, `indent`, `leading`, `leftmargin`, `rightmargin`, `tabstops`

To use HTML formatting in a dynamic text element, the *html* property must be set to true, and the *htmlText* property must be used to populate the field, rather than the *text* property discussed earlier. Try this:

1. Create a new file and save it as *html_and_css.fla* in your *11* folder.
2. Give the file dimensions of 550 × 450 using the Modify→Document menu command.
3. Create a dynamic text field on the Stage. Give it a width of 470 × 390 and position it at (40, 30) on the Stage. Give it an instance name of **`styled_txt`**.
4. Choose "Use device fonts" from the anti-aliasing menu in the Properties panel.
5. Name the first layer **`field`** and add a second layer called **`actions`**.

6. If you wish, you can select the field again and turn on the *multiline* and *html* features using the Properties panel buttons. However, it's better to learn how to do this with ActionScript so you can also do it dynamically.

7. Add the following script to frame 1 of the *actions* layer:

```
styled_txt.multiline= true;
styled_txt.wordWrap = true;
styled_txt.html = true;

styled_txt.htmlText = "<li><b>bold</b></li>";
styled_txt.htmlText += "<li><i>italic</i></li>";
styled_txt.htmlText += "<li><u>underline</u></li>";
```

   This builds the HTML content step by step, although you will see later that you can also load HTML content from an external source.

NOTE

For the remainder of this project, the step-by-step content additions will be kept brief for space reasons, while the corresponding provided sample files will contain more feature-rich examples. Feel free to compare as you go along.

8. Save your movie and test your work. You should see a list with bold, italic, and underlined elements in list format.

9. If you want to see a more detailed example, open the *html_css_01.fla* file in the 11 folder of your working directory. This file uses at least one of most of the supported tags.

10. Once you are finished experimenting, close all open files.

You may have noticed the omission of ordered list tags (`<ol></ol>`) or unordered list tags (`<ul></ul>`) surrounding the list items in the code featured in the final step of the last example. That's because these tags are not supported. All list items will be bulleted by default.

CSS

With HTML tags working in your text file, it's time to step up and style your text with *Cascading Style Sheets* (CSS). Space limitations do not allow an in-depth description of CSS here, so some awareness, or at least an ability to hit the ground running, must be assumed in this context. If you think it will help, you might want to spend a few minutes on the Web brushing up on the concepts behind CSS. A quick description might qualify CSS as a centralized styling system that can be applied to tags project-wide. In a nutshell, you begin by defining a collection of style attributes that can then be applied to many text elements so you don't have to format each one manually.

If you have some experience with CSS, don't get too excited that this will be the answer to every styling need you will ever have in Flash. As with

HTML, support for style properties in Flash is limited. Table 11-3 lists the supported properties, and their ActionScript equivalents, as described in the ActionScript dictionary.

Table 11-3. CSS properties supported by Flash

CSS property	ActionScript property	Usage and supported values
text-align	*textAlign*	Recognized values are *left*, *center*, and *right*.
font-size	*fontSize*	Only the numeric part of the value is used. Units (px, pt) are not parsed; pixels and points are equivalent.
text-decoration	*textDecoration*	Recognized values are *none* and *underline*.
margin-left	*marginLeft*	Only the numeric part of the value is used. Units (px, pt) are not parsed; pixels and points are equivalent.
margin-right	*marginRight*	Only the numeric part of the value is used. Units (px, pt) are not parsed; pixels and points are equivalent.
font-weight	*fontWeight*	Recognized values are *normal* and *bold*.
font-style	*fontStyle*	Recognized values are *normal* and *italic*.
text-indent	*textIndent*	Only the numeric part of the value is used. Units (px, pt) are not parsed; pixels and points are equivalent.
font-family	*fontFamily*	A comma-separated list of fonts to use, in descending order of desirability. Any font family name can be used. If you specify a generic font name, it will be converted to an appropriate device font. The following font conversions are available: *mono* is converted to *_typewriter*, *sans-serif* is converted to *_sans*, and *serif* is converted to *_serif*.
color	*color*	Only hexadecimal color values are supported. Named colors (e.g., blue) are not supported.
display	*display*	Supported values are *inline*, *block*, and *none*.

These properties can be applied using tags and classes, and the anchor tag can add *link*, *hover*, and *visited* states to links.

A style defined to work with a tag begins with the tag itself and is followed by the properties you wish to use, each on a line followed by a semicolon, and all within braces. For example:

```
p {
    font-family: Times,serif;
    font-size: 14px;
}
```

This style would affect all paragraph tags in the text element to which the corresponding style sheet object is applied.

A style defined to work with a class begins with a period and the class name, and the remainder of the structure is the same as you've just seen with tag styles. For example:

```
.headline {
    font-family: Verdana;
    font-size: 24px;
    font-weight: bold;
}
```

This style would affect any applicable tag with a *class="headline"* attribute and value.

Creating and applying styles

There are two ways to build and apply styles. The first is to build the style objects one property at a time in ActionScript, and the second is to load a finished style sheet from an external source. This first example uses the former approach:

1. If it's not still active, open the *html_css_01.fla* file in the *11* folder of your working directory. This file has an assembled HTML string in it, all ready for you to style.
2. Test the movie to see what the HTML will look like without CSS applied. It should resemble Figure 11-6.
3. Close the preview and go back to your main movie. In frame 1 of the *actions* layer, add the following code to the top of the script:

    ```
    var styles:TextField.StyleSheet = new
    TextField.StyleSheet();
    styles.setStyle(".headline",
        {fontFamily: 'Verdana',
        fontSize: '24px',
        fontWeight: 'bold'}
    );
    styled_txt.styleSheet = styles;
    ```

    The first line of the preceding code creates the style sheet object. The second line defines a class style called *headline*. Lines 3 through 6 define the properties of that style, and line 7 applies the style object to the dynamic text field instance.

HTML in Flash
by A. Reader
Flash supports limited HTML tags such as:
• bold
• italic
• underline
Ünicode characters & decimal entitity codes are also supported.
A style can be created this way:
styles.setStyle('p',
{fontFamily: 'Times,Times New Roman,serif',
fontSize: '18px'}
);
A style sheet can be applied using styled_txt.styleSheet = styles;
Consult the companion Web site of this book for more information.

Figure 11-6. HTML text rendered without Cascading Style Sheet formatting

CSS objects must be defined and applied to text elements before the content is added. Styles can be defined and changed later, but if the CSS object itself is applied after the fact, your text will not be styled.

4. Save your work and preview your file. The headline font should now be large, bold Verdana, in contrast with the rest of the text in the field.

HTML in Flash

by A. Reader

Flash supports limited HTML tags such as:

- **bold**
- *italic*
- underline

Ünicode characters & decimal entitity codes are also supported.

A style can be created this way:

```
styles.setStyle('p',
{fontFamily: 'Times,Times New Roman,serif',
fontSize: '18px'});
```

A style sheet can be applied using `styled_txt.styleSheet = styles;`

Consult the companion Web site of this book for more information.

Figure 11-7. The same dynamic text field seen in Figure 11-6, but with Cascading Style Sheet formatting applied

5. To see a more involved example, open *html_css_02.fla*. Several additional styles have been created in this file, and the rendered result should resemble Figure 11-7.
6. When you are finished, close all open files.

The second way to apply style sheets (as well as the HTML content itself) to a text field is to load the content from an external text file. You'll look at that next.

Loading Text

If you have your HTML and CSS documents created already, it can be much easier to load these assets into Flash than to re-create them with ActionScript. Doing so simplifies the whole process greatly.

In the case of CSS, you still need to create the style sheet object and ultimately apply it to the text element, but describing each style and attribute can be done externally:

1. Open *html_css_03.fla*. When loading the assets from an external source, you don't need to build any HTML or CSS beforehand. This file will start you off with a minimum of field attributes.
2. In frame 1 of the *actions* layer, add the following script. It will create the style sheet object the same way you did before, but it will use the *load* method of the style sheet object to load the external file. Only when that load is deemed a success will it then apply the style sheet to the text element, using the same syntax you used before:

```
var main_css:TextField.StyleSheet = new TextField.StyleSheet();
main_css.load("html_in_flash.css");
main_css.onLoad = function(success:Boolean):Void {
    if (success) {
        styled_txt.styleSheet = main_css;
    } else {
        trace("Could not load CSS file.");
    }
};
```

Loading the HTML is very similar. The only difference is that, in this case, you are loading the HTML using standard name/value variable loading techniques. In this case, the source is a text file, but it could also be server output.

You may have used name/value pairs frequently, and not known about it. Often, HTML forms submit data this way, and you may have noticed a URL followed by an ampersand, a variable name, and a value. An example might be:

http://www.domain.com/search.php?name1=value1&name2=value2

To use this approach, your text file must be formatted similarly. Before proceeding with the remaining ActionScript, open the *html_in_flash.txt* text file in your *11* folder. You will see that the file begins with `&content=` and then is followed by the HTML you need. When you are finished, continue with the HTML loading:

3. Add the following to the bottom of the script in frame 1 of the *actions* layer. Remember, your CSS object must be defined and applied prior to the content being added to the text element:

```
var text_lv:LoadVars = new LoadVars();
text_lv.load("html_in_flash.txt");
text_lv.onLoad = function(success:Boolean):Void {
    if (success) {
        styled_txt.htmlText = this.content;
    } else {
        trace("Could not load text file.");
    }
};
```

   As you can see, this structure is almost identical to the loading process for the CSS file. A *LoadVars* object is created, the file is loaded, and only upon success is the *htmlText* property of the text field populated.

4. Save your movie and preview your file. You should see a fully styled document, as depicted in Figure 11-7, by loading the content from external files.

FlashType

Flash 8 has substantially improved the text-formatting and font-rendering capabilities of the Flash Player. It has added additional formatting options such as letter spacing (also known as tracking), as well as provided custom anti-aliasing features. These options combine to make smaller type sizes more legible than ever before. A practical comparison of 9-point type using the older type-rendering engine and the newer advanced type-rendering engine can be seen in Figure 11-8.

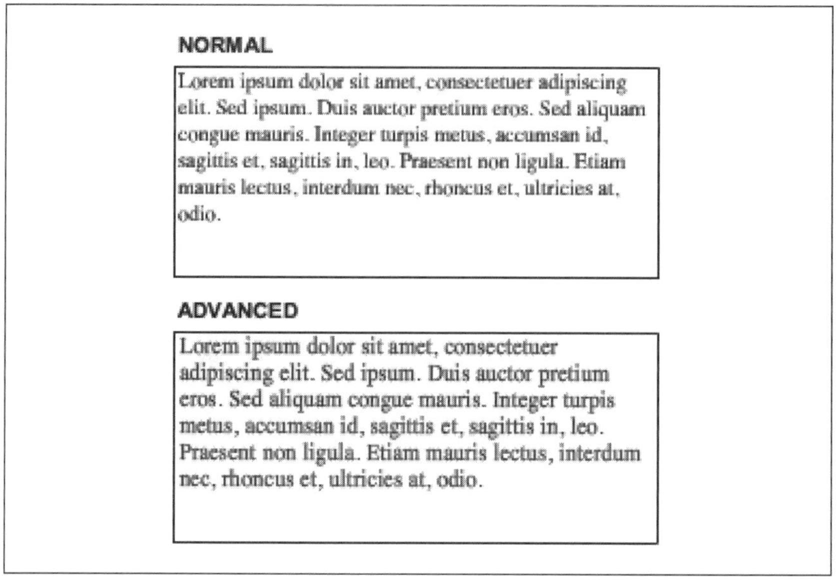

NORMAL

Lorem ipsum dolor sit amet, consectetuer adipiscing elit. Sed ipsum. Duis auctor pretium eros. Sed aliquam congue mauris. Integer turpis metus, accumsan id, sagittis et, sagittis in, leo. Praesent non ligula. Etiam mauris lectus, interdum nec, rhoncus et, ultricies at, odio.

ADVANCED

Lorem ipsum dolor sit amet, consectetuer adipiscing elit. Sed ipsum. Duis auctor pretium eros. Sed aliquam congue mauris. Integer turpis metus, accumsan id, sagittis et, sagittis in, leo. Praesent non ligula. Etiam mauris lectus, interdum nec, rhoncus et, ultricies at, odio.

Figure 11-8. Normal and advanced anti-aliasing options compared

The new text-rendering engine goes by the name of *FlashType*. Although there's more to FlashType, here you'll look at the two biggest parts: the formatting and anti-aliasing controls.

asfunction: ActionScript via Links

It is possible to call ActionScript functions from HTML links, which makes it easy to trigger instructions when interacting with text. Instead of creating invisible buttons that might be layered atop a text element, you can add function calls to links in static text using the Properties panel, or in HTML that is assembled dynamically.

All you need to do is define a function as you normally would, and create a link the way you normally would. However, instead of using a URL in the link, use the *asfunction* protocol.

Just as the *http:*, *mailto:*, and *javascript:* protocols convert links to web address requests, emails, and JavaScript calls, preceding a link with *asfunction:* will cause the link content to be interpreted as an ActionScript function call. The syntax is:

```
asfunction:functionName,stringargument
```

The following example functions similarly to an acronym expander. It will trace the long name of an acronym you click on:

```
function showMsg(msg:String):Void {
    trace(msg);
}
my_txt.htmlText = "You can use <font
color='#990000'><a href='asfunction:showMsg,Hypertext
Markup Language'>HTML</a></font> in Flash.";
```

See *asfunction_01.fla* in the *11* folder of your working directory for a sample of *asfunction* in action.

Formatting

You won't always need to use Cascading Style Sheets to format text in Flash. For example, you won't need the global benefits of CSS to format one instance of text, and at times you may want to take advantage of one or more of the ActionScript formatting options not supported by CSS. To accomplish this, you need to use the *TextFormat* class.

Using the *TextFormat* class is very similar to using the *StyleSheet* class, in that you create a *TextFormat* object, set the values of any properties you wish to use, and then apply it to a text field. *TextFormat* properties are numerous. Among them are *font*, *size*, *color*, *bold*, *italic*, *underline*, *kerning*, *leading*, *align*, *indent*, *leftMargin*, *rightMargin*, *tabStops*, and more.

To demonstrate the use of a *TextFormat* object, you'll use another property and a new Flash 8 enhancement, *letterSpacing*. *Letter spacing*, also known as tracking, is the space that is added to, or subtracted from, the space between all the letters of affected text. Take a look:

1. Create a new file called *flashtype.fla* and save it in your *11* folder.
2. Create a dynamic text element on the Stage and give it an instance name of **dynText1_txt**.
3. Fill the text element with enough text to see changes in its appearance. A few lines should do.
4. Embed your font of choice in the text field you just created. This is an important step to watch for, should problems occur, because several text-formatting options require embedded fonts to work.
5. Add a layer to the top of the timeline and name it **actions**. In the first frame of the *actions* layer, add this script:

```
var txt1_fmt:TextFormat = new TextFormat();
txt1_fmt.letterSpacing = .5;
dynText1_txt.setTextFormat(txt1_fmt);
```

   The first line of the preceding code creates an instance of the *TextFormat* class called *txt1_fmt*. The second line sets the *letterSpacing* property of this *TextFormat* object to .5, adding space between all the characters in the text field to which this format will be applied. The last line applies the format to the dynamic text field you created earlier, *dynText1_txt*.

6. Save your work and test your movie.
7. Your text passage should now have more space between every adjacent letter pair. If the effect is too subtle, increase the *letterSpacing* value in your script until you can clearly see a change. When you are satisfied, return the *letterSpacing* value to .5, as this will help the changes you will make in the upcoming section appear more like they would in a practical situation.

NOTE

For testing purposes, where size considerations are not particularly important, feel free to embed all glyphs. When it comes to creating your final files, however, try to embed as few glyphs as possible to keep file size down.

Custom Anti-Aliasing

Perhaps an even greater improvement to the legibility of small type sizes comes by way of the new custom anti-aliasing controls. When the *antiAliasType* property is set to *advanced*, you can set the thickness, sharpness, and precision with which the type is rendered.

Finesse the anti-aliasing of the text in the file you are presently working on:

1. At the bottom of the script in frame 1, add the following code:

   ```
   dynText1_txt.antiAliasType = "advanced";
   dynText1_txt.thickness = 50;
   dynText1_txt.sharpness = -100;
   dynText1_txt.gridFitType = "subpixel";
   ```

2. Save your work and test your movie. The type should look even better now.

The first line of the preceding script sets the anti-alias type to advanced, making the changes that follow possible. The second line makes the text a bit thicker. This setting can have a value ranging from –200 (much thinner) to 200 (much thicker), making it possible to exert much more granular control over the text than could be achieved by setting the format weight to bold.

The third line similarly affects the sharpness of the text. This value can range from –400 to 400. Notice that, in this case, the value is –100. Softening the text a bit when increasing the thickness can help improve the legibility of fine anti-aliased edges. If you've ever over-sharpened an image in a bitmap-editing application, this analogy will likely be clear. If not, however, experiment with much higher sharpness values—perhaps a succession of 100, 200, and 400—to see the legibility of the text decline.

Finally, the last line sets the grid fit type to *subpixel*. The default setting is *pixel*, which attempts to adjust anti-aliasing thresholds to the whole pixel value. A subpixel value allows adjustments in the fraction of pixels. This may imply that the subpixel setting always looks better because it is more precise, but that is not always the case. When setting custom anti-alias values, always test a variety of settings to achieve the best-looking result.

Although it is typically easier to adjust these settings using ActionScript, both thickness and sharpness can also be adjusted using the Properties panel. With a text element selected, choosing the anti-aliasing menu option "Custom anti-aliasing" will open the dialog seen in Figure 11-9, allowing numerical adjustment of the pictured settings.

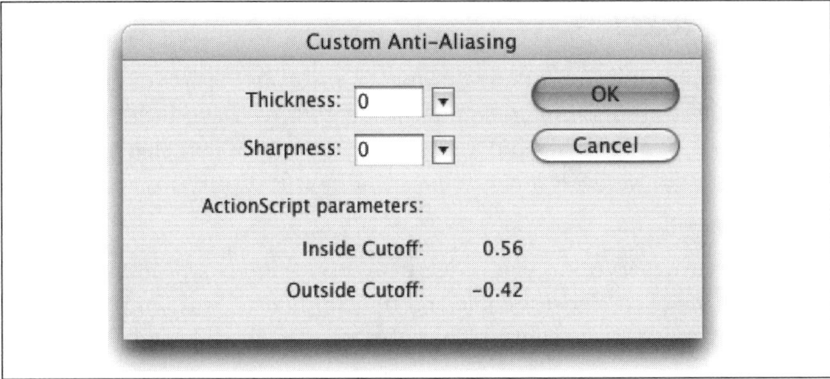

Figure 11-9. The Custom Anti-Aliasing dialog

A pair of intermediate-level bonus source files has been included in the provided source, to let you experiment freely with these settings. The *flashtype_01.fla* file demonstrates the settings at work on a text field with text already included and embedded. The second version of this file, *flashtype_02.fla*, adds to this same demonstration the ability to create text fields on the fly and populate them with ActionScript.

Embedded font symbols

In addition to the code discussed in this chapter, other *TextFormat* properties and *TextField* properties are demonstrated in the *flashtype* sample files. One, the *font* property of a *TextFormat* object, requires *embedded font symbols.*

Embedded font symbols are font outlines that have been embedded into a file's library. This makes it possible to switch among custom fonts at runtime, without having to rely on device fonts that hopefully reside in the user's operating system.

Figure 11-10. Embedding fonts in a document's Library via the Font Symbol Properties dialog

To embed a font symbol, choose New Font from the Library's Options menu (found in the upper-right corner of the Library panel). The dialog pictured in Figure 11-10 will appear. Select the font and style you want to embed, and whether or not you want to include a bitmap version of the font. Bitmap versions of the font can improve legibility at smaller type sizes. Give the font symbol a name that is as descriptive as possible. If the font only has one purpose in your entire project, you can name it something like *logoFont*. However, it's very helpful to base the new font name on the original font name, adding a character such as an asterisk to differentiate the two. This also enables easy reuse of the font symbol across multiple projects.

What's Next?

Text is a broad, and important, category of assets in Flash. Text helps you, as a designer or programmer, communicate with your end user. You've not only learned how to create and format several kinds of text elements in this chapter, but you've even touched on using text to transfer data (with the *LoadVars* class).

But even with everything you've learned here, there is still much more to discover. One of the most reliable and frequently used ways of transferring data, for example, is through the use of XML, which will not be discussed in this book due to scope and space limitations. Consider XML an important topic for self-motivated review.

Similarly, try to expand on what you have learned in this chapter by creating a more advanced application styling scheme. Embed more than one font and then make a style sheet that makes use of each font. Also, create a small interface widget (a pair of buttons or, perhaps, a menu) that will load the appropriate CSS when needed.

Finally, practice calling ActionScript functions from text links using the *asfunction* protocol. This can be a fast and easy way to add interactivity to text because it is not necessary to create buttons in each case.

When you're ready to move on, you'll learn how to load the remainder of the main Flash asset types. You've already learned how to load text, style sheets, and (by extension) data. In Chapters 8 and 9, you learned how to work with external sound and video. In Chapter 12, you'll learn how to load external graphics and other *.swf* files.

In the next chapter, you will:

- Load *.swf* files
- Load bitmaps, including baseline JPEG, progressive JPEG, GIF, and PNG files
- Learn how to use preloading components to make the loading experience more pleasant for the user
- Learn how to write your own preloading code to make your files even leaner
- Discover how event listeners can improve your event management

Loading Assets on the Fly

12

This chapter focuses almost entirely on solving one problem: keeping initial download times to a minimum without compromising too much quality or creativity. This goal can be accomplished in several ways, and each approach has its merits. Perhaps the method that achieves the most successful mix of optimization and quality, however, is loading assets on demand.

Flash projects are often more complex than what we've created so far in this book. Web sites, photo galleries, presentations, printable advertisements, and many other projects can all be created with Flash, and it is rarely an economical use of file size to cram all the necessary assets into one *.swf*. Adding 1 bitmap image to a Flash project may not affect the file size much, but adding 10 can really make a difference.

Splitting projects into multiple pieces and loading each module only when it's required is key to creating Flash content that runs smoothly and loads quickly. You may be thinking that using external assets simply shifts the download burden to a later time. That's true, but the point is that the external content may never be needed and, therefore, may never be loaded.

Another benefit of external assets is that they make complex Flash projects easier to manage and update. A modular structure can speed up development significantly, for a variety of reasons. First, smaller files are typically easier to work with during authoring. This is especially true if a file has a lot of audio or graphics that must be recompressed during each export. Second, if a project is modularized, more than one person can usually work on it simultaneously. Designers, programmers, content developers, and testers can all work together by focusing on individual pieces of the big picture.

Using ActionScript to Modularize Content

Successfully modularizing a Flash project depends largely on what type of content you're working with. For example, it's possible to divide larger projects into smaller *.swf* files. It's also possible to keep many or all bitmaps, sounds, and videos external to your main *.swf* document. In each case, you can load the assets dynamically when needed.

Loading SWFs

Your first project will focus on loading external SWFs using the *loadMovieNum()* command. The related *loadMovie()* command will be examined in just a bit, when you load bitmaps.

Flash allows you to "stack" visual objects in three primary ways:

- Using the *arrange* feature within a timeline layer. You've also had some experience in this book with using the Modify→Arrange→Bring to Front menu command and its related commands to adjust the order of appearance of visual assets within a layer.
- Using the layers in the timeline. As you've seen repeatedly, assets within layers found toward the top of the timeline will appear to be on top of (or in front of, if you prefer) assets within layers found toward the bottom of the timeline.
- Using ActionScript to set the *level* of a scriptable visual asset. Although you may not have had as much experience with this method of ordering movie clips and buttons, this is the subject of this section's mini-project.

To allow ActionScript control over the stacking of movie clips and buttons, Flash uses invisible *levels* that appear above the Stage. In some ways they are similar to timeline layers, but the level of an asset can be changed at runtime, while the timeline layer order cannot. Furthermore, a level can override a layer setting.

For example, imagine a file with movie clips *myClip1*, *myClip2*, and *myClip3* in layers 1, 2, and 3, respectively. Without ActionScript, the stacking order of these movie clips could not be changed at runtime. However, if the level of *myClip1* were set to a number higher than the level of the other movie clips, *myClip1* would appear on top of the other visual assets.

It's also important to understand that the *layer* number has nothing to do with the *level* number. All layers in the main timeline are in Flash's *_level0*. Therefore, placing any asset into *_level1* using ActionScript would cause that asset to appear on top of all the timeline layers, even if the timeline contained 50 layers.

In fact, loading assets into *_level0* will actually replace the main movie. This can be beneficial if you want to link through a linear storyline, replacing timelines chapter by chapter, in an attempt to keep RAM overhead to a minimum. On the other hand, what if you had an ambient soundtrack in the main timeline, or perhaps a chapter-wide navigation system (including Help and other global assets)? Loading a new *.swf* into *_level0* would interrupt the sound playback and/or unload the global interface.

In the latter case, it would be beneficial to feature your global interface and/or ambient soundtrack in the main timeline as you normally might, and then load each animation chapter into *_level1*. This would achieve the goal of never having more than one chapter in RAM at any given time, while ensuring that your global assets are active at all times in the unaffected *_level0*.

Enough description—now try it out for yourself. Start by confirming the *.swf* file you intend to load, and preparing the file into which you will load the external asset:

1. To avoid unnecessary complications with paths in this project, such as the need to traverse folders when locating external assets, both the loading file and the file that will be loaded should be in the same directory. First, make sure that *box_guy_shadow.swf* is in the *12* folder of your working directory. If not, copy the final animation from your *10* folder into the *12* folder.

NOTE

Flash paths are constructed the same way as web site paths. Directories are separated by forward slashes, and you can go up to a higher-level directory by including a ../ at the beginning of the path for every level you want to ascend. For example, the following will go down into an images directory to reach a JPEG:

```
images/loadme.jpg
```

while this path will go up one directory and then down into an adjacent images directory to reach the needed JPEG:

```
../images/loadme.jpg
```

2. Next, create a new file and save it as *load_movie_num.fla* in the *12* folder. Change its file dimensions to 550 × 500 pixels.

3. Create a button in the lower-right corner that will load in the external asset. Give it an instance name of **load_btn**.

4. Your movie only has one layer and one frame, but this is all you need. In frame 1, place the following script:

   ```
   load_btn.onRelease = function():Void {
       loadMovieNum("box_guy_shadow.swf",0);
   };
   ```

   This will load the shadow animation from Chapter 10 into *_level0*. If that's ringing a bell, you've been paying attention. If you haven't noticed a possible issue, you'll soon see it clearly.

5. Save your work and test your movie. Click the button you scripted to load the external *.swf*. If the files were in the same directory, you will see something jarring—not only does your load button disappear, but the Stage size even changes shape. Your root movie has been entirely replaced by the *.swf* file you just loaded. Close the *.swf* and go back to correct the problem.

6. Edit the frame script to load the movie into level 1 (the change is in bold):

```
load_btn.onRelease = function():Void {
    loadMovieNum("box_guy_shadow.swf",1);
};
```

7. Save your work and test your movie. Click the button that loads the external *.swf*. This time, the animation loads into the upper-left corner of your base movie and does not unload the button or change the Stage size. Your base movie remains active in *_level0*, and the new *.swf* is loaded into *_level1*.

Loading assets into levels is fast and easy because no further setup is required. However, it also has limitations. Unless you are adding or replacing entire segments of movies, as in the animation chapters described earlier, you are usually better off loading external assets into movie clips. This is what you will do in the next section.

Loading Bitmaps

Loading bitmaps uses the same techniques as loading *.swf* files. In previous versions of Flash, only external baseline JPEG files could be loaded on the fly. However, Flash 8 now makes it possible to load progressive JPEGs, GIFs, and PNG files.

In this mini-project, you'll examine the *loadMovie()* method. Unlike the level used in *loadMovieNum()*, *loadMovie()* identifies a movie clip as the target into which the external asset is loaded. Try it out with a variety of bitmaps:

1. Open the *load_movie.fla* file in the *12* folder. This will give you a little head start, in that the eight or so buttons you will experiment with have already been created.

2. For scripting flexibility, you will use the *createEmptyMovieClip()* method. This method does exactly what it says: it creates an empty movie clip in the timeline you specify. Add the following line (the simplest use of this method) into the *actions* layer, in frame 1:

```
var container:MovieClip = this.createEmptyMovieClip("container_mc",
1");
```

   Here, this refers to the main timeline. The method also gives the clip an instance name that you specify in the first parameter, and places the clip in the level specified in the second parameter.

3. To start, add a button event handler for the JPEG load button that loads the *water.jpg* file into *container*, the empty movie clip you just created:

```
loadJPG_btn.onRelease = function():Void {
    loadMovie("water.jpg",container);
};
```

NOTE

When storing a reference to a dynamically created movie clip in a variable, you can target the movie clip using the variable or the instance name you gave it during the creation process. In this case, there is little advantage to either method. However, when the script is more complicated—such as when creating many movie clips in a loop—using the variable is much easier.

4. The biggest significance of loading an asset into a movie clip instead of a level is that you can exert more control over it. Anything you can do with a movie clip, you can now do with the loaded asset. To demonstrate, add the following button event handlers for the arrow buttons. They will allow you to move the loaded bitmap around with the buttons:

```
up_btn.onRelease = function():Void {
    container._y -=10;
};
down_btn.onRelease = function():Void {
    container._y +=10;
};
left_btn.onRelease = function():Void {
    container._x -=10;
};
right_btn.onRelease = function():Void {
    container._x +=10;
};
```

5. Save your work and test your movie. The first thing you may notice is that the bitmap loads into the upper-left corner of the movie, just like the *.swf* did when loaded into a level. However, that's just because the *createEmptyMovieClip()* method creates the new movie clip at (0, 0) by default. If you use the arrow buttons, you can see that the clip can be moved around.

6. When you're finished experimenting, close the *.swf* and return to editing the frame script in frame 1.

7. Assign coordinates to the target movie clip to differentiate this mini-project from the use of *loadMovieNum()*. You can add this code anywhere, but inserting it right after line 1 contributes to script clarity:

```
container._x = 20;
container._y = 20;
```

WARNING

If you decide to create a static container movie clip, instead of creating this container on the fly with ActionScript, beware what you place inside it. The loaded asset will replace the content of the container movie clip. For example, don't create a container movie clip that has within it a frame for a slide show, because the frame will disappear when you load the first photo. Instead, create the frame in another movie clip beneath the container.

Similarly, the image will not be cropped or scaled by the movie clip. For example, if you load a 400 × 400-pixel JPEG into a 200 × 200-pixel movie clip, you will still see the entire JPEG. This can be a problem if the larger loaded asset interferes with other assets or interface elements.

In the next project, you will use a component that will automatically scale the asset to fit.

8. Next, add the event handlers that will load the remaining image types:

```
loadGIF_btn.onRelease = function():Void {
    loadMovie("star_move.gif",container);
}
loadPNG_btn.onRelease = function():Void {
    loadMovie("star_move.png",container);
}
```

9. Save your movie and test your work. If you want to compare your file with the provided source, your movie should now look like *load_movie_01.fla*.

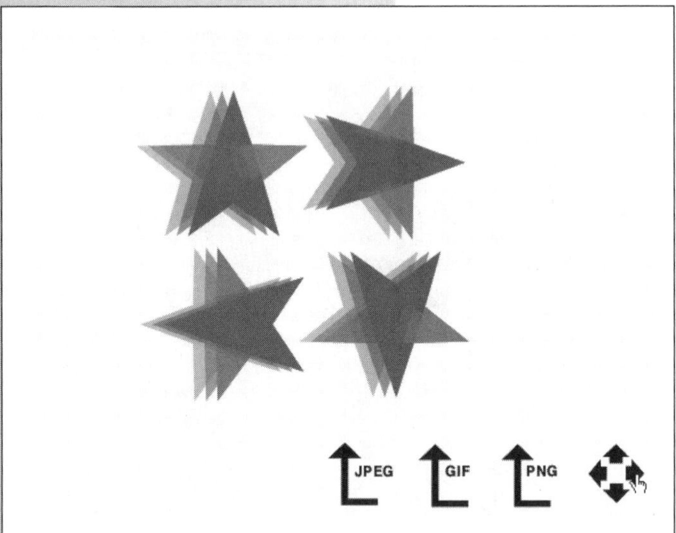

Figure 12-1. External bitmaps loaded into a target movie clip can be manipulated by using ActionScript to control the movie clip

You should now be able to move your loaded bitmaps around the screen, as seen in Figure 12-1 (the movement simulated in this figure is made possible by setting the *_x* and *_y* properties of the target movie clip using the arrow buttons). Each time you load a new bitmap asset type it will replace the previous one, because each method loads the bitmap into the *container* movie clip.

Even with two symbols, three pieces of static text, and three graphics, the parent movie you just worked with is only 1 KB. Why? The *.swf* is tiny because you're loading each of the graphics from an external source. This makes near-instant download of the main file possible. Even over the Internet, loading each graphic will still be a relatively speedy event, and if the user chooses not to download all three graphics, you're ahead of the game.

As good as your file is, it can still be better. It would help if you provided the user with some visual feedback while the graphics are loading. This requires a *preloader.*

Preloading

Although your *.swf* loader is only 1 KB, the graphics it loads average around 50 KB. Other projects are bound to contain assets that are significantly larger. You won't notice any delay working with these assets locally, but if you post these files online the load time will likely be a problem. The *.swf* will load quickly, but external assets might not show up for anywhere from a few seconds to several minutes, depending on the file size and the user's connection speed. Without knowing what's going on, a user may think your project is malfunctioning because it looks like nothing is happening during the load.

To solve this problem, your next project will be to create a *preloader* for the files. A preloader is a widget that uses ActionScript to check the status of the load process and displays it visually so the user always knows when something is loading. The first step will be to use the Flash *ProgressBar* component to do the heavy lifting.

Using Preloader Components

To implement a preloader using components, follow these steps:

1. If you haven't already done so, close the Preview window and close *load_movie.fla*. You'll come back to that file later.
2. Create a new Flash document and save it as *preload_components.fla* in the *12* folder. Change the Stage dimensions to 500 × 375.
3. Create two new layers, for a total of three. Name the first layer **`progressBar`**, the second **`loader`**, and the third **`actions`**.
4. Choose Window→Components to open the Components panel, shown in Figure 12-2.
5. Select the *loader* layer, expand the *UI Components* menu in the Components panel (by clicking on the small arrow), and drag the *Loader* component to the Stage. This creates an instance of this component on the Stage and adds the component to your Library.
6. Using the Properties panel, resize the *Loader* component instance to 500 × 375 (unlocking the aspect ratio constraint if necessary), position it at (0, 0), and assign it an instance name of **`myLoader`**.
7. Select the *progressBar* layer, and drag the *ProgressBar* component to the Stage. Position the instance in the horizontal and vertical center of the Stage. Assign it an instance name of **`myProgressBar`**.

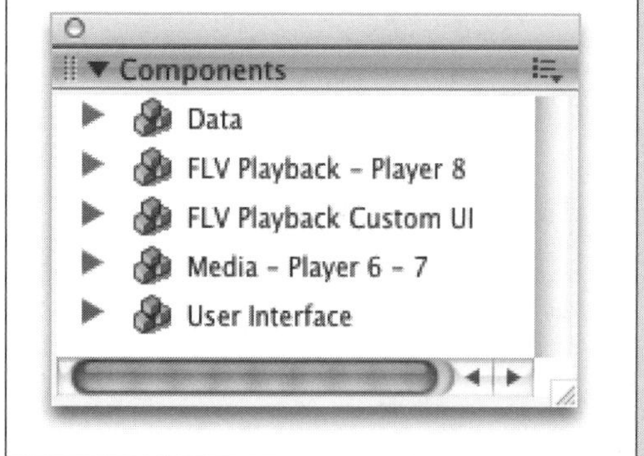

Figure 12-2. The Components panel

The *Loader* component is a bit like the *container* clip you created earlier, in the sense that your external content will load into it. It won't do anything here but scale the loaded asset to fit within the component's own bounding box. The *ProgressBar* component will track the loading progress and display a nice animated bar telling the user how much of the asset has loaded.

To get them to work together, you have to set up the *ProgressBar* component to monitor the *Loader* component's progress, and then you have to tell the *Loader* component what to load:

1. Select frame 1 of the *actions* layer and enter the script that follows:

```
myLoader.autoLoad = false;
myLoader.contentPath = "http://www.flashoutofthebox.com/water.jpg";
myProgressBar.source = myLoader;
myLoader.load();
```

The first line tells the *Loader* component not to load the asset automatically, and the second line tells the *Loader* what to load. The third line tells the *ProgressBar* component to monitor the *Loader*, and the last line starts the loading process.

NOTE

In this step, you're loading a server-based asset (a variant of the water.jpg file with which you've been working), because local assets will load too quickly to give any meaningful feedback. If you don't have an Internet connection at the moment, you can switch the pathname to that of a local file and try this another time. You won't see the progress bar in action, but you will at least see the asset load.

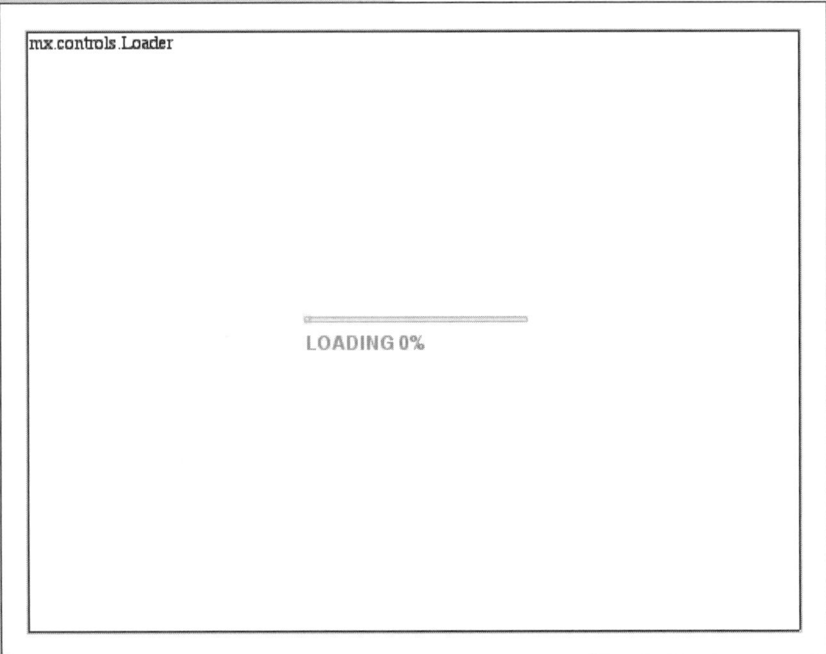

Figure 12-3. The layered components

2. Save and test the movie.

The image loads, and the progress bar displays the load progress nicely. As a quick setup, you've placed the *ProgressBar* component beneath the *Loader*, as seen in Figure 12-3. This way, when the asset loads, the bar becomes hidden. It won't always be easy to set up your files this way, though. For example, in the previous project, you were able to move the target movie clip around and still load in new assets. To hide the progress bar in that case, you would have to build a nested movie clip setup with both the target movie clip and the *ProgressBar* component in a parent movie clip.

In a moment, you'll learn how to clear a preloader so it doesn't have to be hidden at all. However, there's a more pressing problem. Despite the fact that your *preload_components.fla* file has no graphics in it, it is now a whopping 32 KB. As broadband is rapidly becoming the norm, that may not sound like much, but small file size increases can really add up. To put this in perspective, this is 32 times the size of your first loader.

As you've read in Chapters 8 and 9, this increased file size is because the components used in this file are large. Others are significantly larger. Components are designed to have common interface and scripting structures. This makes working with many components very convenient, and the more that are used, the less noticeable the file size increases become. However, using one or two can cause an unwanted exponential increase in download time. Writing your own preloader can help.

NOTE

Don't let the size of some components scare you off, but use them judiciously. In addition to the aforementioned economy of scale introduced when many Macromedia components are used, components also make rapid prototyping much easier. Furthermore, many third-party components are much smaller and can be used as alternatives.

Scripting Your Own Preloader

Your preloader will use text to display the percentage of bytes loaded. Every time 1% of an asset is loaded into your Flash movie, the number in the text field will increment by 1. When the percentage reaches 100%, the asset is fully loaded and displays in the movie. While this isn't the most visually exciting preloader in the world, it does serve the purpose of keeping the user informed and is a good starting point for exploring the visual possibilities of preloaders in your own work.

First, set up the file:

1. Open the *load_movie.fla* file in the *12* folder, and save it as *my_preloader.fla* in the same folder.
2. You'll need to add only one visual asset to this file: a text box into which you'll put the loading information. Select the Text tool and create a dynamic text element about 200 × 30 pixels in size. (The size does not have to be precise; it just needs to be big enough to accommodate the necessary incoming text.) Place it in the lower-left corner of the Stage, and give it an instance name of `info_txt`.
3. Set the text size to 14 point and, to keep file size small, set the font to *_sans*. (Using device fonts may not be as pretty as using custom fonts, but they don't have to be embedded to work.)

Your Stage should now look like the detail shown in Figure 12-4.

Figure 12-4. The dynamic text element on the Stage set up to receive loading information

Now you can start scripting your preloader:

1. Select frame 1 of the *actions* layer and add the following to your script:

   ```
   var my_mcl:MovieClipLoader = new MovieClipLoader();
   ```

   This creates an instance of the *MovieClipLoader* class and stores it in a variable named *my_mcl*. The *MovieClipLoader* class will handle the behind-the-scenes loading and progress reporting for you. All you'll have to do is trap the information it provides, and work it into a state that is meaningful to the user.

NOTE

Like the _mc suffix you used previously, the optional _txt and _mcl suffixes help Flash provide useful code hints in the Actions panel. However, using ActionScript 2.0 static typing (as discussed in Chapter 8) effectively eliminates the need to use these suffixes, because the data type declaration gives Flash all the information it needs. For example, the MovieClipLoader data type tells Flash that this is a MovieClipLoader object. Even more important than providing code hints, Flash can now check for certain types of errors and, if you make a mistake, can alert you when you publish your movie. (If you are still unclear on any part of this concept, see the "Data Types" sidebar in Chapter 8 for more information.)

In any case, though, using the suffixes has no adverse effect, so until you come up with a variable naming convention that you prefer, you may want to continue with this practice.

Now it's time to set up a system that will allow the *MovieClipLoader* object to automatically respond to events that it should respond to, but efficiently ignore unrelated events. This is accomplished by creating an *event listener*. (Briefly, a listener is a generic ActionScript object whose only job is to listen for events and run code in reaction to them. For a detailed look at listeners, see the "Event Listeners" sidebar.)

2. Create, in the same script, a *listener* object that you will later register with the *my_mcl MovieClipLoader* object used to monitor load progress:

   ```
   var my_listener:Object = new Object();
   ```

3. Now set up the event handlers. Start with the *onLoadProgress* event handler to trap the *loadProgress* event. This event is generated throughout the loading process. In addition to broadcasting the loading movie clip reference that is broadcast at all times (so you can tell one load request from another), this event also broadcasts the total file size of the asset (in bytes), and the total amount loaded (in bytes) at the time the event is broadcast.

   From this, you can display any feedback you like. In this case, you're going to display a percentage (*loadedBytes/totalBytes* * 100), rounded to the nearest integer. Fortunately, you don't have to write a rounding conditional that checks if the number's decimal value is above .5 or not. The *Math* object will take care of that for you:

```
my_listener.onLoadProgress = function (mc:MovieClip, loadedBytes:
Number, totalBytes:Number):Void {
  info_txt.text = "Loading: " + Math.round(loadedBytes/totalBytes *
100) + "%";
};
```

NOTE

You may have noticed the use of the plus sign (+) when writing the feedback text. When used with strings (text), the plus sign means concatenate, or join together into a string. Note, too, that a trailing space after the colon is used, but no leading space is used before the percent symbol (%).

Event Listeners

Imagine yourself sitting in a busy airport. If you had to carefully parse every bit of information going on around you, a significant amount of focus would be required and your energy would be unnecessarily drained. So, you compensate by training yourself to listen for any broadcast containing your flight number, your destination city, and perhaps the name of your airline. This is a more efficient way of processing the data around you. It allows you to automatically react to useful information, and discard background noise.

ActionScript can do the same thing using *event listeners*. A listener is simply a standalone ActionScript object that is instructed to listen for specific events and automatically run code when those events occur. This can be very important in the Flash world.

For example, what if you had to write code that constantly checked if any keys were pressed? That would be very inefficient. Instead, the *Key* class can help. The *Key* class is a built-in class that helps you process user interaction via the keyboard. It broadcasts an *onKeyDown* event whenever a key is pressed and an *onKeyUp* event whenever a key is released. You can set up an efficient listener so your code will hear those broadcasts and react. This way, your code responds to known events only when they occur, rather than constantly asking if they have occurred or not.

Listeners are also very helpful when processing information related to the Internet. When you type in a web address in your browser, you are contacting a server; the server receives your request, and then issues a response. This delay between request and response means the calls are *asynchronous*—that is, the results are not available immediately after the request.

In the "Scripting Your Own Preloader" project in this chapter, you face this dilemma. However, instead of forcing Flash to pause while waiting for something to download, you can set up a listener to trap the events automatically issued by the *MovieClipLoader* class. This class broadcasts events when content is being downloaded, when it completes, and when there is an error.

The listener object can capture these events using an event handler syntax that will probably be familiar to you. In this case, *onLoadProgress*, *onLoadComplete*, and *onLoadError* event handlers can be added to the listener, and it can be put to work by being registered with the *MovieClipLoader* object you create. Although this example centers on the *MovieClipLoader* class, this process is the same for any ActionScript object that can work with a listener.

It is good practice to remove a listener using *removeListener()* when it is no longer needed. For tutorial simplicity, this was not included in the code examples in this book. However, the supplemental source file, *my_preloader_02.fla*, shows this practice (as well as additional error checking) in use.

For many more details on listeners, broadcasters, and the design justification for them, see Colin Moock's *ActionScript: The Definitive Guide* and *Essential ActionScript* (both from O'Reilly).

4. Next, set up the *onLoadComplete* event handler to trap the *loadComplete* event generated when loading is complete. You will use this to clear the text field so the load meter will effectively disappear after loading is complete (this same event handler could be used to hide the *ProgressBar* component in the previous project, if you wanted to set up an event listener for that project, too):

    ```
    my_listener.onLoadComplete = function(mc):Void {
        info_txt.text = "";
    };
    ```

5. Finally, set up the *onLoadError* event handler to trap the *loadError* event generated if an asset does not load:

    ```
    my_listener.onLoadError = function(mc):Void {
        info_txt.text = "Error: File did not load.";
    };
    ```

6. Now that you've set up the listener, add it to the *MovieClipLoader* object:

    ```
    my_mcl.addListener (my_listener);
    ```

    That's it for the listener. It took a lot more to explain it than to write it, but it will be worth it. Now you have an efficient mechanism for responding to sporadic events.

7. All that remains is to actually load the external asset so your listener can react. Replace your existing *loadMovie()* methods with *MovieClipLoader* instance methods. Switch the path to the web-based version of the graphic to see the loading in action:

    ```
    //place in JPEG button event handler:
    my_mcl.loadClip ("http://www.flash8projects.com/water.jpg",
    container);

    //place in GIF button event handler:
    my_mcl.loadClip ("http://www.flash8projects.com/star_move.gif",
    container);

    //place in PNG button event handler:
    my_mcl.loadClip ("http://www.flash8projects.com/star_move.png",
    container);
    ```

8. Save your work and test your movie. You should now see loading information in the dynamic text field the first time an asset is loaded. To check your work, compare your script with the complete script in *my_preloader_01.fla*, found in the *12* folder of your working directory.

That's enough scripting for now. As these later chapters become more and more ActionScript-rich, it's a good idea to take a break now and then to let everything sink in.

What's Next?

Keeping your files lean and mean is essential to using Flash effectively on the Web. When developing applications for CD-ROM delivery, as you'll see in Chapter 14, you have a little more flexibility. However, even with the added freedom of not having download times to consider, modularizing your content will still provide worthwhile benefits, such as increased performance and more efficient authoring.

Before continuing, think a bit more about preloaders. Beyond the basic status information offered by standard preloaders, some Flash designers create preloader animations that are entertaining and ease the wait with fun distractions. More ambitious designers integrate preloaders tightly into the design, so the experience appears seamless. Text passages, for example, can be used to parcel out nuggets of information during delays. By the time you're done reading the text, the content you requested has loaded and you're ready to view it.

Try to use the formula in the preloader you scripted to create a clever loading animation. Use the resulting number to set the width of a movie clip, or jump to a corresponding movie clip frame. Let your imagination run wild.

In the next chapter, user interaction reaches a peak. You'll use distance learning as a model to record, store, and submit user responses. You'll learn:

- How to use templates and components to create a simple quiz
- How to save text values to the user's machine and retrieve the information later
- How to submit user input to a server
- How to use a simple PHP script to email the results

e-Learning with Flash

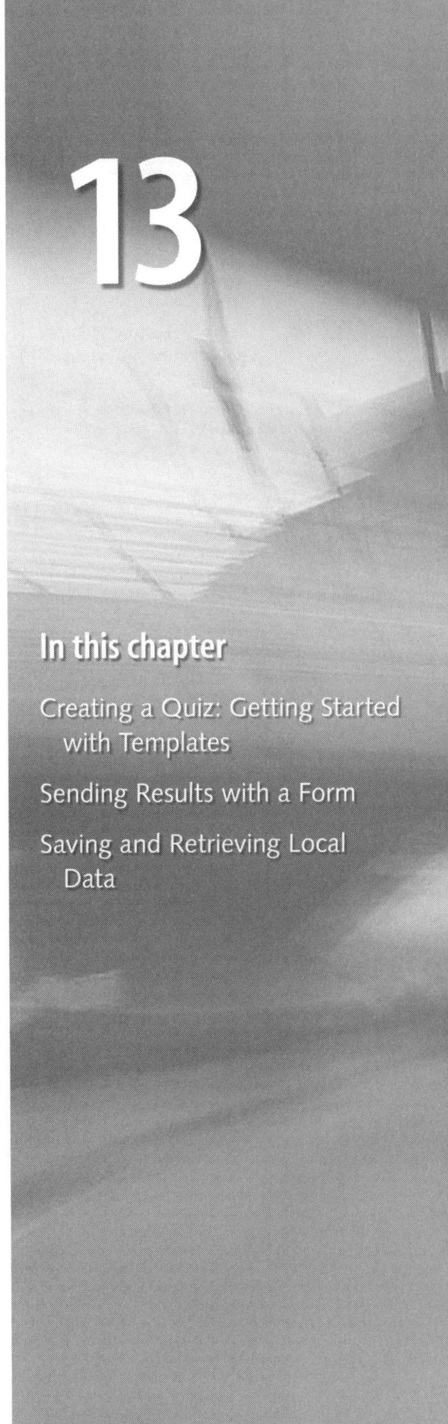

You've learned about basic interactivity and how to create and use button states. You've also seen how to change interface states on the main timeline by simply jumping to another frame or scene. Believe it or not, these basic skills are used in a wide variety of business applications.

Macromedia has researched common uses of Flash and tried to provide ready-made solutions to common requirements. For example, many companies use Flash to present educational material and to inform employees and customers about promotions, procedures, and product information. Flash includes several templates that can be used to quickly create presentations, slide shows, and quizzes, and the functionality of each is built into the template. In this chapter's project, you'll use a template and components to construct a three-question quiz about what you've learned so far.

Creating a Quiz: Getting Started with Templates

The first thing you need to do is choose a quiz template:

1. Use File→New to open the New Document dialog box, and click the Template tab. This displays the New from Template dialog box, as shown in Figure 13-1.
2. Choose *Quiz_style2* from the Templates category in the dialog box and click OK. The quiz template opens.
3. Save the file as *quiz.fla* in the *13* folder.

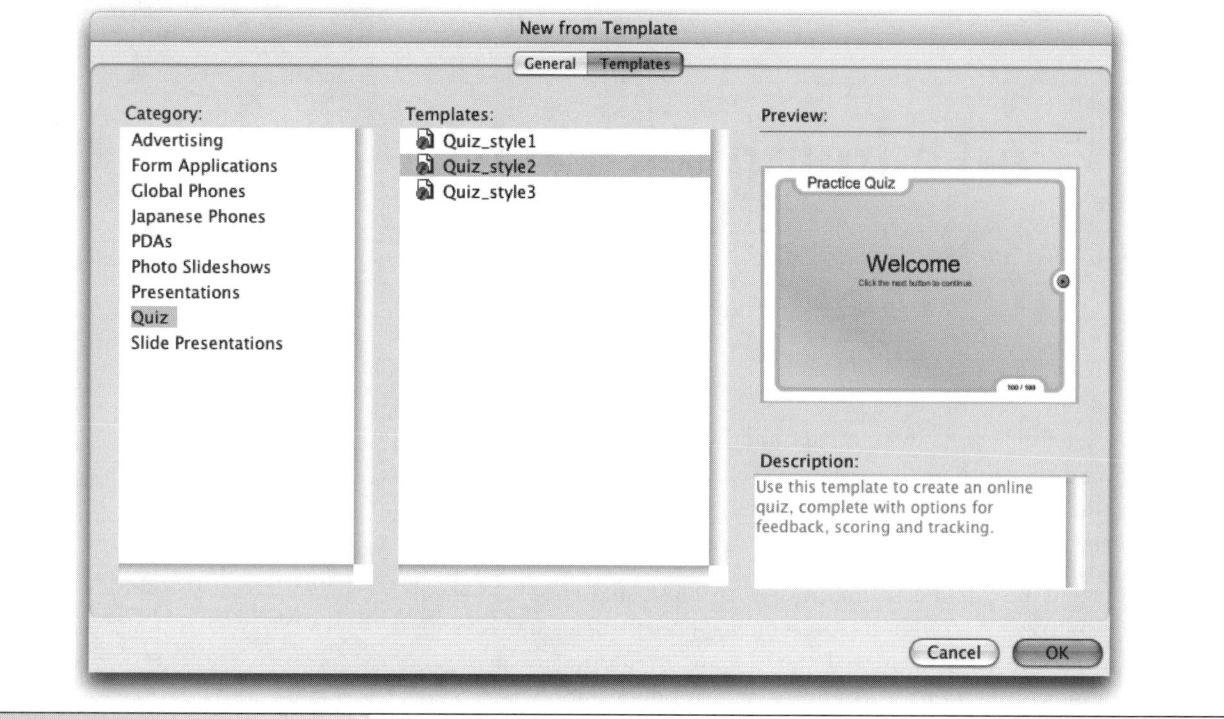

Figure 13-1. The New from Template dialog box

The quiz template has five layers: *Actions*, *Title*, *Interactions*, *Controls*, and *Background*. The *Interactions* layer contains eight frames, six of which contain prebuilt learning *interactions*. Each interaction represents a typical style for a quiz question, such as multiple choice. Frame 1 is the welcome screen for the project, and frame 8 is the results screen. For this exercise, you'll use three learning interaction types: fill in the blank (frame 3), multiple select (frame 6), and true/false (frame 7). Begin designing your quiz:

1. Start by deleting the unneeded frames in all layers. Be sure to select the frame in the number bar above the timeline, rather than in a specific layer. This ensures that all layers will be affected. Since deleting frames causes frames to shift, and frame number references printed here may change, delete the frames in reverse order. Delete frames 5, 4, and 2.

NOTE

Notice the box containing instructions on the left side of the Stage at each frame. Each box is a component. If you've been working through this book sequentially, you've had experience with components already. If not, a component is a preconfigured collection of scripts and assets that you can customize through parameters. For more information, see Chapter 3.

2. Customizing the components found off-Stage on the left is all that is required to program this quiz. First configure the quiz as a whole. At frame 1, select the Quiz Options box, located in the same location (off-Stage left).

WARNING

Within the learning interaction components, locations of panels and other interface elements have not been updated. For example, the Quiz Options box points to an old location for the Components Inspector. It won't take much to figure out the discrepancies, but watch for them.

3. Open the Component Inspector panel, which shows some configurable properties for the quiz (as seen in Figure 13-2). The interface is scalable, so if it is too small, increase the size of the panel using the handle in the lower-right corner. If you have combined the Component Inspector with another panel, or are using the *Flash 8 Projects Workspace*, you may need to separate it again into its own panel group. See Chapter 2 for more information.

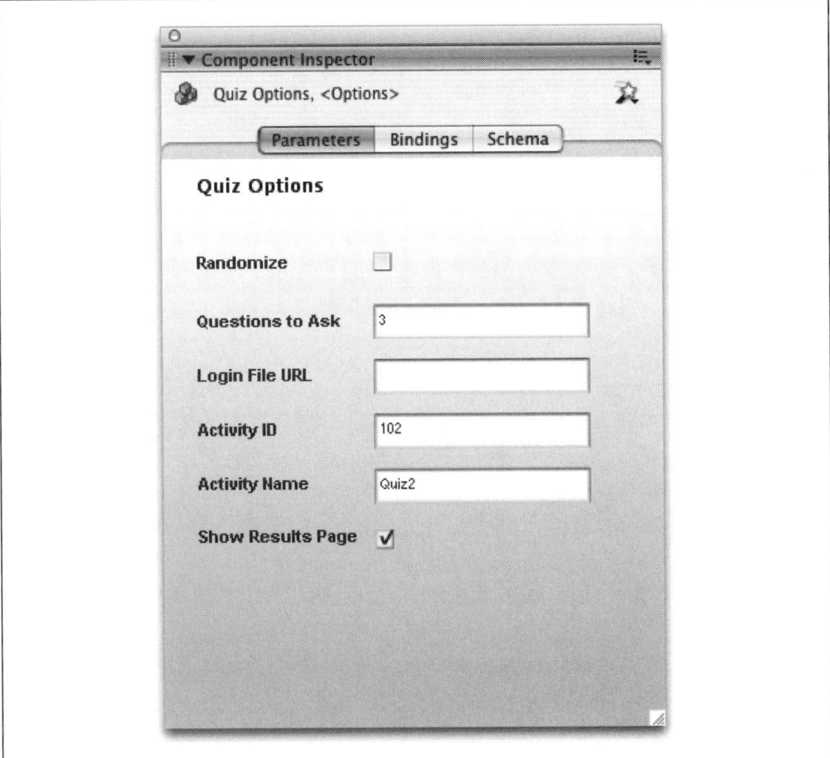

Figure 13-2. The Component Inspector, displaying properties for the quiz component in frame 1

4. In the "Questions to Ask" field of the Component Inspector, enter **3**. Leave the default values for the remaining options unchanged, as they do not apply to this project. If you want to check your progress, compare your file to the *quiz_01.fla* file in the *13* folder.

Once you've set up the quiz basics, you need to customize each learning interaction. Start by configuring the parameters for the first interaction, in frame 2. This is a fill-in-the-blank question:

1. Move the playhead to frame 2 and click on the *FillInTheBlank* interaction component located off-Stage on the left. Unlike in frame 1, more than just the configuration box is selected. For each learning interaction, the first click selects the entire contents.
2. Choose Modify→Break Apart or press Ctrl/Cmd-B once to break apart the clip. Here, and in every remaining case, break apart the interaction only once.
3. Deselect all the assets by clicking somewhere else on the Stage, or pressing Ctrl/Cmd-Shift-A.
4. Select the off-Stage interaction box again. The Component Inspector displays default options for the *FillInTheBlank* interaction, as seen in Figure 13-3.

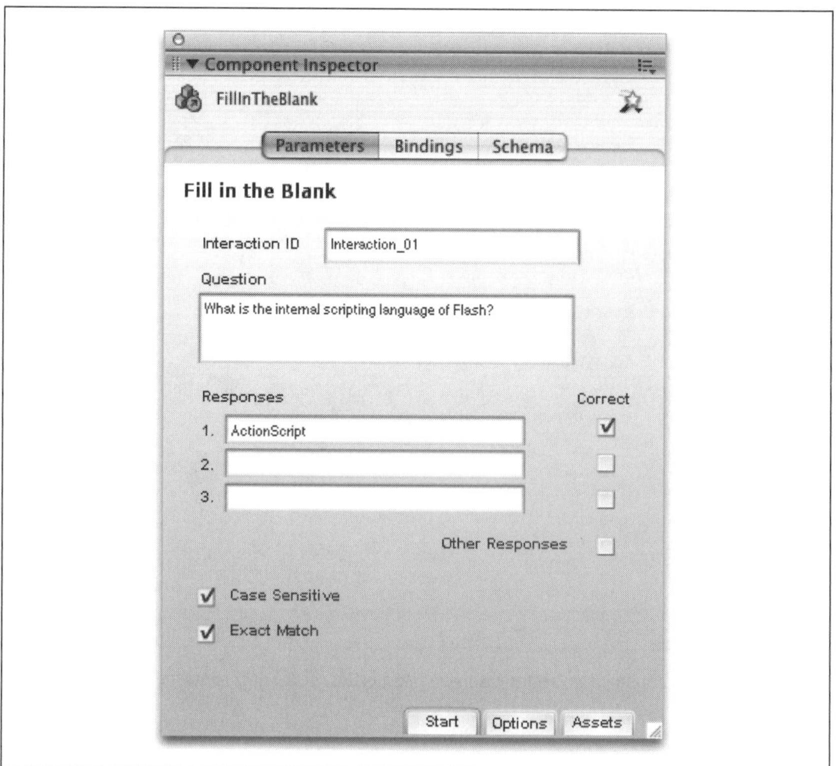

Figure 13-3. The Component Inspector, displaying properties for the fill-in-the-blank learning interaction in frame 2

Start building the quiz by configuring the first interaction:

1. In the Interaction ID field in the Component Inspector, change the ID to **`Interaction_01`**.
2. In the Questions field, replace the placeholder text with **`What is the internal scripting language of Flash?`**
3. In the first Response field, type **`ActionScript`** and mark it correct.
4. Enable the Case Sensitive and Exact Match options to require precise input from the user.
5. Save your work and move on to frame 3.

Continue with the next interaction, and configure the *MultipleChoice* component for question 2:

1. Once again, select and break apart the interaction component, deselect everything, and select the off-Stage box again. The options for this interaction appear in the Component Inspector, as seen in Figure 13-4.
2. In the Interaction ID field in the Component Inspector, change the ID to **`Interaction_02`**.
3. In the Question field, enter **`Which of the following are Flash symbols?`**

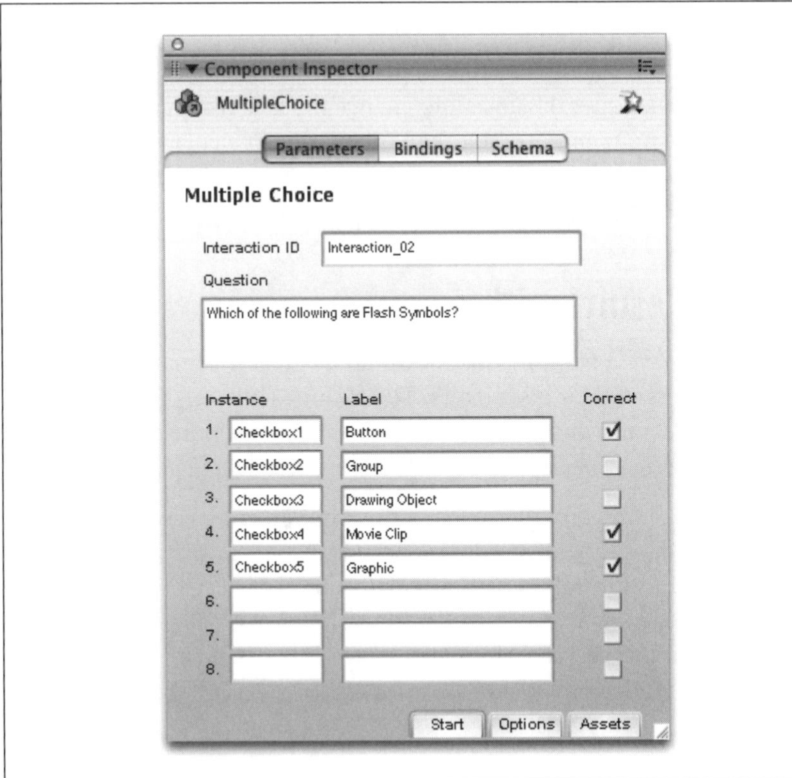

Figure 13-4. The Component Inspector, displaying parameters for the multiple-choice learning interaction in frame 3

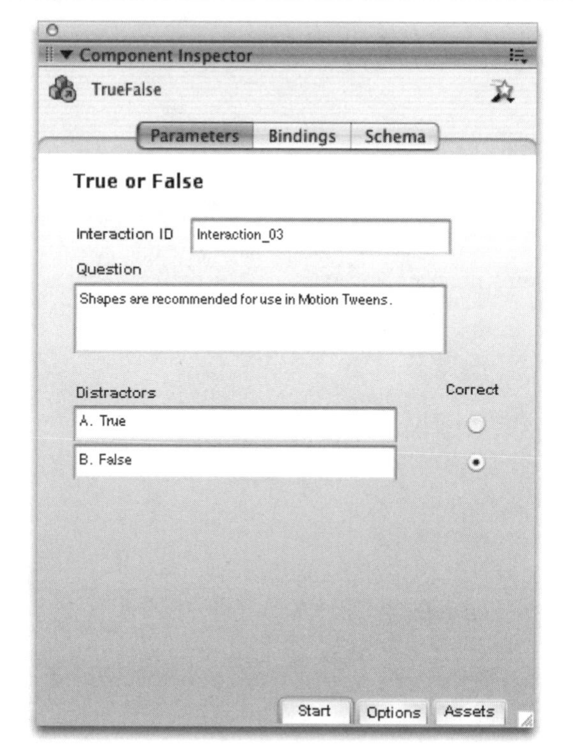

Figure 13-5. The Component Inspector, displaying properties for the TrueFalse learning interaction in frame 4

4. In the Label column, enter **`Button`**, **`Group`**, **`Drawing Object`**, **`Movie Clip`**, and **`Graphic`** for numbers 1–5. Enable the Correct checkboxes for items 1, 4, and 5.

Now for the third and final step, configuring the true/false question:

1. Move to frame 4 and repeat the steps of breaking apart the learning interaction and reselecting the configuration component for editing. This time, you're working with the *TrueFalse* interaction, as seen in Figure 13-5.
2. In the Questions field, enter **`Shapes are recommended for use in Motion Tweens.`**
3. Click the Correct radio button for the false option.
4. Save your work and test the movie. Your file should now be similar to *quiz_02.fla*.

That's it! Start the quiz and answer some questions correctly and some incorrectly. The last screen of the quiz tallies and displays your results.

When you're done, go back and explore the interaction components again. Start with the Options tab. Here, for example, you can change the number of tries the user can take before grading the question, change the feedback text, and weight some questions more importantly than others when calculating the results. The Assets feature lets you use your own text fields and change the labels of buttons, among other things.

Sending Results with a Form

Now that you have a working quiz, it would be great if your students could send their results to their instructors. This requires not only a little setup in your Flash file (commonly referred to as the client-side portion of the solution), but also a server script to send the submitted data via email.

Server scripting is beyond the scope of this book, but a basic PHP example that you can adapt to your needs has been provided so that you can more easily understand it. PHP (which originally stood for *Personal Home Page* but has become known as a recursive form of *Hypertext Pre-Processor*) is a powerful yet simple server scripting language supported by the vast majority of Internet service providers.

For the purposes of this project, a few user-configurable lines in the PHP script will be discussed, but you shouldn't have to change much beyond that.

Creating a Form

Before you get to the server script, you need to create a form that will send the user data to the server. In this project you'll take advantage of what you learned in the previous chapter to load a flexible, reusable form into your quiz. This makes it possible to use the same form in multiple projects. Remember, the more modularized you can make your content, the more you will get out of it.

Here are the steps involved in creating the form:

1. Create a new file and save it as *form.fla* in your *13* folder. In the Modify→Document dialog, give it dimensions of 320 × 330.
2. Name the first layer **`background`**. Add two more layers, and name them **`form`** and **`actions`**.
3. Start by creating the first field. (You will then repeat this process for the remaining fields.)
4. Select the Text tool and draw a text field on the Stage. Convert the text element to an input text field, and give it an instance name of **`sname_txt`** (which stands for a text field for sender name). To keep file size down, choose the *_sans* device font for the field's contents.
5. Grab one of the great new text element corners (introduced in Flash 8) to resize the text field to approximately 220 × 20 pixels. Move the field on Stage to approximately (78, 20).
6. Finally, create a static text element to serve as a descriptive label next to the field. Add the text **`Sender Name`**.
7. As an added interface nicety, switch to the *background* layer and use the Rectangle tool to draw a tinted box below the field and text label.
8. Repeat steps 4 through 7 four more times, using the information shown in Table 13-1.

Table 13-1. Specifications for text fields 2–5

Text label	Instance name	Size	Location
`Sender Email`	`semail_txt`	220 × 20	(78, 45)
`Recipient Email`	`remail_txt`	220 × 20	(78, 90)
`Subject`	`subj_txt`	220 × 20	(78, 130)
`Message`	`msg_txt`	220 × 60	(78, 160)

9. For the last input box, create a sixth text field with no label. Make it a dynamic text element (instead of input, like the previous fields) and give it an instance name of **`status_txt`**. Size it to 300 × 60 pixels, and place it at (10, 260). As a last step, in the Properties panel, disable the selectable option for this field, indicated by the cursor in Figure 13-6.

NOTE

The setup of the form .fla will be detailed in the following steps, but if you prefer, you can open form_01.fla from the 13 folder of your working directory. In this file, the fields and buttons have been created and instance names have been provided, but no scripts have been included. This will save you a bit of time in asset creation but still allow you to add the scripts yourself for practice.

NOTE

These sizes and locations are just approximations to make the creation process a bit easier. Feel free to adjust the values as you go. The values used in the provided source files also differ within a few pixels.

This will prevent the user from editing the status that your form will report for each process.

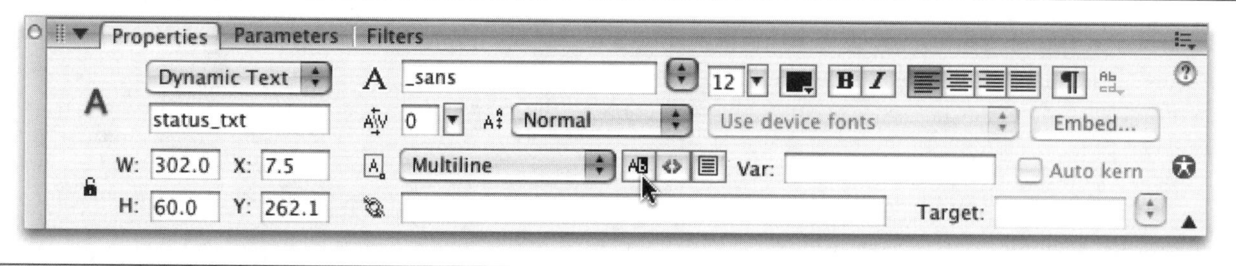

Figure 13-6. Disable the selectable property for the status field to prevent user editing at runtime

10. Finally, in the *form* layer, create a little close button in the upper-right corner and give it an instance name of **close_btn**.

When you're done, save your work and compare your file with *form_01.fla*, seen below in Figure 13-7. You'll start adding buttons in the next step, but notice how the background tints group functionality together and improve the readability of the form. If you want to make any adjustments, do so now and then continue.

Adding buttons

Now it's time to add the buttons to manipulate the form:

1. Open the Components panel and drag the *Button* component to the Stage. (It's found in the *User Interface* components category.)

NOTE

This is just a tutorial step to speed up the process by eliminating the need to create your own custom button. If you are concerned about the file size this component adds, or you want to customize your form's appearance, feel free to create your own button.

2. With the button selected on the Stage, show the Parameters tab in the Properties panel. Change the Label parameter to **Submit**. Give this button an instance name of **submit_btn**.

3. Make a copy of this button and change its Label parameter to **Clear**. Give this button an instance name of **clear_btn**.

The bulk of your form should now be done. You will add more buttons later, but your existing buttons should resemble those seen in the completed form in Figure 13-7. All you need to do now is add ActionScript that compiles the data from the form and sends it to the web server.

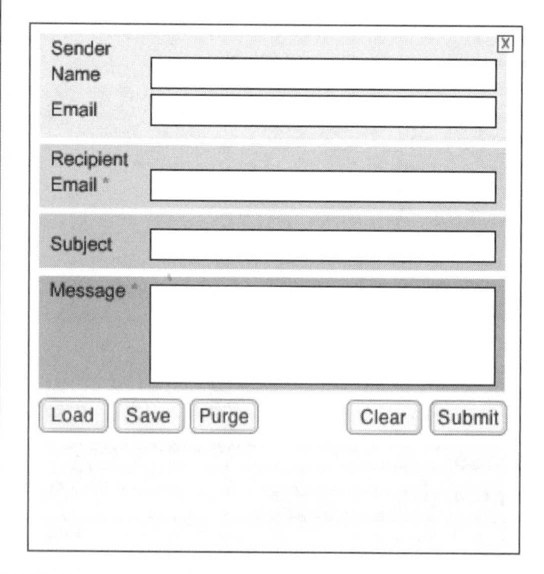

Figure 13-7. The completed form

Compiling and Sending Form Data

Once the user fills out the email information, the data must be sent to the web server for processing. As stated earlier, server-side scripting is beyond the scope of this book, but a complete basic PHP script has been included in the *13* folder on the book's CD-ROM.

In this part of the project, you'll compile and send the form data:

1. In frame 1 of the *actions* layer, start with a script that creates a *LoadVars* object to receive any response from the server. A simple button event handler will do:

   ```
   submit_btn.onRelease = function():Void {
       var eResponse_lv:LoadVars = new LoadVars();
   };
   ```

   The *LoadVars* class makes it easy to send information to, and receive information from, a server. For more information, see the "Loading and Sending Variables" sidebar.

Loading and Sending Variables

There are a few ways to load data from an external source (such as a text file or web server), and similar ways to send the data. One method that you will likely be familiar with is simulating a standard web form and loading or sending standard *name/value pairs*. Name/value pairs are named as they are because a variable's name and value are loaded or sent as a pair, either in a URL or in an object.

After submitting a web form or clicking on a link, you may have seen a URL that looked something like this: *http://www.domain.com/script.php?user=brian*.

This demonstrates the transmission of a variable called *user* and its value, *brian*, to a server script. Just like a web form, name/value pairs can be loaded or sent using the *GET* method, which adds data to a URL (as seen above), or the *POST* method, which sends the data in a hidden object.

Flash makes this process easy using the *LoadVars* class and its *sendAndLoad()* method. Using this class and method, you can specify *GET* or *POST*, send data, and load any result from the server.

The process requires a few simple steps: 1) create a sending *LoadVars* object to send your variables from; 2) create a receiving *LoadVars* object to receive any feedback from the server; 3) create an event handler to wait for the server response; and d) send the data. Here is an example script:

```
var mySend_lv:LoadVars = new LoadVars();
var myReceive_lv:LoadVars = new LoadVars();
myReceive_lv.onLoad = function():Void {
    trace(myReceive_lv.scriptStatus);
};
mySend_lv.user = "brian";
mySend_lv.sendAndLoad("http://www.domain.com/script.
php",myRecieve_lv, "POST");
```

The *onLoad* event handler is required because Internet operations are *asynchronous*. That is, they are not immediately sequential. For example, if you executed the *trace* line immediately after sending the data to the server, there would be no time for the data to be sent, for the server to process the request, or for the server to respond. The event handler effectively means, when a response is received, process it. Using this approach, you don't have to wait around for the server to respond.

You can also improve this example script by adding error checking for the server response. The *LoadVars* example in this chapter takes this extra step.

2. Add to the end of the same object an *onLoad* event handler to capture any server response. Update the *status_txt* field with text from the *scriptStatus* variable that is defined in the script:

```
eResponse_lv.onLoad = function(success):Void {
    if (success) {
        status_txt.text = "Transmission successful.\n";
        status_txt.text += this.scriptStatus;
    } else {
        status_txt.text = "An error occured.\n";
        status_txt.text += this.scriptStatus;
    }
};
```

3. Add to the end of the same *onRelease* event handler a new *LoadVars* object to send the data. Create properties of the object to contain the variable data:

```
var eMail_lv:LoadVars = new LoadVars();
eMail_lv.sname = sname_txt.text;
eMail_lv.semail = semail_txt.text;
eMail_lv.remail = remail_txt.text;
eMail_lv.subj = subj_txt.text;
eMail_lv.msg = msg_txt.text;
```

4. Use the same object to send the data and load any response from the server. Use the correct pathname to your version of the PHP script in the first parameter:

```
eMail_lv.sendAndLoad("flash8projects_email.php", eResponse_lv,
"POST");
```

   Note the use of the receiving *LoadVars* object in the second parameter to catch the response, and notice the use of the *POST* method. The *POST* method is usually superior to the *GET* method because it can send more information and the overall syntax is simpler.

Finally, program three user interface enhancements:

5. First, add as the first line of the *onRelease* handler an instruction that clears the status field each time you submit data. This makes any new server feedback more obvious:

```
status_txt.text = "";
```

6. Second, make it possible to clear all fields with a form reset button:

```
clear_btn.onRelease = function():Void {
    status_txt.text = "";
    semail_txt.text = "";
    remail_txt.text = "";
    subj_txt.text = "";
    msg_txt.text = "";
};
```

7. Third, script the close button to unload this form (remember, you've designed this form to be loaded into another SWF):

```
close_btn.onRelease = function():Void {
        this._parent.unloadMovie();
};
```

If you need a refresher on the this and _parent keywords, see the "Absolute and Relative Target Paths" sidebar in Chapter 6.

8. Your script, so far, should look like this:

```
//send form contents to php script for emailing
submit_btn.onRelease = function():Void {
    status_txt.text = "";
    var eResponse_lv:LoadVars = new LoadVars();
    var eMail_lv:LoadVars = new LoadVars();
    eMail_lv.sname = sname_txt.text;
    eMail_lv.semail = semail_txt.text;
    eMail_lv.remail = remail_txt.text;
    eMail_lv.subj = subj_txt.text;
    eMail_lv.msg = msg_txt.text;
    eMail_lv.sendAndLoad("flash8projects_email.php", eResponse_lv,
"POST");
    eResponse_lv.onLoad = function(success):Void {
        if (success) {
            status_txt.text = "Transmission successful.\n";
            status_txt.text += this.scriptStatus;
        } else {
            status_txt.text = "An error occured.\n";
            status_txt.text += this.scriptStatus;
        }
    };
};
//clear all form fields except name. local shared object not
affected
clear_btn.onRelease = function():Void {
    status_txt.text = "";
    semail_txt.text = "";
    remail_txt.text = "";
    subj_txt.text = "";
    msg_txt.text = "";
};
//unload this form
close_btn.onRelease = function():Void {
    this._parent.unloadMovie();
}
```

To test your movie at this point, you'll need to have access to a server with PHP enabled. If you don't have access to such a setup, you can compare your file with *form_02.fla*.

Server Script Parameters

Although covering server scripting is outside the scope of this text, it will help you adapt the sample script (provided on the CD-ROM) to your needs if you understand three simple parameters.

These parameters can be found at the top of the script, and appear as follows:

```
//***************************
//start customizable variables
$subject = "Demo: Flash 8 Projects for Learning Animation and
Interactivity";
$success_string = "Email sent by server on "; //followed
immediately by date
$failure_string = "Email could not be sent. Check for valid
recipient email address and message.";
//end customizable variables
//***************************
```

The first is the default subject for the email to be sent. This is used only if the user does not fill in a subject of his or her own. You can change this to any valid subject, or remove the text (leaving the two quotation marks) if you want the subject to be blank, the way the user may have intended.

The second is the success string sent back to Flash. If you modify this, remember that the date immediately follows this string. That's why a trailing space is included in the provided context.

NOTE

Remember, semicolons are required at the end of every line in PHP.

The third parameter is the failure string sent back to Flash. Since the email fails to send on the server side for only two reasons, you can include helpful text to let the user know what to look for.

As you get better at ActionScript, you can perform what is called *client-side validation* to try to catch as many errors as possible before even submitting to the server. In any case, it's still a good idea to perform error checking at the server, as well.

Saving and Retrieving Local Data

Frequently, it is useful to save and restore information without relying on server technologies. To do this, Flash uses its own equivalent of the JavaScript cookie or application preference file. These files are called *local shared objects*, and they also go by the acronyms LSO and SOL (because the files use the *.sol* file extension).

Flash Cookies: Local Shared Objects

Local shared objects are very easy to use. Essentially, you create an object, assign it data, and then flush, or write, the information. Flash handles all the file input/output for you to ensure the highest security. Retrieving the information requires the same process in reverse. Security is high because the files are stored in a local directory, the name of which is derived from the file's pathname. Therefore, it is extremely difficult for one file to load information saved by another.

Have you ever filled out a long form on the Web only to run into a server problem or browser crash, losing all the data you entered? In your form, you will make use of LSOs to store the form data for later retrieval, if desired. This can also be very useful during repeated testing. For example, in this case, if you want to test email functionality repeatedly, you need only enter your name and retrieve the sender email, recipient email, subject, and message values through the use of an LSO.

Start by adding buttons to control this feature, and writing the script for the Save button:

1. If it's not open already, open your *quiz.fla* file.
2. Add three new buttons, following the same procedure you used earlier when creating the Submit and Clear buttons. (If you need a review, see the "Adding buttons" passage of the "Creating a Form" section of this chapter.) Assign them the labels **Load**, **Save**, and **Purge** in the Parameters tab of the Properties panel, and give them instance names of **load_btn**, **save_btn**, and **purge_btn**, respectively.
3. Revisit the last frame of the *actions* layer, where you wrote the script for the previous buttons. You will add a few event handlers, starting with the button that will save your local shared object. Open the handler by emptying the status field so you can clearly display any feedback. Then create your first shared object. Use the sender name as the name of the LSO:

```
save_btn.onRelease = function():Void {
    status_txt.text = "";
    var user_so:SharedObject = SharedObject.getLocal(sname_txt.
text);
};
```

4. Continuing the script, check to see if the LSO was found or created successfully. Do this with a simple conditional that checks to see if the variable you tried to populate with the object is now an instance of the *SharedObject* class. If it is not, the creation was not successful.

   Inside the conditional, create properties in the LSO's built-in *data* object. Create one property each for the *Sender Name*, *Sender Email*, *Recipient Email*, *Subject*, and *Message* fields, and populate them with the text from those fields:

```
if (user_so instanceof SharedObject) {
    user_so.data.sname = sname_txt.text;
    user_so.data.semail = semail_txt.text;
    user_so.data.remail = remail_txt.text;
    user_so.data.subj = subj_txt.text;
    user_so.data.msg = msg_txt.text;
    user_so.flush();
    status_txt.text = "Data saved.";
} else {
    status_txt.text = "Couldn't create data based on username.";
}
```

NOTE

Restrictions apply when naming LSOs. See the "Naming Local Shared Objects" sidebar for more information.

5. Save your work and test your movie. Use one word with letters only for the sender name until you understand the naming requirements for LSOs. Although you can't see the result of the save, you should be able to see the positive and negative status strings, depending on what you name the LSO.

Now it's time to create the script that will load the shared object. You will soon see that this code is almost identical to the save code. Of course, instead of loading from the fields and saving to the shared object, the script will load from the shared object and restore its property values to the corresponding fields. Otherwise, however, it's very similar. In fact, it's common practice to include a script to both save and load in the same process. However, the upcoming code has one additional unique attribute.

Naming Local Shared Objects

Local shared objects are Flash's version of cookies—small text files, typically used to save small preference-like bits of information that can be safely stored and retrieved from a secure location.

There are a couple of restrictions that affect the naming of LSOs. They must be named using one word (no spaces are allowed), and the names cannot contain any of the following characters:

```
~ % & \ ; : " ' , < > ? #
```

The first provided sample file in this chapter that saves an LSO, *form_03.fla*, does nothing to validate the proposed *.sol* name. Test this movie and enter a sender name of "Flash 8" (which contains an illegal character because of the space). You will see a status update indicating failure. Attempt another save using "Flash8" (without the space), and the *.sol* will be saved without issue.

Although one option is to list this exception the same way you might indicate required fields, another is to replace any illegal characters. This is very convenient if the new name will not be lost to obscurity over time. For example, the script that follows will replace any illegal character in a proposed *.sol* name with an underscore. However, the new name is derived from the original name, so the same process can be used to retrieve the object.

This handler is included in the final version of the form created in this chapter, and can be seen in use in *form_04.fla*:

```
/*
user name is passed to function, which then swaps any
disallowed characters with underscores.
Function expects string input and returns a string
*/
function cleanSolName(whichName:String):String {
    //bad characters are placed in string. See later
    //note about escaping backslash and quotation mark
var badChars:String = " ~%&\\;:\"',<>?#";
    //counter and new empty strings are initialized
    var charCount:Number = whichName.length;
    var newName:String = "";
    //loop walks through submitted name, char by char
    for (var i:Number = 0; i < charCount; i++) {
        //if name char at this position is found in
        //badChar string, add underscore to new string
        if (badChars.indexOf(whichName.charAt(i)) >
-1) {
            newName += "_";
        //otherwise, add good char to new string
        } else {
            newName += whichName.charAt(i);
        }
    }
    //when loop is finished, new string is complete.
    //return new string to script that called function
    return newName;
}
```

The function is called by sending the desired *.sol* name to the function when saving or loading the object. This replaces any bad name with a legal name where it is needed in the syntax. For example, the first version of the form uses the following syntax to save/load an object:

```
var user_so:SharedObject = SharedObject.
getLocal(sname_txt.text);
```

The second version replaces that syntax with this:

```
var user_so:SharedObject = SharedObject.getLocal
(cleanSolName(sname_txt.text));
```

Since the *SharedObject.getLocal()* method both loads and creates shared objects, it's hard to know whether the object already existed or was newly created. That is, you can't check to see if the object exists without creating it if it doesn't exist. To determine whether the object already existed, you must check to see if a known property of the object exists.

In the following example, after confirming that the object exists, a conditional asks if the known *sname* property has a data type of *undefined*. If the property existed previously, this property will have a *String* data type. However, if the object itself has been created but it has not been populated with properties, the *sname* property thereof will not yet exist.

If this is the case, the script will display status text informing the user that the data was not previously saved under that username. If the shared object does exist, the data fields are filled as expected.

Here is the script to load the LSO:

1. Add the following to the same script in frame 1 of the *actions* layer:

```
load_btn.onRelease = function():Void {
    status_txt.text = "";
    var user_so:SharedObject = SharedObject.getLocal(cleanSolName(
sname_txt.text));
    if (user_so instanceof SharedObject) {
        if (typeof user_so.data.sname == "undefined") {
           status_txt.text = "Couldn't find data based on username.";
        } else {
            semail_txt.text = user_so.data.semail;
            remail_txt.text = user_so.data.remail;
            subj_txt.text = user_so.data.subj;
            msg_txt.text = user_so.data.msg;
            status_txt.text = "Saved data recalled.";
        }
    } else {
        status_txt.text = "Couldn't find data based on username.";
    }
};
```

2. Notice in the previous step that the *Sender Name* field is not restored. This is because you are using the sender name as the name of the LSO as well, so it should not be overwritten or even cleared. Now that you have this functionality in place, edit the *clear_btn.onRelease* event handler to remove the clearing of the *Sender Name* field. The revised script looks like this:

```
clear_btn.onRelease = function():Void {
    semail_txt.text = "";
    remail_txt.text = "";
    subj_txt.text = "";
    msg_txt.text = "";
};
```

NOTE

getLocal() is a method of the SharedObject class itself, rather than an instance of the class, because getLocal() is a so-called class method, not an instance method. See the "Methods" sidebar in Chapter 5 for general information about methods.

3. Save your work and test your file. You should now be able to see the results of the save and load processes. Be sure to clear a field or two between saving and loading so you can watch the restore process.

Finally, it is nice to provide a mechanism to allow the user to eradicate his or her system of all stored shared objects. This code is very similar to the previous event handlers, but it's even simpler as it only needs to clear the LSO:

1. Add the following event handler:

```
purge_btn.onRelease = function():Void {
    status_txt.text = "";
    var user_so:SharedObject = SharedObject.getLocal(cleanSolName(
sname_txt.text));
    if (user_so instanceof SharedObject) {
        user_so.clear();
        status_txt.text = "Data purged from disc.";
    } else {
        status_txt.text = "Couldn't find data based on username.";
    }
};
```

2. Save your work and test your movie. Your file should now be similar to *form_03.fla* and be fully functional.

Clearing outdated feedback

Although the core functionality of your file is complete, there is still one more feature that you can add to improve the experience for the user. At the same time, it will help you practice with the event listeners you learned about in Chapter 12.

Your interface will be enhanced if you remove the status field feedback each time you begin a new process. This will make the information clearer and more meaningful, because older status reports will not linger on the screen, confusing users about the current state of your application.

Add the following code to the end of the last script in the *actions* layer:

```
var textListener:Object = new Object();
textListener.onChanged = function():Void {
    status_txt.text = "";
};
sname_txt.addListener(textListener);
semail_txt.addListener(textListener);
remail_txt.addListener(textListener);
subj_txt.addListener(textListener);
msg_txt.addListener(textListener);
```

This code will create a simple listener that will be trigged by the change of any text field registered with the listener. All it does is empty the status field. After creating the event handler, add the listener to each of the editable fields. Note that the listener is not added to the *status_txt* field because that field is for text output only and will not be changed by the user.

Security

Although a specific path can be specified when invoking *SharedObject.getLocal()*, by default *.sol* files are automatically placed in a folder based on the name of the *.swf* file from which they were created. To browse or remove these files, you can look in the directory in which they are stored. On Windows 2000 and Windows XP systems, you'll find the directory at *C:\Documents and Settings\USER\Local Settings\Application Data\Macromedia\Flash Player\#SharedObjects* (substitute your user account name for *USER*). On Mac OS X systems, it's located at *Macintosh HD/Users/USER/Library/Preferences/Macromedia/Flash Player/#SharedObjects/*.

You may find numerous other *.sol* files on your hard drive, but don't worry. Much like JavaScript cookies, developers often use shared objects to save safe user data on your hard drive. Therefore, Flash-based web sites you've visited may have deposited one or more *.sol* files on your drive. Generally, the *.sol* files are for simple things like your username or the results of a quiz. If a movie needs to save more than 100 KB of data to your hard drive, a message appears in your Flash Player asking you for permission to do so. If you're worried, you can always refuse permission. You can also disable this globally via the same message window.

> **NOTE**
>
> *Macromedia has made some extremely aggressive changes in player security with Flash Player 8. This is slightly less of an issue if all files are on the Internet, but security is especially tight when running files locally that access both local and Internet-enabled assets. For more information, check out the recent changes at Macromedia's web site (http://www.macromedia.com/devnet/flash/articles/fplayer8_security.html).*

The user can access his or her privacy settings from the Flash Player Settings pop-up window. It is accessible at runtime by right-clicking (Win) or Ctrl-clicking (Mac) and choosing Settings from the contextual menu that appears. A user can control additional privacy and security settings via the online Settings Manager on Macromedia's web site. The English-language version is located at *http://www.macromedia.com/support/documentation/en/flashplayer/help/settings_manager.html*.

Also, for many more details on security and privacy (including ways to protect your Flash content), see Chapter 12 of Sham Bhangal's *Flash Hacks* (O'Reilly).

Loading the Form into the Quiz

Building your form in a self-contained file enables you to load it into any other project in which you need to include email support. This is one of the key benefits of modular design.

In most cases, this requires only one simple line of code. However, if you add some functionality, you can get this form to integrate tightly into your quiz. You can have the form automatically read in the quiz tabulation results, and prevent the user from editing those same results before sending off the email.

If you place this code in the form itself, however, you will ruin the modular design you worked so hard to maintain. Instead, issue these instructions remotely, from the host SWF, or quiz, in this case.

First, open your quiz and prepare to load the form:

1. Open the *quiz.fla* file you saved earlier in the *13* folder. (If you want to start with a fresh file, you can open *quiz_02.fla*, or if you want to look at the completed script, you can open *quiz_03.fla*.)
2. Add a keyframe to the last frame in the *actions* layer.
3. Add a layer beneath the *actions* layer, and name it **form**. Add a keyframe to the last frame in the layer.
4. To this keyframe, add a button. Take advantage of the existing symbols and use *btn, nextBtn* (one symbol with a two-word name). It can be found in the Quiz Files→Assets→Buttons folder in the Library.
5. Place the button in the same location as its brethren in the previous frames and resize it to match, if necessary. The button should be approximately 22 × 22 pixels, and should sit at (518, 182). Give it an instance name of **loadForm_btn**.
6. For clarity, add a text label that says **Email Results**.

Now you must script the button to load the form. The form is self-contained, so you won't have to worry about the email code again, but you will need to do a few things. Start by loading in the form:

1. In the last frame of the *actions* layer, add the next five lines of code. After a precautionary *stop()* action, this script immediately creates a movie clip to load the form into, assigns it x- and y-coordinates, and loads the form. There's one difference, though—the x-coordinate is off-Stage. This acts like an invisible preloader, loading the file when you enter the frame and waiting for a button action to populate the form:

   ```
   stop();
   this.createEmptyMovieClip("form_mc", 1);
   form_mc._x = 1000;
   form_mc._y = 46;
   loadMovie("form.swf", form_mc);
   ```

2. Over the next five steps, you'll build an event handler for the button that shows the form. Remember that you're helping the user email quiz results to a colleague or instructor. So, you can practice some intermediate techniques by adapting your modularized form to work in a specific situation.

   First, prevent the user from editing the subject or message of the email, so you can fill in the quiz results yourself. (Obviously, this wouldn't be necessary in another setting if you wanted to allow the user to send any subject and/or message.) Remember that you've loaded the form into the *form_mc* movie clip you created, and the instance names of the text fields you want to control are *subj_txt* and *msg_txt*. Change their *selectable* property to false, so the user can't select, and therefore can't edit, any of the text therein:

```
loadForm_btn.onRelease = function():Void {
    form_mc.subj_txt.selectable = false;
    form_mc.msg_txt.selectable = false;
};
```

3. Then add the following lines, which modify the subject and message fields programmatically:

```
form_mc.subj_txt.text = "Flash 8 Projects Quiz Results";
form_mc.msg_txt.text = "Total Correct: " + QuizTrack.total_correct
+ "\n";
form_mc.msg_txt.text += "Total Wrong: " + QuizTrack.total_wrong +
"\n";
form_mc.msg_txt.text += "Total Score: " + QuizTrack.percent_format
+ "\n";
```

Notice three things: the `+=` shortcut operator to concatenate strings; the ending newline character (`\n`) that adds a carriage return after each line of text added; and the *QuizTrack* object and its *total_corect*, *total_wrong*, and *percent_format* properties. The quiz template you started with makes use of the *QuizTrack* object. If you click on each of the fields on the results screen you're working in now, and then look at the Properties panel, you will see these object properties referenced by the field's variable option. This is shown in Figure 13-8.

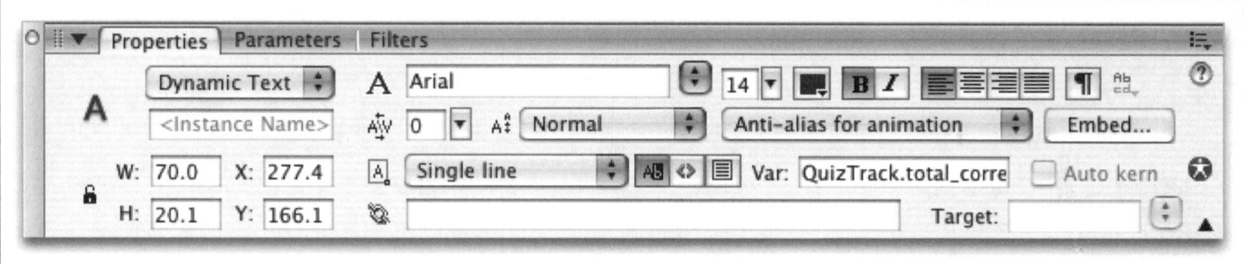

Figure 13-8. The QuizTrack.total_correct text field variable, as seen in the Var: assignment in the Properties panel

4. Now that the locked subject and message fields have been populated, you can show the form on screen. Continue by adding this line to the event handler you assembled in steps 2 and 3:

```
form_mc._x = 75;
```

5. To avoid confusion, after showing the form, hide the button you used to show it:

```
this._visible = false;
```

This allows the user to concentrate on the form and prevents the button from being clicked again unnecessarily.

All you have to do to finish the loading portion of the project is control the disappearance and reappearance of the form through user interaction. The form's close button will automatically unload the form from your project. However, your form preloads silently, not due to user interaction. Therefore, if the user unloads the form, he or she won't be able to load it again unless you change your interface.

So, use a clever trick to further capitalize on the power of modularization. Delete the existing close button event handler and substitute your own. This lets you use the generic form elsewhere, but customize its use here:

> **NOTE**
>
> *Notice the relative paths in use again. Since this new event handler is being added to the close button, its parent is the form itself. This is the movie clip you want to move off-Stage. Similarly, the parent of the form is the quiz, which is where the loadForm_btn resides. This is the button you want to again make visible.*

6. Add these lines to the end of the event handler you've been building. The first deletes the form's close button event handler. The second creates a new one. Instead of unloading the movie, move it back to its initial off-Stage location. Then show the original form display button again:

```
delete form_mc.close_btn.onRelease;
form_mc.close_btn.onRelease = function():Void {
    this._parent._x = 1000;
    this._parent._parent.loadForm_btn._visible = true;
}
```

7. Your finished script should now look like this:

```
this.createEmptyMovieClip("form_mc", 1);
form_mc._x = 1000;
form_mc._y = 46;
loadMovie("form.swf", form_mc);

loadForm_btn.onRelease = function():Void {
    form_mc.subj_txt.selectable = false;
    form_mc.msg_txt.selectable = false;
    form_mc.subj_txt.text = "Flash 8 Projects Quiz Results";
    form_mc.msg_txt.text = "Total Correct: " + QuizTrack.total_
correct + "\n";
    form_mc.msg_txt.text += "Total Wrong: " + QuizTrack.total_wrong
+ "\n";
    form_mc.msg_txt.text += "Total Score: " + QuizTrack.percent_
format + "\n";
    form_mc._x = 75;
    this._visible = false;
    delete form_mc.close_btn.onRelease;
    form_mc.close_btn.onRelease = function():Void {
        this._parent._x = 1000;
        this._parent._parent.loadForm_btn._visible = true;
    }
};
```

8. Save your work and test your movie. Compare your file with *quiz_03.fla*.

Although you can't send an email without the aforementioned PHP server setup, you can at least test the form loading and display states and the local shared object functionality.

What's Next?

Take a few minutes to review what you've accomplished. As a high-level goal, you set out to create a distance-learning tool, realized in Flash. If you know a fair amount about the mechanics of e-learning systems, you may have noticed that the HTML publishing template used by the Flash quiz is SCORM-compatible and works with SCORM 1.2 Tracking. If you look in the File→Publish Settings HTML section, and then investigate the Template menu, you'll see that there are also templates for SCORM 2004 and AICC tracking.

Even if you don't intend to use your work in a dedicated distance-learning management system, you can still create quizzes that submit results. This is possible because of the modularized email form you created. You can now load the form into virtually any project and send email, provided you have a PHP-compatible server to use for this purpose.

Finally, you now know how to save client-side persistent data through the use of local shared objects. This will be very handy when you get to the next chapter and start developing content for distribution via CD-ROM.

First, however, how can you expand on what you've learned in this chapter? Start by experimenting with the quiz types you eliminated at the start of the project. Rather than going back to the quiz template, use the Window→Common Libraries→Learning Interactions menu to open a Library that includes each learning interaction. Add frames to your existing quiz and try out the Drag and Drop, Hot Objects, and Hot Spot interactions.

Next, try out the additional options available in each interaction, and try customizing the assets used. Finally, try saving the quiz results using a local shared object, in addition to the email settings.

In the next chapter, web delivery takes a back seat to handhelds and CD-ROMs. You'll learn:

- How to optimize for previous players (such as Flash 5 and Flash 6) for handheld devices
- How to author Flash Lite content for mobile phones
- How to create standalone projectors that play Flash content without a browser

Flash for CD-ROM and Handhelds

In this chapter, you'll explore two slightly less conventional distribution methods for Flash content. First, you'll see how Flash projects can be created for standalone disc-based delivery without a browser, using projectors. In the second part of the chapter, you'll learn a bit about Flash development for mobile devices, an up-and-coming design area with its own set of special considerations.

Flash on CD-ROM

Although many developers use Macromedia Director, another powerful multimedia authoring program, for CD-ROM development, Flash also offers very basic features suitable for CD-ROM delivery.

It is certainly possible to distribute a CD-ROM project using a browser-based structure to wrap around your Flash content. This requires little extra work or planning, and if your product heavily uses HTML (perhaps repurposed from a related online version), this may be the best way to go. However, if your product is primarily Flash content, the overhead of the browser and Flash Player is unnecessary.

In fact, the added weight of the browser can result in a lesser product, for several reasons (for the sake of this comparison, assume your product is Flash-only):

- The performance of Flash assets in a browser window is worse than in a non-browser environment. When a browser is also running, it must have some attention from the computer, too, so it makes sense that removing it from the mix will boost your playback slightly.
- The browser and any other resources it may require (themes, extensions, other plug-ins, etc.) cause your product to require more RAM.
- The browser can interfere with your product, most notably when it comes to responding to user input. To operate properly, the browser must occasionally receive mouse and keyboard input from the user (such as when the user types a web address in the browser's location

bar, clicks on a button, or uses a keyboard shortcut). Your Flash files may also need to receive user input. Therefore, if your Flash file doesn't have mouse and/or keyboard focus (that is, if it isn't identified as the correct recipient for mouse and/or keyboard events), the browser can intercept user events and your product can seem unresponsive.

Finally, although it would be very surprising if this were not the case, it's still not a good idea to rely on your users having the necessary browser and Flash Player installed. This is particularly true if compatibility issues require a particular browser or version of the Flash Player. Therefore, you should add installers to your CD-ROM, which means you must also follow the necessary licensing and distribution guidelines.

Fortunately, Flash can also create a runtime package that contains all the necessary code to play back your product without relying on additional software. This useful playback engine is called a *projector*.

Projectors

Think of a projector as the Flash browser plug-in without the browser. Gone is the overhead, so RAM use is reduced, performance gets a slight bump, and the user experience is vastly improved for Flash-only projects.

Creating a projector is not much different from creating a *.swf*. The same publishing process is used, and projectors can even be created for both Windows and Macintosh platforms.

You may remember from discussions in earlier chapters how to officially publish your *.fla* files (rather than just creating *.swf* files via the Control→Test Movie menu command, commonly accessed by the Ctrl-Enter/Cmd-Return keyboard shortcut). If not, choose File→Publish Settings and click on the Formats button in the button bar at the top of the dialog. Using this screen, you can specify that one or more file formats be created from your file when it is published. Creating projectors is as easy as enabling the checkbox next to one or both of the projector platform options, as seen in Figure 14-1.

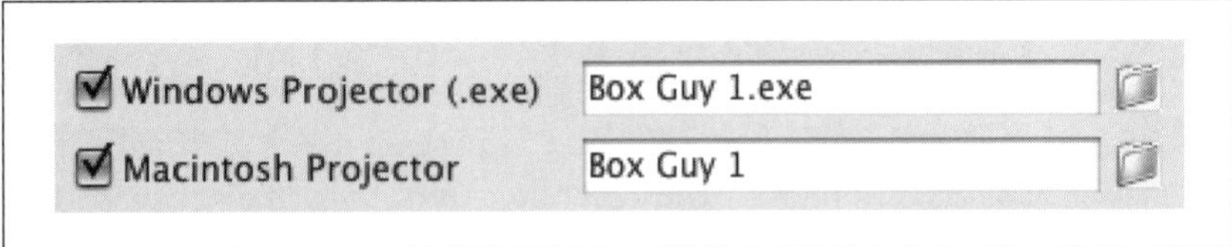

Figure 14-1. The Publish Settings options used to create projectors for Windows and Macintosh platforms

Usually, you don't work hard to make your *.swf* filenames pretty, because the names are rarely seen when the files are loaded into an HTML page or another *.swf*. You should follow some simple naming rules to ensure the widest possible compatibility and ease of use across as many servers as possible, but these rules are usually optional. (The most notable of these suggested rules are to name your files in all lowercase and to avoid spaces and other illegal or inconvenient URL characters.)

When creating a projector, however, you are creating an application whose name the user will likely see and double-click. Suddenly, concise, useful names become a lot more important. Additionally, other applications (e.g., servers or browsers) don't have to process projector names, so you can be freer with your naming conventions.

For example, Figure 14-1 is a screen shot of the publish settings for *box_guy_proj_01.fla*. As that name isn't too friendly, it has been replaced with *Box Guy 1*. On the Windows platform, the dot-three extension is required, so *.exe* (which stands for executable) is added.

> **NOTE**
>
> *Don't worry if you don't see these extensions on your own computer. It is common for operating systems to hide them to simplify what you see in your directories.*

Try creating your own projector now:

1. Open *box_guy_proj_01.fla* from the *14* folder of your working directory.
2. Open the File→Projector Settings dialog, select Format, and confirm that the projector option for your platform has already been set. Also confirm that a user-friendly name is set for the projector.
3. Click the Publish button at the bottom of the dialog. When the progress bar indicates the process is complete, close the dialog by clicking the OK button. That's it—you don't have to change the timeline or ActionScript at all.
4. In the same *14* directory as the file you just opened, find the projector you just created and double-click on it to launch the application.
5. The file will play without the need of the Flash authoring environment or a browser, and it can be distributed to others even if they have neither.

> **NOTE**
>
> *To prevent naming conflicts with files you create in the same directory, the provided projectors are named with additional letters (A, B, C, etc.) rather than numbers (1, 2, 3, etc.).*

New features (or new ways of implementing features) for projectors are very limited. Table 14-1 lists the bulk of them.

Table 14-1. Commands available for projectors

Command	Parameter	Purpose
quit	None	Closes the projector.
fullscreen	*true* or *false*	Specifying *true* sets the Flash Player to full-screen mode. Specifying *false* returns the player to normal menu view.
allowscale	*true* or *false*	Specifying *false* sets the player so that the *.swf* file is always drawn at its original size and never scaled. Specifying *true* forces the *.swf* file to scale to 100% of the player window.
showmenu	*true* or *false*	Specifying *true* enables the full set of context-menu items. Specifying *false* hides all of the context-menu items except About Flash Player and Settings.

Table 14-1. Commands available for projectors (*continued*)

Command	Parameter	Purpose
exec	Path to application	Executes an application from within the projector. The path can contain only the characters A–Z, a–z, 0–9, period (.), and underscore (_). The application to be launched must be in a subdirectory *fscommand* in the same directory as the projector.
trapallkeys	*true* or *false*	Specifying *true* sends all key events to the *onClipEvent(keyDown/keyUp)* handler in the Flash Player.

Try one of the new features now:

1. Continuing with your open file, add the following script in frame 1 of the *actions* layer:

   ```
   fscommand("fullscreen","true");
   ```

   The *fscommand* function is used to provide instructions to playback scenarios beyond Flash. It is primarily used in projectors, as you are using it now, but it can also be used on mobile devices and to talk to an HTML-based scripting language such as JavaScript.

2. Save your file and publish your movie, using the File→Publish menu command.

3. Find the projector in the same location as before, and launch it again.

This time your application provides a fully immersive experience, filling the screen, removing its menu bar, and covering up your desktop. With these added features, however, a few new things are noticeable:

- Your animation has scaled to fill the screen. This can be good or bad, depending on your assets and the file's performance.
- The screen outside the actual Stage has been filled with the Stage color. In this case, it is likely sky blue, but it could also be the default Stage white, potentially causing an effect akin to snow blindness.
- There is no quit button to exit the application. This wasn't useful in a browser, but it is required for good user interface design when in a projector.

Quit your movie using the application standard Ctrl/Cmd-Q, and address these issues one or two at a time.

NOTE

Space constraints prevent Flash-JavaScript communication from being included in this book. However, if you're interested in exploring this technique on your own, fscommand has been replaced for this purpose by the much more reliable ExternalInterface API. You can find a sample file demonstrating its use nested within your main Flash 8 application directory in the /Samples and Tutorials/Samples/ActionScript/ExternalAPI folder.

Begin by fixing the background color and scaling problems:

1. Using the Modify→Document menu command, change the Stage color to black.
2. Add the following to the script in frame 1 of the *actions* layer:

```
fscommand("allowscale", "false");
```

3. You'll add a quit button next, but for the time being, save your work and publish your movie again. Most of the *fscommand* options will not work in a test *.swf*, so you must publish your file to create a projector that can be tested.
4. Launch the new projector and see the result. (If you are checking your progress, your file should now resemble the *Box Guy C* projector in your platform of choice.)

Okay...you've corrected the scale and background color issues, but something new has surfaced. Box Guy, formerly off-Stage left to begin with, is now clearly visible, as seen in Figure 14-2.

Figure 14-2. When viewed in a window larger than the Stage, formerly off-Stage elements are visible and must be masked

When a *.swf* is framed in an HTML page, or scaled to fit the exact dimensions of a player window, off-Stage elements can't be seen. However, when a player window is scaled, or displayed full-screen without scaling, everything in the visible window can then be seen, even if it's outside the actual Stage area.

You'll fix this problem in a moment, but first add a user-friendly quit button:

1. Quit your projector and return to your *.fla* file.
2. Create a new layer just below the *actions* layer and call it **`quit button`**.
3. In this new layer, create a simple button yourself, or, if you prefer, use a button component or a button from another Library to which you have access.
4. Give the button an instance name of **`quit_btn`** and place it in the upper-right corner of your file.
5. Add the following lines to the script in frame 1 (the *fscommand quit* option requires no additional parameters):

```
quit_btn.onRelease = function():Void {
    fscommand("quit");
}
```

6. Save your work.

Next, you will create a mask to prevent your animation from being visible outside the Stage area. It's been several chapters since you've worked with mask layers, so the necessary steps follow:

1. Add a new layer directly below the *quit button* layer, and call it **mask**.
2. Draw a rectangle the full dimensions of the Stage.
3. Double-click the layer icon in the *mask* layer to open the Layer Properties dialog, and set its type to *Mask*.
4. Double-click the layer icons of each layer beneath the *mask* layer in turn, and set each of them to *Masked*.
5. Save your work, publish your movie, and launch the new projector.

Everything should be fine now. Your animation will be visible only inside the Stage area, your screen outside the Stage area will be filled with a nice sedate black that lets you focus on your art, and your new quit button makes it easy for the end user to quit your application. Your end result should now resemble Figure 14-3 and *Box Guy E*. If you have any problems, compare your file to *box_guy_proj_05.fla* in the *14* folder.

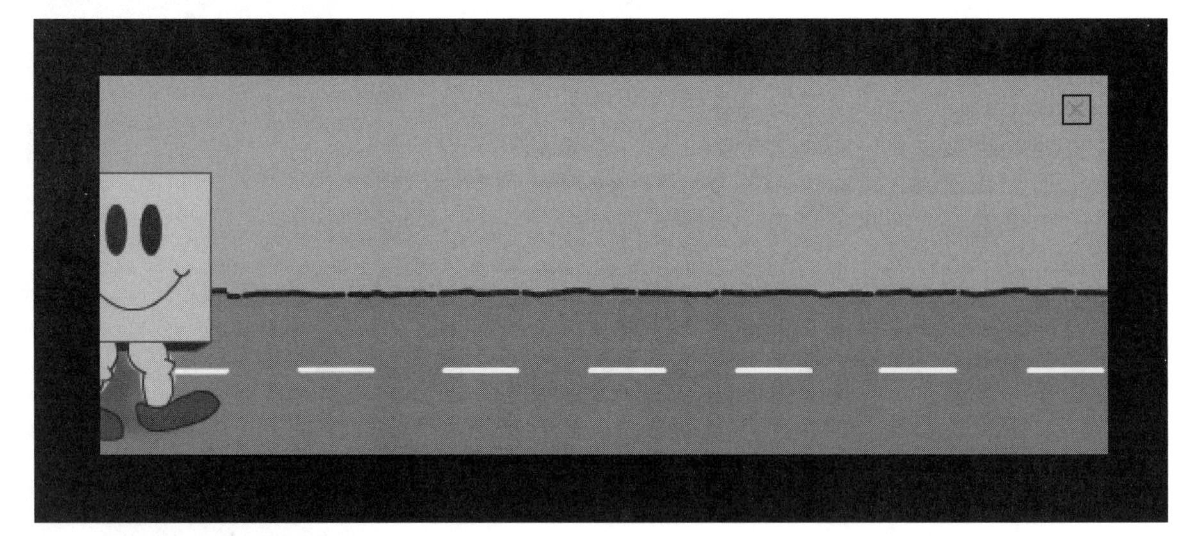

Figure 14-3. The final file is properly masked and includes a convenient quit button

Projector Enhancers

Unfortunately, the options you've just read about and practiced with are about all a Flash projector can do. Without the ability to do more—such as write to the user's hard drive, manipulate operating system settings, or spawn and control windows, just to name a few options—Flash is pretty much worthless for serious CD-ROM development. Even the most basic features are lacking. For instance, a Flash projector can't even center itself on your screen or show a proper window title or application name in its interface.

Fortunately, several third-party applications can add functionality to Flash projectors. One of the best cross-platform options is ScreenTime's *mProjector* (*http://www.screentime.com*). mProjector has almost 200 features for controlling the application, operating system, files, windows, menus, and more. It can even add FTP functionality to your projector, beyond what is possible with Flash 8's new file upload and download capabilities.

If you intend to put a serious effort into developing quality disc-based Flash solutions, a product like mProjector is a must.

Flash on the Run

Just as the Flash Player exists for desktop delivery via browser plug-ins and standalone players, so too can Flash be distributed on many mobile devices. The catch to creating Flash content for mobile devices is that the player technology for these devices lags behind the players used in desktop environments. While desktop users can use Flash Player 8 at the time of this writing, some PDA and handheld users can only play Flash 5 or Flash 6 content. Other devices—primarily cell phones—can only run a new version of the Flash Player called *Flash Lite*, which is roughly equivalent to Flash Player 4.

Even with the technology gap, which continues to close, it's pretty impressive how ubiquitous Flash playback is becoming. With the right planning, you can effectively develop content that can be played on virtually every Flash-enabled device that exists, numbering in the hundreds of millions.

WARNING

With that lofty goal in mind, be sure to test early and often on all target devices to avoid surprises, as platform differences are inevitable. Testing from the outset allows time for product redesign, if necessary.

The last two projects of this chapter will be basic image viewers of sorts. You will make a slide show for use on a PocketPC device, and a New York City Tourism guide that includes descriptive text with images for use on a Flash Lite–enabled cellular phone.

Flash Player for Mobile Devices

Although the functionality of this project will be extremely simple due to space limitations and the need for tutorial clarity, the PocketPC platform allows you to use technology compatible with Flash Player 6. Other platforms (including the CLIÉ, Palm OS, a few Nokia smart phones, and others) also have Flash players, but some can only accommodate Flash 5–compatible content. Be sure to identify your target device and confirm its player support before beginning any project.

To create your slide show, you'll take advantage of Flash's templates and skins:

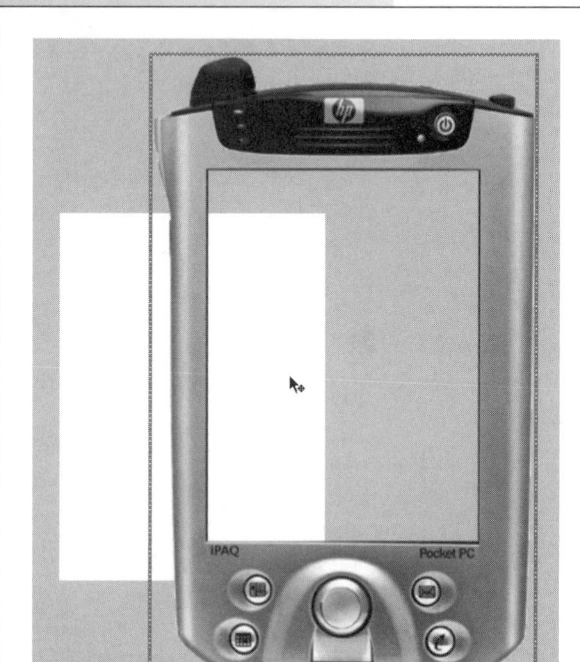

Figure 14-4. The iPAQ 5400 skin for the "Windows Mobile - Full Screen" template

1. Choose File→New and choose the Templates tab to access the "New from Template" dialog box.
2. Choose PDAs from the Category list in the dialog box, then choose "Windows Mobile - Full Screen" from the Templates list.
3. Initially, you will see a fairly standard Stage, although smaller than the normal Flash default. However, in your Library is a device skin to help you see what your content will look like when running on a device in your target audience. In this case, the device skin is derived from the Hewlett-Packard iPAQ 5400.
4. Create a new layer at the bottom of the timeline, and call it **device**. Drag the Library bitmap to the Stage, as seen in Figure 14-4, and position it so that it surrounds the Stage.
5. Next, take advantage of a fabulous trick that will make your authoring easier without affecting your final output. Double-click the layer icon of the *device* layer, and select Guide for the layer type. This will prevent the layer from exporting to *.swf* when the file is published. Now you can design your interface with the device in mind, without worrying about the size of your template. To prevent accidental selection, lock this layer when you've positioned the art to your satisfaction.

NOTE

The guide layer was originally created to allow you to use things like ruler guides and placeholder assets to help you align and position content. However, since the layer is not included when the .swf is published, you can put any helpful content you wish in a guide layer. You can even temporarily disable layers that you intend to keep and use in your final content, just by converting them to guide layers until you need them again.

Buttons for mobile devices

With your skin in place, you can move on to creating the interface buttons. This may seem routine by this point, but there are a couple of nuances that you must consider when developing buttons for mobile devices.

First, unlike the buttons found in a desktop environment, buttons created for stylus-based mobile devices do not use rollover states. Since a stylus, or its equivalent, must be in contact with the screen to function, no rollover is possible. Therefore, when designing your buttons for the PocketPC slide show, create Up and Down states, as seen in Figure 14-5, but do not create separate Over states. (It will do no harm, they just won't be used.)

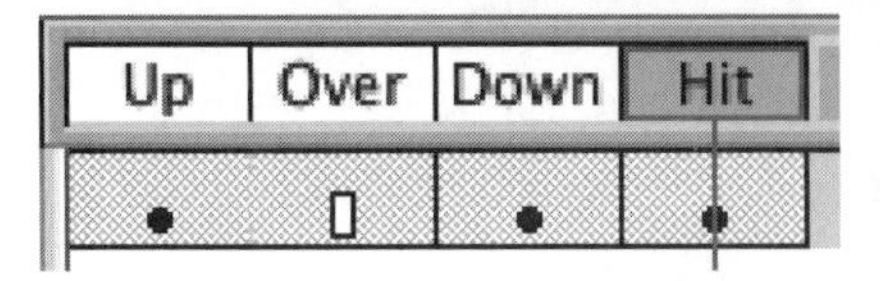

Figure 14-5. Keypad- and stylus-based devices do not use rollover states in buttons

Similarly, remember that you're developing for *handheld* devices. At times, a user may prefer to use a finger rather than a stylus, and your buttons must accommodate this less-precise mode of selection. Therefore, try to make the Hit states of your buttons as large as possible. The visible states of the buttons do not have to be overly large, rendering your design awkward and clunky. Instead, you can enlarge only the Hit states, which remain invisible to the user. Figure 14-6 shows the Hit state of a button (indicated by the overlapping dark and light colors) that is approximately 150% larger than the visible Up and Down states (indicated only by the lighter color).

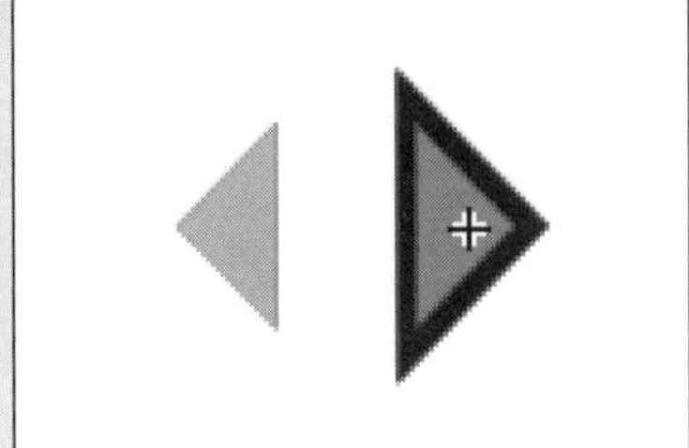

Figure 14-6. For handheld devices, make button Hit states as generous as possible to allow activation by finger, rather than stylus, when needed

Now it's time to build the remainder of the application (if you prefer, you can open *ipaq_02.fla*, which already contains button symbols, and skip to step 5):

1. Add a new layer above your guide layer and name it **buttons**.
2. Create a single arrow- or triangle-shaped button symbol in this layer, following the guidelines for creating buttons for mobile devices discussed previously, and place it in the bottom center of this layer.
3. Make a copy of the button and use Modify→Transform→Flip Horizontal to mirror the first button.
4. Give the left-facing arrow or triangle button an instance name of **prev_btn** and the right-facing arrow or triangle button an instance name of **next_btn**.
5. Select frame 1 of the *Content* layer and use File→Import to Stage to import the *nyc_01.jpg* image. Because this file is one of three sequentially named images, you will kindly be prompted with a question asking if you want to import them all. Answer in the affirmative. Not only will Flash import all three images, but it will also create keyframes for these images in frames 1, 2 and 3, arranging the bitmaps in the timeline in sequential order.
6. Finally, in frame 1 of the *ActionScript* layer, add the following script. The template provides the first comment and instruction. Follow them with the *stop()* action to prevent premature frame advances, and then two button handlers:

```
// this ActionScript sets your content to be full screen
fscommand("FullScreen", true);
//
stop();
//
next_btn.onRelease = function():Void {
    if (_currentframe == 3) {
        gotoAndStop(1);
```

```
    } else {
        nextFrame();
    }
};
prev_btn.onRelease = function():Void {
    if (_currentframe == 1) {
        gotoAndStop(3);
    } else {
        prevFrame();
    }
};
```

NOTE

If you don't understand the use of the double equals sign, or need any other review on conditionals, see Chapter 7 for more information.

The two button handlers in this script are essentially the same. Depending on the button, each click will move the playhead one frame forward or backward until the end of the sequence is reached. At that point, the navigation will loop to the opposite end of the sequence.

Figure 14-7. The finished slide show

7. If you wish, you may add artwork to an additional *background* layer to further spruce up your interface. A very basic example of such an effort can be seen in Figure 14-7.
8. Save your work and test your file.

You should be able to use your mouse to simulate the device stylus and move forward and backward through the three sample images. If your file is not functioning properly, compare your work with the *ipaq_03.fla* sample file provided in the *14* folder on the accompanying CD-ROM.

Of course, this example application is very simple. In the case of the PocketPC device, you can accomplish much, much more because the platform supports files compatible with versions up to and including Flash 6.

How you get your final product onto the target device varies from unit to unit. Typically, you will perform some type of synchronization routine between your desktop and the mobile device. In other instances, you may use a memory card and a desktop card reader to copy the file between machines. Consult the operator's manual for your specific device for more information.

Flash Lite

Flash Lite is a relatively new part of the Flash platform. It is a tiny Flash player designed for inclusion in mobile devices with strictly limited memory capacities and performance limitations—cell phones, for the most part.

Flash Lite content-development constraints are more severe than those encountered when authoring for PDAs and other devices that use the full Flash Player. In the latter scenarios, you are restricted to Flash Player 6, or possibly Flash Player 5, compatibility. When using Flash Lite, you must use ActionScript that is, essentially, Flash 4–compatible. The difference between Flash 4 and Flash 5 may sound subtle, but ActionScript matured quite a bit between these two versions.

The good news is that newer versions of Flash Lite will be more robust, and it looks like major improvements are on the way. At the time of this writing, Macromedia says that Flash Lite 2 will include:

- The Flash 7 code base with support for ActionScript 2.0
- Video playback
- External XML parsing
- Local, persistent data on the device
- Loadable external images and sounds

From Flash 4 to Flash 7 is quite a jump, and many developers are excited about the new feature set. However, several factors suggest that there is still a need for experience with the current version.

First, it is unknown how quickly carriers will adopt the new technology. Second, it is unclear how powerful the new devices will need to be to accommodate Flash Lite 2. If the player size increases substantially, or better processors are required to use it, Flash Lite 2 may not be as widely supported as its predecessors. Finally, there's no information about how existing Flash Lite users can upgrade, if at all. This means that there may continue to be a small, but growing, community of existing users that can't take advantage of new 2.0 content. Finally, at the time being there's no firm release date.

For up-to-date information on Flash Lite, you can check in with the Flash Lite Development Center at *http://www.macromedia.com/devnet/devices/flashlite.html*. For now, however, get your feet wet with the existing version that ships with Flash 8.

Start by creating a small promotional application that might be used by a New York City tourism group. (This is based on the Café Townsend sample file that is distributed with Flash 8, so if you want more practice, you can review that file as well.)

At any time, if you want to bypass these preliminary steps, you can open *nyc_tourism_01.fla* to start with a project-ready file. If this is your preference, skip ahead to the "Adding assets" section. To build the file from scratch, follow these steps:

1. To firmly root yourself in the Flash Lite environment, begin with a template. Create a new file and, whether you use the Flash 8 Startup Screen or the New Document dialog, switch to the Templates section. In the Global Phones category, select the first entry, "Flash Lite 1.1 Symbian Series 60," and click the dialog's OK button. Depending on the features supported by your device, you can create applications that play in the

Content Development Kits and New Profiles for Mobile Devices

Most Flash content for mobile devices can be run either inside a tiny browser inside the device, or within a stand-alone player. Not all devices support both methods, though. To learn more about the specifics of each method, as well as which devices support which features, check out Macromedia's DevNet section covering devices at *http://www.macromedia.com/devnet/devices/*.

Macromedia also offers Content Development Kits (CDKs) and, in some cases, Interface Development Kits (IDKs) complete with documentation, sample files, and even components designed specifically for mobile devices.

Also, at the time of this writing, Macromedia had just released its first supported devices update to Flash 8. A Flash extension with new and updated profiles can be downloaded from *http://www.macromedia.com/software/flash/download/device_profiles/* and installed using the Macromedia Extensions Manager. Keeping your development environment up to date gives you a big leg up when creating new work.

NOTE

Unless you have the specifications of a particular device in mind, starting with a template is the fastest way to get up and running when developing mobile content. Configured templates have been pre-sized and a compatible version of Flash Lite has been chosen for the most common devices. Also, Macromedia updates device profiles periodically to provide you with additional templates. For more information, see the sidebar "Content Development Kits and New Profiles for Mobile Devices."

NOTE

If you prefer to build your file step by step but would rather save time by using existing assets, use File→Import→Open External Library to open the nyc_tourism_01.fla file as a Library. This way, you can choose which assets to create and which to copy into your file when needed.

device's web browser or in the Flash Lite standalone player. This project uses the latter approach.

The first thing you will undoubtedly notice is that the Stage size is much smaller—obviously, to fit in the smaller displays of mobile devices such as cell phones. Take a look, too, at the File→Publish Settings dialog, in the Flash section. You will see that the file's version is specified not as ActionScript 2.0 but rather as Flash Lite 1.1.

2. Use the Modify→Document menu command to set your Stage color to black.
3. Give yourself the frames you will need by adding frames to both existing layers, through to frame 40.
4. You will be adding a few layers of content, so rename the *Content* layer to **`header`** for clarity.
5. In the *header* layer, create an application header that says **`Visit New York City`**. Use any font you like, but remember that legibility is a major issue on small devices. Think about using a bold, clear typeface such as Arial Black. This banner of sorts should be approximately 12–14 pixels tall.
6. When you are satisfied with your header, lock this layer to avoid additional edits.
7. Add a new layer above *header*, and label it **`buttons`**. Create a keyframe in frame 10 to confine the content in this layer to the first 10 frames.
8. In frame 1 of the *buttons* layer, create two buttons. One should say **`New York City Info`** and the other should say **`Sites to See`**. For this project specifically, design the buttons any way you like, but they should appear below a y-coordinate of approximately 160. Also, avoid putting them in the extreme lower-left and lower-right corners. These areas are reserved for another purpose that you'll learn about in a moment. (As a design example, the sample file provided uses stacked buttons that fill the width of the screen.)

WARNING

One important thing to remember here is that most cell phones do not use styluses. Instead, they rely on two-way or four-way navigation keys or a joystick that serves the same purpose. To visually link your keypad manipulations with on-screen buttons, rollover states are used to show the progress of the user's actions.

Down states may also be designed, but many developers choose not to use them so that the buttons will match the static labels that are typically used to identify the phone's reassignable soft keys (explained in the next step).

9. Create another new layer called **`soft key labels`** above the *buttons* layer, and create a keyframe in frame 10. After the user leaves the splash

screen to view content, this layer will be used for labels that will identify the purpose of the two reassignable under-screen keys on most cell phones. These are called *soft keys* because they can be programmed to have different purposes. You can see this in action as they are redefined as you navigate through multiple screens of your own cell phone.

10. In frame 10 of the *soft key labels* frame, create graphics that label the left key **Home** and the right key **Next**. Make these graphics approximately 50 pixels wide and 20 pixels tall, and place them in the extreme lower corners of the Stage. Positioning the graphics this way usually clearly identifies them as labels describing the functionality of the soft keys.

11. Save your work. Your timeline should now look like Figure 14-8.

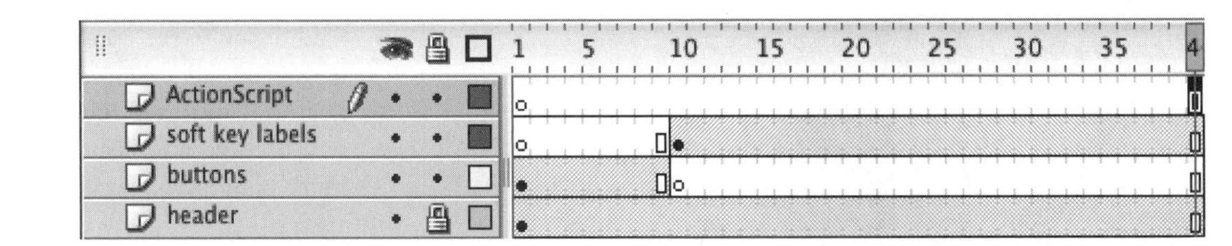

Figure 14-8. The timeline of the New York City Tourism Flash Lite example, as it appears with only buttons included

Now it's time to prepare for content. Your application will display three New York City landmarks and include their names, addresses, and opening hours. The splash page will have two buttons. One will show the application data, and the other will dial the New York City Information Hotline. When viewing the content, the Next button will cycle through the landmarks and the Home button will return to the splash page.

Start with the required text fields:

1. Create a new layer called **site name** directly above the *header* layer.

2. Create a dynamic text field of approximately 174 × 40 pixels, and position it at approximately (1, 145). Give it a *variable name* of **description**. You cannot use an instance name for this project because text field instance names are not compatible with Flash Lite 1.1 (Flash 4 syntax). If you need to review text field variable assignments, see Chapter 7.

3. Create another new layer above *site name* and call it **info**. Create a keyframe in frame 10.

4. In frame 10 of the *info* layer, create another text field, this time of approximately 174 × 18 pixels, and position it at approximately (1, 124). Give it a variable name of **site**.

5. Configure both fields to use the Arial font at size 12, and choose "Bitmap Text (no anti-aliasing)" from the anti-aliasing menu.

6. Save your work.

Next, add the frame labels and keyframes you'll need for navigation:

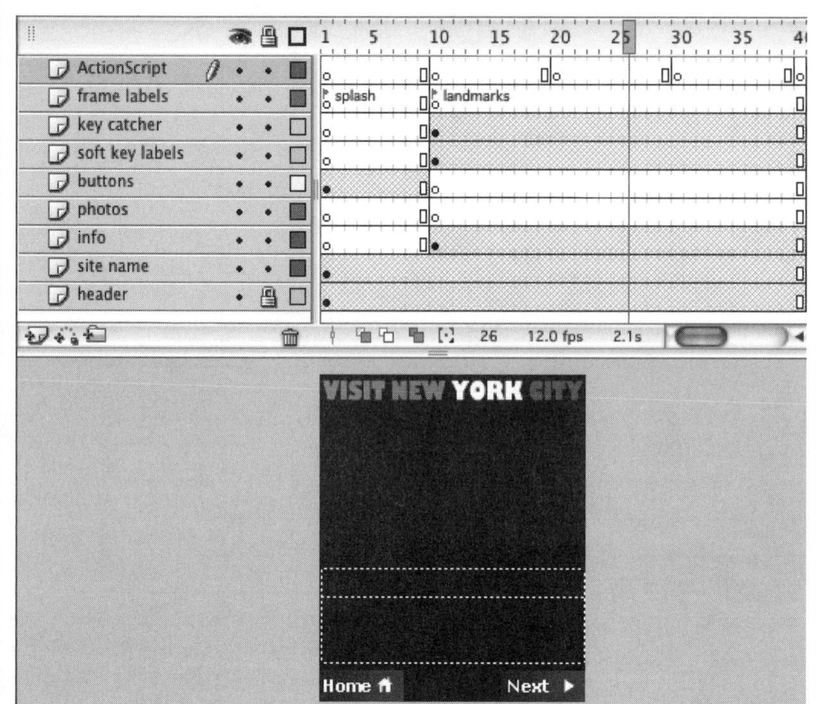

Figure 14-9. The timeline of the New York City Tourism Flash Lite example, as it appears prior to adding content

1. Add a layer directly below the *ActionScript* layer and call it **`frame labels`**. Create a keyframe in frame 10.
2. Give frame 1 the frame label **`splash`**, and give frame 10 the frame label **`landmarks`**.
3. In the *ActionScript* layer, create additional keyframes at frames 20, 30, and 40.
4. Add a new layer above the *info* layer and call it **`photos`**. Create a keyframe in frame 10. This layer will hold your splash and landmark photos.
5. Finally, add a button that you will use to trap the key events sent by the device. You will be using Flash 4 button syntax to trap one key event at a time, so you just need a button of any kind—it will reside off-Stage. Keep file size low by avoiding graphics. Try adding a small text field with no anti-aliasing that says **`key catcher`** to the Up state.
6. Save your work. Your timeline should now look like Figure 14-9, and your file should be similar to *nyc_tourism_02.fla* in the *14* folder of your working directory.

Adding assets

The final stage in completing your file is to add assets and script them:

1. From the *14* folder of your working directory, import *nyc_tourism_splash.jpg*, as well as *nyc_01.jpg*, *nyc_02.jpg*, and *nyc_03.jpg*. You don't want to automatically create keyframes for these images, so use the File→Import→Import to Library option.
2. In frame 1 of the *photos* layer, position the *nyc_tourism_splash* image on the Stage at (0, 120).
3. In frame 10 of the *photos* layer, position the *nyc_01* image on the Stage at (0, 120). Select the image and then choose the Modify→Convert to Symbol menu command. Make your symbol a movie clip, call it

nyc_tourism_mc, and use the 9-point grid icon near the center of the dialog to position the registration point in the upper-left corner of the movie clip.

4. Add the remaining *nyc_0X* images to the movie clip, end to end, so they are all in this order from left to right: *nyc_01*, *nyc_02*, *nyc_03*, and *nyc_01* again. (You will see that the repetition of the first photo is necessary for the tween transition, so you can jump unnoticed from the last frame to the first frame.) When you are finished, return to the main timeline.
5. In frame 10 of the *photos* layer, add a motion tween. It will likely start off with a dotted line indicating an unfinished tween, because you have not provided a destination keyframe. You'll do that now.
6. In frame 20 of the *photos* layer, add a keyframe and position the movie clip at the x-coordinate –176. In frame 30, add a keyframe and position the movie clip at the x-coordinate –352. Finally, add a keyframe in frame 40 and position the movie clip at –528. Your tween should now be complete.
7. Save your work.

All your labor will soon be realized when you add the scripts to your file:

1. Start by scripting the splash page. On the "Sites to See" button, add the following script so that it will take you to the *landmarks* frame when pressed:

```
on(press) {
    gotoAndStop("landmarks");
}
```

NOTE

You may be looking at the previous script and asking yourself why you're departing from best practices and putting the script right on the button, like you did way back in Chapter 4. Because you must adhere to Flash Lite 1.1 (Flash 4–compatible) syntax, this is required. Button instance names didn't exist in Flash 4 days, so you can't remotely add an event handler to buttons using Flash Lite 1.1.

2. On the "New York City Info" button, add the following script:

```
on(press) {
    site = "Call 311 for NYC Info"
    getURL("tel:311");
}
```

The *getURL* command will attempt to dial 311 (New York's Information Hotline) for you. However, not all phones support this action, so you can put a descriptive string in the *site* variable to prompt the user to dial the number manually, if necessary.

3. Now for the *ActionScript* layer. In frame 1, add the following script:

```
stop();
_focusRect = false;
fscommand2("resetsoftkeys");
fscommand2("setquality", "high");
fscommand2("fullscreen", "true");
site = "The Greatest City on Earth!";
```

   The first line prevents the movie from playing automatically. The second line prevents the device from highlighting every selection with a rectangle indicating the focus. Lines 3 through 5 issue instructions to the device. Line 3 resets the programming for the soft keys so they can be programmed with your desired functionality. Lines 4 and 5 set the quality to high and tell the standalone player to display full-screen. Finally, the last line adds a string of text to the Stage-bound *site* variable, displaying it on the screen.

4. In frame 10, add the following lines of code:

```
fscommand2("setsoftkeys", left, right);
stop();
site = "Statue of Liberty";
description = "Ferry, Battery Park to Liberty Island. Open 9:30 -
5:00.";
```

   The first line sets the functionality of the two soft keys to send *PageUp* and *PageDown* events. You will trap these with the aforementioned "key catcher" button in the next step.

5. On the key catcher button, which you've positioned off-Stage, add the following script:

```
on (keyPress "<PageUp>") {
    site = "The Greatest City on Earth!";
    description = "";
    gotoAndStop(1);
}
on (keyPress "<PageDown>") {
    site = "";
    description = "";
    play();
}
```

   Both code segments use button key events to be compatible with Flash 4 syntax. (For more robust key handling, see the "Better Keystroke Detection" sidebar.) The first segment traps the *PageUp* event sent by the Home button. It clears the *description* variable, sets the *site* variable to the splash page text, and navigates to the splash page. The second clears both variables and issues the *play()* command to override the frame script that has stopped the user in each frame. This navigates the user to the next landmark.

6. Now, back to the *ActionScript* layer. In frames 20 and 30, you need scripts that stop user progress and populate the variables, just like you wrote in frame 10:

```
//frame 20
stop();
site = "Empire State Building";
description = "34th St. and 5th Ave. Open 9:30 to Midnight.";

//frame 30
stop();
site = "Central Park";
description = "59th St. and 5th Ave. Open 24 hrs.";
```

7. Finally, in frame 40, add this last line of code:

```
gotoAndStop("landmarks");
```

   This sends the playhead back to the first frame of the sequence so the user can easily page through all the images in a cycle. You needed the duplicate Statue of Liberty because each image tweens in from the right. If you didn't include the first picture again, the navigation script would send the user back to the first image abruptly.

8. Save your work. Your timeline should now look like Figure 14-10, and your file should compare to *nyc_tourism_03.fla*.

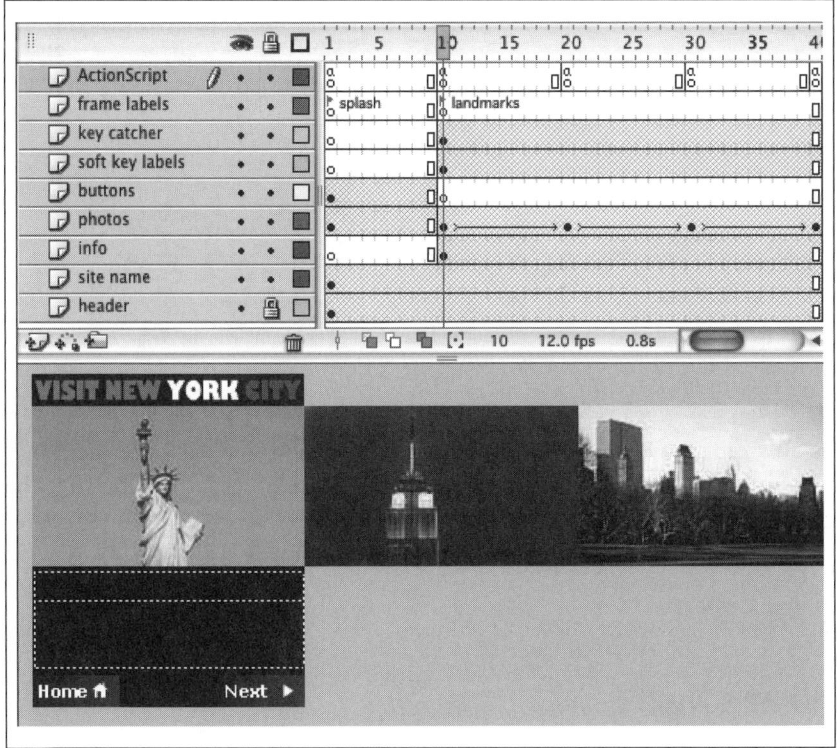

Figure 14-10. The same timeline seen in Figure 14-9, but after the images and tweens have been added

Well, it took more steps than might have been required if you weren't restricted to Flash 4–compatible syntax, but you're all done. You can test your movie now, and you're in for a little surprise.

Because the publish settings (defined by the template) identify the *.fla* as a Flash Lite file, the *.swf* will open up in the Mobile Device emulator. Pick a device and test the file using the on-screen keypad. Figure 14-11 shows what your final product might look like on a Nokia 6680.

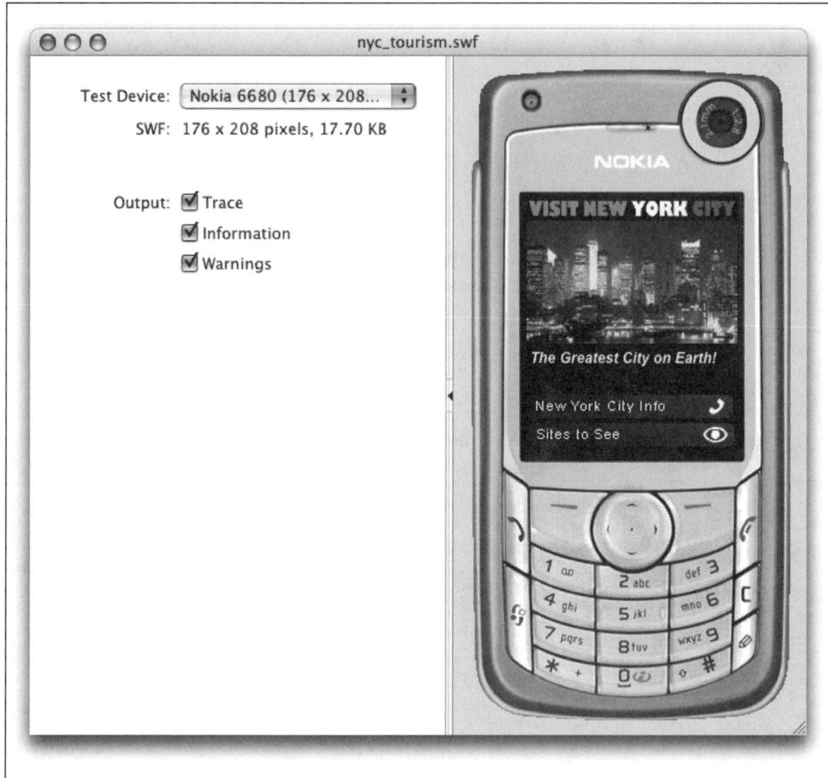

Figure 14-11. The final NYC Tourism promotion as seen in the device emulator playing on a Nokia 6680

If you enable the output checkboxes on the left, you will receive lots of useful information in the Output window. This includes a warning that *fscommand2* actions must be tested on the device, and a warning that the call request may not be compatible with all devices.

Congratulations! You're well on your way to developing Flash content for mobile devices.

What's Next?

By learning about delivering Flash files in ways other than the standard web delivery, you've taken your first major step toward thinking outside the box when it comes to Flash. You've taken this step at a good time, too, because mobile development is a rapidly growing sector of the Flash community.

With that in mind, try to spend as much time as you can keeping abreast of the changes in the mobile authoring space. The next time you consider a mobile device upgrade, think about factoring Flash Lite compatibility into your decision. If you have a compatible device, you can test features that can't be tested in the software-only simulator that ships with Flash.

When you're ready to move on, you'll be embarking on the last chapter of this modest book. Your last experiences within these pages will, ideally, push you further out of your box as you explore custom video and drawing options and learn how to extend Flash's authoring environment.

In the next chapter, you will:

- Export animations to video format for external video processing
- Export interactive Flash files to QuickTime format for interactive video playback in the QuickTime Player
- Use the Drawing API to draw vectors on the fly
- Build your own component
- Review your progress by revisiting ActionScript highlights throughout this book

Better Keystroke Detection

In your foray into Flash Lite development, you saw the ancient method of adding a specific key event to a button. This is fine for down-and-dirty solutions, or when technical limitations prevent more elaborate systems, but it's not a practical approach for more mature applications.

The following code takes a quick look at improved keystroke detection using event listeners. (If you need any review on event listeners, see the sidebar of the same name in Chapter 12.)

This example detects the right and left arrow keys, allowing the user to navigate a file with the keyboard:

```
// create a generic object to act as a listener
keyListener = new Object();

// assign a function to the object's
// onKeyDown property
keyListener.onKeyDown = function():Void {
  // check whether the right or left arrow is pressed.
  // check to see if the constant for the RIGHT
  // key is down when the keyDown event is sent.
  // Test similarly for the LEFT constant.
  // Navigate accordingly.
  if (Key.isDown(Key.RIGHT)) {
    nextFrame();
  } else if (Key.isDown(Key.LEFT)) {
 prevFrame();
  }
}
// register listener with Key class to detect
// key events
Key.addListener(keyListener);
```

Remember, when your application is running in a web browser, the browser itself might intercept keystrokes. The Flash Player traps keyboard events only if it has mouse focus. Users must click the Stage of a movie before the movie's keystroke handlers will become active. Consider forcing users to click a button before entering any keyboard-controlled section of a movie. This ensures that the Flash Player has keyboard focus.

When keystroke detection is no longer needed, you can improve the file's efficiency, and your coding practices, by removing the listener as follows:

```
Key.removeListener(keyListener);
```

Think Outside the Box

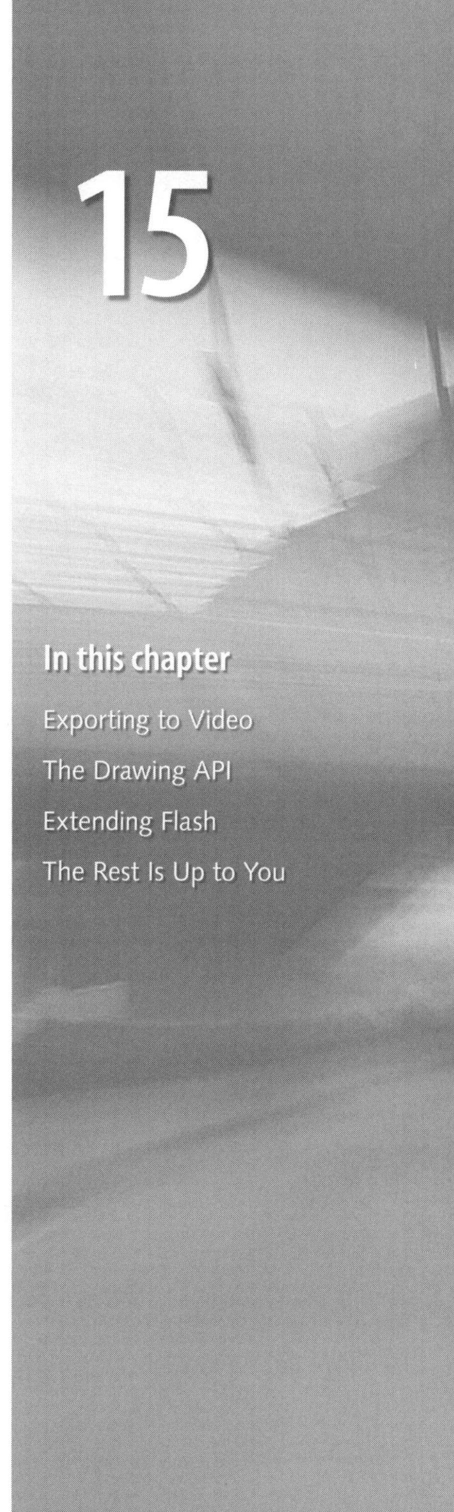

Flash is a powerful tool, and some of its features are often overlooked. In this final chapter, you'll try a few projects that demonstrate some of the application's less common uses.

Exporting to Video

In addition to web- and disc-based animations and applications, Flash can also be used as a limited video production tool. It is not useful as a video-editing program, but it can be helpful when creating video assets to use therein. Flash can export to video in two formats: pixel-based video, for use in a traditional video-editing application, and as a Flash track embedded in a QuickTime movie as part of QuickTime's Media Layer architecture.

Pixel-Based Video

If you're one of the many people who use their computers to create videos, and maybe even DVDs, you may want to use Flash to convert your animations into video format, or to create titles or other simple effects for your videos.

Exporting broadcast-quality video from Flash requires a little preparation. Bearing that in mind, try adapting your first animation for video export:

1. Open the *animation_complete.fla* file from the *03* folder in your working directory.
2. Choose File→Save As, and save the animation as *animation_video.fla* in the *15* folder. This will allow you to modify your document freely without overwriting the original.
3. Use Modify→Document to change the frame rate of your original movie to 30 frames per second. Flash's default frame rate is 12 fps, but high-quality video typically runs at 30 fps. (The exact rate for broadcast TV in the United States is 29.97 fps, but it differs slightly in other countries.)

4. Before exporting, test your movie. Depending on how fast your computer is, your movie will play at up to twice the speed it used to play, which is too fast.

5. To fix this, you must add frames to your animation. This will simultaneously slow down the animation to normal speed and make it much smoother. The *.swf* version started out as a 4-second animation: 48 frames at 12 fps. To achieve that length again, you must end up with 120 frames at 30 fps.

6. Somewhere between frame 1 and frame 12, where the first box scaling occurs, click in the bar where the frame numbers are visible above all the layers. Clicking here ensures that no single frame is selected and prevents you from accidentally adding frames to only one layer.

7. Add 18 frames to the animation by pressing F5 18 times. The final keyframe that was in frame 12 should now be in frame 30, as seen in Figure 15-1.

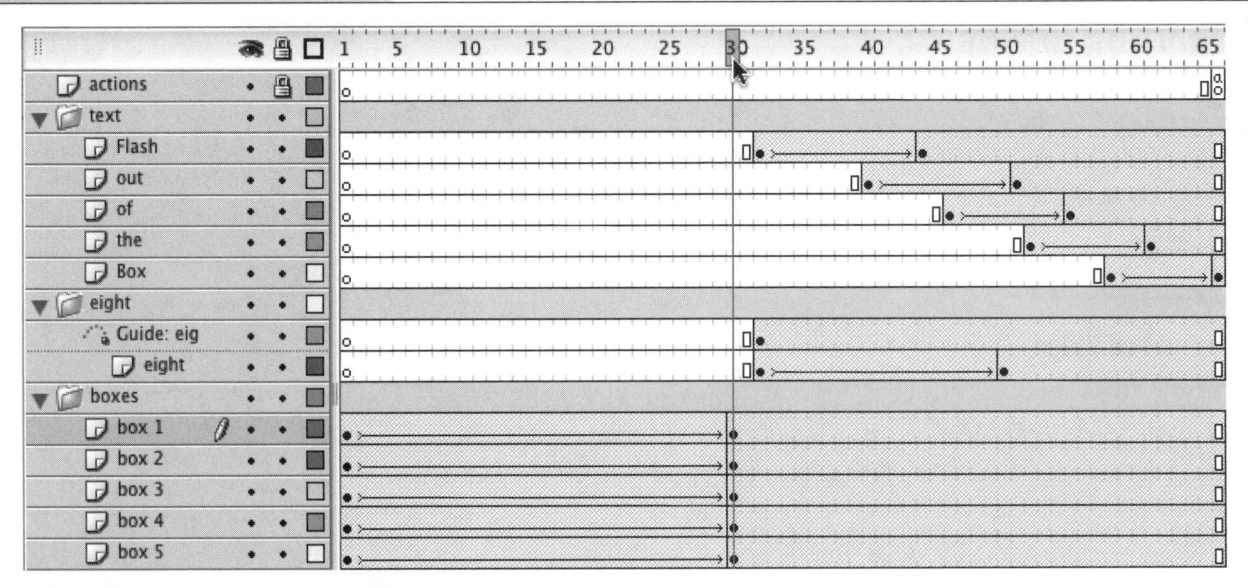

Figure 15-1. The timeline, after adding the first group of frames to match the new frame rate

8. Next, add 10 frames to the tween of each word. (Because of the layer structure, this will automatically tween the number 8.) Again, click in the numbered frame bar above all the layers to avoid accidentally selecting and adding frames to only one layer. Remember that these tweens are staggered, so try not to accidentally lengthen each tween more than once. Looking at Figure 15-1 as an example, good points at which to insert new frames include frames 35, 44, 51, 55, and 61.

9. All that remains to reach your desired 4-second animation is to add a few more frames to the end, so the entire animation concludes at frame 120.
10. Save your work. If you want to check the file, compare it to *animation_video_02.fla*.

With the adjustments made, you're ready to create a QuickTime movie from your Flash file:

1. Choose File→Export→Export Movie to open the Export Movie dialog box.

NOTE

You will notice two QuickTime formats listed. "QuickTime Video" will rasterize your file into a linear, pixel-based format, like most digital videos you see. This video can then be edited in a variety of applications. "QuickTime" will embed your file as a Flash track within a layered QuickTime movie, compatible with QuickTime Media Layer–savvy applications.

2. In the Save As field, specify **`animation_video.mov`** as the filename and choose "QuickTime Video" from the Format drop-down list.
3. Save your file in the *15* folder of your working directory.
4. The Export QuickTime Video dialog box, shown in Figure 15-2, will open.
5. Enter **500** in the Width field, to match the Stage dimensions. If the "Maintain aspect ratio" option is enabled, the Height field will adjust accordingly.

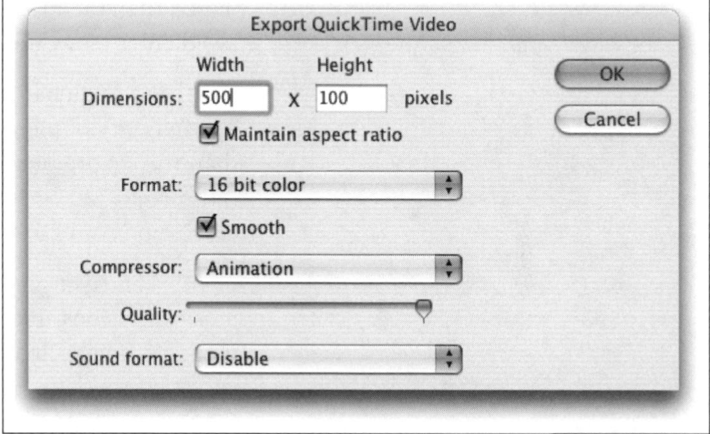

Figure 15-2. The Export QuickTime Video dialog

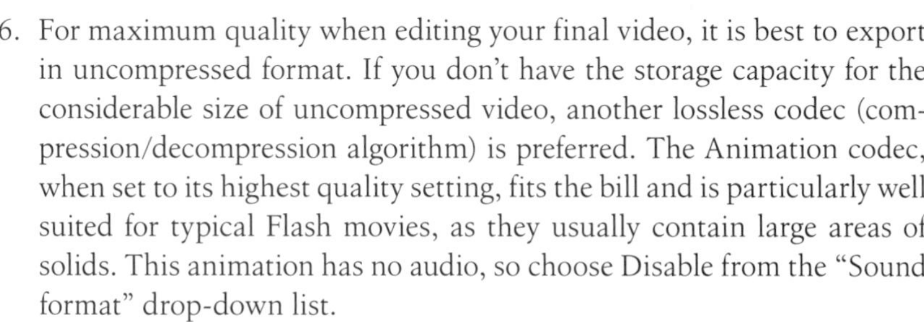

6. For maximum quality when editing your final video, it is best to export in uncompressed format. If you don't have the storage capacity for the considerable size of uncompressed video, another lossless codec (compression/decompression algorithm) is preferred. The Animation codec, when set to its highest quality setting, fits the bill and is particularly well suited for typical Flash movies, as they usually contain large areas of solids. This animation has no audio, so choose Disable from the "Sound format" drop-down list.
7. Click OK to export the QuickTime video.
8. Locate *animation_video.mov* in the *15* folder and double-click it to preview your file in the QuickTime Player.

You now have a video that can be integrated into most video-editing environments.

There are a few things to remember when planning such a process. Space prevents an in-depth analysis of each of these items, but here are a few quick points to consider:

1. Exporting to rasterized (pixel-based) video ignores all scripts, so you can't use ActionScript to control your animation.
2. Movie clips won't play, so you need to use graphic symbols instead, and you can't rely on movie clip control (see number 1).
3. Advanced: If you must use scripts or movie clips, you can bring the Flash file into Director and export to QuickTime from there. However, as of this writing, Director MX 2004 only supported up to Flash Player 7 *.swf* output. So, you won't be able to take advantage of Flash 8–specific features.
4. Although HDTV is changing the television horizon, the NTSC color palette used for analog television broadcast in the United States is more muted than the RGB color palette. Try to design in the NTSC palette to avoid color blowouts.
5. Another thing changing with the wider use of HDTV is aspect ratios. The majority of televisions, however, still use rectangular pixels, rather than the square pixels of a computer monitor. To achieve the standard full-screen 720 × 480 final size, compensate by starting with Stage dimensions of 720 × 540.
6. Finally (and yet another thing changing with the improved HDTV), most televisions underscan the information provided, effectively cropping the image. It is typical to allow yourself a 5–10% bleed of the width on the left and right, and the same percentage of the height on the top and bottom, to make sure important art is viewable. The area within these boundaries is commonly called the *safe area*. It is also a good idea to allow another safety margin of 5–10% within that region for important text. This is called the *title safe area*.

QuickTime Media Layer

As Flash video technologies have improved, creating interactive or vector/pixel hybrid video projects directly within Flash has become increasingly common. This allows you to use the latest versions of ActionScript, Flash, and FLV formats for the best quality/feature mix.

However, there may be instances when you want to combine Flash and QuickTime. QuickTime's ability to contain many different tracks of many different asset types—sometimes referred to as the *QuickTime Media*

Layer (QTML) architecture—makes this possible. For example, you may want to capitalize on a particular video quality or codec but add a password-protection scheme directly into the video, or you may want to embed a custom-made controller, high-quality text overlays, or other elements directly into a video. All of this is possible by exporting a Flash file into a QTML track.

Version support

There are significant limitations, however. QTML files won't behave the same in all situations. For example, many types of tracks are ignored in more traditional video environments, so they should not be used the way pixel-based QuickTime video files are used. Further, the QuickTime version current as of this writing supports only Flash 5 ActionScript. This means that if you intend to create a hybrid of Flash vectors and video for an interactive QuickTime asset, you must limit your programmed features to those that are supported by that generation of ActionScript.

An easy way to do this is to set your file to export a *.swf* compatible with Flash Player 5, prior to beginning the project:

1. Create a new Flash document, and save it temporarily using any filename and location. (You will move on to a video project in a moment; this step is just to familiarize you with Flash 5 output.)
2. Select the File→Publish Settings menu command.
3. Select the Flash button in the middle top navigation bar (between Formats and HTML).
4. Select "Flash Player 5" from the Version menu, as shown in Figure 15-3.

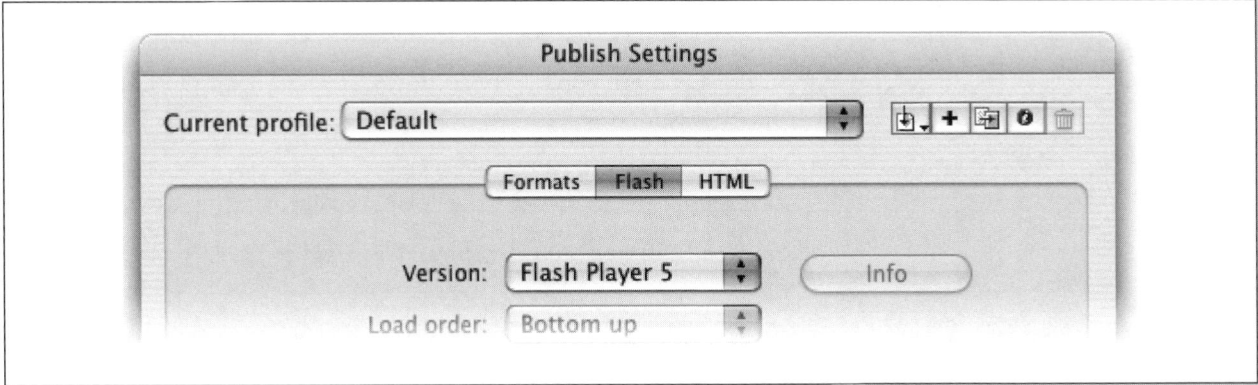

Figure 15-3. The Publish Settings dialog box

5. Next, open the Actions panel and look at the ActionScript menu on the left. Many entries are highlighted in yellow, as seen in Figure 15-4, indicating that they are not supported in the version of the Flash Player you have selected.

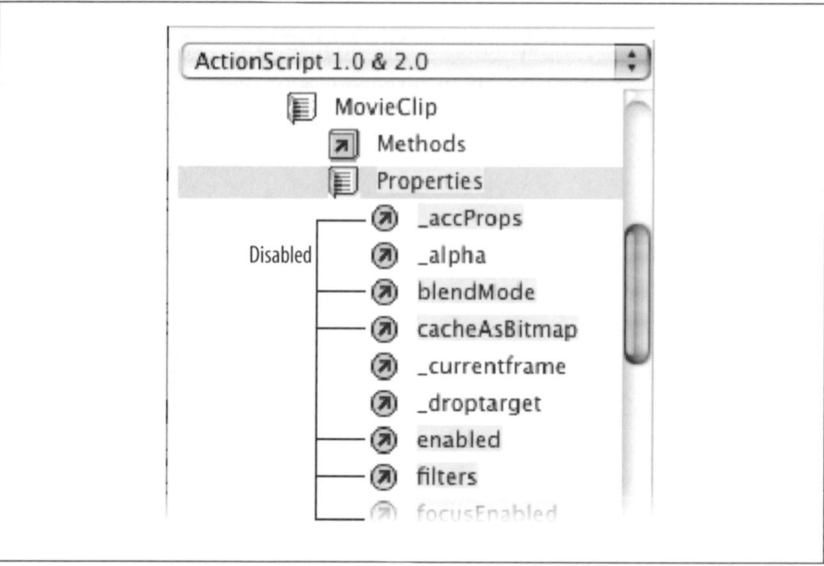

Figure 15-4. The Actions panel, highlighting features disabled by the Flash Player setting chosen in the Publish Settings dialog

If you avoid the highlighted entries, your file will usually work fine when embedded in a QuickTime movie. Most of the ActionScript compatible with Flash Player 5 will work in QuickTime. However, some things, such as *fscommand* actions, are not understood. These commands are designed primarily for issuing instructions to a standalone projector for disc-based playback of Flash files, which you learned about in Chapter 14.

Exporting the QTML track

Now apply what you know to exporting your file:

1. If it's not still open, reopen the *animation_video.fla* file.
2. Choose File→Export→Export Movie to again open the Export Movie dialog box.
3. This time, in the Save As field, specify **animation_qtml.mov** as the filename and choose "QuickTime" from the Format drop-down list.
4. Save the file in your *15* folder. The Export QuickTime dialog will open.
5. In the first part of this project, you'll create a Flash track that you can later add to an existing QuickTime document. Therefore, you don't need to worry about the QuickTime alpha and layer compositing features, a controller, or playback features. This animation has no sound, so you don't need to compress it in QuickTime. Be sure to turn on the "Flatten (Make self-contained)" setting, though, as shown in Figure 15-5, so your movie doesn't rely on any other assets and can function entirely on its own.

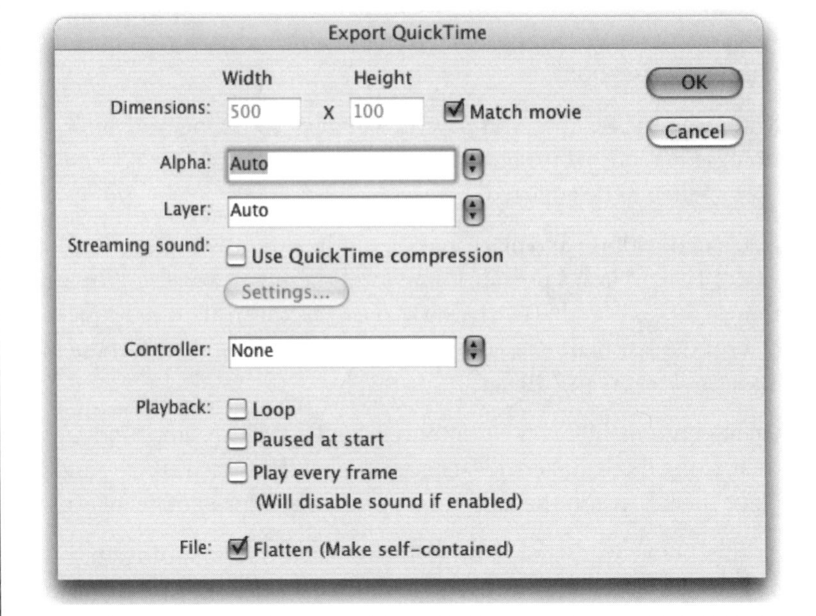

Figure 15-5. The Export QuickTime dialog

6. Click OK to export the movie. Open the file in the QuickTime Player, and you'll see that the quality of the vectors is preserved. This is now a Flash track inside a QuickTime layer, rather than a Flash animation that has been rasterized into pixels, frame by frame.

Many developers prefer to composite QuickTime layers in a QTML-savvy editing application. However, if you know you want to merge a Flash track with a video track, and you have all the assets ready, you can do so right in Flash.

Exporting merged video and SWF tracks

The difference between this next project and the video work you did in Chapter 9 is that the video you work with here will neither be entirely embedded nor an external FLV that is loaded at runtime. Instead, you will link to a video during authoring, and then export the Flash and video tracks together into a QuickTime file.

> **NOTE**
>
> *To review the sample code associated with this project, you must have the .mov and .fla documents in the same directory. Since enough room exists on a CD to duplicate these files, this step has been taken for you. However, if you don't want duplicate files on your hard drive, feel free to move either file into a new directory. For clarity, the steps discussed herein will be based on the provided CD directory.*

To export merged video and SWF tracks:

1. Create a new Flash document, and save it as *linked_video.fla* in the *15* folder of your working directory.
2. Choose File→Publish Settings and specify Flash Player 5 compatibility in the Version menu.
3. Set the document properties to a Stage dimension of 320 × 275 and a background color of black.

> **NOTE**
>
> *In authoring mode, you can preview the video live, but without sound. Since you must export the file as a QuickTime file, testing the .swf will not include the video.*

4. Import the *nero.mov* video, just as you did in Chapter 9. This time, however, choose the "Linked QuickTime video for publishing to QuickTime" option.

5. The same dialog that you saw in Chapter 9, telling you how many frames are required to show the video, will display. Click Yes and allow the timeline to be adjusted.

6. Add a marker layer and place markers at the three distinct sections of the video. Using Flash's default frame rate, these will be at approximately frames 50, 511, and 703. (If you want to factor in the soundtrack, you can set the last marker at approximately frame 798.) Name these markers **nero**, **archie**, and **dinner**, respectively.

7. Create buttons that you will program to play, pause, stop, and move to each of the three makers you created. Label them accordingly, and then place them beneath the video at a *_y* value of approximately 260.

8. At this point, you would normally give each button an instance name and assign each one an event handler in a frame script. However, ActionScript compatible with Flash Player 5 (required for export to the QuickTime format) did not support button instance names. So, revert to the basic use of applying handlers directly to your buttons. Select the play button and add this script to the Actions panel:

```
on (release) {
    play();
}
```

9. Add the same event handler directly to each of the other buttons, adding the following instructions:

```
//PAUSE: stops the timeline but allows you to continue later, if
desired
stop();

//STOP: both stops and resets to frame 1
gotoAndStop(1);

//NERO: goes to the frame label "nero"
gotoAndPlay("nero");

//ARCHIE: goes to the frame label "archie"
gotoAndPlay("archie");

//DINNER: goes to the frame label "dinner"
gotoAndPlay("dinner");
```

10. Now you can export your movie as QuickTime again. For now, continue with all the default settings, as you did previously, but this time enable the "Paused at start" playback option. The result should resemble Figure 15-6.

Figure 15-6. Your animation playing in the QuickTime Player

The video will be paused, and the play, pause, and stop buttons should work as described. The Nero button will jump to the start of the video, when Nero the lionfish appears (skipping the title). The Archie button will jump to the first appearance of Archie the shrimp, and the Dinner button will jump to the beginning of the lionfish feeding.

Notice, however, that the background beneath the buttons is not black, as it was in the *.fla*. This is because you used the default Flash/QuickTime *Alpha* and *Layer* compositing options. By default, the Alpha setting will make the Flash Stage transparent, and the Layer setting will place the Flash file above all other video tracks during export.

As an experiment, re-export using the same process as before, but change the Alpha setting to Copy. Be sure to press the play button so you can hear the audio source, but you will see no video. This is because the Flash track has been made opaque, but it's still in the top layer. Finally, re-export using Copy and Bottom for the Alpha and Layer settings, respectively. Now the Flash layer is opaque, and beneath the video.

NOTE

If you didn't get the same results, compare your work with the provided .fla and final .mov files. (If, after copying files, you find it necessary to re-establish the link to the external video file, simply right/Ctrl-click on the video in the Library, and edit its properties.)

The Drawing API

One of the most important ideas to come away with after reading this book is that a world of creativity exists beyond the basic uses of Flash. As you become more and more comfortable with ActionScript, for example, you will find yourself replacing timeline techniques with scripting, and building things you never thought you could. For example, what if you wanted to draw something based on user input, and therefore couldn't draw the shape using traditional tools?

In this case, ActionScript offers a way to create lines, curves, and fills programmatically. The Drawing API (application programming interface) needn't be as intimidating as it sounds. It's really just a collection of commands that define line and fill styles, how to position points, and how to connect them. A simple example to draw a three-pixel-wide, black line dynamically might look like this:

```
// Create a new empty clip to act as the drawing canvas
this.createEmptyMovieClip("canvas_mc", 1);
// Create a stroke that is 3 pixels wide, black, with 100% alpha
canvas_mc.lineStyle (3, 0x000000, 100);
// Start line at x:20, y:20
canvas_mc.moveTo(20, 20);
// Draw a horizontal line 100 pixels long to x:120, y:20
canvas_mc.lineTo(120, 20);
```

Of course, you can create much more complex works of art than this example implies. For example, you are not restricted to creating straight lines; you can also create Bezier curves and manipulate their control points.

For now, however, try to create some simple eye candy that keeps four moving circles connected with lines.

Start by creating four circles and positioning them on the Stage in random locations:

1. Create a new Flash document, and save it as *connect_the_dots.fla* in the *15* folder of your working directory.
2. Using the Oval tool, draw a small circle, 10 × 10 pixels, with a dark fill and no stroke. Convert it to a movie clip and call it **circle**.

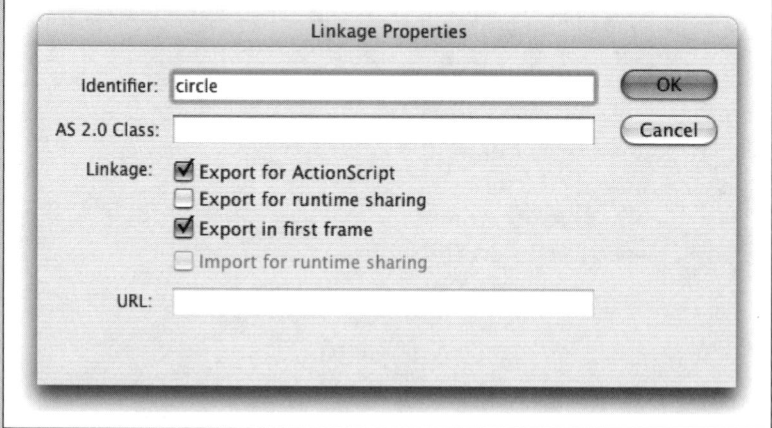

Figure 15-7. The Linkage Properties dialog

3. You will soon add this circle to the Stage dynamically, so you must give it a name with which it can be identified. Right/Ctrl-click the symbol in the Library and select the Linkage option. In the Linkage dialog, name the identifier **circle**, as seen in Figure 15-7.
4. Now you can add four circles to the Stage. Create a *for* loop that repeats its contents until its counter variable is exceeded. (To look at the script in its entirety while reading, open the *connect_the_dots_01.fla* file in the *15* folder.) In this case, you will create four circles as the value of *i* increases from its initial value of 0, adding 1 each time until the loop fails at 4 and the script continues. Remember, the semicolon allows multiple instructions on a single line, and the ++ increments the variable as if you said `i = i + 1`. For clarity, the closing brace is included here,

but everything in the next few steps (until indicated) will appear inside the loop:

```
for (i = 0; i < 4; i++) {
}
```

5. Inside the loop, you will do everything you must to make each circle behave similarly, but independently of each other. First, attach the Library movie clip called *circle* to the main movie, and store a pointer to it in the *ref* variable for easy reference. Each time you dynamically create or attach a movie clip, it should have a unique instance name and must reside in its own level. Use the value of *i* in the loop to create these unique names and levels:

```
ref = this.attachMovie("circle", "circle" + i, 100 + i);
```

6. Next, position each circle on the screen randomly. The first line of the code snippet below shows the simple way to assign the *_x* value. The Stage width is 550 pixels, so you can simply create a random number between 0 and 550. However, this method has been deprecated in favor of the more standards-compliant way of generating a random number using the *Math* object. Similarly, the technique used for the *_y* value shows how to use any size Stage and make sure the movie clip is never partially off the Stage (as would be the case for 0 or 550, for example).

   To begin, the routine for creating a random number between 0 and 1 is stored in the predefined *Math* object. Therefore, you need only call it to get a random number. Since this number is a fraction, you can then get a number in your desired range by multiplying that range by the new number. Since you're working with *_y* values here, your range needs to be the Stage height minus the height of the circle (400 – 10). However, this might result in values from 0 to 390, so to prevent the clip from being off the top of the Stage, you must offset this range by half the height of the clip:

```
ref._x = random(550);
ref._y = (Math.random() * (Stage.height - ref._height)) + (ref._
height / 2);
```

7. Now you need to send each circle moving in a different direction. Randomly pick a number of pixels to add to the *_x* and *_y* of each circle. Pick a number from 0 through 10, but then subtract 5:

```
ref.dirX = (Math.random() * 10) - 5;
ref.dirY = (Math.random() * 10) - 5;
```

   This gives you a possible range of –5 through 5. Then, store that value in an independent variable that is *inside* each circle. (Remember, any time you manipulate *ref*, you are working with one circle.)

8. Finally, create an event handler for each circle to execute its code every time that circle receives an *enterFrame* event. Don't forget that using this inside the event handler means you are referring to the circle to which it

is attached. The first two lines are simple. Just add the random number of *_x* and *_y* pixels chosen in the last step to each circle's current location.

The next section may look complicated, but it's just a simple conditional statement. If the circle is moving in a positive x direction and it's past the right edge of the Stage (in this case, 550), *or* it's moving in a negative x direction and it's past the left edge of the Stage (0), just reverse its direction by multiplying the current direction by –1. Remember from your look at conditionals that && means *and* and || means *or*:

```
ref.onEnterFrame = function():Void {
    this._x += this.dirX;
    this._y += this.dirY;
    if ((this.dirX > 0 && this._x > Stage.width) || (this.dirX < 0
&& this._x < 0)) {
        this.dirX *= -1;
    }
    if ((this.dirY > 0 && this._y > Stage.height) || (this.dirY < 0
&& this._y < 0)) {
        this.dirY *= -1;
    }
}
```

9. Test your movie. You should see four independently moving circles, with no connecting lines. If you want to check your work, or follow along with the finished example, open the *connect_the_dots_01.fla* file in the *15* folder.

10. The last step is to add the connecting lines. Start by creating an empty movie clip to serve as a canvas for the dynamically drawn lines. Notice that the use of this refers to the current timeline, so the keyword refers to the main movie again, not one of the circles:

```
this.createEmptyMovieClip("canvas_mc", 1);
```

11. Next, create an *enterFrame* event handler that updates the lines as fast as your frame rate allows. First, clear the canvas so you don't draw an entirely new set of lines each time the handler is called. Then, define a line style. In this case, the script calls for a 1-pixel-wide, dark blue line with an alpha of 100 (i.e., opaque). Finally, draw lines from the first circle to the second circle, the second circle to the third circle, the third circle to the fourth circle, and the fourth circle back to the first circle:

```
canvas_mc.onEnterFrame = function():Void {
    canvas_mc.clear();
    canvas_mc.lineStyle(1, 0x000099, 100);
    canvas_mc.moveTo(circle0._x, circle0._y);
    canvas_mc.lineTo(circle1._x, circles1._y);
    canvas_mc.lineTo(circle2._x, circles2._y);
    canvas_mc.lineTo(circle3._x, circles3._y);
    canvas_mc.lineTo(circle0._x, circles0._y);
}
```

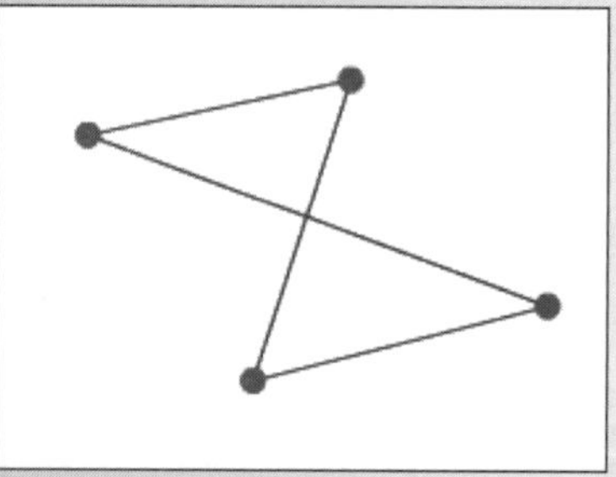

Figure 15-8. The Drawing API connects these movie clips at runtime

12. Test your movie and compare it to *connect_the_dots_01.fla* in the *15* folder. It should look something like Figure 15-8.

Extending Flash

Although it's not nearly as extensible as Director or Photoshop, for example, Flash can still be extended beyond its out-of-the-box configuration. Flash extensions are essentially limited to the authoring environment, but when it comes to enhancing the authoring experience, Flash is very flexible and allows you to create custom commands, tools, panels, behaviors, and more. (This limitation also has the side benefit of keeping the runtime player lean and the end-user experience standardized.)

Space limitations prohibit an exhaustive look into all of the possibilities, but this book will still give you some experience in extending Flash. In Chapter 2 you created a basic command using the History panel, and in this chapter you will make your own simple component.

Building Your Own Component

You've used components several times in this book. Components are valuable tools that can both help an ActionScript novice build rich interactive experiences and assist ActionScript veterans with rapid prototyping. However, you've also seen that stock components—particularly the Flash v2 components that ship with Flash 8 and Flash MX 2004—can add considerably to your file size. In larger projects delivered over broadband this can be relatively unnoticeable, but in small projects the size changes can be significant.

So, this project will be to adapt the preloader script you wrote in Chapter 12 and build your own smaller version of a component.

The first step in creating a component is to package the assets and ActionScript necessary for the component as a self-contained unit. Start by turning your preloader script and its associated text field into a movie clip:

1. Open *my_preloader_03.fla*, located in the *15* folder. This file contains the preloader script you created earlier, without the buttons and other extraneous material. Save it as *my_component.fla* in the *15* folder.

2. Select frame 1 of the *actions* and *text* layers, then right/Ctrl-click and choose Copy Frames from the contextual menu.

3. Press Ctrl/Cmd-F8 to open the Create New Symbol dialog box. Create a movie clip symbol and name it `My Loader Self`. The name you use for this movie clip becomes the name of the component that appears in the Components panel later. You will make two versions: one version will load assets into itself, and the second version will load assets into a remote target.

4. In Edit mode for *My Loader Self*, right/Ctrl-click on frame 1 of *Layer 1* and choose Paste Frames from the contextual menu. The frame

contents and layer names that you copied earlier will be pasted into the timeline.

5. Position the text field at (0, 0), so the clip's registration point can be used to align instances of the component on the Stage. The registration point is the only thing you'll see when you drag this component on-Stage, and if you know the registration point is in the upper-left corner of the text field, you can use it to accurately position the component.

Your preloader script was originally written to load a specific image (*water.jpg*) into a specific place (the *container_mc* clip). To use the existing script in a component, the code has to work in any situation. To pull this off, you need to generalize the code by making the name and path of the file into which the component will load configurable options:

1. In Edit mode for *My Loader Self*, select frame 1 of the *actions* layer and open the Actions panel.
2. Modify the *loadClip()* statement in the preloader script by replacing the hard-coded pathname of the demo water image with the following variable (change shown in bold):

```
my_mcl.loadClip (fileToLoad, container);
```

3. As an additional nicety, change the depth in which the asset loads from the previous hard-coded `1` (change again shown in bold):

```
var container:MovieClip = this.createEmptyMovieClip("container_mc",
this.getNextHighestDepth());
```

The last step simply ensures that Flash renders the movie clip in front of all other objects on the same level and layer in the current movie clip, increasing the chances that you won't have to fool around with stacking order when you use your component. However, the *fileToLoad* variable is important. You may have noticed that you haven't defined this variable anywhere. That's because this placeholder variable will be defined within the Flash interface, in the Component Parameters panel.

Now turn the symbol into a component:

1. Right/Ctrl-click on the *My Loader Self* symbol in the Library and choose Component Definition from the contextual menu. The Component Definition dialog box shown in Figure 15-9 opens.
2. In the Parameters section of the dialog box, you need to define the *fileToLoad* variable you used earlier. Click the Add Parameter button (the + sign) to create a new parameter.
3. Enter a descriptive string like **`File to load:`** in the Name field for the parameter, and press Enter/Return.
4. In the Variable field, enter the variable name, **`fileToLoad`**. As is true with nearly all ActionScript, case matters, so type it exactly the same way you did in the script.

5. Skip over the Value field for a moment. From the Type drop-down list (which is used to specify the data type for the variable), choose String.
6. Finally, enter **path/asset.ext** into the Value field. This is an optional step—many developers leave string default values blank, which is one way to remind the user that a path can be specified, and that any asset Flash can load externally is supported (in Flash 8, that means SWF, JPG, GIF, and PNG files). The Component Definition dialog box should now look like Figure 15-9.

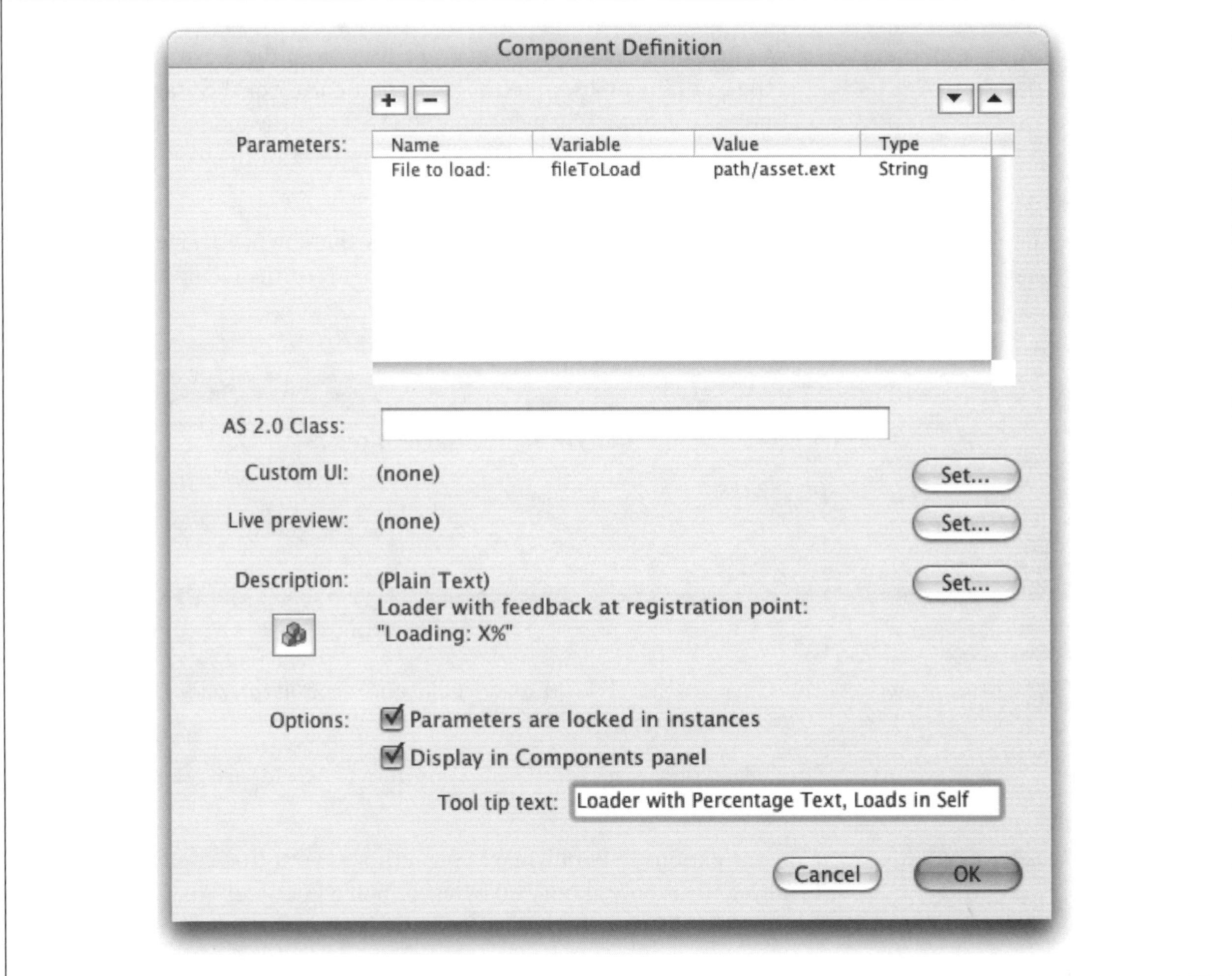

Figure 15-9. The Component Definition dialog box

Your component is now functional, but don't stop just yet. In case you share this component with others, make the user experience friendlier:

1. Click the Set button next to the Description label and enter some descriptive text that will be displayed in the Flash authoring interface when this component is selected. Try something like **Loader with feedback at registration point: "Loading: X%"**. (The sample file has

more descriptive text, if you want to get ideas later.) Click OK to set the text.

2. Back in the Component Definition dialog box, in the Options section, check the "Display in Components panel" option and type **`Loader with Percentage Text, Loads in Self`** into the "Tool tip text" field. As a tool tip, this text should be shorter than the description.

3. Click OK to close the dialog box. Notice that the icon for the *My Loader Self* symbol in the Library panel has changed to a component icon. All that's left to do now is to put in the parameter values.

4. Get a fresh start by deleting everything from the Stage and dragging in the component anew, to the upper-left corner of the Stage. (This is not necessary, but it will help show you that no other code is at work during your test.) Remember, the registration point of this component will be the registration point of the loaded asset.

5. Select the component and show the Component Parameters tab in the Properties panel, as seen in Figure 15-10, or the Component Inspector (Window→Component Inspector).

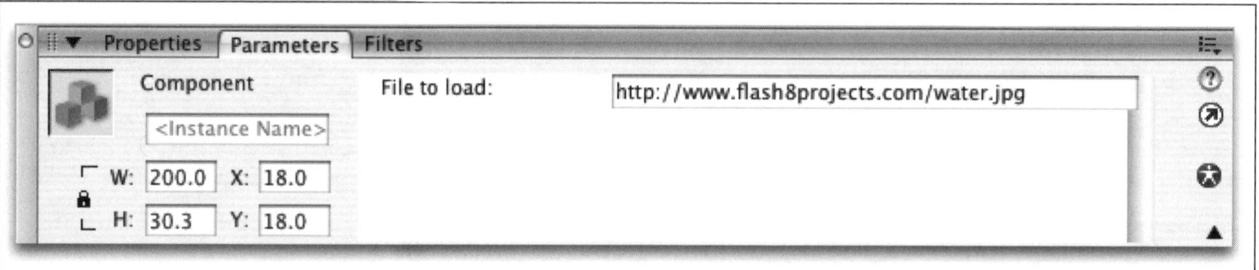

Figure 15-10. The Component Parameters tab

6. Click in the "File to load" field and type ***`http://www.flash8projects.com/water.jpg`***.

7. Save your work and test your movie. Compare your file to *my_component_02.fla*.

Congratulations. Not only have you authored your first component, but the resulting file is only about 500 bytes, or half a kilobyte! That's approximately 1/64th of the size of the component you set out to rewrite. Good work!

Further customizing your component

The drag-and-drop simplicity of this component is great, but the loading status information always appears where the asset is loaded. What if you wanted to replicate the multi-graphic example you created in Chapter 12, where the text always appeared in the lower-left corner, regardless of the asset load location?

Add one more parameter to your component to make the load target configurable as well:

1. Go back to your file in progress and right/Ctrl-click on the component to begin editing.
2. Select frame 1 of the *actions* layer again and open the Actions panel.
3. Modify the *loadClip()* statement once again, this time replacing the load target. Replace *container* with *whereToLoad* (change again shown in bold):

   ```
   my_mcl.loadClip (fileToLoad, whereToLoad);
   ```

4. You no longer need the first line, so delete the following text:

   ```
   var container:MovieClip = this.createEmptyMovieClip("container_mc",
   this.getNextHighestDepth());
   ```

5. Right/Ctrl-click on the component in the Library, and choose the Component Definition option again.
6. Add a parameter to tie in with your new variable. Enter **Where to load:** in the Name field, **whereToLoad** in the Variable field, and **_parent.container.mc** in the Value field, and make sure String is selected in the Type drop-down menu.
7. Edit the descriptive text and the tool tip string to change the references to the asset loading into the component itself. Instead, mention in both places that the asset is loaded into a remote location. OK the dialog to go back to the Library.
8. Rename the component **My Loader Remote**.
9. Go back to the main timeline. Create a movie clip in the upper-left corner of the Stage and give it a symbol and instance name of **container_mc**. You can now move your component to any location you want, and the asset will still load in the targeted component.
10. Save your work and test your movie. Your file should now resemble *my_compononent_03.fla*.

The preceding code won't work if you specify **1** for the *whereToLoad* parameter. Although you can still use the *loadClip()* method to load into a level, the component will not understand the string "1" as a level.

For maximum flexibility, the user of the component could specify a level number instead of a string without worrying about the component's implementation. You can modify the code to convert the *whereToLoad* parameter to a number, if necessary, by replacing this code:

```
my_mcl.loadClip (fileToLoad, whereToLoad);
```

with this:

```
if (isNaN(parseInt(whereToLoad))) {
    // treat destination as movie clip object
    my_mcl.loadClip(fileToLoad, whereToLoad);
} else {
    // treat as level number
    my_mcl.loadClip(fileToLoad, parseInt(whereToLoad));
}
```

An ambitious developer might also warn the component user if the specified target clip or level doesn't exist. However, a full discussion of writing custom components is beyond the scope of this book. This project's goal is to help you understand universal issues, such as how to define parameters to generalize your components. If you'd like to try to add support for level numbers, you can compare your attempt with *my_component_04.fla*.

Adding Your Component to the Flash Interface

All that remains is for you to export the component so that it can be stored in the Flash install directory and accessed via the Components panel:

1. Continuing from where you left off, right/Ctrl-click on *My Loader Self* in the Library and choose Export SWC File from the contextual menu.
2. In the Export File dialog box, name the file **`My Loader Remote.swc`** and save it in the *15* folder. (Feel free to export *My Loader Self*, too, if you want to use both components.)
3. Save and close your file.

Now you have a compiled component that, once installed, will appear in the Components panel. Add it to the Flash install directory and test it:

1. Locate *My Loader Remote.swc* in the *15* folder and copy it to the clipboard.
2. Paste a copy of *My Loader Remote.swc* into the Flash 8 components configuration folder. The location of this folder can vary from Flash version to Flash version and operating system to operating system, but at the time of this writing the most probable locations for Flash 8 component installation were as follows:

   Windows

   C:\Program Files\Macromedia\Flash 8\<language>\Configuration\Components

   Mac

   Macintosh HD/Applications/Macromedia Flash 8/Configuration/Components

   For additional locations, consult the Macromedia web site.

3. It's a good idea to create a subfolder in the *Components* directory, named *Custom* or something similar, into which you can put components that you install by hand. This will keep things organized.
4. Back in Flash, open the Components panel's Options menu and choose Reload. The new *My Loader Remote* component should appear in the list.

If your new component doesn't appear in the Components panel, you may need to restart Flash.

Last but not least, test the new component in a new file and make sure it does what it's supposed to:

1. Create a new Flash document and save it as *component_test.fla* in the *15* folder.
2. Drag the *My Loader Remote* component onto the Stage.
3. Create a movie clip in the upper-left corner and give it an instance name of **container_mc**.
4. In the Properties panel's Parameters tab, enter **http://www.flash8projects.com/water.jpg** in the "File to load" field. If the "Where to load" field does not already contain *_parent.container_mc*, enter that text in the field.
5. Save and test your movie.

There is one small catch to using the loading components you've created: they only work with Flash Player 7 or later. Although ActionScript 2.0 can be used when exporting to Flash Player 6 format, that version of the player doesn't support recent classes such as *MovieClipLoader*.

When creating Flash content, it's best to decide which version of the Flash Player you'll be publishing to prior to starting your project. Many of the most powerful features of ActionScript are supported only in Flash Player 7 or later, but you can still accomplish a reasonable amount of goals with Flash Player 5 compatibility.

Intermediate to Advanced Component Features

There are several additional options that can be explored when creating your own components. Some are user-interface related, such as the Live Preview option for components with a significant visual portion and the ability to create a custom interface so you don't have to rely on the Component Parameters tab or the Component Inspector panel. Others include the ability to add actions for your own components to Flash's Actions panel and help for your own components to the Macromedia Help system.

ActionScript Spotlights

If you take one thing away with you after reading this book, it should be that the power to unlock Flash's true potential comes through learning ActionScript. The Flash interface provides many ways to get started creating wonderful art, animations, designs, and even basic applications and prototypes. Flash 8 offers the Flash designer a greater number of interface-based tools than any previous upgrade, including its filters, blend modes, custom easing, and more. Yet even the best timeline artists have only scratched the surface of what is possible.

The following list covers some of the key ActionScript highlights presented throughout this book. Whenever possible, try to revisit these topics and continue to hone your ActionScript skills.

Chapter 3:

- "Your First Script"
- "Frame Scripts"
- "Semicolon;"

Chapter 4:

- "Scripting Your Button"
- "Easy Scripting with Script Assist"
- "Components and Behaviors"
- "Event Handlers"
- "Code Hints"
- "Comments"

Chapter 5:

- "Properties"
- "Methods"
- "Functions"

Chapter 6:

- "Controlling the Character with ActionScript"
- "Absolute and Relative Target Paths"
- "Movie Clip Event Handlers"

Chapter 7:

- "Scriptable Masks"
- "Timeline Versus ActionScript Animation"
- "Variables and Scope"
- "Conditional Statements"
- "Operators"

Chapter 8:

- "Scripting Your Own Sound Control"
- "Data Types"

Chapter 9:

- "Scripting Your Own Video Control"
- "Null"

Chapter 10:

- "Bitmap Filter Effects: Using ActionScript"
- "Blend Modes: Using ActionScript"
- "Arrays"
- "Loops"

Chapter 11:

- "Custom Anti-Aliasing"
- "CSS"

Chapter 12:

- "Using ActionScript to Modularize Content"
- "Scripting Your Own Preloader"
- "Event Listeners"

Chapter 13:

- "Flash Cookies: Local Shared Objects"
- "Sending Results with a Form"
- "Loading and Sending Variables"

Chapter 14:

- "Flash Lite"
- "Projectors"

Chapter 15:

- "The Drawing API"
- "Building Your Own Component"

If the early looks at ActionScript 3 (in alpha release at the time of this writing) are any indication, more will soon be possible with Flash than ever before. Look for Rich Shupe's *Learning ActionScript 3*, an upcoming title from O'Reilly.

These tasks vary in complexity and require at least a minimal amount of comfort with XML. Coverage is outside the scope of this text, but there are a few online resources dealing with the creation of components and other Flash extensions that include these features. See the appendix for details.

One additional feature that is likely within the grasp of even a moderately determined entry-level user is the packaging of a component or other extension for installation through the Macromedia Extensions Manager. This software should be included with your Flash installation, but it can also be downloaded from Macromedia's web site, free of charge. By creating a small XML file, you can package your component or extension into an installer that will automatically place your software in the appropriate directory, making manual installation unnecessary. Sample files are distributed with the Extensions Manager, so if you're up to it, try bundling up your component for distribution.

The Rest Is Up to You

Well, that's all folks. The projects in this book have been designed to cover a wide range of topics to give you a varied look into the world of Flash. In the best of circumstances, the experience has been positive and you've learned some things that will carry through in your own work.

Please visit this book's companion web site, *http://www.flash8projects.com*, for additional information, sample code, supplemental projects, additional resources, updates, and possible errata. Send in your questions and examples of your own work and contact the author and others in the Flash community.

What's Next?

You may be asking yourself why this section exists in the last chapter of the book. It has been included here for two reasons. First, you shouldn't finish this book without trying to take this final chapter one or two steps forward, just as you have with each prior chapter. Second, the appendix of this book is chock-full of useful information—if you sometimes gloss over appendixes, you should give this one a look.

Before continuing, try to come up with one use of Flash that you consider to be "outside the box," even if only because of your current experience level. Pushing yourself to learn will drive you to create. Try creating a segment for use in a home movie or DVD, or a mobile experience using the Flash Lite Player. Open your imagination.

Next, try to expand the features of your preloader component. For example, try adding an event handler so the loading process is triggered with a mouse click. When you've added one or more features, try preparing it for installation via the Macromedia Extensions Manager. (See "Intermediate to Advanced Component Features" for more information.)

Finally, move on to the appendix and explore the many additional resources available to you.

In the appendix, you will find lots of useful information and resources, including:

- A look at some of the more notable preferences you should be acquainted with
- An overview that describes how to create custom keyboard shortcut sets
- A brief list of tips for troubleshooting problems and getting the most out of this book
- A small collection of online and printed resources to help you continue your progress

Tips and Resources

This appendix contains a small collection of basic tips and resources, with information ranging from how to configure your preferences to what web sites and books to explore next. Also included in these pages are some pointers that may help you if you're having any trouble with any of the sample files provided on this book's companion CD-ROM. Finally, suggested areas of continuing study, as well as a glimpse into ways that you can extend the Flash authoring environment, round out this text.

In this appendix

Preferences

With any application as feature-rich as Flash, you are likely to gain some efficiencies, or even capabilities, by exploring the Preferences options. Flash, however, is better than some other applications when it comes to including user-definable features. Some of the highlights of each of Flash's Preferences categories will be briefly discussed here, but you may want to take a few minutes to look around for yourself.

General

The General category, shown in Figure A-1, contains miscellaneous preferences that apply to the application at large. For example, you can define whether or not the Startup Screen is displayed, switch between document-level and object-level undo, and specify how many levels of undo are supported. (The latter will affect RAM consumption, authoring performance, and the History panel.)

In the General tab, you can also specify some application-level settings that can help you work in Flash the way you do in other programs. You can decide whether new documents should open in tabs or new windows, how certain tool options are presented, whether entire frame spans are selected when clicked or just the keyframe in which the click was made, and what color is used to show highlighted selections.

NOTE

You can further adapt Flash to your working habits by changing tool configurations and keyboard-shortcut mappings, as discussed later in this appendix.

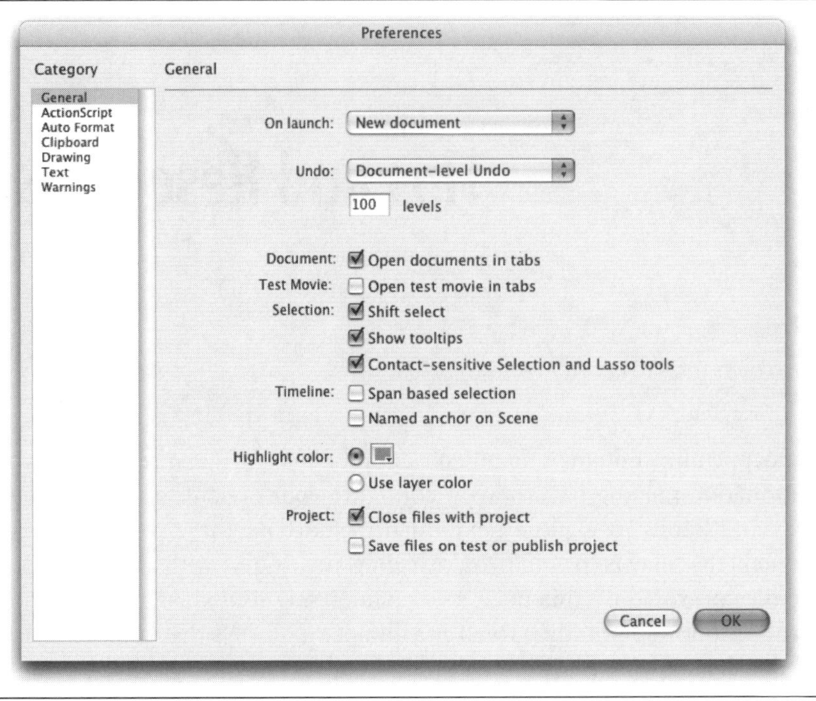

Figure A-1. The General Preferences tab

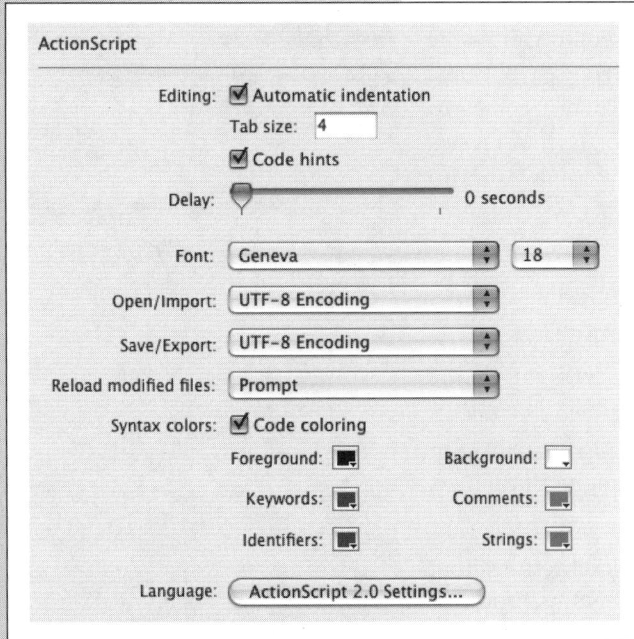

Figure A-2. The ActionScript Preferences tab

ActionScript

The ActionScript Preferences category, shown in Figure A-2, allows you to choose how your scripts will be formatted, including font, font size, and the colors used when syntax coloring. The latter will help you easily differentiate variable names from properties, for example. This is also where you define ActionScript 2.0 class paths, to tell Flash where it can find your custom classes during compiling.

Auto Format

The Auto Format category, shown in Figure A-3, is a useful and often overlooked category of preferences that can help beginners learn ActionScript syntax and keep scripts clean and easy to read. It allows you to set five options that will change the way the interface reformats scripts for you, when asked to do so. These options let you define your own style of coding, which is helpful because you will see a variety of style preferences when reading tutorials, sample code, and other resources.

For example, some coders prefer to start a function or logical statement with the brace on the first line, as examples appear in this book:

```
function f(x) {
    if (x <= 0) {
        return 1;
    } else {
        return x * f(x - 1);
    }
}
```

Other developers prefer to put these braces on their own lines, as seen here:

```
function f(x)
{
    if (x<=0)
    {
        return 1;
    } else
    {
        return x*f(x-1);
    }
}
```

Auto Format

- [ ] Insert { on line after if, for, switch, while, etc.
- [ ] Insert { on line after function, class, and interface keywords
- [ ] Don't cuddle } and else
- [ ] Insert space after function name in function calls
- [x] Insert spaces around operators

Preview:

```
function f(x) {
  if (x <= 0) {
    return 1;
  } else {
    return x * f(x - 1);
  }
}
```

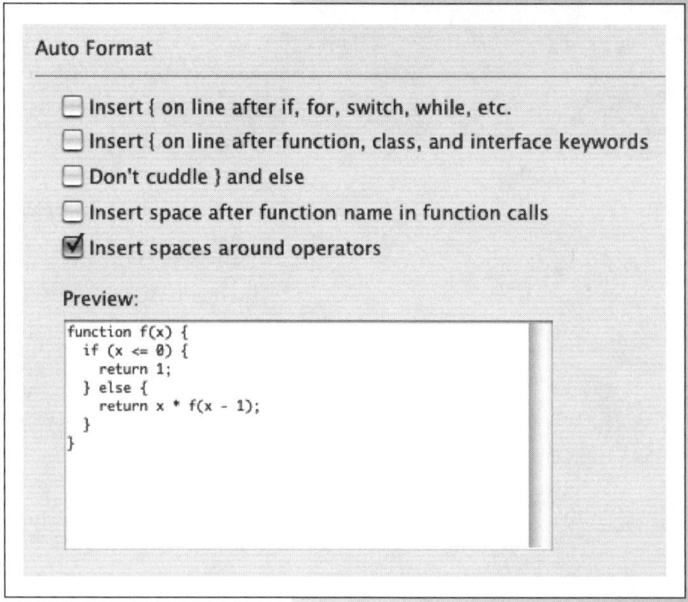

Figure A-3. The Auto Format Preferences tab

Another difference between the two formats above is that the first inserts spaces around operators, while the second format does not. This, too, can be defined as a preference.

Clipboard

The Clipboard Preferences category is another, perhaps subtler but no less useful, way of defining how Flash works with other programs. Here you can define how certain asset types are shuttled through the clipboard, including settings such as graphics resolution, gradient quality, and whether FreeHand text is maintained as editable blocks or rendered as shapes.

Drawing

Drawing preferences include Bezier curve preview and cursor options, and tool sensitivity presets such as how to connect lines, smooth curves, and recognize shapes and lines, and even how accurate your clicks must be to select objects. Many of these settings can be overridden on a case-by-case basis, but defining them in the Preferences panel can save time on a global level.

Text

Text preferences include the default orientation of text that you specify as vertical, and, most importantly, which font is used by default when a custom font is not found during authoring. This is called *font mapping* and will also be discussed in the "Troubleshooting" section of this appendix.

Warnings

One of the best user-interface-related preferences is the ability to identify which warning messages you want to see when a relevant situation arises. Unlike many programs that force you to view and dismiss all alerts, Flash lets you prevent certain alerts from displaying, if preferred. Typically, you will start with all warnings enabled.

However, you may want to edit a large group of files for which you don't have a required font, or that must be exported to a specific player version, or that you are converting from Flash MX 2004 to Flash 8 file formats. All of these changes would ordinarily issue alerts, but in the Warnings Preferences tab you can temporarily disable these warnings to speed up your editing, and then re-enable the options later if you wish.

Customizing the Tools Panel

One of the ways of extending Flash is by creating supplemental tools. The PolyStar tool, found grouped with the Rectangle tool, is an example of a tool that has been added to Flash out of the box, as a demonstration. When you add new tools, you can use the Customize Tools Panel dialog (accessible via the Edit→Customize Tools Panel menu command on Windows or the Flash Professional→Customize Tools Panel menu command on Mac OS X) to place them where you want them.

Even if you don't get as far as adding tool extensions to your interface, you may want the items in the Tools panel grouped differently. For example, you may want to group shape or selection tools together, or even remove tools you don't use often. The Customize Tools Panel dialog, shown in Figure A-4, lets you reorder tools in the Tools panel and add or remove tools.

Figure A-4. The Customize Tools Panel dialog box

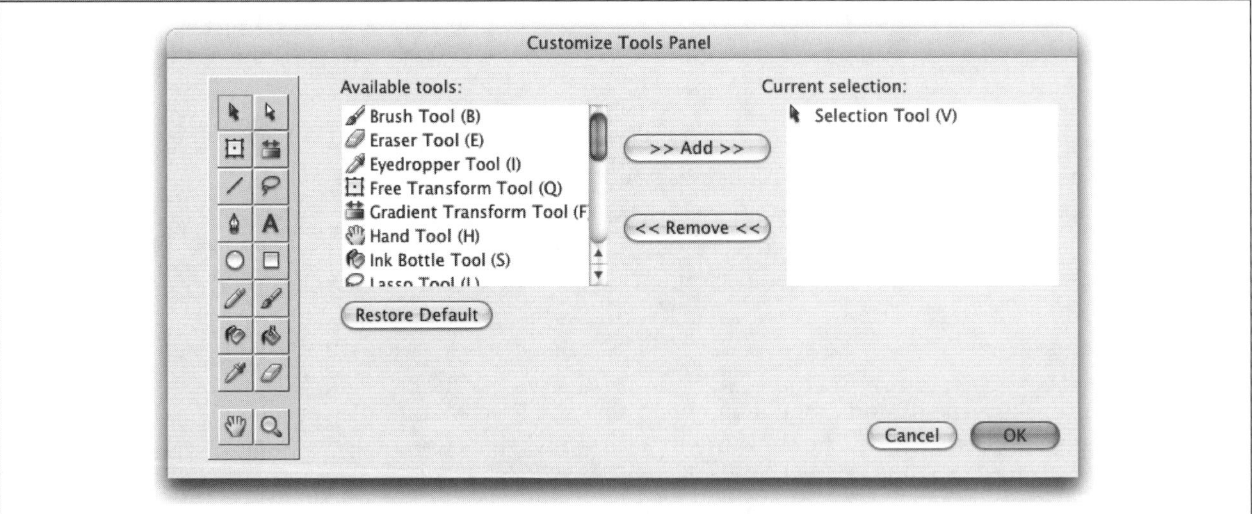

Customizing Keyboard Shortcuts

Many commands and features in Flash already have corresponding keyboard shortcuts, such as pressing V to activate the Selection tool. However, you may want a speedier way to run a command or open a custom panel set. As a general example, Figure A-5 shows the process of adding a keyboard shortcut to a menu command that doesn't already have a corresponding shortcut.

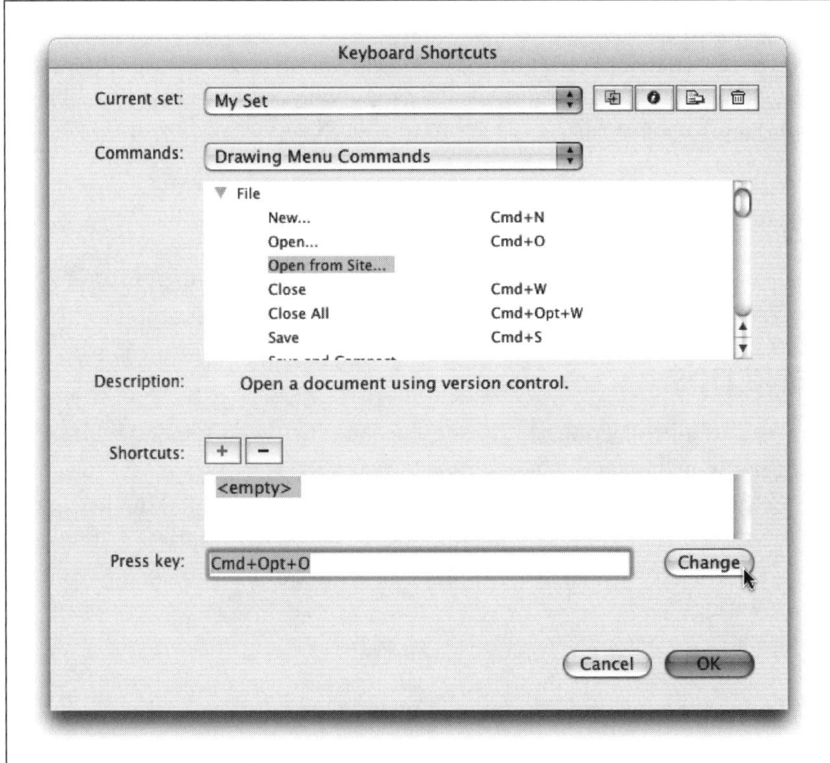

Figure A-5. The Keyboard Shortcuts dialog box

You can also reassign shortcuts, as seen in this procedure:

1. Choose Edit→Keyboard Shortcuts (Win) or Flash Professional→Keyboard Shortcuts (Mac) to open the Keyboard Shortcuts dialog, shown in Figure A-5.
2. Click the Duplicate Set button in the dialog box, name the new keyboard shortcut set something like **`My Set`**, and click OK. This preserves the original shortcuts, rather than overwriting them, and provides you with a set that you can modify freely.
3. In the Commands section of the dialog box, expand the File menu and select Close All (which closes all open documents and Libraries).

4. In the Shortcut section, click Add Shortcut, and press the keys you want to use as the new shortcut. For example, you might press Shift-Ctrl-W (Win) or Shift-Cmd-W (Mac). The keys you press appear in the Press Key field.
5. Click the Change button. This opens a message warning you that the shortcut is already assigned to the Work Area command, an infrequently used feature.
6. Click Reassign.
7. Click OK to close the dialog box.

Now, when you have more than one document or more than one Library open, you can simply use this keyboard shortcut to close all your Flash files at once.

You can even reconfigure many or all shortcuts at once to match other programs that you may be more familiar with. For example, you can choose a shortcut set more in line with Photoshop, FreeHand, or Illustrator.

Basic Tips

Here is a small collection of tips that haven't already been mentioned in the main body of this text. They may help you with your progress in learning the Flash interface and make your scripting a little easier. This list is just the tip of the iceberg, and is merely meant to get you started in the right direction. Feel free to visit the companion web site for this book and submit your own tips!

In the meantime, here are some useful tidbits:

- Pressing F4 will hide or show all open panels.
- After copying an item to the clipboard, Edit→Paste in Place (Ctrl/Cmd-Shift-V) will paste that item in its former location, rather than the geographical center of the screen.
- To maintain a complete undo history, Flash maintains file changes even when items are deleted from the file. This can cause unnecessarily large *.fla* file sizes. In most cases, you can reduce the file size by using the File→Save and Compact menu command. This is the equivalent of using the Save As command, without having to rename your file. It will purge your file of unneeded information.

WARNING

Be careful when using the Save and Compact feature. It will purge your History list, and you will not be able to recover the list or backtrack through previously recorded edits.

- Using File→Save As, you can save a copy of your file in a version that will be compatible with Flash MX 2004. Bear in mind, however, that all Flash 8–specific features will be lost.
- If you find yourself frequently reusing a file setup, you can save that setup as a template using File→Save as Template. In doing so, you can give the template a name and specify the category in which the template should be found. From then on, the template will be available to you as were the other templates used in this book.
- Pressing Ctrl/Cmd-F while editing a script will give you a simple find and replace dialog that will work within a single script. However, if you use the same keyboard shortcut when the Actions panel does not have user focus, or use the Edit→Find and Replace menu command at any time, the more powerful application-wide Find and Replace dialog will appear, as seen in Figure A-6. Not only can you search and replace among all scripts in a document with this dialog, but you can also specify whole word, case sensitive, and regular expression searches, and search text fields, labels, and parameters. You can even find and replace non-text items, including fonts, colors, symbols, sounds, videos, and bitmaps.

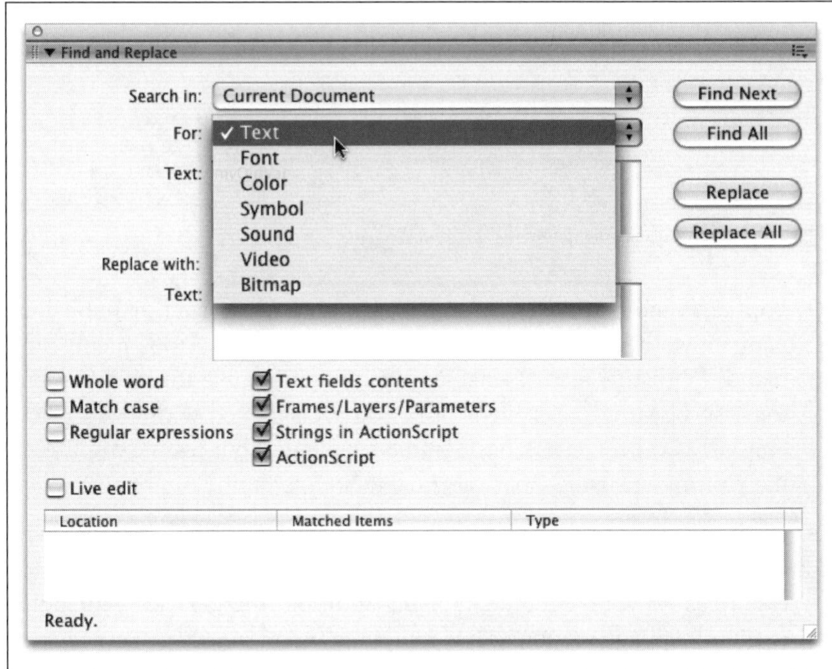

Figure A-6. The application-wide Find and Replace dialog

- If you have trouble finding something in your movie, try using the Movie Explorer panel (Window→Movie Explorer), seen in Figure A-7. The Movie Explorer will show you an outline view of the structure of your document, and you can specify which types of element are included therein. You can quickly edit any item by double-clicking it, and Movie Explorer can even show you frame and symbol instance scripts to help you identify at a glance which item to edit. This is especially useful if you start out by adding scripts directly to buttons and movie clips, rather than defining event handlers in frame scripts.

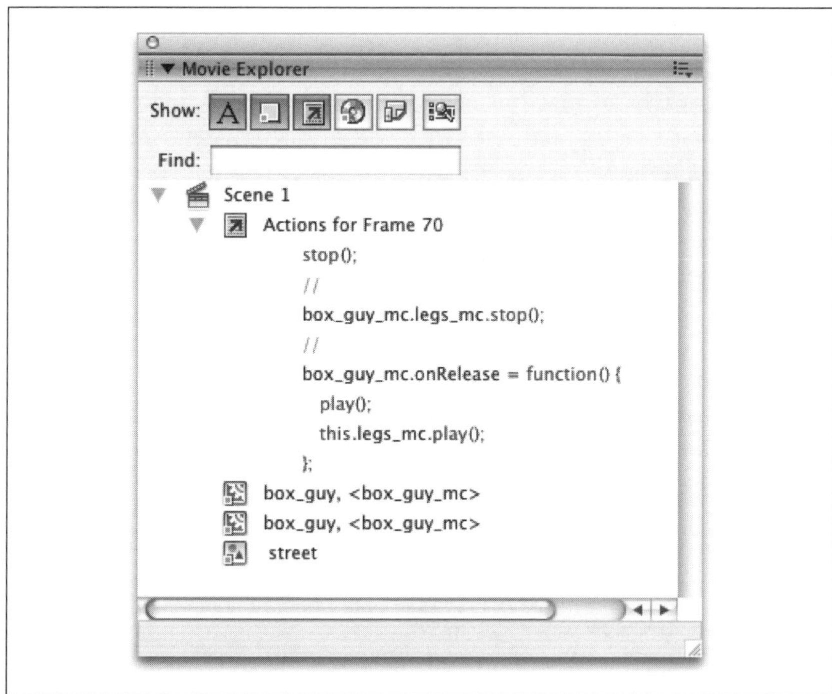

Figure A-7. The Movie Explorer panel

- You can quickly preview button states without testing or publishing your movie by using the Control→Enable Simple Buttons menu command. With this feature enabled, you won't be able to select the buttons, so be sure to disable it once you are satisfied with the preview. Similarly, you can check basic frame scripts without testing or publishing your movie using Control→Enable Simple Frame Actions.
- Flash 8 has a fairly impressive spell checker, accessible via the Text→Check Spelling menu command. It allows you to check many different areas of your document, using multiple dictionaries—including foreign-language dictionaries—following many rules that govern what is checked and how. These options are configured in the companion Text→Spelling Setup dialog, seen in Figure A-8.

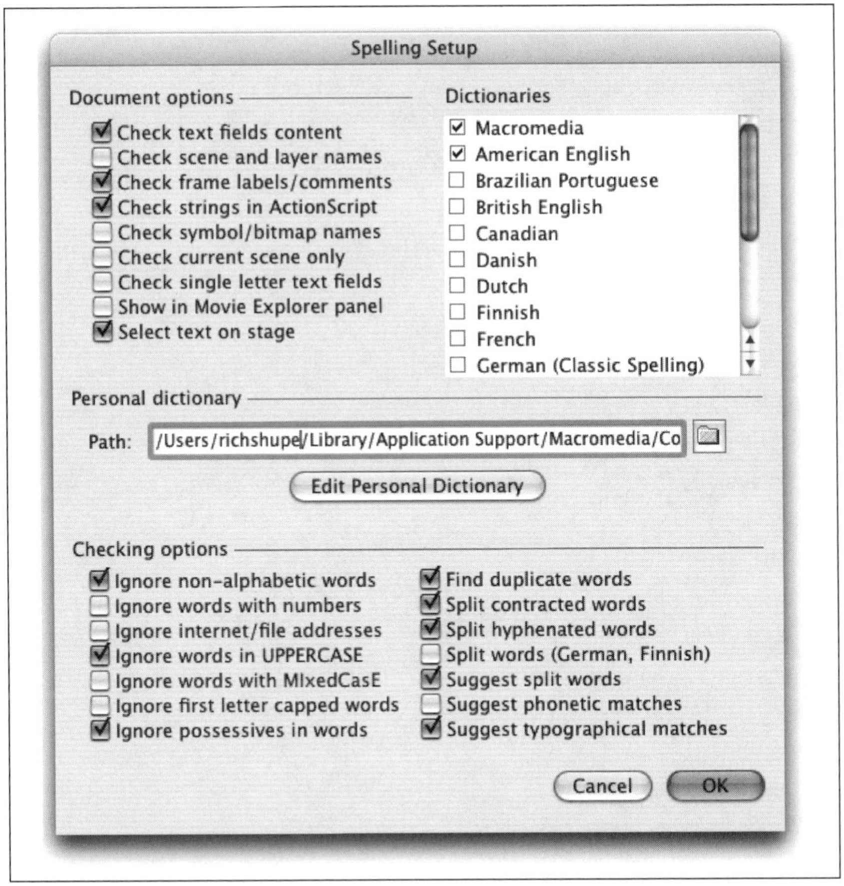

Figure A-8. The Spelling Setup dialog box

Flash 8 Basic Versus Professional

As stated in the Preface and throughout this text, several of the projects herein assume you are using, or evaluating, Flash 8 Professional. Table A-1, featured in Macromedia's product literature, itemizes features included in each version.

Table A-1. Comparison of Flash 8 Professional and Flash 8 Basic

	Flash 8 Professional	Flash 8 Basic
Expressiveness		
Filters (Graphic Effects)	•	
Blend Modes	•	
Advanced Easing Control for Animation	•	
ActionScript 2.0	•	•
Object-based Drawing Mode	•	•
FlashType Text Rendering Engine	(advanced options)	•
Templates	•	•

Table A-1. Comparison of Flash 8 Professional and Flash 8 Basic (*continued*)

	Flash 8 Professional	Flash 8 Basic
PDF and EPS (Adobe Illustrator 10) Support	•	•
Data Components	•	
UI Components	(advanced set)	(basic set)
Mobile Authoring		
Publish to Flash Lite	•	
Interactive Mobile Device Emulator	•	
Mobile Templates	•	
External Players	•	
MIDI Ring Tone Support	•	
Professional Video		
Embedded Video	•	•
External Video	•	
Advanced Video Import Workflow	•	
Advanced Video Component	•	
Stand-alone Video Encoder	•	
Flash Video Exporter Plug-in for QuickTime	•	
Advanced Encoding Options	•	
Embedded Cue Points for FLV Files	•	
Alpha Channel Support	•	
User Experience		
Script Assist (Formerly Called "Normal Mode")	•	•
Advanced Library	•	•
Spell Checking and Search/Replace	•	•
Advanced Video Component	•	
Project Panel	•	
Extensibility Architecture	•	•
SWF Metadata	•	•
Accessibility	•	•

Troubleshooting

You may glide through this entire text with nary a problem. However, don't feel bad if you have your fair share of glitches. Here are some of the common issues you may run into, and how you might address them:

Missing source files

Early in this book, it was recommended that you copy the source directory from the CD-ROM to a designated directory on your hard drive. If your hard drive space is limited, you may also consider copying files one chapter at a time. If you need to delete provided files from your drive to make room for new files, they will always be there on the CD. Finally, if you're really in a pinch for space, you can open files from the CD and save them locally only when needed. In any case, try to designate one directory as your source directory, whether it remains on the CD-ROM or exists on your hard drive. To simplify references to the parent source directory, it has been called your *working directory* throughout this book. Usually, files have been provided in many stages of development to guide you through each project. They have been named sequentially with numeric suffixes to make it a little harder for you to overwrite them with your own files. However, if you do, don't worry. Simply copy them over again from the CD-ROM.

Missing or differing menu commands or keyboard shortcuts

Flash development is largely identical on both Windows and Macintosh platforms, although some of the keyboard shortcuts and locations of menu commands vary slightly. If you're having trouble with a particular step, check to see if any platform-specific information has been included, and that you're using the right keyboard shortcut. Typically, keyboard shortcuts are identified by platform, or the Windows command is listed first, followed by the Macintosh equivalent (e.g., Ctrl/Cmd-V).

Missing features

This book assumes that you are using, or evaluating, Flash 8 Professional. If you are using the Basic version, some features may be missing. (See "Flash 8 Basic Versus Professional" for details.)

Components animate through many visible states
Static typing does not generate expected warnings

These problems may occur if your file is not configured to use ActionScript 2.0. Open the File→Publishing Settings dialog and, under Flash, make sure ActionScript 2.0 is selected.

Seemingly correct scripts generate unexpected errors, including "Statement must appear within on/onClipEvent handler"

Check to make sure you are placing the code in the appropriate place. The context sensitivity of the Actions panel makes it easy to add a script to the wrong location. Click in a frame to add a frame script. To add a script to a movie clip or button, be sure it's the only item selected. An easy way to check that you're adding your script to a logical location is to check the string that follows "Actions" in the title bar of the Actions panel. It will say Frame Script, Movie Clip, Button, or something similar, depending on your selection.

Seemingly correct scripts don't work, but don't generate errors

This can occur for many reasons, but one likely reason is that the script calls for an instance name, and you have not named the movie clip or button. Add instance names to symbols in the Properties panel. See the "For Instance" sidebar in Chapter 6 for more information.

Other possible causes for this problem may be that the item you wish to control has not yet loaded or is not in the frame where you wish to manipulate it. Scripts always load from the top layer to the bottom, but you can change the order in which assets are loaded in the Publish Settings dialog. Try switching the load order from Bottom Up to Top Down. If the script starts to work, you may not be giving the assets enough time to load before referencing instances in your scripts. Similarly, make sure an instance is in the frame where you first define its event handlers and properties.

Some components work and others don't

This may be because you are using a mixture of old and new components. As of Flash MX 2004, Macromedia switched to the v2 component architecture to take full advantage of ActionScript 2.0. Older components may not be compatible with this architecture. Similarly, v2 components require ActionScript 2.0 and will not work in files set to compile with ActionScript 1.0. See "Components animate through many visible states," earlier in this list.

X- and y-coordinates in the project instructions don't yield intended results
X- and y-coordinates in the source files match the project instructions

Flash features two ways to reference x- and y-coordinates of a Stage-bound asset: by the asset's registration point and by its upper-left corner. If your x- and y-coordinates are not what they you expect them to be, open the Info panel. The tiny nine-dot grid near the center of the panel has two active dots. The upper-left dot will set the coordinate system to use the upper-left corner of a symbol when citing positions. The center dot will use the asset's actual registration point (even if it's no longer at the center of the asset after an edit). Try switching this selection to see if your numbers match the project and/or source files.

A missing font warning appears

This simply means that you don't have the fonts necessary to edit the relevant text fields without changing the font used. If you make no edits to affected text files, you can still edit other portions of the file, and the fonts will be unchanged. You can then acquire the correct font and publish your file without incident. If you don't expect to be able to acquire the font, you can use the Missing Fonts alert dialog to substitute another font for publishing only. (The alert will appear automatically when you display on the Stage a scene containing a missing font. Clicking Select Substitute Fonts will open the Font Mapping dialog, which you can also access via the Edit→Font Mapping/Flash Professional→Font

Mapping menu command.) This will not edit your file, so it will allow you to adjust the font later, if desired. As a result, however, the warning will show every time the font is missing.

A warning asks if you want to abort a script because it is running slowly
: You should always say yes to this warning. Usually it means you've made an error when creating a loop or referring to a variable, and you're stuck in a very large or infinite loop structure. It's best to heed the advice of the alert and try to find the problem. If you don't abort the script, Flash will continue to try to execute the script and may freeze. If this happens, you may need to force quit the application.

If this list doesn't address the problem you're having, first consult the companion web site for this book, *http://www.flash8projects.com*. If you don't find an answer to your question there, contact the publisher at *bookquestions@oreilly.com*.

Areas of Continued Study

As you can imagine, it's not possible to discuss every aspect of Flash development in one book. In addition to the inevitable space limitations imposed upon any single topic, many skills require additional familiarity with the Flash interface, and/or additional experience with ActionScript. However, it's still important to continue your learning, so here are five suggested topics worth exploring. Portions of most of these topics will likely be covered in one or more resources listed later in this chapter:

Flash screens and forms
: Flash 8 Professional's screens features provide a streamlined development metaphor better suited to slide shows and forms than the default Flash timeline. Available when creating a new document, Flash screens are used to create screen-based presentations à la Microsoft PowerPoint. Flash forms are used to develop user interfaces visually à la Microsoft Visual Basic.

XML
: Flash has a built-in XML parser, and it can send and receive data in XML format. For details, see the discussions of the *XML*, *XMLnode*, and *XMLSocket* classes in *ActionScript: The Definitive Guide* (O'Reilly).

Accessibility
: Accessibility features allow users with visual, aural, and mobility impairments to experience your Flash content. Not only will taking advantage of these features expand your potential audience, but some sectors are required to comply with Federal Section 508, which mandates their support. See Macromedia's web site (*http://www.macromedia.com/resources/accessibility/flash8/*) for more information on how to make your content accessible to all users.

Printing

End users can click the web browser's Print button to print the contents of the browser window, but more advanced printing of Flash content requires ActionScript. You can perform basic printing using the *print()*, *printNum()*, *printAsBitmap()*, and *printAsBitmapNum()* commands. For additional features, such as spooling multiple pages to the printer at once, check out the *PrintJob* class.

Creating your own extensions and components

Skilled developers can create commands and tools for use in the Flash authoring environment. The Flash JavaScript Dictionary (*http://www.macromedia.com/support/documentation/en/flash/documentation.html#flashjsdict*) includes the necessary information to get started customizing the Flash authoring environment. Also, more details on component development, a topic just touched on in this text, are available at *http://www.macromedia.com/support/documentation/en/flash/documentation.html#usingcomps*. The next section in this appendix will highlight a scant dozen or so such extensions, from a handful of developers, to give you an idea of what's possible. Be sure to visit the companion web site for this book, *http://www.flash8projects.com*, for more information about these, and other, extensions.

Extending Flash

Although not nearly as extensible as Director, Flash allows you to extend its authoring interface through custom components, tools, panels, commands, and more. The JavaScript Flash application programming interface (JSFL API) is a JavaScript-based syntax for controlling much of the Flash interface. You can learn to write your own extensions using JSFL, or take advantage of the many existing extensions.

Of course, an appendix could hardly contain an exhaustive list of extensions for your consideration, so what follows is a mere sampling, in a variety of categories and in no particular order, for you to evaluate. See the "Resources" section of this appendix for more information on extending Flash.

Flashloaded Components

Flashloaded
P.O. Box 47619
939 Lawrence Ave. East
Toronto, ON M3C 3S7
Canada
(647) 438-7519
(647) 438-7520 (fax)
http://www.flashloaded.com

Flashloaded is one of the best commercial component vendors around, offering a wide variety of components that add prebuilt functionality in the areas of text, 3D, navigation, image manipulation, menus, and more. Some components, such as the ultimateScroller (a superior scrolling component that improves font legibility and includes easing) and the legendary Bit Component Set (the industry-leading replacement component set for users who don't want the size overhead of Flash's built-in components), improve on functionality that is already available in Flash. Other products provide features that aren't easily achieved, such as 3D simulations and advanced tree navigation systems. The components are all very reasonably priced and easy to use. For detailed reviews of six Flashloaded components, visit this book's companion web site (*http://www.flash8projects.com*).

Flashloaded Sound & Video

Flashloaded
See "Flashloaded Components" for contact information.

Other useful products offered by Flashloaded include video and sound loops for use in your Flash projects. The VideoPacks are very well made, seamless video loops that come in a variety of sizes, from 350 × 150 to 800 × 600. Using single frames of video in each frame of a movie clip creates video loops that are compatible with every version of Flash. This makes it easy to integrate the loops into any file and to change the tempo of the loops to match your preferred frame rate. Flashloaded's SoundPacks are also well made and are available in a variety of moods, tempos, and musical styles and for a variety of uses, including intros, effects, button sounds, and even voices.

Fonts for Flash

http://www.fontsforflash.com

Fonts for Flash offers the largest single collection of fonts optimized for Flash. The company specializes in pixel fonts, which provide superior clarity at small font sizes without anti-aliasing. Fonts are available for the Mac and PC and include serif, sans-serif, display, dingbat, extended, condensed, and many more styles. A number of free fonts are available for testing.

AccRepair

Hiawatha Island Software Incorporated
6 Chenell Drive Suite 280
Concord, NH 03301
(603) 229-3055
(603) 223-9741 (fax)
http://www.hisoftware.com/macromedia_flash/Index.html

AccRepair is an innovative tool that allows you to scan your Flash files for ways to improve accessibility for the widest possible user base (see Section 508 of the Rehabilitation Act, available at *http://www.section508.gov/index.cfm?FuseAction=Content&ID=14*). It can test for text elements that have been made accessible but that are improperly configured, it can test the tab order provided for keyboard navigation through your application and related issues, and it can test for static text elements that should be made dynamic for better screen reader compatibility. It can also make some repairs to your files for some of the issues detected. Running AccRepair is an excellent first step in making all your Flash assets accessible to all users.

Hi-Caption

Hiawatha Island Software Incorporated
See "AccRepair" for contact information.

Hi-Caption is another accessibility product available from Hiawatha Island Software. It allows you to take transcripts of your linear media and add captions for display in your Flash files. It includes a caption-creation package as well as a caption-viewer component, and it uses XML as a data standard. Hi-Caption also syncs well with existing Flash components. Adding closed captions to your applications has never been easier!

Zoomifyer

Zoomify, Inc.
P.O. Box 8008
Santa Cruz, CA 95061
(831) 420-0400
(831) 420-0401 (fax)
http://www.zoomify.com

Zoomifyer is a fabulous software suite that will display your high-resolution images in a variety of on-screen sizes, up to and including their native resolutions, with intuitive zoom and pan controls. You begin the process by simply dragging and dropping your image onto a standalone converter. The converter creates a folder of multi-resolution tiles and a data file, and the Zoomifyer viewer reassembles the tiles at runtime. Very easy to use, and with a very small file-size overhead, Zoomifyer allows the user to zoom in to great image detail, without the accompanying file size of very large images. Appropriate image tiles are loaded on a need-to-use basis, keeping your applications lean and mean—all with little to no scripting. Best of all, a free version, Zoomifyer EZ, is available for you to try and use. This is a must for anyone who needs to present images with great clarity.

Sorenson Squeeze

Sorenson Media, Inc.
4179 Riverboat Road, Suite 208
Salt Lake City, UT 84123
(801) 313-8150
(801) 313-8151 (fax)
http://www.sorensonmedia.com

Sorenson Squeeze is an excellent standalone video-encoding application. It is sold in a variety of configurations, from a complete suite that offers a comprehensive list of supported formats to a version that is specifically designed for Flash video. Squeeze can encode videos into SWF files for embedding videos, or into more useful external FLV files that can be loaded into your SWF files at runtime. Videos can be encoded using the Sorenson Spark codec for compatibility with Flash versions prior to 8 or, with an optional plug-in, using On2's VP6 codec for Flash 8. It has many useful features, including batch processing, a watch folder, one-pass variable bit rate encoding, and a large list of presets.

On2 Flix

On2
1560 Broadway, 10th Floor
New York, NY 10036
(646) 292-3533
(646) 292-3534 (fax)
http://www.on2.com

Flix is an excellent standalone video-encoding application created with Flash designers and developers in mind. It is simple yet powerful and provides an impressive array of features. Flix can encode videos into SWF and FLV files for Flash Versions 3 through 8, and it can create audio-only files and vectorized versions of your videos for interesting effects. It can batch process, add overlays and players, and add simple scripts to SWF files it creates. Repeated tests also confirm that it is the fastest encoder on the market at the time of this writing.

gProject

gskinner.com
http://www.gskinner.com/products/gProject/

gProject is a Project panel replacement for the Professional versions of Flash MX 2004 and Flash 8. Projects are a way to organize larger applications that typically use multiple FLA and/or SWF files, external ActionScript files, and more. gProject allows you to publish and save groups of files and easily access just about every file used in a project. It adds some really great features, the most useful of which is the ability to read and write to directories from within the panel. This feature allows you to create and open new files, look at modification dates, and carry out similar actions without ever leaving the Flash IDE. gProject also offers multiple compile options, support for testing frameworks (ASUnit and AS2Unit), the ability to manipulate class files, and more. It even does a few nice smart things, such as maintaining a list of recently opened files and allowing you to adjust your preference settings, map custom keyboard shortcuts, pin directories, and more. If you plan on working with large projects in Flash Professional, gProject is a must.

Swift 3D Xpress

Electric Rain, Inc.
5171 Eldorado Springs Dr.
Boulder, CO 80303
(303) 543-8230
(303) 543-8225 (fax)
http://www.erain.com/products/Xpress/

Swift 3D Xpress is an extension that allows you to quickly create simple 3D simulations right within Flash. Swift 3D Xpress will take any vector asset from your Stage and intelligently mimic 3D behaviors within the Flash 2D environment. Best of all, no 3D experience is necessary to use the product. You can extrude, rotate, and similarly manipulate objects with ease. You can also dip into the gallery of prebuilt drag-and-drop materials, lighting schemes, and animations to kick-start your creativity. If you want to take your 3D simulation to the next level, you can add shadows, specular highlights, reflections, and even transparency. Once you're finished with your object, Swift 3D Xpress will transfer the final asset back to Flash's Stage as a movie clip. If you really dig this extension, you can graduate to its senior standalone counterpart, Swift 3D.

FlashAmp

Marmalade Multimedia
http://www.marmalademedia.com.au

FlashAmp is a fabulous standalone application that will analyze amplitude and/or spectral data in sounds and export Flash-friendly data files for your programming needs. Using the arrays it generates, you can map frame-specific values of amplitude and/or up to 16 bands of frequencies to your animation. Using FlashAmp, you can synchronize sound with Flash events better than ever before, including lip-syncing with surprising ease. The standard and Pro versions support batch processing for greater efficiency and normalizing for higher sound quality. You can even set your dB output scale to match a useful range that will make your programming easier.

For example, if you want to show frames within a 10-frame animation, set the scale to 0–10. If you want to manipulate alpha values, set the range to 0–100. Or, if you want to control rotation, set the range to 0–360. What you do with the easy-to-use numeric output that FlashAmp generates is entirely up to you.

Resources

The Flash community is one of the most prolific and generous of any such collective. Here are a few select resources, grouped into a few categories, to start you on your journey. Take what you need from these sources, and give what you can to the growing community.

Online

It would be impractical, if not impossible, to list all the online resources available to the interested Flash user. However, here are a small number of resources for you to look into. The companion web site for this book, indicated at the end of this list, will maintain a larger list of online destinations, including those contributed by readers.

Tutorial and open source sites

These superior sites, among many others, help you by developing original tutorials and open source files (as well as hosting contributions from readers, in some cases), all free of charge. Again, the inclusion of just these few sites is in no way a slight to any other generous web sites. Many of the finest gems online can also be found in the blogging community, so be sure to check the blog aggregators later in this list.

- Flash Creations (*http://www.flash-creations.com*)
- Kirupa (*http://www.kirupa.com*)
- gotoAndLearn (*http://www.gotoandlearn.com*)
- ActionScript.org (*http://www.actionscript.org*)
- InformIT.com (*http://www.informit.com/guides/guide.asp?g=flash*)

Macromedia

This list is a subset of resources published by Macromedia. Macromedia's Flash resources are, of course, vast, and searching the main web site can also yield positive results.

- Flash Support (*http://www.macromedia.com/support/flash/*)
- Flash Developer Center (*http://www.macromedia.com/devnet/flash/*)

- Flash Learning Guides (*http://www.macromedia.com/devnet/flash/learning.html*)
- Flash Documentation (*http://www.macromedia.com/support/documentation/en/flash/*)
- Flash Exchange (*http://www.macromedia.com/exchange/flash/*)
- User Group Program (*http://www.macromedia.com/usergroups/*)
- Events Listing (*http://www.macromedia.com/cfusion/event/*)

Blog aggregators

The fastest-growing and fastest-moving sources of information on Flash are probably developer blogs. There are far too many to list here, but fortunately, there are two popular Flash-heavy aggregators that collect blog topics from all over the world. Starting your search at one of these sites may result in more targeted hits than if you were to search the Web at large. The Macromedia XML News Aggregator (MXNA) has been included here because Macromedia does not host most of the featured content.

- Macromedia XML News Aggregator (*http://weblogs.macromedia.com/mxna/index.cfm*)
- Full as a Goog (*http://www.fullasagoog.com*)

Companion web site

Be sure to look at the companion web site for this book for updates, errata, additional resources, bonus projects, and more.

Flash 8 Projects (*http://www.flash8projects.com*)

Books

Much like online resources, there are quite a few Flash books on the shelves these days. Since their average cost of $40 or more will likely prevent you from buying them all, here are my official recommendations for more advanced Flash topics:

ActionScript: The Definitive Guide (O'Reilly)
: Affectionately known as ASDG, this book is exactly what it says—the definitive guide for ActionScript. The author, Colin Moock (*http://www.moock.org*), is a very well respected ActionScript guru. Although the current edition of this book, *ActionScript for Flash MX: The Definitive Guide*, only covers ActionScript 1.0, it is still an excellent resource for learning ActionScript syntax and deep underpinnings of the language. It covers ActionScript programming in a comprehensive and intelligent way, including a detailed reference section. Keep an eye out for the third edition of ASDG, which is currently in development.

For details on OOP development in ActionScript 2.0, see Colin's latest book, *Essential ActionScript 2.0*.

Essential ActionScript 2.0 (O'Reilly)
: The title says it all. This book covers the in and outs of ActionScript 2.0, including object-oriented design, object-oriented programming, and design patterns. This is a valuable resource for serious scripters. With the impending introduction of ActionScript 3.0, a shift in coding techniques has brought the long-term worth of ActionScript 2.0 into debate. However, there is still significant value in becoming familiar with this version for a variety of reasons, including the maintenance of legacy code, as well as the impending introduction of Flash Lite 2.0 for mobile devices, which will be based on ActionScript 2.0.

Flash Hacks (O'Reilly)
: Sham Bhangal's *Flash Hacks* is a fun and informative exploration of a wide variety of Flash-related topics, from animation to ActionScript. You'll learn how to optimize content and code, protect your SWF files from prying eyes, simulate 3D, and more. This is a great resource to bring beginners up to speed with the larger Flash universe and to reinvigorate the creative spark in more experienced developers.

Index

A

B

C

D

E

Q

R

S

About the Authors

Rich Shupe is a Certified Macromedia Professional and the founder and CEO of Force Mass Acceleration (*http://www.fmaonline.com*), a New York–based multimedia development company and training facility located in midtown Manhattan. He has trained digital professionals for more than a decade and is a frequent lecturer and trainer at FlashForward, Macworld, and other industry events. He is on the faculty of New York's School of Visual Arts, teaching in both the undergraduate and masters programs, and has taught at many other academic institutions both in the United States and abroad.

Rich was first turned on by what would become Flash when it was still called FutureSplash Animator, yet he is still just shy of middle age. His company, FMA, is a leading developer of digital supplements for educational texts and creates web sites, CD-ROMs, kiosks, DVDs, and installations for clients and artists of all kinds, using Flash, among other fine tools and technologies.

Rich is also the author of *The Director Xtras Book* (Ventana) as well as a monthly Flash article for DevX (*http://www.devx.com*) covering almost anything Flash-related for all skill levels. He has contributed (writing or editing) to several now-ancient texts, including *InterActivity Magazine*, the *Apple Enhanced CD Factbook* (Apple), *Multimedia Sound and Music Studio* (Random House), and others. He also created and published *Reflex Magazine* back in his "heyday."

Robert Hoekman, Jr., is the cofounder of 33Inc.com, and is an Interface Designer and Usability Specialist for GoDaddy.com.

In the past several years, Robert has worked in corporate environments as an interaction designer and Flash developer, and has designed for audiences ranging from music-memorabilia collectors to executives at Fortune 1000 companies.

Robert is the author of *Flash User Experience Best Practices* (Lynda.com), a book on Flash design basics called *Flash Out of the Box* (O'Reilly), contributing author for *Flash MX 2004 Magic* (New Riders), and author of the extensive series of articles called "10 Minutes With Flash" (InformIT).

Colophon

The cover fonts are Adobe Syntax and Linotype Birka. The text and heading fonts are Linotype Birka and Adobe Myriad Condensed; the sidebar font is Adobe Syntax; and the code font is TheSans Mono Condensed from LucasFont.

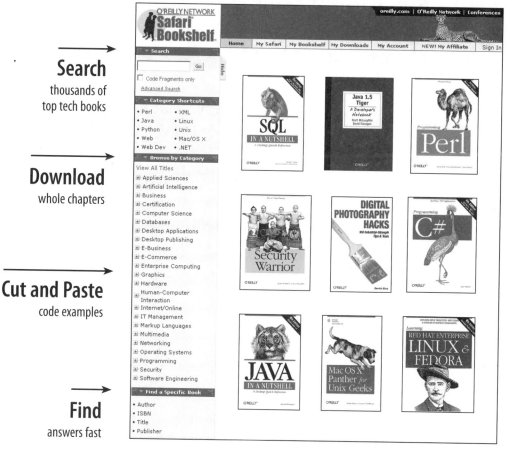